The
SPSS GUIDE to
Data
Analysis

Marija J. Norušis

Rush-Presbyterian-St. Luke's Medical Center

SPSS Inc.

For more information about the SPSS^{X}™ system and other software produced and distributed by SPSS Inc., please write or call

Marketing Department
SPSS Inc.
444 North Michigan Avenue
Chicago, IL 60611
(312) 329-3500

Preface

"The business of a poet is to examine not the individual but the species; to remark general properties and large appearances. He does not number the streaks of the tulip, or describe the different shades of verdure of the forest; he is to exhibit . . . such prominent and striking features as recall the original to every mind." (Samuel Johnson, *Rasselas.*)

It is not often that anyone compares a statistician to a poet. Yet it is fitting to do so. The statistician, like Johnson's poet, searches for "general properties and large appearances." The goal of data analysis is to describe the species based on observations of individuals. The data analyst must identify patterns from thousands of fragments and then speak of the whole. For that is what is of interest.

In this book we consider how to proceed from individual observations to the whole. There are many ways in which the fragments may be assembled, and these can result in different views of the whole. Statistics books differ in what parts of the assembly process they emphasize. This book tries to give students the skills that they need to become informed consumers or producers of statistical information. Therefore this book emphasizes what the statistical process is all about: how to conduct studies, what the results mean, and what can be said about the whole from the pieces.

Since computers are routinely used for data analysis today, this book also introduces students to SPSS^X. Students can thus practice using the tools for analyzing data that the professionals use, and gain experience in analyzing data the way professional researchers do. They need these skills if they pursue graduate degrees, and equally if they enter the working world.

Using this Text

This book is in four parts: preparing data for analysis, describing data, testing hypotheses, and examining relationships. Examples from the NORC General Social Survey are used throughout. Of course, the best way to learn about anything is to actually do it. That's especially true for data analysis, so each chapter closes with exercises that reinforce and extend the material in three main areas: syntax, statistical concepts, and data analysis. These exercises test understanding of both the mechanics of statistical analysis and the interpretation of the results. The data used in the data analysis exercises (a subset of the General Social Survey data) are available from SPSS Inc. If the complete General Social Survey data are available, they can be used equally well. Appendix B contains selected answers to the exercises. Appendix A explains how to correct some of the errors commonly made by users of the SPSS^X system.

Acknowledgments

I wish to thank the members of the SPSS staff who have participated in the preparation of this book. I have benefited from their expertise. Many reviewers have offered helpful comments and suggestions, for which I am grateful. Finally, I wish to thank Professor James A. Schoenberger for encouraging my writing efforts.

Marija J. Norušis

Contents

8 SUMMARIZING DATA   86

9 COUNTING RESPONSES FOR COMBINATIONS OF VARIABLES   106

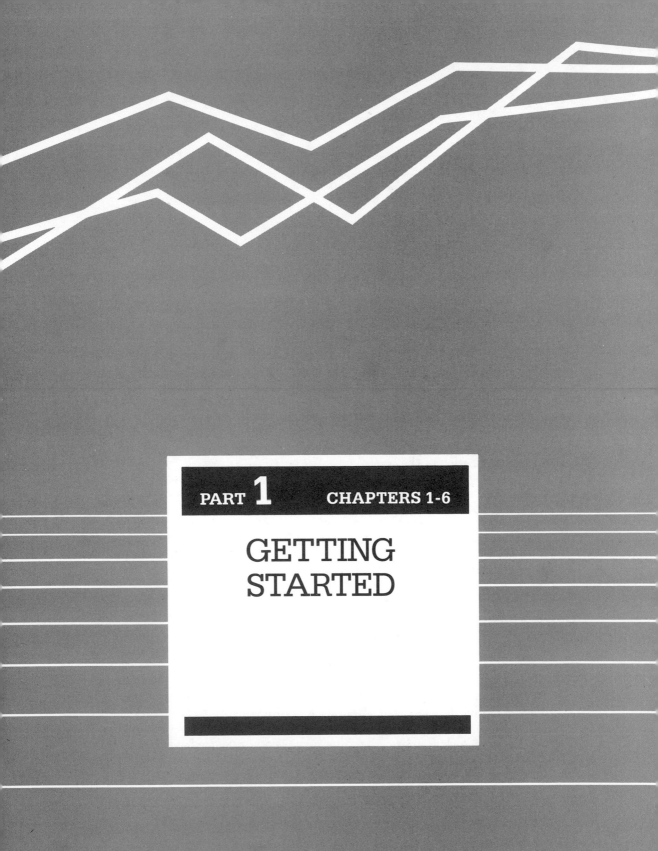

PART **1**   CHAPTERS 1-6

GETTING STARTED

1 Introduction

Perhaps you're reading this book because you've realized the importance of collecting, analyzing, and interpreting data. Either by choice or assignment you're about to begin on a research project and you want to do it well. You want to design a good study, analyze the results properly, and prepare a cogent report which summarizes what you've found. You know that in education, business, medicine, and other disciplines, data are pivotal for decision making. You also know that using a computer for data analysis is essential. You don't want to waste your time poring through data with a hand calculator. If this is the case, you can proceed to the section "About this Book," which describes the organization of the book.

Or perhaps you're reading this book because you have to. It's an assignment. The statistics course is a requirement. The university thinks you should know something about statistics. You're not sure. You think a course in medieval astrology may be just as useful and probably more interesting. You may or may not enjoy using the computer, but it seems that you must use it. Forced unions of authors and readers can be difficult for both; perhaps it will help ease our relationship if we look at some of the reasons you'll profit from learning about data analysis.

WHAT ARE DATA?

In common usage "data" are any materials which serve as a basis for drawing conclusions. Drawing conclusions from data is an activity in which everyone engages—bankers, scholars, politicians, doctors, and corporate presidents. In theory, we base our foreign policy, methods of treating diseases, and corporate marketing strategies on "data." There are many sources for data. We can conduct our own surveys or experiments, look at information from surveys other people have conducted, or examine data from all sorts of existing records—such as stock transactions or election tallies.

Acquiring data is not enough. We must determine what conclusions are justified based on the data. That's known as "data analysis." People and organizations deal with data in many different ways. Some people accumulate data but don't bother to evaluate it objectively. They think they know the answers before they start. Others want to examine the data but don't know where to begin. Sometimes people carefully analyze data, but the data are inappropriate for the conclusions that they want to draw. Unless the data are correctly analyzed, the "conclusions" based on them may be in error. A superior treatment for a disease may be dismissed as ineffectual; you may lose your life savings by purchasing stocks which don't perform well; or you may target your marketing campaign to the wrong audience, costing your company millions of dollars. The consequences of bad data analysis can be severe and far reaching. That's why you want to know how to analyze data well.

What Does Data Analysis Involve?

You can analyze data in many different ways. Sometimes all you need to do is describe the data. For example, how many people say they are going to buy a new product you're introducing? What proportion of them are men and what proportion are women? What is their average income?

In other situations you want to draw more far-reaching conclusions based on the data you have at hand. You want to know whether your candidate stands a chance at being elected, or whether the new drug is better than the one usually used. You don't have all of the information you would like. You have data from some people, but you would like to draw conclusions about a much larger audience.

Why Use Computers?

Computers simplify many tasks, including data analysis. By using a computer to analyze your data, you greatly reduce both the possibility of error and the time required. Learning about computers and preparing data for analysis by computer does require time, but in the long run it substantially decreases the time and effort required. Using a computer also makes learning about data analysis much easier. You don't have to spend time learning formulas. The computer can do the calculating for you. Your effort goes into the more interesting components—generating ideas, choosing analyses, and interpreting their results. Using a computer to analyze data doesn't mean that you'll need to know less about the concepts underlying data analysis. You should be able to learn more about them and understand them better. This book doesn't emphasize formulas. It emphasizes understanding what data analysis is all about. The computer can be used to calculate results. You must know what they mean.

WHAT IS SPSS^X?

The computer program you will learn to use for analyzing data is called SPSS^X. With it you can perform many types of statistical analysis and data management tasks. SPSS^X is the latest version of SPSS software, which for years has been widely used by researchers and students alike. Learning how to use it is easy. You just give the system some simple English-like commands, and it does the rest. You don't have to know much about computers to use it. You do have to know how to run jobs on your particular computer. In Chapters 4 and 5 we'll talk about how this is typically done, but if you've never used the computer you'll have to get help at that point.

SPSS^X is always under development. The PLOT procedure, used in Chapters 20 and 22, was added to the system in Release 2 of SPSS^X, and is not available on some computers.

ABOUT THIS BOOK

This book is divided into four parts: designing a study, describing data, testing hypotheses, and describing relationships. The order of the book parallels the steps involved in conducting a research project. The steps are similar for most types of studies—it doesn't matter whether you want to gauge consumer reactions to a new product, pilot a novel method of teaching, or study the reasons for absenteeism in your company. To help you understand the concepts being introduced, we analyze an actual study.

Designing a Study

The first step is determining what data will be collected from whom, and how. Since you'll be using a computer for analyzing data, you must make sure that the data are recorded in such a way that they can easily be entered into a computer. The next step is actually entering the data into a computer and preparing the data for analysis. This requires gaining some familiarity with computers and with computer programs which are used to analyze data. That's what the first part of the book is about.

Describing Data

Once you've prepared a data file, you're ready to start analyzing the data. The first step in data analysis is describing the data. You look at the information you have gathered and summarize it in various ways. You count the number of people giving each of the possible responses. You describe the values by calculating averages and seeing how much the responses vary. You look at several characteristics together. How many men and how many women are satisfied with your new product? What are their average ages? You also identify values which appear to be unusual—

ages in the 100's, incomes in the millions—and check the original records to make sure that these values are not due to errors in coding or entering the data. You don't want to waste time analyzing incorrect data.

Testing Hypotheses

Sometimes all you need to do is describe your data. You have information available for everyone or everything that you're interested in drawing conclusions about. That's usually not the case. Instead, you want to test hypotheses about much larger groups of people or objects than those included in your study. You want to know what proportion of all of the users of your product are satisfied with it. You want to know whether buyers of your product differ from nonbuyers. Are they younger, richer, better educated? You want to draw conclusions about all buyers and non-buyers based on the people you have included in your study. To do this (and understand it) you have to learn something about statistical inference. The second part of the book shows you how to draw conclusions about populations based on samples. You learn how to test whether you have sufficient evidence to believe that the differences or relationships you find in your sample are true for the whole population.

Describing Relationships

You often want to determine what the relationship is between two variables. For example, what is the relationship between dollars spent on advertising and sales? How can you predict how many additional sales to expect if you increase your advertising budget by 25%? Or what is the relationship between the dosage of a drug and the reduction in blood pressure? There are many different ways to study and model the relationship between pairs of variables. You can compute indexes which estimate how strong the relationship is. You can build a model which allows you to predict values of one variable based on the values of another. That's what the last part of the book is about.

2 Designing a Study

How should you proceed if you want to explore an idea?

- What information do you want to obtain?
- Who or what do you want to be able to draw conclusions about?
- Who will you include in your study?
- Will it be an experiment or a survey?

If it's an experiment:

- How will you decide who goes into which group?
- How will you decrease the chance that the subjects or experimenters influence your results?
- How will you choose a comparison group?

You must state your ideas clearly if you plan to evaluate them. This advice applies to any kind of work and especially to research design and statistical analysis. Before you begin working on design and analysis, you need to have a clearly defined topic to investigate.

ASKING A QUESTION

You may have a general suspicion that smoking less makes people feel better. Or you may have an idea for a study method that will make people learn more. Before you begin a study about such intuitions, you should replace vague concepts such as "feeling better" or "smoking less" or "learning more" with definitions that describe measurements you can make and compare. You might replace "feeling better" with an objective definition such as "the subject experiences no pain for a week." Or you might record the actual dosage of medication required to control pain. If you're interested in smoking, you need a lot of information to describe it. What does each of the subjects smoke—a pipe, cigars, or cigarettes? How much tobacco do the subjects consume in a day? How long have they been smoking? Has the amount they smoke changed?

On the other hand, you must balance your scientific curiosity with the practical problems of obtaining information. If you must rely on people's memory, you can't ask questions like "What did you have for dinner ten years ago?" You must ask questions that people will be able to answer accurately. If you're trying to show a relationship between diet and disease, for example, you can't rely on memory of what people ate at individual meals. Instead, you have to be satisfied with overall patterns that people can recall. Some information is simply not available to you, however much you'd like to have it. It's better to recognize this fact before you begin a study than when you get your questionnaires back and find that people were not able to answer your favorite question. If you think about your topic in advance, you can substitute a better question, one that will give you information you can use, even if it's not the information you *wish* you could have.

What Information Do You Need?

A critical step in any study is the decision about what information you are going to record for each participant. Of course, you can't record every possible piece of information about your subjects and their environment.

Therefore, you should think hard about what information you will try to get. If you accidentally forget to find out an important characteristic of your subjects, you may be unable to make sense of the patterns you find in your data. When in doubt, it is usually better to record more information than less. It's easy to leave unnecessary variables out of your data analysis, but it's often difficult (and expensive) to go back and gather additional information. For example, if you're studying what types of people are likely to buy a high-priced new product, you may not be able to adequately describe buyers versus nonbuyers if you forget to include information about income.

DEFINING A POPULATION

When you conduct a study, you want your conclusions to be far reaching. If you're a psychology student, you may want your results to apply to all laboratory rats, not just the ones in your lab. Similarly, if you're doing a market research survey on whether people in Los Angeles would buy disposable umbrellas, you may want to draw conclusions about everybody in the city. The people or objects about whom you want to draw conclusions are called a **population.** One of the early steps in any study is nailing down exactly what you want your population to be.

Defining a population may seem straightforward, but often it isn't. Suppose that you are a company personnel manager, and you want to study why people miss work. You probably want to draw conclusions only about employees in your particular company. Your population is well defined. However, if you're a graduate student writing a dissertation about the same topic, you face a much more complicated problem. Do you want to draw conclusions about professionals, laborers, or clerical staff? About men or women? Which part of the world is of interest—a city, a country, or the world as a whole? No doubt, you (and your advisor) would be delighted if you could come up with an explanation for absenteeism that would apply to all sorts of workers in all sorts of places. You're not likely to come up with that kind of explanation, though, and even if you do, you're not likely to come up with the evidence to support it.

All kinds of people miss work because they're sick, but unlike others, the president of Major Corporation probably doesn't need to stay home waiting for a phone to be installed. The afternoons he takes off to play golf with his buddies are probably not recorded in the personnel office as absenteeism, either. People miss work for lots of reasons, and the reasons are quite different for different kinds of employees. Be realistic, and study only a part of the labor force. Absenteeism among laborers in auto factories in Detroit, for example, is a problem with a well-defined population about which you'd have a fighting chance to draw some interesting conclusions.

Even when the population of interest seems to be well defined, you may not actually be able to study it. If you're evaluating a new method for weight loss, you would ideally like to draw conclusions about how well it works for all overweight people. You can't really study all overweight people, though, or even a group that is typical of all overweight people. People who don't want to lose weight or who have been disheartened by past efforts to reduce may not agree to try yet another method. You will probably be able to try out your new method only on people who want to lose weight. These people form your population, then, not all overweight people.

Remember that a population defined realistically in this way may be lighter, younger, or healthier than the ideal population, all overweight people. Therefore, your conclusions from studying people who want to lose weight don't necessarily apply to people who are not motivated. For example, the treatment may have some unpleasant consequences, such as making people want to chew on the nearest thing available, like gum, a pencil, or the corner of a desk. People who really want to lose weight will be willing to put up with such minor inconveniences to reach their goal. People who don't much care about their weight may toss in the scale quickly. Thus, the new treatment may work quite differently for those who are motivated versus those who are not.

Sampling

Although you may want to draw conclusions about all rats or all residents of Los Angeles, you certainly don't want to have to train all of the world's rats or personally visit every Los Angeles home. What you want to do is study *some* rats or people, draw conclusions based on what you've observed in them, and have the conclusions apply to the population in which you're really interested.

The rats or people (or other creatures or objects) that you actually observe in your study are called the **sample.** You can select a sample from a particular population in countless ways. How you do it is very important, because if you don't do it right, you won't be able to draw conclusions about your population. That's a pretty serious shortcoming! For the most part, interesting studies are those that allow you to draw conclusions about a much larger group of subjects than those actually included in the sample.

Random Samples

What is a good sample? A sample is supposed to let you draw conclusions about the population from which it's taken. Therefore, a good sample is one that is similar to the population you're studying. But you should *not* go out and look for animals, vegetables, or minerals that you think are "typical" of your population. With that kind of a sample (a **judgment** sample) the reliability of the conclusions you draw depends on how good your judgment was in selecting the sample—and there's no way to assess the selection scientifically. If you want to back up your research judgments with statistics (one of the reasons, I hope, why you are reading this book), you need a **random sample.** Statisticians have studied the behavior of random samples thoroughly. As you will learn in later chapters, the very fact that a sample is random means that you can determine what conclusions about the population you can reasonably draw from the sample.

? *So what is a "random sample," if it's so important?* It is a sample that gives every member of the population (animal, vegetable, mineral, or whatever) a fair chance of being selected. Everybody or everything in the population has the same chance. No particular type of creature or thing is systematically *excluded* from the study, and no particular type is more likely to be *included* than any other. Each unit is also selected independently: including one particular unit doesn't affect the chance of including another. ■ ■ ■

If you are interested in the opinions of all the adults in Los Angeles, do not rely on a door-to-door poll in midafternoon or ask questions of people as they leave church services on a rainy Sunday. Such samples exclude many of the types of people you want to draw conclusions about. People who have jobs are usually not home on weekday afternoons, so their opinions would not be included in your results. Similarly, people standing in the rain may express different opinions—especially about umbrellas, for example—than they would if they were warm and dry. Polling in the rain would lead you to a bad guess about the proportion of the city's residents interested in your new product, umbrellas that are disposable. To make things worse, you *can't tell* what the effects of excluding dry people will be. You can't tell whether your observed results are biased one way or another, and you can't tell by how much. You might even be on target, but you don't know that, either.

From any particular random sample, of course, the results are not exactly the same as the results you would get if you included the entire population. Later chapters will show you how statistical methods take into account the fact that different samples lead to somewhat different results. You will then understand how much you can say about a population from the results you observe in a sample.

Volunteers

To make it easier to have people participate in your study, you may be tempted to rely on volunteers. But you should not rely on any special types of people, and volunteers are one of those special types. Many studies have shown that people who volunteer are different from those who don't. Often, volunteers are different in important ways.

For example, when Ann Landers conducts a survey by asking people to write in and express their opinions, she is relying on people who write to her voluntarily. These people are probably quite different from the people who don't. The people who do bother to write in about topics like having children or dealing with noisy neighbors or interacting with the opposite sex form a special type of sample.

The results from this kind of voluntary sample don't even apply to the population of all people who read the column, and the results certainly don't apply to any wider population. Who is likely to take up a pen and write to a columnist? Certainly not students cramming for finals. Most likely, the respondents are people with time on their hands, people who have very strong feelings one way or another, and people who read papers that carry that particular column. (Then, too, the respondents are limited to people who can read and write.) You can't generalize the results of a columnist's survey like this to *any* larger group.

Similarly, if you stand in a shopping center with your newly invented disposable umbrella in one hand and a clipboard in the other, and you wait for people to voluntarily come up and talk to you, your results probably won't apply to any well-defined larger group. Only when a sample is selected randomly, so that all members of the population have the same likelihood of being included, can you relate the sample results back to the target population. Sampling strategies are important in many different kinds of studies.

USING SURVEYS

Two categories of studies that are often undertaken are **surveys** and **experiments.** Other categories of studies are also done, but these two differ in a fundamental way. In a survey, unlike an experiment, you just record information about the participants (or perhaps ask them to record the information themselves.) You ask questions or take measurements. You don't actually do anything to the people. In fact, you try as much as possible not to exert any influence.

To conduct a good survey, you must phrase your questions so they don't suggest "correct" answers. If you're interviewing a person, you must make sure that you don't smile and thus encourage a particular response. For the same reason, you must not frown or even raise an eyebrow when you disapprove. In legal jargon, you must not "lead the witness."

You must also make sure that you question all people with the same eagerness and not elicit more thorough information from one type of person than from another. If you think too much education makes people neurotic, you must make sure that you question those who have advanced degrees and those who don't with the same fervor about their neuroses. You must be careful not to dig deeper in the learned people's psyches than in the unlearned ones.

You can get survey data in two different ways. You can conduct your own survey, or you can get the data from a survey that somebody else has already done.

Conducting Your Own Survey

The great advantage to conducting your own survey is that you can tailor it for your own research project. You can ask the questions you want to ask in the way you want to ask them. You can choose exactly the population you want to study and select just the kind of sample you need. You can control the training of interviewers, and you can deal with all of the problems that come up during the survey itself. In short, you can do everything possible to make sure the survey will help you answer your questions.

Doing all of these things takes a great deal of time and often a great deal of money. If you're going to invest a lot of time and money in a study, you owe it to yourself to get expert advice. Show your plans to someone who has actually carried out similar surveys, and ask for advice—*before* you take any big steps like printing the questionnaires.

A book on data analysis—like this one—can't tell you all you need to know to carry out a serious survey. But Chapter 3 does tell you some of the principles for designing the form for a questionnaire to simplify the task of analyzing your data.

Analyzing an Existing Survey

Without a doubt, the best way to get survey data is to design and carry out a survey focused on precisely the research questions you want to study. Realistically, though, you often have to settle for "re-using" a survey that somebody else has carried out. In fact, that is the strategy of most of the examples in this book (see Chapter 3). Using data from a survey that wasn't designed for your study is often called **secondary analysis** to distinguish it from the **primary analysis** that was the purpose of the original survey.

Secondary analysis lets you do research that you couldn't otherwise do all on your own. But you must keep in mind that the data were not collected specifically for your own interests. The survey questions may not have measured exactly what you wanted them to, but you're stuck with them nonetheless. Remember to interpret them as they were asked, not as you wish they were asked.

When you plan to use existing data, you don't have to worry about the thousands of details that go into conducting a survey. Instead, you have to make sure that the survey was carried out properly in the first place. Was it conducted by a reputable organization? Were the questions well phrased, was the sample well chosen, were the forms carefully processed? Most important, have *you* formulated research questions that you can reasonably hope to answer with the existing data?

DESIGNING EXPERIMENTS

Unlike a survey, an experiment involves actually doing something to the subjects rather than just soliciting answers to questions. For example, instead of asking people whether they think that vitamin C is effective for preventing colds, you might give them vitamin C and observe how many colds they develop. Sometimes you study the subject before and after your experimental treatment. Sometimes, instead, you take several groups of subjects, do something different to each of the groups, and then compare the results.

Experimentation on people poses ethical questions that deserve careful thought. Many responsible institutions have committees that regulate experiments involving human subjects. If an experiment exposes a subject to risks, such as possible side effects from a new drug, you must certainly inform the subjects in advance. Usually you must have them sign forms to give their consent.

In experiments as well as surveys, the subjects must come from the population you're interested in. (As you've probably gathered by now, proper sampling is much easier with laboratory animals than with people in a survey!) When you design an experiment, you need to fret about some other things as well. For example, to compare different treatments or techniques, you must make sure that the groups receiving them are as similar as possible. Again, randomness is the key. The best way to make groups similar is to assign subjects to the groups randomly. This procedure doesn't guarantee that the groups will be exactly the same, but it does increase the likelihood.

Random Assignment

Random does not mean "any old way." You can't assign subjects to groups according to whatever strikes your fancy or let others make the assignment decisions for you. On the contrary, randomness requires a very specific, systematic approach to minimize the chance of groups being distorted with particular types of individuals. If you allowed school teachers to select which of their students receive personal computers, for example, they might select well-behaved students to reward them for past efforts. These students may be more intelligent or more diligent than the students who don't get to use the special equipment. Any

Table 2.1   A table of random numbers

8588	5171	0775	7818	8683	3168	1557	8319	8733	0678
7185	8645	1537	3754	0201	2450	5757	3479	6619	7297
1053	9728	3028	8725	4855	0218	8771	8711	5227	0172
751⑦	0826	7257	5527	2668	8157	9188	9087	3322	9672
3551	3316	3584	9439	0011	7365	7787	2771	1246	3253
0540	5837	3791	5113	9965	1547	8996	2194	5726	7744
8465	5569	3735	9040	5370	9659	3204	8690	7635	0260
7596	3890	9413	0714	3739	6928	9430	1803	4582	6382
1975	2561	0757	4942	9724	4448	1938	8763	8070	4775
6568	4150	2359	9998	8336	1032	2512	4846	5662	0727
5663	0845	9992	1232	1894	8111	1875	5363	6654	4690
5752	0513	5976	5158	3309	6280	9070	4958	4529	9911
5289	1813	2026	5226	5053	6380	5452	2842	9163	0307
1025	1437	1879	5550	9449	7903	5308	6931	6937	2185
4487	6412	5533	7740	2590	2580	0091	1993	1185	7311
7362	1779	3391	5349	7330	6562	8946	2329	3123	8516
7848	7974	6174	8014	7262	2689	8035	8546	0975	4533
8752	9071	8844	8708	4724	9788	9572	1540	3772	0495
8139	0471	5303	2611	9669	3966	0300	6057	2510	0498
7405	7764	6131	6204	8835	0345	0011	2385	0941	1822

evaluation of the effect of personal computers would be tainted by the differences between the students.

A good way to assign people, animals, or objects to the groups is to use a table of random numbers. You can't just make up a table of numbers that you think are random. You're likely to have certain number biases. Unlike experimenters, random number tables don't have birthdays, license plates, children, or any other reasons to prefer one number over another. In a properly constructed table of random numbers, every number from 0 to 9 has the same chance of appearing in any position in the table.

The table of random numbers in Table 2.1 has the numbers grouped into fours, but the grouping is just for convenience. It has no other significance. To randomly assign subjects to groups, you start at an arbitrary place in the table and assign the digit at that place to the first subject. Each new subject gets a digit from successive places in the table. If you start at the circled location in Table 2.1, for example, the first subject gets the number 7, the next subject the number 0, and the next subject the number 8. Since everything is random, it really doesn't matter whether you read the table across or down. However, once you've selected a starting point, stay in sequence. Using the table in this systematic way prevents you from choosing "favorite" numbers as starting points or as the next numbers in the sequence. You can never be too careful when you're trying to be random.

You use the numbers you assigned to the subjects to assign them to experimental groups. For example, if you have two groups, you can assign subjects with even numbers to one and subjects with odd numbers to the other. This procedure should result in about the same number of subjects in the two groups. But if you want the groups to be exactly equal in size, you can assign two- or three-digit random numbers to each of the subjects. Then arrange the numbers in order, from smallest to largest. Subjects with numbers in the lower half go to one group, and subjects with numbers in the upper half go to the other. You can use all sorts of systems with a random number table to assign subjects to groups, even in very complicated experimental designs.

? *Why is randomness so important? Does it really matter?* Yes, it does. Unless you use a procedure that assigns your subjects randomly, the results of your study may be difficult or impossible to interpret. Many assignment schemes that appear random to the inexperienced investigator turn out to have hidden flaws. On one occasion, researchers at a hospital compared two treatments for a particular disease. Patients who were admitted on even-numbered days received one treatment, and those admitted on odd-numbered days received the other. That assignment sounds random enough, but it failed. The number of patients admitted with the disease on even days gradually became larger than the number admitted on odd days. Why? What happened is that some of the physicians figured out the scheme and made it a point to admit their patients on days when the procedure they preferred was being used. Such biases make it possible for the patients admitted on even and odd days to be quite different. You can't rely on the results of such a study that used nonrandom assignment.　■■■

"Blind" Experiments

In experiments, as in surveys, you must not bias your observations or treatments with your own opinions or preconceptions about which group or treatment should yield better results. Some events, of course, are not disputable, such as the fact that a rat has died. However, when making observations that are not as clear-cut, such as assessing the happiness of a person's marriage, it is all too easy to let unreliable judgment creep in—even though you're trying to be objective and "scientific."

Not only you as an experimenter but also your subjects (especially if they're humans) can influence the outcome of an experiment without even trying. An example of a biasing influence is the **placebo effect,** a well-known effect in medical research. The placebo, such as a brightly colored pill that has no real effect, and a (costly) pep talk from a sympathetic physician are enough to cure many ailments. In an experiment on alertness, for example, if students know that the vitamin supplements they get with their math lessons are intended to make them less sleepy during class, they may actually feel more alert (or more drowsy if they have a bias against the experiment's success). In an experiment on anxiety, if the patients believe that the pill they are getting is the most important drug since penicillin, they will feel more tranquil than if they believe that they are just getting breath mints.

The placebo effect can occur in many kinds of experiments, not just in medical research. To avoid the effect, prevent subjects from knowing which experimental group they're in, and don't tell them anything about the expected results. Keep them "blind" as much as possible. Ethical considerations require that they know about any risks and that they give "informed consent." However, you can still design the treatments to avoid biasing the results. For example, if one treatment requires a group of people to take pills, make sure that all of the other groups get pills too, even if they're just sugar.

The people who record the experimental results should also be unaware of the assignment of subjects to groups. They, too, should be "blind." Make sure they know exactly what to measure, such as weight without clothes, learning time to the nearest second, anxiety on a particular scale. But avoid explaining more than they need to know. If you satisfy their curiosity by explaining what is going on while the study is in progress, you will never be sure whether they unconsciously affected the results. Explain the issues after the study is complete. You don't want anybody's prejudices to influence the measurements. Even if you're making the observations yourself, you can still keep yourself blind by not knowing which subject is in which experimental group. Have an assistant assign the subjects randomly to the various groups, leaving you pure and untainted.

Medical studies are often characterized as being single blind or double blind. When only the subjects don't know which groups or treatments they've been assigned, the experiment is called **single blind.** And when the experimenter and the subjects don't know the assignment, the study is called **double blind.** Double blind studies are the most reliable.

Control Groups

If you're conducting a study to evaluate a new experimental method or treatment, make sure you include a group that *doesn't* receive the new treatment. This **control group** will provide you with measurements to which the results of the new treatment can be compared. If you're evaluating a new instructional method, for example, the appropriate control treatment may be the standard instructional method. If you're doing a medical experiment, the appropriate control treatment may be the standard medication or procedure for a particular ailment.

Don't compare the new treatment's results just to historical information or "commonly held beliefs." Experimenters may be tempted to do so, but then they run into a variety of problems. For example, a surgeon who is pioneering a new technique can't simply compare the survival rates of patients who were given the new operation with those of patients from previous years. Differences may occur for many reasons. Current patients may have been diagnosed earlier than previous patients, so they have a better chance of surviving. Another possibility is that the surgeon's skills may have improved with time, making the newer patients more likely to survive.

All kinds of things are different between groups that are treated at different times. You don't know—you can't know—what all of these things are and how they affect a study. To avoid this problem, make sure that a control group is part of your study's design, and don't rely on historical controls.

WHAT'S NEXT?

This chapter has briefly discussed some important points to think about when designing a study. There are many others. For further discussion of basic design issues, read N. M. Bradburn and S. Sudman's *Asking Questions* (1982) and B. Williams' *A Sampler on Sampling* (1978).

The next chapter of this book focuses on survey research. You will learn about an extensive study that includes a question on how people feel about life in general. You will also learn how to set up questionnaire forms so they are useful for interviews and for data analysis.

Summary

How should you proceed if you want to explore an idea?

You should carefully formulate a question and decide exactly what pieces of information are necessary to answer the question.

You must determine what the population of interest is and select a random sample of objects or people from the population.

You must be sure that you don't unintentionally bias your sample by making it more likely that some members are included than others.

You must collect your information in an objective fashion. The procedure for gathering the information must be objective and standardized. Questions must be unambiguous.

If several different conditions are being compared, you must ensure that the subjects are randomly allocated to the groups.

You must prevent the subjects and investigators from allowing their personal prejudices to influence the outcome of the investigation.

EXERCISES

1   If there are 50 children in a classroom and you wish to select 10 of them randomly to participate in a study, how would you go about selecting the sample?

2   A candidate for political office is interested in finding out what percent of a city's voters support him. He has obtained bids from two survey organizations to conduct a poll for him. Both organizations plan to canvass about 1000 residents. The first, using a register of households, proposes to select a random sample of 400 households and then question all family members. The second plans to randomly select 1000 people from the population. Explain to the candidate which poll will probably be more informative and why.

3   Your former high school principal is interested in why some of his graduates are successful and others not. He commissions you to develop a plan for studying this question.

   a.   What is your population?

   b.   Discuss several ways for selecting a sample.

   c.   How would you define "success?"

   d.   If you do a mailing to graduates and receive questionnaires returned as "undeliverable," discuss problems with just throwing them away.

   e.   If you've decided to do a survey by mail, how will you deal with people who do not return your form. That is, how will you deal with the problem of non-response?

   f.   What do you think of the strategy of distributing questionnaires at a class reunion?

4   Which of the following procedures should result in a random sample of a city's adult population?

   a.   "Random-digit dialing."   A computer places calls to randomly generated phone numbers.

   b.   Random selection of 10 places of employment and then random selection of employees within each.

   c.   Selecting every fifth person entering a grocery store.

   d.   Randomly selecting children in all schools and then including their parents in the study.

5   In the 1936 Presidential race between Roosevelt and Landon, the *Literary Digest*, a magazine which ran the largest polls of that time, predicted a Landon victory on the basis of 2,376,523 mail questionnaires (out of about 10,000,000 mailed). In fact, Roosevelt won by a margin of 19 percentage points. What possible reasons can you think of for their missing the mark so badly?

6   In the 1954 clinical trial of the Salk polio vaccine, many different study designs were considered.

   a.   One possible approach would be to select a random sample of children and vaccinate them. What problems do you see with this approach?

   b.   Another approach would be to vaccinate a group of children whose parents have volunteered them for the study, and then compare the polio rate for vaccinated children with the rate for unvaccinated children in the same area. What problems do you see with this approach?

c. Many trials of medical agents must rely on volunteers. Can you think of a better strategy than giving all of the volunteers the new treatment and then comparing their results to known results in the general population?

d. Knowing that polio is an epidemic disease in which clusters of cases occur, what do you think of vaccinating only all children in Chicago and then comparing their rate to all non-vaccinated children in Detroit?

7 U.S. employment and unemployment statistics are based on results from the monthly Current Population Survey. One of the questions not included in the survey is, "Were you unemployed?" What would be wrong with asking the question in that way?

8 Suppose you want to determine how self-made millionnaires differ from the general population.

a. What problem do you see with just taking a random sample of the population?

b. There are more complex types of random samples than those in which each unit has the same chance of inclusion. (In all of them, however, every member of the population has a *known*, non-zero chance of inclusion and this chance is taken into account in analyzing the data.) Suggest an alternative sampling strategy to deal with the problems you mentioned in (a).

9 List some problems you see with attempting to take random samples from large populations. What happens when you can't identify all the members of your population?

3 Designing Forms for Studies

How should you design the form that will be used for recording the data?

- What information will you gather for each respondent?
- How will you record the answers?
- How will you assign codes to answers?
- How will you indicate that a respondent refuses to answer a question or that the information is unavailable?
- How will you prepare the form to make it easy to enter the information into the computer?

Because it's much easier to follow explanations when they are tied to an example, the remainder of this book focuses on one large-scale study, the General Social Survey, or GSS. The General Social Survey is conducted by the National Opinion Research Center, NORC, a social science research organization at The University of Chicago. By examining parts of the General Social Survey in this book, you will learn about form design and coding, data entry, and especially about statistical analysis of the results. This chapter discusses design of the forms for collecting the data.

THE GENERAL SOCIAL SURVEY

The General Social Survey is administered every year to a sample of about 1,500 persons. This sample represents the population of adults living in the United States but not in institutions such as mental hospitals and college dormitories. Members of the military are also excluded. An interviewer visits each selected household and questions the chosen person, the **respondent,** about present and past experiences, behavior, and opinions.

The method that the National Opinion Research Center uses to select people for inclusion in the sample is complex. It involves first selecting a random sample of cities and counties, then a random sample of neighborhoods, then a random sample of households, and finally a person within a household. In this book, this sampling scheme will be treated as equivalent to a random sample of the population.

The General Social Survey was designed to include questions on many different topics, particularly questions previously asked on older surveys during the 1940s, 1950s, and 1960s. Having data for the same questions asked over the years lets people study how attitudes and opinions have changed. Data from the General Social Survey are distributed at nominal cost and are widely used by researchers and students. (See *General Social Surveys, 1972-1985: Cumulative Codebook.*)

Is Life Exciting?

So many questions are included in the General Social Survey that it would be hard to show the analysis of all of them. Instead, we will focus on one of the questions:

In general, do you find life exciting, pretty routine, or dull?

We'll look at responses to this question and see how they relate to responses to several other questions, such as those about education, age, sex, marriage, and belief in life after death. But before looking at the actual data from these questions, let's start at the beginning.

DESIGNING THE FORM

Before you accumulate survey data, you must design an appropriate form. For many questionnaires, the respondent fills out the form. However, an interviewer might fill it out, or the respondent might fill out some parts and the interviewer might fill out other parts. For the General Social Survey, a trained interviewer fills out the form. This procedure adds to the cost of the study but makes it easier to control the way in which the questions are presented. In any case, the form must clearly specify what information is to be recorded and how it is to be recorded. To minimize the number of errors that occur when the form is used, you should make it easy to understand and reasonably simple.

Take the time to design your form so that the information from it can be easily entered into a computer. If you don't think about the data entry in advance, you'll be stuck with boxes of forms and no easy way to start analyzing them. You'll spend needless hours or even days recopying numbers from one form to another. This kind of work is boring, thankless, and—to make things worse—it is bound to increase the number of errors in the data. You won't make this mistake twice; plan ahead and don't make it at all. Enough warning. Let's proceed.

Arranging the Form

Figure 3.1 shows a form like the one used for recording the results of a General Social Survey interview. Only some of the questions are shown, and they are rearranged from the original. In addition to the questions themselves, the form has numbers at the right margin. These numbers, each followed by a slash, describe how the information will be stored in the computer. The last item on the form, the record number, has a similar use. Chapter 4 discusses the meaning of all these numbers in detail.

Interviewers fill out this form, or one like it, in the homes of the respondents. Interviewers are trained to read each question *exactly* as it appears, without varying a word and without indicating approval or dismay at the respondents' answers. All of the respondents must be asked the questions in the same say. If you design a survey study and you don't insist that your interviewers ask the questions in a standard way, differences in their personalities or attitudes can contaminate the results.

As shown in Figure 3.1, there is a place on the form to record each piece of information. The *way* it is to be recorded is also clearly specified. For example, instead of asking directly for a person's age, the interviewer is to request the actual month, day, and year of birth. Some people, especially as they grow older, have unpredictable systems for altering their ages at each birthday. Asking for the date of birth, instead of asking directly for age, increases the likelihood of a correct answer. The computer will calculate the exact age later. Never ask interviewers or respondents to calculate anything themselves. Get the raw numbers, and let the machine do the arithmetic. If you're interested in the ratio of a person's weight to height, for example, the interviewer or respondent should record the weight and height, and you should leave the ratio to the computer. This procedure saves your time and increases the accuracy of the results. Computers divide better than distracted people with calculators.

Coding the Data

The answers to some questions are numbers. If you ask how much people weigh, how many cigarettes they smoke daily, or how many brothers and sisters they have, the answers will be numbers, and you can simply leave space on the questionnaire form to write in each one. You should leave enough room for the biggest number possible, even if you don't expect to get it. If you ask enough people how many children they have, for example, you will certainly find somebody who has 10.

When the answer to a question isn't a number, you should try to figure out in advance what answers are possible. Respondents would then select among the alternatives. If you don't think of the possible responses before the survey, you'll be in serious trouble. For a question about how people view life in general, if you let people supply their own alternatives, you'll probably end up with as many different answers as there were people. How are you going to analyze "Kinda OK," "Could be worse," "Great, except for my job," "Today exciting, yesterday not"? You would spend hours deciding what to do with a few hundred of such answers. By forcing people to choose among specific alternatives, (such as "Exciting," "Pretty routine," "Dull"), you can get data that are easier to analyze.

? *What if you really are interested in the way people say things on their own?* Sometimes you simply don't know in advance what people will say, and you want to allow them to say exactly what they please. You can certainly have interviewers write down exactly what the respondents say, word for word. Questions like these, which don't specify the possible responses, are known as **open-ended questions.** A computer won't be much help in analyzing open-ended questions directly, though, so you should either study the answers and assign codes to them before you enter your data or else ask the same questions again in a different way, with specified choices for responses.   ■ ■ ■

Figure 3.1 Sample form with questions from the General Social Survey

1. Case Number ☐☐☐☐   01-04/

2. What is your date of birth?

   ☐☐   ☐☐   ☐☐☐☐   06-13/
   Month Day   Year

   Numerical Notations of Months

January	01	May	05	September	09
February	02	June	06	October	10
March	03	July	07	November	11
April	04	August	08	December	12

3. Circle Respondent's Sex: 15/

   Male.......1   Female.....2

4. Are you currently--married, widowed, divorced,
   separated, or have you never been married?

   Married.........1   Separated.......4   16/
   Widowed.........2   Never married...5
   Divorced........3

5. On the whole, how satisfied are you with the work you
   do--would you say you are very satisfied, moderately
   satisfied, a little dissatisfied, or very dissatisfied?

   Very satisfied..........1   17/
   Moderately satisfied....2
   A little dissatisfied...3
   Very dissatisfied.......4
   Don't know.............8

6. Taking things all together, how would you describe your
   marriage? Would you say that your marriage is very happy,
   pretty happy, or not too happy?

   Very happy...........1   Not too happy........3   18/
   Pretty happy.........2   Don't know...........8

7. In general, do you find life exciting, pretty routine,
   or dull?

   Exciting.............1   Dull.................3   19/
   Pretty routine.......2   No opinion...........8

8. Do you believe there is life after death?

   Yes..............1   Undecided........8   20/
   No...............2

9. What is the highest grade in elementary school or
   high school that you finished and got credit for?
   CODE EXACT GRADE.

   No formal school....00   7th grade........07   22-23/
   1st grade..........01   8th grade........08
   2nd grade..........02   9th grade........09
   3rd grade..........03   10th grade.......10
   4th grade..........04   11th grade.......11
   5th grade..........05   12th grade.......12
   6th grade..........06

10. IF FINISHED 9TH-12TH GRADE OR DON'T KNOW:
    Did you ever get a high school diploma   24/
    or a GED certificate?

    Yes 1
    No...................2
    Don't know...........8

11. Did you ever complete one or more years of college for credit--not including schooling such as business college, technical or vocational school?

    Yes 1
    No..............2   25/
    Don't know.......8

    IF YES TO PREVIOUS QUESTION:

12. How many years did you complete?

    1 year...........13   6 years...........18   26-27/
    2 years..........14   7 years...........19
    3 years..........15   8 or more years....20
    4 years..........16   Don't know........98
    5 years..........17

13. Do you have any college degrees?

    Yes................1   28/
    No.................2
    Don't know.........8

    IF YES TO PREVIOUS QUESTION:

14. What degree or degrees? CODE HIGHEST DEGREE EARNED

    Associate/Junior college............2   29/
    Bachelor's..........................3
    Graduate............................4
    Don't know..........................8

15. In which of these groups did your total family income, from all sources, fall last year--1983-- before taxes, that is. Just tell me the letter.

    A. Under $1,000 01   31-32/
    B. $1,000 to 2,999.................02
    C. $3,000 to 3,999.................03
    D. $4,000 to 4,999.................04
    E. $5,000 to 5,999.................05
    F. $6,000 to 6,999.................06
    G. $7,000 to 7,999.................07
    H. $8,000 to 9,999.................08
    I. $10,000 to 12,499...............09
    J. $12,500 to 14,999...............10
    K. $15,000 to 17,499...............11
    L. $17,500 to 19,999...............12
    M. $20,000 to 22,499...............13
    N. $22,500 to 24,999...............14
    O. $25,000 to 34,999...............15
    P. $35,000 to 49,999...............16
    Q. $50,000 or over.................17
       REFUSED.........................97
       DON'T KNOW......................98

    TOTAL INCOME INCLUDES INTEREST OR DIVIDENDS, RENT, SOCIAL SECURITY, OTHER PENSIONS, ALIMONY OR CHILD SUPPORT, UNEMPLOYMENT COMPENSATION, PUBLIC AID(WELFARE), ARMED FORCES OR VETERAN'S ALLOTMENT.

16. Would you say your own health, in general, is excellent, good, fair, or poor?

    Excellent.........1   Poor.............4   33/
    Good..............2   Don't know.......8
    Fair..............3

    RECORD NUMBER...........................|1| 40/

For questions that require choosing among alternatives, think about all the possibilities. Make sure nothing falls through the cracks. Anticipate the unusual. For example, if you want to ask about housing, remember that not everyone lives in a house or an apartment. It is especially important to make provisions for responses such as "Don't know" or even "None of your business." Don't leave it up to an interviewer to decide what to do when somebody can't or won't answer a difficult question. Anticipate these problems, and write clear instructions on the form in the places where such answers can occur. Whenever there is a real possibility of answers that don't fit into your coding scheme, include an "Other" category, and leave space on the form for writing out the unusual answers. You may be able to do something with this written information later.

On the General Social Survey form, all acceptable answers to a question are listed. Each answer has a code with it, a number that represents that answer. For the exciting-routine-dull-life question, a code of 1 is circled for the answer "Exciting," 2 for "Pretty routine," and 3 for "Dull." The code number 8 is reserved for the answer "Don't know." These numerical values are the **coding scheme** for the variable. For each respondent, one of these numbers will go into the computer to represent the answer to this question.

Coding schemes are arbitrary. A code of 3 could just as well have been assigned to the Exciting response, and a code of 1 to Dull. What's important is that each possible response has a code that is different from the others. For example, you wouldn't code the states of the union by their first letters, because the first letters for the names of many states are the same.

Tips on Form Design

Here are a few hints about things you can do, when designing your form, that will make your life a lot easier when it comes time to analyze the data. Some of these hints are about the arrangement of the form, and some are about coding.

Split up complicated questions. Some questions are best asked in parts. Questions 9–14 in Figure 3.1 were carefully designed to find out a respondent's level of education. Instead of just asking for total years of education, the General Social Survey asks about the highest year completed in grammar school or high school and then (separately) asks about college. This is so that someone who spent five years mastering first grade won't count them as five years of education. Because years of education don't always correspond to diplomas and degrees, the General Social Survey also asks for the highest degree received.

Record numbers when you can.   Record information in as much detail as possible, using actual numbers. Don't group family size into small, medium, and large. Instead, get the exact number of people in the family. Later, you can use the computer to create categories like small, medium, and large based on the exact numbers. If you've recorded only the categories, you won't be able to try different grouping schemes or to analyze the data in more detail.

You may notice that the General Social Survey question about income doesn't follow this advice. That's because income is a sensitive matter for many people, and they may refuse to give their income as an exact dollar amount; or they may not know their yearly income to the nearest dollar. The General Social Survey softens the question by letting the interviewer hand a card to the respondent with preprinted income categories. That way, the respondent never needs to give an exact figure. Analyzing income categories may be harder than analyzing the exact incomes—but the problem would be even worse if people refused to answer at all or if they gave false answers.

Use a numeric coding scheme.   When items require coding, assign numbers instead of letters to the responses. Numbers simplify both data entry and data analysis. For example, coding sex as 1 and 2 is simpler than coding sex as M and F.

Put an identification number on the form.   You can use the identification number to locate forms that you later find to have errors or unusual values. Even if you're running a confidential survey and each form isn't linked to a particular person, put an identification number on the respondent's form *before* you enter the data into the computer. Then enter the identification number with the rest of the data. This number links the paper form and the computer record.

COLLECTING THE DATA

You figure out the questions you want to ask and the way you want to record the answers, and you design a clear form that's easy to use. Then you can go ahead and use it for collecting the data. In many studies, much of the work comes here. Remember that the interviewers must carry out your well-designed survey exactly as you specified. They must ask the questions in a standardized way, without leading the respondents, and they must use your coding schemes by entering the proper types of information in the right places. Unless the interviewers (or you yourself) gather the data well, all the work you did to prepare the study and any work you do to analyze it will be for naught.

WHAT'S NEXT?

When you have the completed forms from your study, you need to enter the data into a computer so that the computer programs can then carry out your instructions for data analysis. Chapter 4 describes how to enter the data.

Summary

How should you design the form that will be used for recording the data?

Indicate a specific place on the form to record each piece of information.

Include an identification number on the form for each respondent.

Record the actual values for numeric data.

If necessary, assign codes to possible answers.

Assign special codes for missing or unavailable information.

Split up complicated questions into parts.

Make sure the data can be entered into a computer directly from the form.

EXERCISES

1 In question 3 at the end of Chapter 2 we discussed a study to identify why some high school graduates are more "successful" than others. Choose 5 measures of "success." Write the question, answers, and coding scheme you will use for obtaining the information.

2 A survey was conducted to examine voter preference in a mayoral campaign. The three viable candidates are Jane, Harry, and Rich. The following table contains responses for six of the persons interviewed:

Person	Sex	Age	Candidate	Registered to vote	Employment status
Rogers	male	52	Harry	yes	looking
Boyd	male	25	Rich	doesn't remember	full time student
Paul	female	38	Svetlana	no	not on market
Kelley	male	no answer	Marija	yes	employed
Shoot	female	45	Rich	no	laid off
Harman	female	68	undecided	yes	retired

a. Decide how you will code each of the variables.

b. Using your coding scheme, code the cases in the table.

3 What improvements would you make to the following form which was designed to measure insomnia after administration of a drug?

```
Name_____

Age   1. under 20      Race_____        Sex_____
      2. 21-70
      3. 71-99
      4. other


How well did you sleep last night?_____


Did you wake up during the night? 1. yes 2. no 3. maybe

Do you think you slept better last night than you
usually do?

        1. Yes, much
        2. Yes, somewhat better
        3. Yes, but not much
        4. No

How many hours did you sleep last night?

        1. more than 8
        2. 4-8
        3. less than 4

Describe your dreams if they troubled you.
```

4 Devise coding schemes for the following variables:

a. miles driven to work per year

b. hours of television viewing per month

c. favorite type of television program

d. daily alcohol consumption

e. grandfather's income

f. the respondent's income

g. attitude toward violence on television

5 Here are some additional questions from the General Social Survey. Suggest coding schemes.

a. Were you living with both your own mother and father around the time you were 16?

b. What hours do you usually work?

c. How often do you attend religious services?

d. Many people who want to volunteer for service in the armed forces do not have the necessary basic skills like reading, writing and arithmetic. Do you think the armed forces should refuse to accept such volunteers, or should they accept them and give them the necessary education?

6 Improve the following coding schemes and questions:

a. Circle the number of meals you typically eat in a restaurant each week:

    1. 0-1
    2. 1-3
    3. 5-6
    4. more than 7

b. What type of restaurants do you eat at?

    1. inexpensive
    2. expensive
    3. very expensive
    4. all of the above

c. Which of the following influence your selection of a restaurant?

    1. cost not food not service
    2. food not cost not service
    3. service not cost not food
    4. cost and food not service
    5. food and service not cost
    6. service and cost not food
    7. other

d. Rate the last restaurant you ate at on the following scale:

    _____
    0   75

e. Given economic contingencies and inflation, as well as cost escalation, difficulties in staff acquisition, in conjunction with variegated consumer consumption preferences, how would you optimize restaurant performance in this establishment?

4 Setting Up Your Data File

What is a data file, and how do you go about creating one?

- Should you do anything with the forms before you enter data from them into the computer?

- How should your data be arranged in the computer file?

- How does the computer know which number in the data file corresponds to which question?

- What is a text editor, and how do you use one?

- What is a backup copy, and why should you bother to make one?

The data from the General Social Survey are easy to analyze because much of the difficult work has been done by others. Selecting the sample, designing the form, training the interviewers, cleaning up the data, and entering it into the computer have all been done by experienced professionals.

Users of the General Social Survey receive a computer tape that contains all of the data, and they get an excellent codebook that describes the data. All they need to do is give a few simple commands to a computer, and they're ready to analyze the survey as they want. Many universities have the survey data in a computer file (more about that later), which makes the data even simpler to use. But if you're collecting your own data, you'll have to consider some of the problems you can encounter in getting it ready to analyze.

REVIEWING AND PREPARING FORMS FOR DATA ENTRY

After you've collected your data but before you enter it, you should check through the forms to see if anything strange has happened. People who fill out forms or respond to questionnaires are very creative in coming up with ways to confound your expectations. They forget to answer questions, refuse to answer questions, answer questions twice, and make up their own alternatives rather than choose from the ones you gave them. You need to find out about these problems and decide how to handle them before anyone tries to enter your data into the computer.

Make sure that the special codes for missing and illegible answers are entered on the forms. You may have to expand the master list of the codes to include new ones for unanticipated situations. If your study was conducted shortly after a blizzard, for example, you may find that snow removal ranked unexpectedly high among people's concerns. If you didn't have a preassigned code for snow removal, you may want to include one, so you can distinguish it from the rest of the "Other" concerns.

Remember, if *you* can't decipher a questionnaire, neither will the person who enters the data into the computer. Even if you enter the data yourself, you'll do a better job if you decide what to do with the problems in advance, before you have a computer terminal staring at you impatiently.

ENTERING DATA INTO A COMPUTER FILE

This book can't tell you much about getting access to your computer—establishing an account, getting a password, finding a terminal, and so on—since these steps vary greatly from one computer center to another. Most computer centers are helpful in showing the ropes to newcomers. Once you've learned about your computer center, you can begin entering your data.

If you enter data through a computer terminal, you'll have to transfer the information from your forms into a computer file. A **computer file** is a place where you can store information in a computer and retrieve it whenever you need to. You can think of a file as a sheet of paper, and your terminal as a typewriter. Each line you type on the page becomes a line in the file. Lines in a file are also called **records.** Unlike a sheet of paper, though, a computer file can hold a very large number of lines.

Assigning Positions in the File

Every character on a typewriter has the same width. You can line up a column of numbers in a report by making sure that they're the same number of spaces from the left margin, where each line begins. In a computer file, you can also line up a column of numbers. In fact, this tidy practice is so important for computer files that the convention is to describe each space in a line as forming its own column. The first character you type on a line, even if it's a blank space, is in column 1; the second is in column 2; and so on. (A computer screen that's like a TV usually displays 80 columns. Terminals that print characters on paper sometimes have more.)

Data Formats

For a data-analysis program like SPSS[X] to find and identify individual pieces of information (such as each case's response for the fifth question), you must first arrange the data in an orderly way in the file. (A **case** is typically one of the persons from your study.) With an orderly data arrangement, you can easily tell the computer the layout of your file when it comes time for analysis (see Chapter 6). Several different systems of arranging data are common.

Fixed Format

The most useful method of arranging data when you have a lot of it for each case is **fixed format.** To use a fixed format, you put each piece of information in the same column locations for each case. For example, you might place the month of birth in columns 6 and 7, the day of birth in columns 8 and 9, and the year of birth in columns 10 through 13. The month of birth would be in the same two columns for all of the cases. That way, the computer program for data analysis will know where to find it.

When the birth month is a one-digit number, for January through September, you can place either a blank or a zero in column 6. The computer interprets blanks and zeros before a number in the same way.

The number of columns you must leave to record each piece of information depends on how big that response can be. In the previous example, both month and day of the month are allowed two columns. Year gets four columns if it is recorded completely (1986, rather than just 86). You would probably record a year with four digits to allow for people born in the 1800s. You want to tell the difference between somebody born in 1975 and somebody born in 1875. Three digits would be enough, but four are easier to read.

Choosing the number of columns for the date of birth is simple, since you know that months, days, and years fall within certain limits. You can't have a month that is 274 or a day that is 3,922. Two columns are always enough for month and for a day. If you're recording a family's income in dollars, however, figuring how many columns or positions you should allow isn't nearly as easy. Five digits are enough for most people, since not many families have incomes of $100,000. (You don't have to worry about the dollar sign and the comma. You should just enter the *number*.) However, it's possible that you'll have families with incomes in the hundreds of thousands or even higher. To allow for incomes in the billions, you would need 10 columns (9999999999). Most of the time, however, it would be quite reasonable to code incomes over a million dollars as 999999. In any event, you must decide in advance how many columns to leave for each question on the form. If there's *any* possiblity of encountering numbers that won't fit, decide in advance what you'll do with them.

Put the Format on the Form

If you can, put the column locations for each piece of information onto the form itself; you'll make data entry easier and more reliable. Look again at the form in Chapter 3, also in this chapter's Figure 4.1 The numbers in the right margin indicate where in the computer file to put each piece of information. The identification number is in the first four columns, the date of birth in columns 6 through 13, sex in column 15, marital status in column 16, and so on for the rest of the questions. If the information on a form doesn't fit into a single line of the computer file, you can split the information across several lines. If you do this, also put a number on each line to identify its position within the case. Each of these lines is a different record. The data from our example form do fit into a single record, so the record number (indicated at the end of the form) is 1. The record number itself is entered into column 40, though you can do without it on forms like this, which use just a single record.

Multiple Records

If your information does *not* fit in a single record, you must figure how many records you need and how the information should be arranged in each of them. To each piece of information, assign a record location—the line it is on—and a column location—its position on that line.

Although the actual layout of the multiple records varies, every record should contain the case identification number and a record number, preferably in the same columns of each record. This arrangement makes it easy to check that no records are missing for any case. It also makes it easy to determine where records gone astray really belong.

Freefield Format

When you arrange your data in a fixed format, each type of information must always be in the same location. When entering a number into the computer, you must make sure it's in the location you've designated. If a number creeps over one column too far, you'll be in trouble when the computer tries to interpret it.

You can use a method of entering data that does *not* depend on fixed column locations. Instead, it relies exclusively on the sequence in which information is entered. This method is called **freefield-format** data entry.

The scheme is simple and consistent. For each form you enter the pieces of information ("values") in the same sequence, and you separate adjacent values with one or more blanks. Column location doesn't matter at all. The number of records used to enter the form doesn't matter, either. You can even start entering a new form in the middle of a line (a particularly unwise practice). The computer simply reads the pieces of information and assigns them as answers to the questions in order, until it reaches the end of the list of questions—and then it starts again at the top of a form.

When entering data in freefield format, it's easy to lose track of where you are on a form. You can't look at the screen, see that you're in column 15, and know you should be entering the respondent's sex. For data analysis, the computer will expect a certain order, such as month, day, year. If you accidentally skip the month of birth, the computer will misinterpret all of the numbers from that point on. It will think that the next number you entered—the day—is the month. It will interpret the number you entered after that—the year—as the day; and on and on. The entire sequence is off.

If you're lucky and just omit some numbers, the computer can tell you that you don't have enough. Then you can go search for the missing ones. However, you can *really* cause problems if you left out one number and entered another twice. Then the computer assumes everything is fine since it has the right number of pieces of information. Everything in between your two mistakes will be garbled, and you won't know about it.

Freefield format is useful if you're not entering very many pieces of information for each respondent. In those situations, you can locate errors without much trouble, and the comfort of not having to keep track of columns when entering the data is worth it. But when you have a large or complicated form, it's always worthwhile to assign fixed positions to each piece of information.

TEXT EDITORS

If you use a computer, you will almost certainly need to learn how to use a program called a **text editor.** A text editor (or just *editor* for short) is a program that lets you create or modify files on the computer. You can type data into a file, modify (or *edit*) the data in a file, and store new files containing your modified data. Every editor works in its own way. We're going to look at editors in general and then work through a couple of particular examples. Even if you'll be using a different editor, the examples should still give you a good idea of what a text editor does.

? *If you want to analyze data statistically, why do you need a text editor? You're not dealing with "text," you're analyzing numbers, right?* That may be true, but when you analyze your data, you work with files, and an editor is a basic tool for working with them. You use an editor with your **data file** if you enter the data into the computer yourself. You also use an editor with the SPSS^X **command file,** which contains the commands telling SPSS^X how to analyze your data. You have to create such a file before you can do any analysis.

Your text editor is the most basic tool you use when you work with a computer. Take some time, play with it, and learn how to use it well. ■ ■ ■

How to Use a Text Editor

To create a file on the computer, you have to do the following things in one way or another:

1 First you have to get the computer's attention. Find a computer terminal, find the power switch, and turn it on. If the terminal is connected over a phone line, you have to dial a phone number. Hit the Return key or the Enter key until the computer responds.

2 Identify yourself. On most systems, you type in an "account number" or a "user identification." You probably need to type a secret password, also. You find out these things when you're authorized to use the computer.

3 Run the text editing program. Typically this involves typing in the name of the text editor and pressing the Return key or the Enter key. On some systems, such as WYLBUR, you are always in the editor and don't have to do anything special to run it.

4 Enter your data or make your changes. With **full-screen editors,** you can enter or change a whole screen of data at one time. With **line editors,** you must work with one line at a time, pressing the Enter key or Return key after each line.

5 Save the file. Additions or changes you make with the editor affect only a temporary copy of your file. You can store the copy in the computer to create a permanent file (usually with a command such as SAVE).

Examples

Let's take the form from Chapter 3 and see how you might enter the data from it using two different text editors to create a new data file. Figure 4.1 shows a filled-out questionnaire. The two editors are WYLBUR, which runs on IBM computers with OS operating systems, and EDT, which runs on VAX computers with the VMS operating system. (An **operating system** is a kind of master program that does things such as scheduling other programs and providing access to files.) WYLBUR is an example of a line editor, and EDT is normally used as a full-screen editor.

WYLBUR

On computers with operating systems in the OS family from IBM, WYLBUR is one of the more widely used text editors. WYLBUR is a line editor. It is also a complete"environment": it manages your entire session on the computer, so there is no separate text-editor program to run.

When you use WYLBUR, an important key on your terminal is the Return key or the Enter key, whichever you may have. We'll indicate this key as (RETURN). Another important key is the one marked Attention or Break, which we'll indicate as (ATTN).

Here's how your session might go. You dial the phone and establish a connection between your terminal and WYLBUR. WYLBUR asks for your account and password; you type them in, hitting (RETURN) after each. WYLBUR sends you a **prompt,** a brief message indicating that the system is ready to accept a command. The prompt is usually the word COMMAND?, although it might be just the question mark. The exchange may continue like this:

```
COMMAND?  (ATTN)
   1.   ?
```

(In this and later examples, the material that you enter is **boldfaced,** and the material that WYLBUR produces is in regular type.) By pressing the (ATTN) key, you indicate to WYLBUR that you want to enter data. (Pressing it again would indicate that you're finished entering data and want to issue a command.) Since this is the beginning of your session, you haven't yet been working with any file, so WYLBUR asks for line number 1 of a new file. Now you simply type in the numbers from the questionnaire. Be careful to put each number in the proper column, as the questionnaire shows. The identification number goes in columns 1–4, month of birth in 6–7, day of birth in 8–9, and so on. For the form in Figure 4.1, you would enter the data like this:

```
COMMAND? (ATTN)
    1.    ? 0001 08241952 152912 12112014 161        1 (RETURN)
    2.    ?
```

Notice how the values are carefully lined up in the columns indicated on the form. The form indicates that the case identification number goes in columns 1–4, so the identification number for this case, 0001, is in the first four columns of the line. After you've enter many cases, the values should all line up neatly under one another, and the exchange between you and the computer will look something like this:

```
    1.    ? 0001 08241952 152912 12112014 161        1 (RETURN)
    2.    ? 0002 04141941 213111 12111412 141        1 (RETURN)
    3.    ? 0003 09011967 118111 12129999 112        1 (RETURN)
    4.    ? 0004 10251911 221928 12129999 093        1 (RETURN)
(more cases here)
  422.    ? 0591 06121959 212111 12111613 152        1 (RETURN)
  423.    ? (ATTN) ***

COMMAND? SAVE MYFILE.DATA
MYFILE.DATA SAVED ON DISK01

COMMAND? LOGOFF CLEAR
```

When you've entered all the cases, you press (ATTN) at the very beginning of a line to indicate that you're through typing in data and you want to give WYLBUR a command. WYLBUR prints three asterisks and then sends you its regular prompt, COMMAND?. Your command to WYLBUR is to SAVE the entered data in a file named MYFILE.DATA. WYLBUR creates this file with your data in it and prints a message confirming what it has done. It tells you the name of the place where it stored your file—a storage device named DISK01. Your next command is LOGOFF CLEAR, which disconnects you from WYLBUR. Your session is over; you have successfully created a data file.

EDT

On VAX computers that run the VMS operating system, the standard text editor is named EDT. You can use EDT either as a line editor or a full-screen editor, and you can switch back and forth. When you use EDT as a full-screen editor, you can move the **cursor** to any point on the screen and enter data or make changes, directly at that point. The cursor is a box or similar marker that shows you where the next character you type will appear.

Figure 4.1 A form with answers filled in

1. Case Number   ⬚0⬚0⬚0⬚1⬚   01–04/

2. What is your date of birth?

   ⬚0⬚8⬚ ⬚2⬚4⬚ ⬚1⬚9⬚5⬚2⬚   06–13/
   Month Day   Year

      Numerical Notations of Months

   January   01   May   05   September 09
   February 02   June   06   October   10
   March   03   July   07   November   11
   April   04   August   08   December   12

3. Circle Respondent's Sex: 15/

   Male......①   Female.....2   .

4. Are you currently—married, widowed, divorced,
   separated, or have you never been married?

   Married........1   Separated.......4   16/
   Widowed........2   Never married..⑤
   Divorced.......3

5. On the whole, how satisfied are you with the work you
   do—would you say you are very satisfied, moderately
   satisfied, a little dissatisfied, or very dissatisfied?

   Very satisfied.........1   17/
   Moderately satisfied...②
   A little dissatisfied...3
   Very dissatisfied.......4
   Don't know............8

6. Taking things all together, how would you describe your
   marriage? Would you say that your marriage is very happy,
   pretty happy, or not too happy?

   Very happy...........1   Not too happy........3   18/
   Pretty happy.........2   Don't know...........8

7. In general, do you find life exciting, pretty routine,
   or dull?

   Exciting............①   Dull.................3   19/
   Pretty routine.......2   No opinion...........8

8. Do you believe there is life after death?

   Yes.............1   Undecided........8   20/
   No.............②

9. What is the highest grade in elementary school or
   high school that you finished and got credit for?
   CODE EXACT GRADE.

   No formal school....00   7th grade........07   22–23/
   1st grade..........01   8th grade.........08
   2nd grade..........02   9th grade........09
   3rd grade..........03   10th grade........10
   4th grade..........04   11th grade........11
   5th grade..........05   12th grade.......⑫
   6th grade..........06

10. IF FINISHED 9TH–12TH GRADE OR DON'T KNOW:
    Did you ever get a high school diploma   24/
    or a GED certificate?

    Yes ....①
    No...................2
    Don't know..........8

11. Did you ever complete one or more years of college for
    credit—not including schooling such as business
    college, technical or vocational school?

    Yes ....①   25/
    No..............2
    Don't know.......8

    IF YES TO PREVIOUS QUESTION:

12. How many years did you complete?

    1 year...........13   6 years...........18   26-27/
    2 years..........14   7 years...........19
    3 years..........15   8 or more years...⑳
    4 years..........16   Don't know........98
    5 years..........17

13. Do you have any college degrees?

    Yes..............①   28/
    No.................2
    Don't know.........8

    IF YES TO PREVIOUS QUESTION:

14. What degree or degrees? CODE HIGHEST DEGREE EARNED

    Associate/Junior college...........2   29/
    Bachelor's.........................3
    Graduate...........................④
    Don't know.........................8

15. In which of these groups did your total family
    income, from all sources, fall last year—1983—
    before taxes, that is. Just tell me the letter.

    A. Under $1,000 01   31-32/
    B. $1,000 to 2,999.................02
    C. $3,000 to 3,999.................03
    D. $4,000 to 4,999.................04
    E. $5,000 to 5,999.................05
    F. $6,000 to 6,999.................06
    G. $7,000 to 7,999.................07
    H. $8,000 to 9,999.................08
    I. $10,000 to 12,499...............09
    J. $12,500 to 14,999...............10
    K. $15,000 to 17,499...............11
    L. $17,500 to 19,999...............12
    M. $20,000 to 22,499...............13
    N. $22,500 to 24,999...............14
    O. $25,000 to 34,999...............15
    P. $35,000 to 49,999...............⑯
    Q. $50,000 or over.................17
       REFUSED.........................97
       DON'T KNOW......................98

    TOTAL INCOME INCLUDES INTEREST OR DIVIDENDS, RENT,
    SOCIAL SECURITY, OTHER PENSIONS, ALIMONY OR CHILD
    SUPPORT, UNEMPLOYMENT COMPENSATION, PUBLIC AID(WELFARE),
    ARMED FORCES OR VETERAN'S ALLOTMENT.

16. Would you say your own health, in general,
    is excellent, good, fair, or poor?

    Excellent........①   Poor.............4   33/
    Good.............2   Don't know.......8
    Fair.............3

    RECORD NUMBER...........................|1| 40/

Important keys for using EDT, or any full-screen editor, are the four cursor keys (marked with arrows) that you use to move the cursor around the screen. You'll also use the (RETURN) key like the one on a typewriter, and you'll need to know how to type **control sequences.** Typing a control sequence simply means holding down the key marked CTRL, on the left side of the keyboard, while typing some other key. To type CTRL-Z, you just hold down CTRL, type the letter Z, then release both keys.

EDT also uses the keys on the **keypad,** a special group of keys at the right of the keyboard. Each of these keys stands for a specific command, and you can issue that command simply by pressing its key. There's an obvious disadvantage to using an editor that relies on special keys: you have to learn which key does which command. Until you do, you'll be constantly referring to a manual or a chart. However, you can get started with just a few commands, which you'll learn quickly. As you continue to use the editor, you'll find that you gradually pick up the other commands. Once you know them, you can use them efficiently. While you're learning, you can easily get help by pressing the HELP key. (On the keyboard of the series VT100 and VT200 terminals, the HELP key is marked PF2.)

To start your EDT session, you must log on to the VAX computer. Turn on the terminal and press the (RETURN) key. The computer will ask for your user name and your password, and then it will display its prompt, the dollar sign ($).

EDT, unlike WYLBUR, expects you to name your file before you create it. Let's say you want to call your data file MYFILE.DAT:

```
$ EDT MYFILE.DAT
Input file does not exist
[EOB]
*
```

EDT has started running as a line editor. It has told you that the file you named, MYFILE.DAT, does not yet exist. That makes sense—you're about to create it. The EOB stands for End Of Buffer, which means technically that you are at the end of this file that does not exist. Finally, the asterisk (*) is the EDT prompt, telling you that EDT is ready for a command.

Type C or CHANGE to change from line editing to full-screen editing. Then press (RETURN). The screen clears, and you can type:

```
0001 08241952 152912 12112014 161     1 (RETURN)
0002 04141941 213111 12111412 141     1 (RETURN)
0003 09011967 118111 12129999 112     1 (RETURN)
0004 10251911 221928 12129999 093     1 (RETURN)
```
(and so on for all the data)

Check the data as you enter it. If you find a mistake, move the cursor to it, and delete the bad characters with the Delete key. Then type in the correct data. The characters you type are always inserted before the position of the cursor. When you get to the bottom of the screen and press

(RETURN) after the last line, the whole display moves up to make room for a new line.

When you've entered all the data, type CTRL-Z as explained above: hold down the CTRL key and type a z. This switches you back into line editing so you can give the command to save your file and leave the editor. EDT will give you its prompt, the asterisk. You then type EXIT and press (RETURN):

```
0591 06121959 212111 12111613 152        1 (CTRL-Z)

*EXIT (RETURN)
```

You use the EXIT command to save the file and take you safely out of EDT. The next prompt you'll get will be the dollar sign.

TIPS ON ENTERING DATA

It's easy to make mistakes when you type in your data. Here are some tips that will make it easier for you to find and fix these mistakes:

- Line up the data for each case so that the same types of information always appear at the same positions on the line. If you have room, leave a blank space between the pieces of information or between groups of them so that they're easier to spot. In other words, use *fixed format*, as discussed above.

- Start each case on a new line. If you have too much data for a case to fit on a single line, go ahead and use more than one line per case; but never put more than one case on a line. (You can't, if you use fixed format.)

- Put the case ID number at the beginning of *each line* of the file. If you are using more than one line per case, repeat it on each line.

- If you are have more than one line per case, also number each line *within* the case.

- Save your data file frequently as you enter the data. That way, you'll have a permanent copy of most of your data even if something goes wrong while you're working.

- Make a **backup copy,** an extra copy of the data to use if your original data file is somehow lost or destroyed.

WHAT'S NEXT?

Once the data file is complete, you're ready to start the analysis phase of the study. The next chapter describes how to run SPSS^X, and the following chapter describes how to tell SPSS^X the layout of your data file.

Summary

What is a data file, and how do you go about creating one?

Always check your forms for legibility and completeness before entering data from them into the computer file.

Assign codes to answers before entering data into the computer file.

Start each case on a new line in the computer file. If necessary, you can use more than one line for a case.

Unless your file is quite small, use fixed format: put the answer to any one question in the same columns for all cases.

Use a text editor to enter data into a computer file and to save the file, or to change data in an existing computer file and to save the modified file.

Make a backup copy of your data file as a spare. You can use it if you make a mistake or if the computer malfunctions and your file is damaged.

EXERCISES

Concepts

1 Sometimes a question simply doesn't work. Respondents or interviewers misunderstand it, or respondents refuse to answer it, or they simply don't know the answer. Discuss the problems of revising such questions at the following stages in the study:
   a. While designing the form.
   b. While proofreading the printed forms.
   c. After trying out a few questionnaires on people like those who will answer it. (Preliminary tests like this are called "pretests.")
   d. After receiving the first completed questionnaires and noticing the problems.
   e. After beginning to analyze the data.

2 Discuss how likely it is that bad questions will be *detected* at each of the stages in the previous question. Do your answers to questions 1 and 2 suggest any procedures you could use to improve the questions in your study?

3 Compare the advantages of entering your data into the computer in fixed format, versus free format.

4 Text editors include powerful commands for deleting or modifying lines, and for moving lines around within the file. In view of this,
   a. Why is it important to enter an identification number on every line in the data file?
   b. Why is it important to make a second copy (a "backup") of the data file?

Data Analysis

1 "Play" with your text editor for ten minutes or more. Try at least to learn how to:
   a. delete a line.
   b. add a new line at the end of the file.
   c. add a new line in the middle of the file.
   d. move a line from one place to another in the file.
   e. leave the editor without saving the file.
2 Using the text editor, enter the data for the first four cases used in this chapter into a file on your computer. Be sure to save the file before you leave the editor. Choose any name you like for the data file.

5 Running SPSS[x]

How do you tell SPSS[x] the way you want it to analyze your data?

- What kind of commands does SPSS[x] recognize?
- How should these commands look? Does spelling matter? What about spaces between words?
- Is punctuation important in entering commands?
- What is a command file, and how do you create one?
- Once you've set up a command file, how do you tell SPSS[x] to carry out the commands in it?

Now that you've got a computer file containing your data, you have to tell SPSS^X how you want to analyze it. In this chapter we'll go over the way you use commands to tell SPSS^X what to do, and then we'll look at the steps you take to actually run an SPSS^X program.

SPSS^X COMMANDS

SPSS^X is a tool. It does what you tell it to do. You communicate with it by giving it **commands.** A command is simply a word or group of words that SPSS^X recognizes and knows how to obey. The name of a command is always the first word on a line, and it always begins in the first column. Other information may follow and may even continue onto other lines— but if so, the information on the other lines must be indented so it won't be mistaken for the start of new commands. A simple job might use these three SPSS^X commands:

```
FILE HANDLE GSS / (system-specific information)
GET FILE=GSS
LIST CASES=10
```

Most of the time, a command pretty well says what it does. The LIST command in this example lists the values of the data in 10 cases. Other commands, like FILE HANDLE, are less obvious at first, but they supply information that SPSS^X needs to do your bidding. Important things to remember about SPSS^X commands are:

- The name of a command must begin in column 1 and must be spelled correctly. Otherwise, SPSS^X won't recognize it. Most commands include additional information, or **specifications.**

- The specifications on a command are separated by blank spaces, or sometimes by special characters such as ( ) / = .

- You can add blank spaces around the special characters ( ) / = .

- You can add *extra* blank spaces anywhere a *single* blank space is allowed.
- You can type commands in upper case or lower case.
- You can use as many lines as you want for entering a command, as long as the lines after the first begin after column 1. However, you can't split a single word across two lines.

Since you can perform many types of statistical analysis using SPSS^X, its language contains many commands and subcommands. You'll learn only a few of them in this book. But you'll learn all of the most common commands.

The SPSS^X Language

The name of a command by itself is rarely enough to convey exactly what you want done. On most commands, therefore, you enter additional information, specifications, to describe exactly what you want. You have to enter the specifications in a way that SPSS^X can understand, of course. Here is an example of an SPSS^X command with specifications:

```
LIST VARIABLES = AGE
  / CASES = 10
  / FORMAT = NUMBERED
```

Keywords are words that SPSS^X understands. Most of the words on this command are keywords. Except for command names, you can usually abbreviate keywords to their first three letters. LIST is a keyword that is the name of the command itself. It cannot be abbreviated. VARIABLES, CASES, and FORMAT are keywords used as **subcommands.** They supply specific information relating to the command. NUMBERED is another keyword, used here with the FORMAT subcommand. Such keywords usually have an obvious meaning. Here, NUMBERED simply means that SPSS^X should number the cases that it lists.

AGE is not a keyword. It is a variable name. We'll discuss variables in Chapter 6. The important thing about names such as this is that SPSS^X doesn't recognize them until you define them. And you must always spell them exactly the same as in the definition. Again, though, it doesn't matter if you use upper or lower case. The above example is only correct if AGE was defined on a previous command.

Specifications are often numbers. In the example, the number 10, after the subcommand CASES, indicates that 10 cases should be listed.

What else? Don't forget the punctuation. The **slash** character (/) separates the different subcommands. Other commands may require parentheses. We'll point these out as we come to them. Finally, the equals sign (=) typically separates a subcommand from its specifications.

You can frequently get away with leaving off the equals sign, but it's safest to include it.

By putting everything in lower case, abbreviating keywords, and leaving off the equals signs, you could write the example LIST command as

```
list var age/cas 10/for num
```

This form is a lot shorter, but it's harder to read. In this book, you'll generally see commands spelled out for clarity.

? *Do you have to memorize all of these things to use SPSS^X? How many subcommands and keywords and specifications does it take to use a command?* It takes only a bare minimum. For example, to list a whole data file, you can just use the command

```
LIST
```

When you don't enter all the possible specifications, SPSS^X uses its **defaults.** A default specification is one that will be used unless you specify something else. For the LIST command, the defaults are to list all the variables and all the cases and not to number the cases. These are the things that happen if you type just LIST. Most of the time, you can rely on the defaults to give you the most commonly requested information. ■ ■ ■

THE SPSS^X JOB

To do anything useful with your data, you usually need at least three SPSS^X commands:

1 A command to identify your data file.

2 A command to specify how the data file should be read.

3 A command to indicate what you want to do with the data.

Usually, though, you have more than three commands. Sometimes you have many more, since it's convenient to do several tasks at once.

You type your job—the group of commands you want SPSS^X to process—into a computer file with the same text editor you use for entering data. However, you give the command file another name. Every file must have its own name, and if you save your commands into a file with the same name as your data file, the command file replaces the data file.

After setting up your command file, you **run,** or submit, the commands. That is, you instruct your computer to turn your commands over to the SPSS^X program for processing.

The exact way in which you do this depends on what kind of computer you use and (equally important) on what kind of operating system is in control of the computer. As a result, the exact procedures you follow may be slightly different from the ones discussed below. Don't worry—there's always someone who can help. Most problems at this level are easily solved. (After you've run a few jobs, you're likely to find that *real* beginners come to you for advice.)

STEPS IN RUNNING SPSS[X]

Let's go through the basic steps:

1 Create the file containing the data you want to analyze. Or just find out the name of the existing file that you want to use—like the GSS file for the General Social Survey examples in this book.

2 Create a command file that contains your SPSS[X] commands.

3 Instruct your computer to run the SPSS[X] program, telling it the name of your command file so SPSS[X] will know what to do.

4 Look at the **listing** created by your job to see the results. The listing is the output, which shows the results. It may be placed in a new computer file of its own, it may appear on the screen of your terminal, or it may be automatically printed.

At some point—either in Step 2 or Step 3, depending on your computer— you need to tell SPSS[X] the name of the data file you created or found in Step 1. With most operating systems you put the name of the data file on the SPSS[X] FILE HANDLE command. With the IBM OS family of operating systems, you enter special commands called Job Control Language, or JCL, to identify your data file at the time you run SPSS[X].

We'll go through some examples. Things will probably be a little different on your system, but these examples should give you a feel for what's involved in running SPSS[X].

An IBM OS Operating System

On a computer with one of the IBM OS operating systems, such as MVS, you use JCL to specify the files and other resources your job will need. JCL looks formidable at first, but you'll soon learn that you can use mostly the same JCL lines over and over again for different jobs, changing only a few details, such as file name.

It's convenient to put the JCL in the same file as your SPSS[X] commands. You can use a text editor (such as WYLBUR, described in

Chapter 4) to create a file containing both the SPSS^X commands and the JCL. A simple job might look like this:

```
//LISTDATA JOB (accounting information),NORUSIS,REGION=512K
//   EXEC SPSSX
//GSS  DD  DSN=SPSDATA.GSS84,DISP=SHR
GET FILE=GSS
LIST CASES=10
//
```

The commands that begin with // are JCL. The two lines beginning with GET and LIST are SPSS^X commands (see Chapter 6).

The next step is to actually *run* the job. If you're using WYLBUR or a similar text editor to set up your job, you can run the job directly from the editor. The file you are editing should be the command file. If not, first tell WYLBUR to USE that file. Then just type the WYLBUR command RUN. Let's say your command file is named LIST.JOB:

```
COMMAND? USE LIST.JOB
COMMAND? RUN
```

Remember to save your command file in case you want to modify the job and run it again.

Finally, you want to see the results, the output. On IBM OS systems, the output will typically be printed without your having to do anything special.

A VAX VMS Operating System

On a VAX system (and many other types of computers), you use your text editor to create a command file. Let's say you named the command file LIST.SPS. It might look like this for a simple job:

```
FILE HANDLE GSS / NAME='GSS84.DAT'
GET FILE=GSS
LIST CASES=10
```

After saving this file as LIST.SPS and exiting the text editor, you get the dollar-sign prompt and can then run the job with the following command after the prompt:

```
$ SPSSX LIST.SPS
```

When you run the job this way, you don't need to look for the output. It just comes to your terminal.

WHAT'S NEXT?

The next chapter shows you how to tell the computer about your data, and from there it's on to getting the results.

Summary

How do you tell SPSS[X] the way you want it to analyze your data?

SPSS[X] commands are made up of keywords that SPSS[X] automatically recognizes, variable names and labels that you supply, and punctuation.

You must spell out the first word of a command name in full. Otherwise, you can abbreviate keywords with their first three letters.

A command must begin in column 1. You can continue a command onto additional lines, but they must be indented so they won't be mistaken for new commands.

You can enter commands in upper or lower case, and you can vary the number of spaces between words as you like.

Commands are punctuated with slashes, parentheses, and equals signs. Slashes and parentheses are required. The equals sign is sometimes optional, but it's best to enter it when you're not sure.

You enter your commands into a command file by using a text editor. When you tell your computer's operating system to execute the SPSS[X] program, you must usually give the system the name of your command file. (Details vary from one computer system to another.)

EXERCISES

Syntax

1   We used the following short job in this chapter to show the form in which you enter SPSS[X] commands:

```
FILE HANDLE GSS / (system-specific information)
GET FILE=GSS
LIST CASES=10
```

Find the one mistake in each of the following variations on this job:

a.
```
file handle=gss / (system-specific information)
   get file=gss
   list 10 cases
```

b.
```
FILE HANDLE  GSS / (system-specific information)
GET      FILE gss
   LIST        cases 10
```

c.
```
FILE HANDLE GSS
   / (system-specific information)
GET
   FILE GSS
LIST
CASES=10
```

2 You have collected your data and entered it into a data file, using a text editor. Now you want to use the editor to set up a command file containing the SPSS^X commands to analyze your data. Should you specify the same name for the command file that you used for the data file? Why?

Data Analysis

1 Using a text editor, set up a command file containing the three commands shown above. Find out what information is needed on the FILE HANDLE command to identify the GSS system file (either the one accompanying this book, or one obtained from some other source).

(If your computer uses the IBM OS operating system, omit the FILE HANDLE command. Supply the necessary JCL to run the SPSS^X program and read a GSS system file.)

2 Run the SPSS^X job that you set up in the previous exercise. Print the output from the job.

Defining Your Data

*How do you tell SPSS[X] what's in your data file—
which answers correspond to which questions?*

- How do you tell SPSS[X] the name of your data file?

- How do you tell SPSS[X] what variables are in your data file and where they are located in the records?

- How do you distinguish values that represent missing data, such as questions that weren't answered?

- How do you make SPSS[X] label your output, so you'll be able to remember what the variables and their response codes mean?

- Do you have to supply all this information every time you use the data file?

You know where your data are and how they're organized. Now you must tell the computer. To make it easier to describe the data, we'll need some simple jargon: *cases*, *variables*, and *values*.

CASES

Each person who participates in a survey or experiment is known as a **case.** (Another word often used is *observation*.) Actually, a case need not be a person. It can be anything. If you're doing experiments on rats, the case is the individual rat. You might record such things as learning time, food consumed, or weight of the animal. If you're studying the beef content of hamburgers, each hamburger is a case. For a hamburger, you might measure the place it was bought, the cost, and the weight of the beef. The case (or observation) is the unit for which you take measurements.

VARIABLES AND THEIR VALUES

Think back to the way you conduct a survey. You ask each person for the same type of information: date of birth, sex, marital status, education, views on current life and afterlife. Although you ask everybody the same questions, the answers naturally vary from person to person. Some respondents are men; others are women. Some are single; others are married, widowed, separated, or divorced. Each of the items you ask about (more specifically, each item for which you record an answer) is known as a **variable.** The answer a particular person gives is known as the **value** for that variable. Year of birth is a variable; responses such as 1952 or 1899 are values for year of birth.

These concepts (cases or observations, variables, and values) are fundamental for any kind of data analysis. Think about them one more time, and make sure you understand how they relate to one another. The questions you ask, or types of information you record, are variables. Each individual answer or piece of information is a value. The people or things you test in the study are cases, or observations. For each case, you have one value for each variable.

IDENTIFYING YOUR DATA FILE

Before you can read your data file with SPSS[X], you must describe what file you want to read and how you want to read it. You can use the FILE HANDLE command to identify the file, and you can use the DATA LIST command to specify how you want it read (what the variables are and where they are in the file).

The FILE HANDLE Command

You must enter a FILE HANDLE command for every file you want to read with SPSS[X]. This command lets you give a file a nickname to use during your SPSS[X] job. If your computer requires a file name that's complicated or hard to remember, you only have to give that name once in your job and then use the nickname. For example, if your data are in a file called MYFILE.DAT, you might specify:

```
FILE HANDLE GSSDATA / NAME='MYFILE.DAT'
```

The FILE HANDLE command may look different on your computer, or you may not even need to use it in your SPSS[X] program.

To learn about using FILE HANDLE, find out what kind of computer you are using and what type of operating system it has. (Remember than an operating system does such things as scheduling other programs and providing access to disk files.) One common family of operating system on IBM computers is known as OS. When you run SPSS[X] on a computer that has an OS operating system, you don't need a FILE HANDLE command at all. Instead, you use the Job Control Language, or JCL. JCL is part of the operating system, and you can use it to specify which files you're going to need. You saw an example of JCL in Chapter 5. With SPSS[X], you might use the following JCL command to assign the nickname GSSDATA to a file named MYFILE.DAT:

```
//GSSDATA DD DSN=MYFILE.DAT,DISP=SHR
```

With other operating systems, you do use the FILE HANDLE command. Most of the time, you use it to provide only the name of the data file, like this:

```
FILE HANDLE GSSDATA / NAME='MYFILE.DAT'
```

If you want to use more than one file in a single job, you can simply enter a separate FILE HANDLE command for each file and use a different nickname with each one. Then, when you need a specific file, just refer to it by the particular nickname you gave it.

Like all other SPSS[X] commands, the FILE HANDLE command must start in column 1 and must be spelled correctly. Refer to Chapter 5 for the general rules about SPSS[X] commands.

The DATA LIST Command

Use the DATA LIST command to describe the variables and their location in the data file. The first thing you have to do on the DATA LIST command is identify the data file you're going to define, using the nickname from its FILE HANDLE command (or from the JCL):

- Move to the beginning of a new line of the file into which you're entering commands. Type the words DATA LIST starting in column 1.

- Next, enter the keyword FILE, an equals sign, and the nickname you chose for your file.

At this point, you have:

```
FILE HANDLE GSSDATA/ NAME='mydata.dat'
DATA LIST FILE=GSSDATA
```

But you're not finished yet with the DATA LIST command.

Identifying Your Variables

The next thing you must tell the computer is where each variable is located. You must tell it that the identification number for each case is in columns 1 through 4, the month of birth is in columns 6 and 7, the day in columns 8 and 9, the year in columns 10 through 13, and so on for the rest of the variables you'll use.

You need a convenient way to refer to the variables. Assign each one a name to use throughout the SPSS^X job. For example, you can call the identification number ID, the month of birth BMONTH, the day of birth BDAY, and the year of birth BYEAR. Names for all the variables (along with their column positions) are in Table 6.1. (More about the "Missing codes" later.) Table 6.1 shows the variable names assigned by the people who run the General Social Survey.

Variable Names

You could have given the variables in Table 6.1 many different names. When naming your children or pets, you are free to use any name you please. On the other hand, when requesting a license plate you must follow a few rules, so that license plates will all be different but can all be made the same size. Variable names are like license plate numbers in these ways: they have to be different, and they have to fit in a certain amount of space. When you name variables:

- Give every variable a different name.

- Don't use more than eight characters.

- Start the name with a letter, from A through Z. (The rest of the characters can be letters or numbers.)

- Choose names that help you remember what the variable is: AGE rather than X1, RACE rather than VBQZ.

Table 6.1 Variables in the data file

Description	Columns	Missing codes	SPSS^X variable name
Case number	1−4	(none)	ID
Birth month	6−7	97−99	BMONTH
Birth day	8−9	97−99	BDAY
Birth year	10−13	9997−9999	BYEAR
Sex	15	7−9	SEX
Marital status	16	7,9	MARITAL
Satisfaction with job	17	7−9	SATJOB
Happiness with marriage	18	7−9	HAPMAR
Life's excitement	19	7−9	LIFE
Life after death	20	7−9	POSTLIFE
Highest grade	22−23	97−99	YRSEDUC
High school diploma	24	7−9	HSDEGREE
Any college	25	7−9	ANYCOLL
Years of college	26−27	97−99	YRSCOLL
Any degrees	28	7−9	ANYDEG
What degrees	29	7−9	COLLDEG
Family income	31−32	97−99	INCOME
Condition of health	33	7−9	HEALTH
record number	40	(none)	(none)

■ Don't use names from the following list:

```
ALL    EQ   LE   NOT     TO
AND    GE   LT   OR      WITH
BY     GT   NE   THRU
```

All of these are words that mean something special to SPSS^X. ALL, for example, means "all variables" in some situations. If you had a single variable named ALL, you might get more output than you bargained for.

Naming Variables on a DATA LIST

Once you've assigned names to all of your variables, you must tell your choices to the computer. To do this, list all of the variable names and their columns on the DATA LIST command.

You signal that you're starting to describe the variables by typing a slash. After the slash, you type a variable name followed by its column numbers. If a variable is in a single column, just give the one number. If a variable is in several columns, give the first and last column numbers, and separate them by a hyphen—just as in Table 6.1. The complete DATA LIST command for our example looks like this:

```
DATA LIST FILE=GSSDATA / ID 1-4 BMONTH 6-7 BDAY 8-9 BYEAR 10-13
    SEX 15 MARITAL 16 SATJOB 17 HAPMAR 18 LIFE 19 POSTLIFE 20
    YRSEDUC 22-23 HSDEGREE 24 ANYCOLL 25 YRSCOLL 26-27 ANYDEG 28
    COLLDEG 29 INCOME 31-32 HEALTH 33
```

You list all of the variables and the column number or numbers for each. If the descriptions go on for more than one line, be sure to indent all the lines after the first.

Don't worry about the number of spaces you need to separate pieces of the command. You can have more than one space anywhere that a single space is used. You must have at least one space between a variable name and its column numbers. Otherwise, the column numbers would look like part of the variable name. If you like, you can even enter your variables as a table like this:

```
DATA LIST FILE=GSSDATA
    /  ID        1- 4
       BMONTH    6- 7
       BDAY      8- 9
       BYEAR     10-13
       SEX       15
   ...and so on.
```

Except for spacing, which doesn't matter, this is the same command as the one before.

Defining Cases from Multiple Records

If you entered the data for each case on more than one line in your data file, you have to tell SPSS[X] how many lines, or records, to expect. Use the keyword RECORDS on the DATA LIST command to indicate the number of lines for each case. If you have five lines for each case, type:

```
DATA LIST FILE=GSSDATA RECORDS=5 /
```

You also need to indicate *which* record contains the data for each of your variables. This is simple. All you have to do is put a slash between the variables that are on different records, and give the number of the next record directly after the slash. For example, if you have three records with the variables AGE and SEX on the first record, and the variables HEIGHT and WEIGHT on the second, type

```
DATA LIST FILE=NICKNAME RECORDS=3 /1 AGE 2-3 SEX 4 /2 HEIGHT 3-4
    WEIGHT 9-11
```

The number 1 after the first slash tells the computer that the variables coming up, AGE and SEX, are on the first record. The number 2 following the second slash tells the computer that you are about to start defining the second record. You can skip records if you don't plan to analyze the variables on them. If you don't need HEIGHT and WEIGHT from the second record, but you want to use a variable called SUNTAN from the third record, you can type:

DATA LIST FILE=NICKNAME RECORDS=3 /1 AGE 2–3 SEX 4 /3 SUNTAN 9

The system for describing your data with DATA LIST is very flexible:

- You don't have to define all the variables in your data file, only the ones you want to use.
- You don't have to read variables from each record. The RECORDS keyword tells SPSS^X how many total records are used, and the number following each slash tells SPSS^X which record contains the variables you're about to define.
- You don't have to define variables in their order on a record. You can define SEX before AGE, even if AGE comes first on record 1.
- However, you do have to define the *records* in order. You can't define variables on record 2 and then go back to record 1.

? *Is all this multiple-record business like indenting—when you use more than one line for a command?* No, now we're talking about data for a case using more than one line in the *data file*. The number of lines you use for each case in the data file has nothing whatever to do with the number of lines it takes to enter your DATA LIST command in the *command file*. The slashes and record numbers on the DATA LIST command refer to the arrangement of variables in the data file. It's quite likely that you will have so much to enter on the DATA LIST command that *it* will have to be split across two or more lines; but that is a completely different matter. To use a second line for the DATA LIST command, just remember to indent it. To indicate on a DATA LIST command that you're about to describe variables on the second line of each case in the data file, enter /2 on the command.   ■ ■ ■

String Variables

Most of the time, the data you analyze with SPSS^X are numbers. Whenever possible, you should use numbers to code your data, even if you start out with words or names. If you're stuck with words instead of numbers, you can go ahead and define variables that contain words instead. These are called **string variables,** or sometimes **character variables.** (Instead of being numbers like good, honest variables, they are just strings of characters.)

String variables don't have to be words, of course. They can be letters or punctuation marks or random characters. They can even be strings of numbers. The point is that SPSS^X doesn't know or care what the values of a string variable mean. It will not try to do arithmetic with them. It just treats them as strings of characters. Two things are especially important when you have string variables:

1 Whenever you define a string variable on a DATA LIST, you have to tell SPSS[X] that the variable's values aren't numbers. Otherwise SPSS[X] will try to read them as numbers and complain when it can't.

2 Whenever you type the *values* of a string variable, in your SPSS[X] job, you must enclose them in quotes.

On a DATA LIST, you indicate that a variable is a string variable by putting (A), for Alpha, after its name and position. For the last DATA LIST above, suppose that SEX was coded as either M or F, for Male or Female. M and F are not numbers, so you'd have to make SEX a string variable. The DATA LIST would then look like this:

```
DATA LIST FILE=NICKNAME RECORDS=3 /1 AGE 2-3 SEX 4 (A) /3 SUNTAN 9
```

The (A) after SEX 4 indicates that the values for SEX (in the 4th column) may not be numbers, and that SEX should therefore be treated as a string variable. On other SPSS[X] commands, you have to refer to the M and the F as 'M' and 'F'.

DATA LIST for Freefield Data

As explained in Chapter 4, you can enter your data in freefield format if that's convenient. (It's usually convenient when you have only a few variables.) In freefield format, the data for each variable aren't necessarily in particular columns. Instead, they're separated from each other by one or more blank spaces. Every data value must be present.

If you're using freefield format, the DATA LIST command is slightly different from the one described above. It's simpler. All you have to do is include the keyword FREE on the DATA LIST command, before the slash. It doesn't matter whether FREE comes before or after FILE=NICKNAME, so long as it's before the slash. Then you just list the variable names in their order in the file:

```
DATA LIST FREE FILE=MYDATA/ ID BMO BDAY BYEAR ...
```

You don't have any column numbers associated with each of the variables. You do, however, use (A) for string variables. You don't use the RECORDS keyword, or additional slashes, on a DATA LIST FREE command, because SPSS[X] doesn't care what record the variables are on or what columns they're in. It just reads values one after another and assigns them in order to the variable names you typed on the DATA LIST command.

Including Your Data in the Command File

When you don't have much data, and your data records are no longer than 80 characters, you can include them in your command file:

```
DATA LIST / NAME 1-8 (A) AGE 10-11 SEX 13
BEGIN DATA
Johnson  35 2
Murphy   51 1
END DATA
```

There is no file name on the DATA LIST commmand, and the actual data follow BEGIN DATA and are followed by END DATA.

THE ACTIVE FILE

When you ask SPSS^X to do something with your data (perhaps print it out or calculate statistics), it uses the information on the DATA LIST command to read the data and convert it into a form the computer can calculate with. In this form, the data are called the **active file.** SPSS^X uses the active file for all of its processing. When you supply labels for the data, as described below, they are also put into the active file. When you change the data by using SPSS^X commands (see Chapters 10 and 12), you again change the active file. Your original data file remains safe and intact, with the same information you put into it.

MISSING DATA

For each variable in our survey, a special code indicates when information is missing. For some questions, several codes indicate missing values. For example, if the interviewer forgot to ask a question, you can use a code that means No answer. If the respondent refused to answer or didn't remember the answer, the information is still missing, but you probably want to distinguish this situation from a simple mistake. (People who refuse to answer sensitive questions are often a distinctive group.) You use the MISSING VALUES command to tell the computer what codes indicate that information is missing. As you'll see once we start looking at data analysis, missing values must be treated in special ways. SPSS^X allows you to specify up to three different codes to indicate missing values.

The General Social Survey uses the codes in Table 6.2 to indicate different types of missing data, depending on how many columns are occupied by a variable (also see Table 6.1).

Table 6.2 Missing-data codes for the General Social Survey

	Refused answer	Didn't know answer	No answer recorded
1 column	7	8	9
2 columns	97	98	99
3 columns	997	998	999
and so on			

You tell SPSS[X] that these codes represent missing information with the MISSING VALUES command, like this:

```
MISSING VALUES BMONTH (97,98,99) BDAY (97,98,99)
  BYEAR (9997,9998,9999) SEX (7,8,9) ...
```

After each variable name, enter in parentheses the codes for missing values. If you used the same codes for several variables, you can list all of the variable names that have the same codes and then give the codes once. For example, type

```
MISSING VALUES BMO BDAY (97,98,99)
```

instead of

```
MISSING VALUES BMO (97,98,99) BDAY (97,98,99)
```

User-Missing and System-Missing Values

In the example above, SPSS[X] treats codes 97, 98, and 99 as missing because you told it to, by entering a MISSING VALUES command. Data that are missing for this reason are called **user-missing,** because you (the user) specified them as missing.

Sometimes SPSS[X] must treat data as missing regardless of whether you tell it to or not. Perhaps a case in your data file is simply missing some variables. Perhaps somebody's fingers slipped and entered a person's age as YP instead of 60. When things like this happen, SPSS[X] assigns a special value called the **system-missing** value. Statistics are never computed with system-missing values, because they aren't proper values at all.

? *What good are missing values? Why do we have to fool with them?* Most of the time, you can't really do anything with missing values, but you don't want to throw away the whole cases they came from. Other variables in those cases may have perfectly good values. And you may change your mind about user-missing values. People who don't know who they will vote for are sometimes useless for your analysis, but sometimes they're the most interesting people of all.

Nobody wants missing values in their data, but they always turn up. One of the first things you should do with a new data file is get a general idea of how many missing values there are, and why. You can do that with frequency tables, which you'll see in Chapter 7. ■ ■ ■

VARIABLE LABELS

Although you try to choose a variable name that describes the variable, it's hard to be really descriptive in just eight characters. The variable name POSTLIFE is fine for an eight-character name, but it could refer to many different types of questions. How long can a goldfish last if it's sent through the mail? How many years did POST magazine publish? What kind of animal would people like to be reincarnated as?

You can clarify your variables by using the VARIABLE LABELS command. This command lets you have a label printed on your output whenever you use the corresponding variable in your analysis. Most of the time, SPSS[X] can print up to 40 characters of information as a variable label. You don't *have to* use these extended labels. They're often helpful, though, especially if other people, not familiar with your own creative names, must read your output.

To assign a label to the POSTLIFE variable, type:

```
VARIABLE LABELS POSTLIFE 'Belief in life after death'
```

If you want to give labels to several variables, you can list them all on the same VARIABLE LABELS command. For example, you can type:

```
VARIABLE LABELS POSTLIFE 'Belief in life after death'
                MARITAL  'Marital status'
                LIFE 'Is life exciting or dull?'
```

You give each variable name, followed by at least one comma or blank space, and then the label enclosed in apostrophes or quotation marks. (If you want to include an apostrophe as part of a label, enclose the label in quotation marks. If you want to enter a quotation mark as part of a label, enclose the label in apostrophes.) Don't split a label between two lines.

VALUE LABELS

When you look at your output, you'll find it much easier to remember what a particular variable measures or describes if you use the VARIABLE LABELS command. However, a variable label doesn't tell you anything about the coding scheme for the variable. Even if you've assigned a label like "Belief in life after death" to the POSTLIFE variable, you won't be able to tell that a code of 1 means Yes, a code of 2 means No, and a code of 8 means the respondent was undecided. If you want the computer to tell you how many people gave each of the possible responses, you'll find it easier to read the output if labels tell you what the response codes mean. Obviously, the computer can't tell you what the codes mean unless you tell the computer first.

Use the VALUE LABELS command to assign labels to each of the codes. Type:

```
VALUE LABELS POSTLIFE 1 'Yes' 2 'No' 8 'Undecided' 9 'Missing'
```

This command assigns the label Yes for a code of 1 on the variable POSTLIFE, the label No for a code of 2, the label Undecided for a code of 8, and the label Missing for a code of 9. You must enclose each of the labels in quotes or apostrophes. The labels should be short, 20 characters long at the most, because there's only a certain amount of space for them on SPSS[X] output. You can't continue a single label from one line to the next. If it doesn't fit on a line, put it all on a new line.

When you have several variables with the same coding scheme, you can list all of the variable names together before you start identifying the codes:

```
VALUE LABELS POSTLIFE GUNLAW 1 'Yes' 2 'No' 8 "Don't know"
```

You can also assign different labels to different variables on a single VALUE LABELS command. Separate the labels for one variable from the labels for another with a slash. For example, type:

```
VALUE LABELS POSTLIFE 1 'Yes' 2 'No' 8 "Don't know"
             / LIFE 1 'Exciting' 2 'Pretty routine' 3 'Dull'
                8 "Don't know"
             / SEX 1 'Male' 2 'Female'
             / MARITAL   1 'Married' 2 'Widowed' 3 'Divorced'
                4 'Separated' 5 'Never married'
```

Remember how we considered the possibility that SEX could be coded as M or F and would then be defined as a string variable? If you do that, you have to put the M and the F in quotes everywhere you use them in your SPSS[X] job. The VALUE LABELS command would look like this:

```
VALUE LABELS SEX 'M' 'Male' 'F' 'Female'
```

Looks silly, but that's what you have to do with string variables.

AN EXAMPLE: DEFINING THE GENERAL SOCIAL SURVEY DATA

Figure 6.1 contains all the SPSS[X] commands needed to describe the data file we've been discussing.

- The FILE HANDLE command identifies the data file and gives it a nickname.
- The DATA LIST command gives names to the variables and specifies their locations in the data file.
- The MISSING VALUES command indicates which codes have been used where no valid data exists for the variables.
- The VARIABLE LABELS command furnishes long descriptive labels for each variable.
- The VALUE LABELS command describes the meanings of individual values that are not obvious.

Figure 6.1 Commands for defining the survey data

```
FILE HANDLE GSSDATA / (system-specific information)

DATA LIST FILE=GSSDATA / ID 1-4 BMONTH 6-7 BDAY 8-9 BYEAR 10-13
   SEX 15 MARITAL 16 SATJOB 17 HAPMAR 18 LIFE 19 POSTLIFE 20
   YRSEDUC 22-23 HSDEGREE 24 ANYCOLL 25 YRSCOLL 26-27 ANYDEG 28
   COLLDEG 29 INCOME 31-32 HEALTH 33

MISSING VALUES SEX, MARITAL, SATJOB, HAPMAR, LIFE, POSTLIFE,
   HSDEGREE, ANYCOLL, ANYDEG, COLLDEG, HEALTH (7, 8, 9) /
   BMONTH, BDAY, YRSEDUC, YRSCOLL, INCOME (97, 98, 99) /
   BYEAR (9997, 9998, 9999) /

VARIABLE LABELS ID 'Identification number' BMONTH 'Month of birth'
   BDAY 'Day of birth' BYEAR 'Year of birth' SEX "Respondent's sex"
   MARITAL 'Marital status' SATJOB 'Satisfaction with job or housework'
   HAPMAR 'Happiness of marriage' LIFE 'Is life exciting or dull?'
   POSTLIFE 'Belief in life after death'
   YRSEDUC 'Years secondary education' HSDEGREE 'High school degree?'
   ANYCOLL 'Any college?' YRSCOLL 'Years college education'
   ANYDEG 'Any college degree?' COLLDEG 'College degree'
   INCOME 'Total family income' HEALTH 'Condition of health'

VALUE LABELS SEX 1 'Male' 2 'Female'
   MARITAL 1 'Married' 2 'Widowed' 3 'Divorced' 4 'Separated'
           5 'Never married' 9 'No answer' /
   SATJOB 1 'Very satisfied' 2 'Moderately satisfied'
           3 'A little dissatisfied' 4 'Very dissatisfied'
           8 "Don't know" 9 'No answer' /
   HAPMAR 1 'Very happy' 2 'Pretty happy' 3 'Not too happy'
           8 "Don't know" 9 'No answer' /
   LIFE 1 'Exciting' 2 'Pretty routine' 3 'Dull' 8 "Don't know"
           9 'No answer' /
   POSTLIFE 1 'Yes' 2 'No' 8 "Don't know" 9 'No answer' /
   HSDEGREE, ANYCOLL, ANYDEG 1 'Yes' 2 'No' /
   COLLDEG 2 'Associate' 3 'Bachelors' 4 'Graduate' /
   HEALTH 1 'Excellent' 2 'Good' 3 'Fair' 4 'Poor'
           8 "Don't know" 9 'No answer' /
```

THE LIST COMMAND

After all the work of setting up this command file, you'd probably want to see some evidence that it all works. One of the simplest things you can do with SPSS^X is list the values of your variables. You do this with the LIST command, which we looked at briefly in Chapter 5. To list all the data on your file, you can simply add the command

```
LIST
```

to the end of your command file. With a big file like the one for the General Social Survey, this is too much information. But you can use the CASES subcommand and the VARIABLES subcommand to specify how many cases and which variables you want. If you use both subcommands, separate them with a slash. Adding the command

```
LIST CASES=5 / VARIABLES=SEX MARITAL LIFE
```

to the end of the above command file produces the following listing.

Figure 6.2 Output from the LIST command

```
    SEX   MARITAL     LIFE

     2        2         2
     2        5         1
     2        3         1
     2        1         2
     1        3         1

NUMBER OF CASES READ =      5    NUMBER OF CASES LISTED =      5
```

SAVING AND USING SYSTEM FILES

The DATA LIST command tells SPSS^X how to read the information in a data file. The computer reads the information and converts it into **binary format,** a format that uses zeros and ones inside the computer to manipulate numbers. Converting the information from the data file can require a lot of processing, so it's often desirable to save the data in the binary format.

SPSS^X saves data in binary format in a **system file.** Along with the actual data, a system file contains:

- The names you've given your variables.
- All the variable labels and value labels you've assigned.
- The missing values you've specified.

It also contains some other information that's less important to us now.

? *What kind of a file is this "system file"? Is it a disk file? A command file? A data file?* The word *file* is used a lot with computers—that's for sure—because a file is a collection of information, and information is what computers deal with. A system file is a special kind of file that's used by SPSS^X. You can't edit a system file with your text editor. It may or may not be a disk file; that simply depends on whether the device in which the information is physically stored is a disk. A system file isn't a command file, although it does contain a lot of information that you entered into the command file. Nor is it the same as what's usually called a *data file.* It's more than a data file, because in addition to the data it has information taken from the command file.

In simplest terms, a system file is a copy of all the information that SPSS^X makes available to its statistical procedures—in a form it can use efficiently. ■ ■ ■

Once you enter the DATA LIST, VARIABLE LABELS, VALUE LABELS, and MISSING VALUES commands to define your data, and you enter all of the data themselves into a data file, it's a good idea to save an SPSS^X system file. We'll see why soon.

How to Save a System File

Saving a system file is easy. It usually takes just a couple of additional commands. First, of course, you have to define your variables and enter all of the labels you want to save in the system file. The additional commands you need are a FILE HANDLE command to describe the system file and a SAVE command to do the actual saving. (If you're using an IBM OS operating system, which doesn't require file handles, you'd describe the system file in your JCL.) It all works like this:

```
FILE HANDLE GSSDATA / (system-specific information about data file)
FILE HANDLE GSS      / (system-specific information about system file)
DATA LIST FILE=GSSDATA / ID 1-4 BMONTH 6-7 BDAY 8-9 BYEAR 10-13
   SEX 15 ...
MISSING VALUES SEX, MARITAL, ...
VARIABLE LABELS ID 'Identification number' BMONTH 'Month of birth'
   BDAY 'Day of birth' ...
VALUE LABELS SEX 1 'Male' 2 'Female'
   MARITAL 1 'Married' 2 'Widowed' ...
SAVE OUTFILE=GSS
```

The second FILE HANDLE command identifies the system file to the operating system. The SAVE command saves the system file, and the OUTFILE subcommand specifies a file handle, GSS.

How to Read a System File

After you've saved a system file, what do you do with it? It's out there with all the data and labels. When you want to use it again, just GET it, like this:

```
FILE HANDLE GSS / (system-specific information)
GET FILE=GSS
```

Now you have an active file containing the data, labels, and missing-value codes you had defined when you saved the system file. You can go on and do your analysis. You don't have to enter a DATA LIST command or any of the other commands in Figure 6.1.

In the rest of this book, the examples start out with the GET command to read a system file instead of a DATA LIST command to read a data file. You get the same results if you use DATA LIST and the other commands every time, but GET is a lot easier. Remember, though:

- Use DATA LIST to read a data file.
- Use GET to read a system file.

If you saved the file with the SPSS^X SAVE command, you can read it with the GET command. And you can't read it any other way! System files are in a special format that only makes sense to SPSS^X. If you created the file in any other way, you have to use DATA LIST to read the data. Then, if you like, you can save a system file, and after that you can use the GET command.

WHAT'S NEXT?

You've learned to tell SPSS^X how to read the variables in your data file, how to label them, how to list them, and how to save them in an efficient form for future use. That's a lot of preparation, but it lets you do some complicated things very easily. Now you can begin to analyze the data.

Summary

How do you tell SPSS^X what's in your data file—which answers correspond to which questions?

The FILE HANDLE command identifies a file that SPSS^X should use (such as a data file) and assigns a nickname for referring to it.

The DATA LIST command gives the nickname of the data file and then specifies the names and locations of the variables in the file.

The MISSING VALUES command specifies data values that should be omitted from your statistical analysis because they represent data that are missing.

The VARIABLE LABELS and VALUE LABELS commands supply descriptive labels that SPSS^X can use to make your output easier to understand.

The SAVE command saves all your data, variable names, variable and value labels, and missing-value specifications in an SPSS^X system file. The GET command retrieves all of this information for later use.

EXERCISES

Syntax

1 What is wrong with the variable names on the following DATA LIST commands? Modify each command so that it is acceptable.

   a. DATA LIST FILE=DATA / FIRSTNAME 1-8 LASTNAME 10-20 SCORE 21-25

   b. DATA LIST FILE=DATA / ID 1-4 84GRADE 6-8 85GRADE 9-11 86GRADE 12-14

   c. DATA LIST FILE=DATA / EDUC 1-2 DEGREE 3 PAEDUC 4-5 DEGREE 6 MAEDUC 7-8 DEGREE 9

   d. DATA LIST FILE=DATA / ALL 1 SOME 2 NONE 3

2 Suppose that you have a data file in which each case requires 3 lines of data. Write a DATA LIST command to read two variables, SEX and RACE, from columns 11 and 12 of the first record, and one variable, VOTE, from column 40 of the third record. All three variables are numeric. Do not read anything from the second record.

3 Correct the errors in each of the following commands:

  a. VARIABLE LABELS MARITAL Marital status
                         AGEWED Age at first marriage

  b. VARIABLE LABELS SPEDUC 'Spouse's education'

  c. VALUE LABELS 1 'Married' 2 'Widowed' 3 'Divorced' 4 'Separated'
     5 'Never married'

  d. VALUE LABELS SEX M 'Male' F 'Female'

Concepts

1 a. Is it true that any data which can be read as a numeric variable can also be read as a string variable? If not, give an example of a value which could be read as a number but not as a string.

  b. Is it true that any data which can be read as a string variable can also be read as a numeric variable? If not, give an example of a value which could be read as a string but not as a number.

2 a. In the following question, do you think that code 8 should be declared as a missing value? Why or why not?

Do you agree or disagree with the policies of Mayor Smith?

Agree........... 1
Disagree........ 2
Don't know...... 8

  b. In the following question, do you think that code 2 should be declared as a missing value? Why or why not?

Do you agree or disagree with the policies of Mayor Jones?

Agree........... 1
Uncertain....... 2
Disagree........ 3

  c. What is the advantage of being able to specify user-missing values? Think of a response to a question that would sometimes be regarded as missing, and sometimes as valid. (Don't use an example from this chapter.)

Data Analysis

1 a. Think of four variables for a study you might be interested in conducting. Make up data for a dozen or so cases, on the four variables. Enter the data into a data file.

  b. Write the DATA LIST command needed to read your data file.

  c. Write VARIABLE LABELS and (if appropriate) VALUE LABELS commands for your study.

  d. Run a job including the DATA LIST, VARIABLE LABELS, and VALUE LABELS commands. Include a LIST command to print a list of the values in your data file. Check to make sure they agree with what you entered. If not, correct your job and run it again.

PART **2**   CHAPTERS 7-12

DESCRIBING DATA

Counting Responses for a Single Variable

How can you count the various responses people give to a question?

- What is a frequency table, and what can you learn from it?
- How can you tell from a frequency table if there have been errors in coding or entering the data?
- What are percentages and cumulative percentages?
- What is a bar chart, and when do you use it?
- How can you tell if a variable is measured on a nominal, ordinal, interval, or ratio scale?

You're finally ready to get answers to your questions. How many people find life exciting? How many believe in a life after this one? How many marriages are happy? How many people are satisfied with their jobs?

COUNTING FREQUENCIES

You can answer all of these questions and many similar ones by just counting the number of times various answers occur. For example, to find out how people view life, all you have to do is count the number of people who selected response 1 (Exciting), response 2 (Pretty routine), and response 3 (Boring).

Fortunately, since you're analyzing the survey with SPSS^X, *you* don't have to count anything. Tell the computer to count. Run the following job (if you're not sure how, you may want to refer back to Chapter 5).

```
SET WIDTH 80
FILE HANDLE GSS / (system-specific information)
GET FILE=GSS
FREQUENCIES VARIABLES=LIFE
```

The FREQUENCIES command counts the number of times each of the codes occurs. You supply the names of the variables for which you want counts; everything else is done for you.

? *Where did all these commands before* FREQUENCIES *come from?* To run SPSS^X, you have to set up a command file with your text editor, as we discussed in Chapter 5. We talked about the FILE HANDLE and GET commands in Chapter 6. They tell SPSS^X how to read a system file containing the GSS (General Social Survey) data. SET WIDTH is just a way to specify the maximum width of the output from SPSS^X (see Chapter 5).

You'll need to use either a DATA LIST or a GET command in your jobs, depending on whether you use a raw data file or a system file. SET WIDTH 80 is not necessary, although you may want to use it if you have a terminal with an 80-column screen. ■ ■ ■

Figure 7.1 A frequency table

FILE: 1984 General Social Survey

LIFE   Is life exciting or dull?

VALUE LABEL	VALUE	FREQUENCY	PERCENT	VALID PERCENT	CUM PERCENT
Exciting	1	684	46.4	46.8	46.8
Pretty routine	2	704	47.8	48.2	95.0
Dull	3	73	5.0	5.0	100.0
Don't know	8	5	.3	MISSING	
No answer	9	7	.5	MISSING	
	TOTAL	1473	100.0	100.0	

VALID CASES   1461   MISSING CASES   12

Interpreting a Frequency Table

When you run a job with the above FREQUENCIES command, you get back something very much like Figure 7.1. It's called a **frequency table** because it tells you how frequently each of the responses occurs. The first line in the figure identifies the file, here the 1984 General Social Survey. The next line identifies the variable. The variable name, LIFE, and the variable label, Is life exciting or dull?, appear here. Then starts the actual frequency table.

Each line of the frequency table describes a particular code. For each code, the first column, called VALUE LABEL, is the explanatory label you attached to the code. If you didn't give a value label to a code, this space is left blank. The second column, headed VALUE, is the actual code used to represent the response in the data file. The third column, headed FREQUENCY, is the number of cases who chose that response.

The first line of this table is for the first code, which corresponds to a person saying life is exciting. This response has a code of 1 and an explanatory label, Exciting. You can find the number of cases who gave this answer (684) in the third column.

The last lines at the bottom of a frequency table describe the codes used for missing responses, if there are any. For the exciting-routine-dull question, two codes designate missing values. When a person couldn't decide whether life was exciting or not, the interviewer assigned the code 8, which stands for Don't know. From Figure 7.1, you can see that only five people were plagued with indecision. The second code used for missing values is 9. It is used when no response was found on the questionnaire. The interviewer may have forgotten to ask the question or to record the answer. In both of these situations, code 9, which stands for No answer, is used. From the last line of Figure 7.1, you see that seven questionnaires had no answer for this question.

Checking the Data

If you find codes in the frequency table that are not supposed to occur in the data—say a value of 6 for the exciting-routine-dull question—you must go back and look for the cases with the offending values. Maybe the data were entered incorrectly, or maybe the answer on the form was wrong. Go back and check. Unless you clean up the data, all subsequent analyses will be incorrect. Finding these bad codes is one important reason why you should run frequency distributions before beginning other analysis. (Another reason is simply to get a good, basic look at your data so you won't be surprised later.)

PERCENTAGES

If you tell a friend that 684 people find life exciting, chances are your friend will reply, "Yeah? Out of how many?" The number itself isn't very informative. It means one thing if 100,000 people were questioned, and another if 685 people were questioned. A group of 684 people out of 100,000 suggests that the excited people are a very small minority. But if 684 out of 685 people find life exciting, that's almost everyone.

One way to make a count more meaningful is to express it as a percentage of the entire sample. The percentage tells how many people out of each 100 gave the response you're talking about. Two out of 5 is 40%—and so is 400 out of 1,000.

You can find percentages in the fourth column of your SPSS^X frequency table. The 684 people who found life exciting were 46.4% of the total sample of 1,473. Almost half of the people questioned found life exciting. (You can find the total number of cases in your study by looking at the line labeled TOTAL at the bottom of the frequency table. The first number in that line, under the column labeled FREQUENCY, is the total number of cases. As you can see, 1,473 people were part of the 1984 General Social Survey.)

Similarly you can see from Figure 7.1 that 47.8% of the people found life pretty routine. A mere 5% of the sample found life dull. The five people who couldn't decide whether life is exciting or dull were about one-third of 1% of the sample. The seven missing answers are about a half of 1% of the total sample. The sum of the percentages across all possible codes is 100%.

Valid Percentages

Sometimes you wish to compute percentages using only cases who actually answered a question. Suppose you ask 100 people whether life is exciting or routine, and 25 say that it's exciting, 25 say that it's routine, and 50 tell you to bug off. It's a bit misleading, though it's correct, to state that 25% of those people think that life is exciting. A naive reader or listener would probably assume that the other 75% of the people find life unexciting. That's not really true, since the remaining 75% includes people who declined to answer, as well as those who find life routine. You can describe the results better by saying that half of the people *who answered the question* find life exciting, and half find life routine. You should also mention that half of the people in your sample refused even to answer the question.

You find the percentages based only on the cases who actually answered the question (so-called **valid cases**) in the column labeled VALID PERCENT in the frequency table. For our example, since so few cases had missing responses, the columns labeled VALID PERCENT and PERCENT are almost identical. If you have many cases with missing values, the two columns can be quite different. Since cases with codes declared missing are not included in the calculation of the "valid" percentages, the word MISSING appears for them in the VALID PERCENT column instead of a percentage.

Bar Charts

The last column, labeled CUM PERCENT, is also valuable, but we'll appreciate its value better in looking at the frequency table for another variable later on. Before doing that, let's consider an optional, visual way of examining frequency counts. Look at Figure 7.2, which is a frequency table of the responses to the question about marriage. You can see that 56% of the sample were married (on the date the survey was taken), 10% were widowed, 11% were divorced, and 19% were never married.

To transform this frequency table into a picture, you merely add the word BARCHART to your FREQUENCIES command.

```
FILE HANDLE GSS / (system-specific information)
GET FILE=GSS
FREQUENCIES VARIABLES=MARITAL / BARCHART
```

When you run a job with this command in it, the result looks like Figure 7.3. The display is called a **bar chart** because each line in the frequency table is turned into a bar. The length of the bar depends on the number of cases. (The actual frequency is given inside the bar.) At a quick glance, you can tell how often each of the responses was selected. You can also see whether one of the responses was an overwhelming favorite, and which responses are about equally likely.

Since computer screens and printers have a limited ability to show detail, responses that have similar frequencies may end up with bars of equal length—even though the actual frequency counts are slightly different. In this example, the bars for Widowed and Divorced have the same length, although the actual frequencies are a bit different. This doesn't really matter. The point of a bar chart is to provide a visual summary of the data, and such minor distortions do not distort the

Figure 7.2 A frequency table on marriage

```
FILE:      1984 General Social Survey

MARITAL    Marital status

                                            VALID     CUM
     VALUE LABEL          VALUE  FREQUENCY  PERCENT  PERCENT  PERCENT

Married                     1       829      56.3     56.3     56.3
Widowed                     2       154      10.5     10.5     66.7
Divorced                    3       166      11.3     11.3     78.0
Separated                   4        42       2.9      2.9     80.9
Never married               5       282      19.1     19.1    100.0
                                  -------   ------   ------
                          TOTAL    1473     100.0    100.0

VALID CASES     1473    MISSING CASES     0
```

Figure 7.3 A bar chart

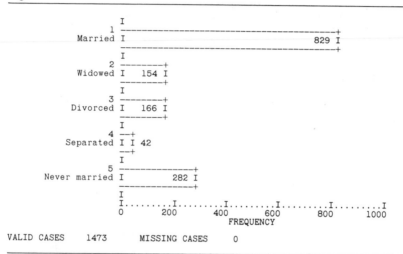

```
VALID CASES     1473    MISSING CASES     0
```

overall impression. If you want precision, look at the numbers, not the chart.

Cumulative Percentages

The last column in the frequency table is entitled CUM PERCENT. To see what this column tells you, look at the frequency table for another variable, EDUC, which shows the highest year of school completed.

```
FILE HANDLE GSS / (system-specific information)
GET FILE=GSS
FREQUENCIES VARIABLES = EDUC
```

> ? *Where did this* EDUC *variable come from? The questionnaire in Chapter 3 had two variables, one with highest year of elementary and high school and one with highest year of college.* EDUC was made by combining the variables named YRSEDUC and YRSCOLL back in Chapter 6. Although these variables were combined into EDUC before the data were distributed, you can do similar things yourself. Combining, shuffling, and otherwise altering variables is easy on a computer. More about that in Chapters 10 and 12. ■ ■ ■

From Figure 7.4, can you tell what percentage of the sample completed fewer than 8 years of school? Since there is a separate entry in the table for each year of school completed, the number you want is the sum of the percentages of those whose highest year completed was 0, 1, 2, 3, 4, 5, 6, or 7. You can compute this with a calculator using the VALID PERCENT column. But don't bother. Just look at the entry in the CUM PERCENT column for 7 years. It tells you that 5.9% of the sample stopped at 7 or fewer years of school. The cumulative percentage for a response is the sum of the valid percentages for that response, plus all responses that precede it in a frequency table. By looking at the cumulative percentage for the value of 11, you can tell that 28% of the sample had 11 or fewer years of school.

LEVELS OF MEASUREMENT

All frequency tables produced by the FREQUENCIES procedure contain a column with the cumulative percentages. For years of education, cumulative percentages are very useful and easy to interpret. For some variables, such as marital status, race, state of birth, or father's occupation, cumulative percentages are of little use or interest (although they are printed anyway). Look again at Figure 7.2, the frequency table for marital status. The cumulative percentage for code 3—Divorced—is 78%. It's the sum of the valid percentages for the categories Married, Widowed, and Divorced. If you had interchanged the coding scheme for Married and Never married—that is, if you had assigned a code of 1 to Never married and a code of 5 to Married, leaving the other codes alone—the cumulative percentage for code 3 would be the percentage of people who were *never* married, were widowed, or divorced. That is something completely different.

Categories.   If you think about the numbers used to code marital status, you'll realize that the particular number assigned to a category conveys no *numerical* information. The fact that Never married is assigned a bigger number (code 5) than Divorced (code 3) means nothing. The codes just represent the categories.

Figure 7.4 A frequency table for education

FILE: 1984 General Social Survey

EDUC   Highest year of school completed

VALUE LABEL	VALUE	FREQUENCY	PERCENT	VALID PERCENT	CUM PERCENT
	0	3	.2	.2	.2
	1	3	.2	.2	.4
	2	4	.3	.3	.7
	3	9	.6	.6	1.3
	4	11	.7	.7	2.0
	5	11	.7	.7	2.8
	6	19	1.3	1.3	4.1
	7	26	1.8	1.8	5.9
	8	77	5.2	5.2	11.1
	9	58	3.9	3.9	15.0
	10	99	6.7	6.7	21.8
	11	91	6.2	6.2	28.0
	12	491	33.3	33.4	61.4
	13	108	7.3	7.3	68.7
	14	121	8.2	8.2	76.9
	15	74	5.0	5.0	82.0
	16	149	10.1	10.1	92.1
	17	40	2.7	2.7	94.8
	18	31	2.1	2.1	96.9
	19	20	1.4	1.4	98.3
	20	25	1.7	1.7	100.0
No answer	99	3	.2	MISSING	
	TOTAL	1473	100.0	100.0	

VALID CASES   1470   MISSING CASES   3

Ordered Categories.   Sometimes the order of numbers is significant. Think about the exciting-routine-dull variable. The responses to the question can be arranged in a meaningful order. If we arrange them in terms of decreasing excitement, then the response Exciting comes first, followed by the response Pretty routine, and finally the response Dull. Of course, we could have arranged the responses in the other order as well (from low excitement to high excitement). In both orders, the response Pretty routine falls between the others. It means nothing that the Widowed response falls between Married and Divorced, because there is no *order* to those categories; but it does mean something that Pretty routine is between Exciting and Dull.

Numbers.   Although the codes assigned to the exciting-routine-dull variable are ordered from high to low, we can do little else with the actual codes. They merely convey order. Someone who was bored with life (code 3) didn't differ by two "excitement units" from someone who found life exciting (code 1). Subtracting or dividing the codes makes no sense.

The education variable is different. The numerical code assigned to each category is not merely a code. It *is* the highest grade completed. It's a real number, and we can treat it as such. For example, someone with 8 years of education has twice the number of years of education as someone with 4 years. Someone with 16 years of education has 4 more years than someone with 12. We can add, subtract, and divide the codes, and understand the results.

Nominal, Ordinal, Interval, and Ratio

Variables can be classified into different groups based on how they are measured. Marital status, degree of excitement, and years of education are all different types of variables. Marital status is called a **nominal** variable since the numerical code assigned to the possible responses convey no information. They are merely labels or names. (That's why the level of measurement is called *nominal*—from the Latin word for "name.") Birthplace, color of hair, position on the football team, and species of animal are all examples of nominal variables. Codes assigned to possible responses merely identify the response. The actual code number means nothing.

If the possible responses can be arranged in order, as with the exciting-routine-dull variable, the variable is called **ordinal**: its codes have an order, nothing more. (*Ordinal* is from—you guessed it—a Latin word meaning "order.") Variables such as job satisfaction, condition of health, and happiness with one's social life, all of which are usually measured on a scale going from much to little, are ordinal variables. The numbers assigned to the responses allow you to put the responses in order. But the actual distances between the numeric codes mean nothing.

Body temperature can be measured and recorded on a scale that is much more precise than job satisfaction. The interval, or distance, between values is meaningful everywhere on the scale. The difference between 100 degrees Fahrenheit and 101 degrees Fahrenheit is the same as the difference between 102 degrees and 103 degrees. Since temperature measured on the Fahrenheit scale does not have a true zero, however, you can't say that an 80-degree day is twice as hot as a 40-degree day. A temperature of zero does not mean there is no heat. The zero point is determined by convention. (If you insist, I'll admit that temperatures do have an absolute zero point; but that has very little to do with the measurement of body temperatures.) Thus body temperature can be called an **interval** variable.

The last type of measurement scale is called a **ratio** scale. The only difference between a ratio scale and an interval scale is that the ratio scale has an absolute zero. Zero means *zero*. It's not just an arbitrary point on the scale that somebody happened to label with zero. Height, weight, distance, age, and education can all be measured on a ratio scale. Zero education means no education at all. On a ratio scale, the proportions, or ratios, between items are meaningful. A 200-pound person is twice as heavy as a 100-pound person. A 1,000-meter race is twice as long as a 500-meter race.

I suppose there's no need to tell you what language the words *interval* and *ratio* come from.

? *Why all the fuss? Why have we spent all this time describing these "levels of measurement?"* The reason is straightforward—the way in which you analyze your data depends on how you've measured it. Certain analyses make sense with certain types of data. Even something as simple as interpreting cumulative percentages requires you to know what scale your data are measured on. You've seen that cumulative percentages don't make much sense for variables measured on a nominal scale. In the next chapter, you'll learn some additional techniques for describing variables measured on different scales. ■■■

MORE ABOUT THE FREQUENCIES PROCEDURE

You use the SPSS[X] FREQUENCIES procedure to:

- Make a frequency table.
- Make a bar chart.
- Make a histogram (described in Chapter 8).
- Calculate descriptive statistics (also described in Chapter 8).

A Frequency Table

To make a frequency table type

```
FREQUENCIES VAR=YOURVAR
```

where YOURVAR is the name of the variable for which you want to make the frequency table. Notice that we have abbreviated VARIABLES to VAR. SPSS[X] keywords other than command names can be abbreviated to three or more characters.

If there are several variables for which you want frequency tables, list all of their names separated by at least one blank or a comma.

```
FREQUENCIES VAR=YOURVAR1 YOURVAR2 YOURVAR3
```

A Bar Chart and a Frequency Table

To make both a frequency table and a bar chart, add a slash and the word BARCHART:

```
FREQUENCIES VAR=YOURVAR / BARCHART
```

A Bar Chart without a Frequency Table

If you want to make a bar chart, but don't want to get a frequency table, add a slash and the words FORMAT = NOTABLE:

```
FREQUENCIES VARIABLES=YOURVAR / FORMAT=NOTABLE / BARCHART
```

A Frequency Table in a Condensed Form

If you want to make a table and print it in a condensed format, use the CONDENSE keyword. This format takes up less space than the usual one.

```
FREQUENCIES VARIABLES=YOURVAR / FORMAT=CONDENSE
```

WHAT'S NEXT?

You've seen that using the FREQUENCIES procedure is a handy way get a good impression of all your data. In Chapter 8, you'll see how you can use FREQUENCIES to collapse your data with a new type of picture and summarize it with single numbers.

Summary

How can you count the various responses people give to a question?

A frequency table tells you how many people (cases) selected each of the responses to a question. For each code, it contains the number and percentage of the people who gave each response, as well as the number of people for whom responses are not available.

If you find codes in the frequency table that weren't used in your coding scheme, you know that an error in data coding or data entry has occurred.

Variables are classified into different categories based on the coding scheme:

If there's no order to a coding system, and a particular code only identifies a category, the variable is measured on a nominal scale.

If the categories can be ordered on some basis, the variable is measured on an ordinal scale.

If you can interpret the actual distances between the ordered categories, the variable is measured on an interval scale.

If you can interpret distances and can also speak of a zero value, the variable is a ratio variable.

EXERCISES

Syntax Exercises

1 When you run the following command

```
FREQUENCIES LIFE
```

you get this error message:

```
>ERROR   10040  LINE   3, COLUMN 13, TEXT: LIFE
>Error in FREQUENCIES command.
>THIS COMMAND NOT EXECUTED.
```

Indicate what's wrong with the command and write it correctly.

2 How can you simplify the following set of commands?

```
FREQUENCIES    VAR=LIFE
FREQUENCIES    VAR=MARITAL
FREQUENCIES    VAR=SEX
FREQUENCIES    VAR=RACE
```

3 You run the following command

```
FREQENCIES VAR=LIFE
```

and get the error message

```
>ERROR       1 LINE   3, COMMAND NAME: FREQENCIES
>Text appearing in the first column is not recognized as a command.  Is it
>spelled correctly?  If it was intended as a continuation of the previous
>command, the first column must be blank.
```

Fix the command.

4 Fix the following commands:

a. FREQUENCIES VAR=LIFE/BARCHART LIFE

b. FREQUENCIES VAR=LIFE BARCHART

c. FREQUENCIES VAR=LIFE/
   BARCHART

Statistical Concepts

1 For which of the following variables would frequency tables be useful?

a. calories consumed per day

b. ideal number of children for a family to have

c. belief in life after death

d. mileage on family automobile

e. political party membership

f. ID numbers of the forms

2 Below is a frequency table for the job satisfaction variable from the General Social Survey. Fill in the missing entries:

SATJOB   Satisfaction with job or housework

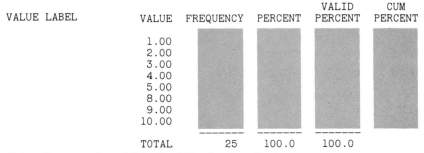

VALUE LABEL	VALUE	FREQUENCY	PERCENT	VALID PERCENT	CUM PERCENT
Very satisfied	1		37.7		45.9
Moderately satisfied	2	423	28.7	35.0	81.0
A little dissatisfie	3	146	9.9	12.1	
Very dissatisfied	4	84	5.7	7.0	100.0
Not applicable	0	208	MISSING		
No answer	9	57	3.9	MISSING	
TOTAL		1473	100.0	100.0	

VALID CASES   1208   MISSING CASES

3 The following data represent the number of periodicals read by 25 college students: 1, 1, 1, 1, 1, 1, 2, 2, 2, 3, 3, 3, 3, 3, 3, 3, 4, 4, 5, 5, 5, 5, 8, 9, 9, 10.

a. Fill in the following frequency table:

VALUE LABEL	VALUE	FREQUENCY	PERCENT	VALID PERCENT	CUM PERCENT
	1.00				
	2.00				
	3.00				
	4.00				
	5.00				
	8.00				
	9.00				
	10.00				
TOTAL		25	100.0	100.0	

b. Using the same data, fill in the following bar chart:

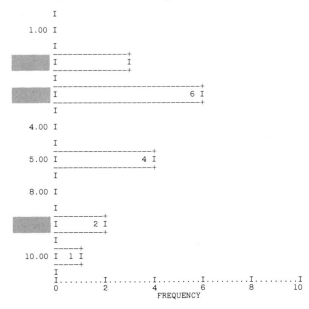

4 For which of the following variables would cumulative percents be readily interpretable?

   a. number of adults in a household

   b. brand of car ownership

   c. college major

   d. number of illnesses during the past year

5 Which scale of measurement (nominal, ordinal, interval or ratio) are the following variables measured on?

   a. ethnic origin

   b. satisfaction with family life

   c. breed of dog

   d. likelihood of buying a product

   e. days of hospitalization

   f. hours worked per week

Data Analysis

1 Make frequency tables and bar charts for HAPMAR (happiness of marriage) and RACE. On the output, indicate how the different columns of the frequency table are calculated.

2 a. How many people are very happy with their marriage?

   b. What percent is this of all currently married people who answered the question?

   c. What percent of the total sample are happily married people?

   d. What percent of the married people who answered the question are either very happily married or pretty happily married?

   e. Can you tell from the tables what percent of people in the various race categories are happy with their marriage?

3 Explain why there are two different codes for missing values for the HAPMAR variable. Do they convey different information?

4 Give an example of a question which may be answered by looking at the cumulative frequency column for HAPMAR.

8 Summarizing Data

How else, other than by making a frequency table, can you summarize the responses to a question?

- What is the mean? The median? The mode? What does each of them tell you about the distribution of a variable?

- When is each of these statistics most appropriate? What characteristics of the data make each one more or less useful?

- How can a graphical display summarize the distribution of a variable? What kinds of graphical displays are used, and what are the advantages of each?

- Aside from the mean, median, and mode, what other statistics might provide helpful information?

- In what way can you describe how concentrated—or how dispersed—the values are?

In the previous chapter, you saw that a frequency table is a convenient way of looking at the responses to a question. Frequency tables are easy to read, and they provide complete and detailed information about the answers. You know exactly how many people gave each of the responses. But sometimes that's just too much information.

DESCRIPTIVE STATISTICS

Think about a variable like age, height, or weight. If you recorded actual heights in inches or weights in pounds, a lot of different responses are possible. The more finely you measured the variables, the larger the number of possible responses. If you recorded height only to the nearest foot, the number of different heights is fairly limited. However, if you measured height to the nearest millimeter, it's possible that everyone in your sample had a different measurement. What would happen if you made a frequency table for such a variable? You'd probably end up with an enormous table with a lot of different values. Most of the codes in the table would show only a single case with that particular value. In fact, if every case had a different value, you'd end up with nothing more than a list of all the responses. That kind of frequency table doesn't do much for you. You need some way to summarize the data further.

Nominal Variables

The actual way to get further summaries depends on how the variable is measured. If you have a frequency table that shows the number of people who were born in each of 400 cities, you may not be able to summarize further at all. Since the name or ID number of the city is a nominal variable, you can't very well group the cities into larger categories without further information, such as what state they're in. In other words, you can't really summarize a name effectively. All you can do with the name or ID number is *count* the number of people for each one.

If you're going to report the results to an audience that has a short attention span, you might organize the frequency table so that it goes from the most popular city to the least popular. Then you could mention only the "top ten" cities. The "top" city has a statistical term you can use to describe it—the **mode.**

Nominal variables with many categories simply don't lend themselves to summarization by computer. If you need to summarize, you have to rearrange the coding system. For example, you can combine cities in the same state, or you can group them by population. You can then make frequency tables based on the new, more compact classification. (Chapter 10 tells you how to use the computer to rearrange your coding system.)

Ordinal Variables

It's easier to summarize an ordinal variable than a nominal variable. If you make a frequency table and decide that you have too many categories (Extremely exciting, Greatly exciting, Moderately exciting, Mildly exciting, Slightly exciting, Almost but not quite exciting, ...), you can *combine* adjacent categories. One way to do this is to convert all the different codes that stand for varying degrees of excitement to a single code—Exciting. Similarly, you can combine the various codes for Routine, and for Dull. The frequency table for the less elaborate coding scheme will be easier to read and probably just as informative.

A variable with ordered categories also gives you more choice in descriptive statistics. You can still report the mode (the category that has the largest number of cases) for an ordinal variable, as you can for a nominal variable. The mode, remember, tells you which response occurred most frequently. In addition, there's another number, often more descriptive, that you can compute for an ordinal variable. It's called the **median.** The median is the "middle" value, the value that divides the observations into equal halves. Notice that you can't have a middle value unless it makes sense to put the values in order. That's why the median is a useful statistic for ordinal variables but not for nominal variables.

If you ask five people to rate the President's performance on a scale of 1 to 5, and you get the answers 1, 1, 3, 4, 5, the median answer is *3*. The value *3* divides the five responses into equal halves, when they're placed in order like this. The median is the middle observation when the values are ordered from smallest to largest (or largest to smallest, for that matter). The median provides you with some idea of what a *typical* response is.

What if you have an even number of observations? There may not be a single median, since two numbers are in the middle. That's true. With the numbers 1, 2, 3, 4, the numbers 2 and 3 are equally in the middle. If this happens, you can still calculate the median. Find those two middle numbers, and figure out what number would be in the middle of them:

- Add the two middle numbers together.
- Take half of their sum. This is the median.

In this example, you would add the middle numbers 2 and 3 to get 5. Half of 5, or 2.5, is then the median of 1, 2, 3, 4. SPSS^X does this for you automatically. ▪▪▪

Figure 8.1 A frequency table for AGE

FILE: 1984 General Social Survey

AGE   Age of respondent

VALUE	FREQ	PCT	CUM PCT	VALUE	FREQ	PCT	CUM PCT	VALUE	FREQ	PCT	CUM PCT
18	2	0	0	42	21	1	55	66	14	1	85
19	20	1	1	43	25	2	56	67	25	2	87
20	23	2	3	44	23	2	58	68	24	2	88
21	37	3	6	45	20	1	59	69	9	1	89
22	29	2	8	46	18	1	60	70	18	1	90
23	50	3	11	47	19	1	62	71	12	1	91
24	47	3	14	48	22	1	63	72	14	1	92
25	39	3	17	49	21	1	65	73	6	0	93
26	32	2	19	50	8	1	65	74	15	1	94
27	44	3	22	51	16	1	66	75	9	1	94
28	37	3	25	52	21	1	68	76	14	1	95
29	33	2	27	53	14	1	69	77	13	1	96
30	28	2	29	54	17	1	70	78	6	0	96
31	28	2	31	55	19	1	71	79	4	0	97
32	37	3	33	56	19	1	72	80	6	0	97
33	39	3	36	57	19	1	74	81	12	1	98
34	31	2	38	58	24	2	75	82	8	1	98
35	37	3	40	59	16	1	76	83	5	0	99
36	41	3	43	60	27	2	78	84	4	0	99
37	38	3	46	61	20	1	80	85	2	0	99
38	31	2	48	62	20	1	81	86	2	0	99
39	24	2	50	63	15	1	82	87	1	0	99
40	28	2	51	64	13	1	83	88	2	0	100
41	25	2	53	65	18	1	84	89	7	0	100

MISSING DATA

VALUE	FREQ	VALUE	FREQ	VALUE	FREQ
99	6				

VALID CASES   1467   MISSING CASES   6

Interval or Ratio Variables

If your variable is measured on an interval or ratio scale, there are many different ways to summarize it. You could still make a frequency table, but it would probably be unwieldy and not particularly informative.

```
FILE HANDLE GSS / (system-specific information)
GET FILE=GSS
FREQUENCIES VARIABLES = AGE / FORMAT = CONDENSE
```

Look at Figure 8.1, which is a frequency distribution for the AGE variable. It looks different from the previous tables since it's printed in a condensed format, which we mentioned at the end of Chapter 7. Both the valid percent and the cumulative percent are rounded to the nearest integer. The percent based on all cases, including missing, does not appear. If this table had not been printed in condensed format it would continue for many pages, and you would have a hard time looking at it. Even in condensed format, it doesn't really grab your attention.

HISTOGRAMS

The frequency table contains all of the information about the AGE variable—too much information to scan easily. A bar chart sure wouldn't help, since it would have as many bars as there are different values. What you could do is make another frequency table in which each line represents not a single age but several ages. For example, you can count the number of people in their teens, twenties, thirties, forties, and so on. This is a more manageable way to look at the data. You could then use a modification of the bar chart, called a **histogram,** to display the number of cases occurring in each of the decades. To make both a frequency table and a histogram, type:

```
FILE HANDLE GSS / (system-specific information)
GET FILE=GSS
FREQUENCIES VARIABLES = AGE
 / HISTOGRAM MINIMUM(10) MAXIMUM(90) INCREMENT(10)
```

Figure 8.2 is the histogram for the AGE variable. The first line represents cases in their teens; the second represents cases in their twenties; and so on. For each ten-year group of ages, the histogram shows a row of stars, or asterisks (*), whose length depends on the number of cases that belong to the group. The actual number of cases appears in the column labeled COUNT. (The number of cases each asterisk represents is shown at the top of the table. In this example, each asterisk represents 8 cases.) The middle value for each interval is printed in the column labeled MIDPOINT. For example, the midpoint age for people in their forties is 45, and there were 222 cases in the sample with ages in the forties. If you add up all of the counts in Figure 8.1 for ages 40 to 49, you get the number 222. Try it.

? *Why did it take such a long specification to get the histogram?* It doesn't really. Just a slash and the word HISTOGRAM on the FREQUENCIES command will tell SPSS^X to produce a histogram. The MINIMUM, MAXIMUM, and INCREMENT specifications are optional. They determine the lowest and highest values shown, as well as the size of the interval. We used them here so that the groups would come out in convenient intervals: teens, twenties, and so on. If we'd just said HISTOGRAM, SPSS^X would have made up its own intervals. ■ ■ ■

By looking at Figure 8.2, you get a pretty good idea of the ages of the people in your sample. You see that not many people were in their teens. This is because the General Social Survey was restricted to adults 18 or older. The greatest numbers of people were in their twenties and thirties. The numbers of people in their fifties and sixties were similar. As expected, there were not very many people in their eighties. You could tell all of this from the frequency table, but not so easily.

The number of intervals you should use in a histogram depends on the data. If the intervals are very wide, you may not be able to see

Figure 8.2 A histogram for AGE

```
    COUNT    MIDPOINT    ONE SYMBOL EQUALS APPROXIMATELY  8.00 OCCURRENCES

       22      15.00    ***
      371      25.00    ********************************************
      334      35.00    ******************************************
      222      45.00    ****************************
      173      55.00    ********************
      185      65.00    ***********************
      111      75.00    **************
       49      85.00    ******
                        I....+....I....+....I....+....I....+....I....+....I
                        0        80       160      240      320      400
                                          HISTOGRAM FREQUENCY

VALID CASES    1467    MISSING CASES    6
```

Figure 8.3 Another histogram for AGE

```
FILE:      1984 General Social Survey

AGE        Age of respondent

    COUNT    MIDPOINT    ONE SYMBOL EQUALS APPROXIMATELY  4.00 OCCURRENCES

        0      12.50
       22      17.50    ******
      186      22.50    ************************************************
      185      27.50    ************************************************
      163      32.50    *****************************************
      171      37.50    *******************************************
      122      42.50    ******************************
      100      47.50    *************************
       76      52.50    *******************
       97      57.50    ************************
       95      62.50    ************************
       90      67.50    ***********************
       65      72.50    ****************
       46      77.50    ***********
       35      82.50    *********
       14      87.50    ****
                        I....+....I....+....I....+....I....+....I....+....I
                        0       40       80       120      160      200
                                          HISTOGRAM FREQUENCY
VALID CASES    1467    MISSING CASES    6
```

important differences. On the other hand, if they are too narrow, you may have more detail than you want to see. Often it's a good idea to make several histograms and see which one summarizes the data most clearly.

```
FILE HANDLE GSS / (system-specific information)
GET FILE=GSS
FREQUENCIES VARIABLES = AGE
 / HISTOGRAM MINIMUM(10) MAXIMUM(90) INCREMENT(5)
```

Figure 8.3 is a histogram for age in five-year intervals: 15–19 years, 20–24 years, 25–29 years, and so on. Even though this histogram shows more detail than the other one, it's not really more informative. A grouping of cases into decades of age seems to be sufficient.

Differences between Bar Charts and Histograms

As you've noticed, a histogram looks pretty much like a bar chart. SPSS^X prints boxy bars for bar charts and rows of stars for histograms, but that's not important. There are only two real differences:

1 In a bar chart, each bar represents a single code, while in a histogram the asterisks often represent the frequencies of several codes.

2 Bar charts and histograms treat codes with *no* cases (frequencies of zero) in different ways.

To make a bar chart, you don't have to assume anything about what the codes actually mean. If you're using the codes from 1 to 3, and there are no cases with the value of 3, there simply is no bar for that code. Since you can use whatever codes you want for nominal and ordinal variables, there's no way that the computer can tell what codes were possible but did not occur. If a value has no cases, no line appears for it in a frequency table, and no bar in a bar chart.

On the other hand, if the variables are measured on an interval or ratio scale, you do want to know when some of the values do not occur in your data. When this happens, a histogram leaves a space for them with no stars. If there were no people in their thirties in the sample, the line for the thirties decade would remain in the histogram, but it would have no stars. If you made a bar chart of the ages, no space would be left for the thirties. The "holes" in the histogram tell you that some possible values didn't occur at all. That makes it easier for you to see what the real distribution of values looks like. It is essential to know about the "holes" when you have an interval or ratio variable.

Uses of Histograms

When are the special characteristics of a histogram useful? Histograms are useful whenever:

- A variable has many different values.
- It's reasonable to group adjacent values.

Never use a histogram to summarize a nominal variable. If you have codes from 1 to 121 that identify different religions (see Appendix J of the General Social Survey *Codebook* if you can), it makes no sense to group the codes into intervals. The Hungarian Reformed Church (code 1) probably has little to do with the Evangelical Congregational Church (code 2), so there's no logical reason to combine them in a histogram. And there are simply too many codes to make a bar chart.

By looking at a histogram, you can see the *shape* of the distribution:

- How often the different values occur.
- How much spread or variability there is among the values.
- Which values are most typical of the data.

These things are important, first of all, because they tell you a lot about your data. Also, some of the statistical procedures that we'll be using later don't work properly unless the data come from particular types of distributions.

Different Types of Distributions

A variable like age can have many different types of distributions, depending on what population you study. If you're studying first-graders, their ages are fairly similar. If you made a histogram of the ages, you'd most likely end up with two lines of stars, one for 5-year-olds and one for 6-year-olds, with a few stray stars for 7- or 8-year-olds.

On the other hand, if you study college freshmen, the distribution of the ages spreads out more. Although the majority of college freshmen are either 18 or 19, there are always a few younger students who skipped grades, and surprisingly often there is an octogenarian catching up on what he or she missed. You find people in all different age groups in this sample. Some values are more likely than others, but many different ones occur.

Finally, if you're studying the entire U.S. population, your sample includes people of all ages. The histogram of their age distribution would not look anything like that of the first-graders or of the college students.

MORE DESCRIPTIVE STATISTICS

If you want to describe the distribution of ages in each of the three samples just referred to, you can always show the three histograms. That's a fine way to display the results. But often you want to summarize the data even further. You'd like to be able to report some numbers that describe the distributions more precisely.

What sorts of descriptions might these be? The mode—the most frequently occurring value—is the simplest way we can represent "typical." For a nominal variable, it's about the only thing we can use. The median—the middle value when values are arranged from smallest to largest—is another way of representing "typical." Of course, you can only calculate the median for a variable that's measured at least on an ordinal scale. There's no way you can arrange religions and find a "middle" one. (Strictly speaking you can calculate a median for nearly anything. What I really mean is that you can only make sense of a median when the variable is measured at least on an ordinal scale.)

In addition to the mode and the median, there are other handy statistics you can use to describe your data.

Other Percentiles

The median is the value that splits the sample into two equal parts. Sometimes, though, it's useful to look at values that split up the cases in other ways. What's the value that cuts off the bottom quarter of the cases, or the top quarter? These values are called **percentiles** since they tell the percentages of cases above and below them. The median is the 50th percentile, since 50% of the cases have larger values and 50% have smaller values. The 25th percentile is the value that splits the cases so that one quarter of them have values below it. (It follows that 75% of the cases exceed the 25th percentile.) If you've made a frequency table, you can locate percentiles in the cumulative frequencies column. However, there's a simpler way to go about it.

```
FILE HANDLE GSS / (system-specific information)
GET FILE=GSS
FREQUENCIES VARIABLES=AGE / FORMAT=CONDENSED
 / PERCENTILES 25 50 75
```

This job asks for the 25th, 50th, and 75th percentiles for the AGE variable. As shown in Figure 8.4, 25% of the cases have ages less than or equal to 29; 50%, less than 40; and 75%, less than 58.

The Average or Arithmetic Mean

For interval and ratio variables, the arithmetic **mean,** or average, is usually a better measure of central tendency than either the mode or the median. It's simple to calculate. Just add up all of the values and divide the sum by the number of cases. Since you're using SPSS^X for analyzing the data, you don't even have to bother doing that. Just type

```
FILE HANDLE GSS / (system-specific information)
GET FILE=GSS
FREQUENCIES VARIABLES=AGE / STATISTICS MEAN MEDIAN MODE
```

and SPSS^X prints the mean, median, and mode for the AGE variable. As shown in Figure 8.5, the mean value for age is 44, the median is 40, and the mode is 23.

Why are all of these "typical" values different? There's no reason for these numbers to be identical, since they all define "typical" in different ways. The mode is the value that occurs most often; the median is the middle value when the numbers are arranged from smallest to largest; and the mean is the familiar "average" value. ■ ■ ■

Mean, Median, or Mode?

For AGE, the mean and the median values are pretty similar. The mode is quite different. Which number should you report if you are describing the age data?

Usually the mode is a poor measure of central tendency for an interval or a ratio variable. Looking at Figure 8.4, you can see that age 23 does have the highest frequency (50 cases), but many other ages have large frequencies as well. If you look at the percentage, you'll see that only 3% of the sample is 23 years old. So you can pretty much eliminate

Figure 8.4 A frequency table with percentiles

FILE: 1984 General Social Survey

AGE Age of respondent

VALUE	FREQ	PCT	CUM PCT	VALUE	FREQ	PCT	CUM PCT	VALUE	FREQ	PCT	CUM PCT
18	2	0	0	42	21	1	55	66	14	1	85
19	20	1	1	43	25	2	56	67	25	2	87
20	23	2	3	44	23	2	58	68	24	2	88
21	37	3	6	45	20	1	59	69	9	1	89
22	29	2	8	46	18	1	60	70	18	1	90
23	50	3	11	47	19	1	62	71	12	1	91
24	47	3	14	48	22	1	63	72	14	1	92
25	39	3	17	49	21	1	65	73	6	0	93
26	32	2	19	50	8	1	65	74	15	1	94
27	44	3	22	51	16	1	66	75	9	1	94
28	37	3	25	52	21	1	68	76	14	1	95
29	33	2	27	53	14	1	69	77	13	1	96
30	28	2	29	54	17	1	70	78	6	0	96
31	28	2	31	55	19	1	71	79	4	0	97
32	37	3	33	56	19	1	72	80	6	0	97
33	39	3	36	57	19	1	74	81	12	1	98
34	31	2	38	58	24	2	75	82	8	1	98
35	37	3	40	59	16	1	76	83	5	0	99
36	41	3	43	60	27	2	78	84	4	0	99
37	38	3	46	61	20	1	80	85	2	0	99
38	31	2	48	62	20	1	81	86	2	0	99
39	24	2	50	63	15	1	82	87	1	0	99
40	28	2	51	64	13	1	83	88	2	0	100
41	25	2	53	65	18	1	84	89	7	0	100

M I S S I N G   D A T A

VALUE	FREQ		VALUE	FREQ		VALUE	FREQ
99	6						

PERCENTILE	VALUE		PERCENTILE	VALUE		PERCENTILE	VALUE
25.00	29.000		50.00	40.000		75.00	58.000

VALID CASES   1467   MISSING CASES   6

Figure 8.5 Central tendency

MEAN	44.005	MEDIAN	40.000	MODE	23.000

VALID CASES   1467   MISSING CASES   6

the mode as a good number to report in this situation. Though it satisfies one of the definitions of "typical," it ignores much available information about the data.

Although the median is a good measure of "typicalness" (called **central tendency** in more formal language), it ignores a lot of the information that you've collected about a variable measured on an interval or ratio scale. For example, the median of the five ages 28, 29, 30, 31, 32 is 30. The median for the five ages 28, 29, 30, 98, 99 is also thirty.

The actual values of ages above and below the median are ignored. The median is 30 regardless of whether everyone is close to 30 or whether the values vary quite a bit.

When should you report the median, and when should you report the mean? If a variable is measured on an ordinal scale, the median is the statistic of choice. If a scale doesn't have intervals of equal length, it doesn't make sense to compute a mean. For a variable measured on an interval scale, the mean and the median are both useful numbers to report. The mean makes maximum use of the data since all of the values are actually used in computing it. (Remember, you add up *all* the numbers, then divide by how many numbers there are.) In some situations, however, the mean may not really represent the data well.

Suppose you ask five people how many parking tickets they've received in the last year, and you get the following replies: 2, 5, 6, 7, 90. The mean number of tickets for this sample is 22. (Verify this: the sum is 110, and 110 divided by 5 is 22.) That statistic does not describe the data well. The person who never feeds a meter is making the people in the sample look more delinquent than they really are. The median, 6, describes the data better.

Whenever there are cases that have values much larger or smaller than the others, the mean may not be a good measure of central tendency. It is unduly influenced by extreme values (called **outliers**). In this situation, you should report the median and mention that some of the cases had extremely large or small values. For example, you could say "The median number of tickets for the sample is 6. Eighty percent had 7 or fewer tickets a year. One person reported 90 tickets."

HOW MUCH DO THE VALUES DIFFER?

Measures of central tendency provide information only about "typical" values. They tell you nothing about how much the values vary within the sample. Suppose you ask 10 students on the Dean's List and 10 students on academic probation how many hours of TV they watched last week, and you get the answers shown in Table 8.1.

The average number of hours for the two groups of students is the same—5 per week. However, the distributions of values differ. All of the Dean's List students watched between 4 and 6 hours of TV during the week. There's little variation in the numbers from student to student. The students on probation, however, differ from each other much more. Some seem to have devoted themselves entirely to scholastic pursuits, while others watched a lot of TV.

How can you measure this variability? One of the more obvious ways is to report the smallest and largest values in each of the samples. The minimum number of hours in the first sample is 4 and the maximum is 6. In the second sample, the minimum number of hours is 0 and the maximum is 15. The distance between the largest and smallest values is

Table 8.1 A TV log

	Dean's List students	Probation students
	Hours	Hours
	4	0
	4	0
	5	0
	5	0
	5	0
	5	3
	5	10
	5	10
	6	12
	6	15
Sum	50	50
Mean	5	5

called the **range.** For the first sample, the range is 2, while for the second sample, it is 15. That's quite a difference. By comparing the ranges of the two samples, you can tell that the students in the second sample differed more from each other than those in the first.

The range is not a particularly good measure of variability, though. It depends only on the smallest and largest numbers and pays no attention to the distribution of the numbers in between. For a variable measured on an ordinal scale, it's the best you can do. For a variable measured on an interval or ratio scale, you can compute some better measures.

THE VARIANCE

For each case, you can compute how much it varies from the mean of all the cases. Just subtract the case's value from the overall mean. For the first case in Table 8.1, the difference is:

4 (the case's value) − **5** (the mean) = −**1.**

This indicates that the person watched one less hour of TV than the average number. Table 8.2 shows the differences for all of the data. From the table, you can see that the differences are much smaller for the Dean's List students than for the students on probation.

Table 8.2 The TV log with differences from the mean

	Dean's List students		Probation students	
	Hours	Difference	Hours	Difference
	4	−1	0	−5
	4	−1	0	−5
	5	0	0	−5
	5	0	0	−5
	5	0	0	−5
	5	0	3	−2
	5	0	10	5
	5	0	10	5
	6	1	12	7
	6	1	15	10
Sum	50	0	50	0
Mean	5	0	5	0

How can you use these differences to measure variability? The simplest tactic that comes to mind is just to add up the differences and compute a mean difference for each group. Like many great ideas we've all had, this one has a flaw. The sum of the differences from the mean is always zero. Some of the differences are positive, and some are negative, so when you add up all of the positive and negative numbers the result is always zero. You need a better way to assemble all of the differences from the mean.

There are several ways to do this. For example, you could treat all the differences as if they were positive and compute a mean difference for them. It turns out, though, that a better way by far is to:

- Square the differences.
- Add them up.
- Then divide the sum by the number of cases minus one.

This measure is called the **variance.**

? *Why divide by the number of cases minus one, instead of just the number of cases?* You are working with a sample taken from a larger population, and you are trying to describe how much the responses vary from the mean of the entire population. However, since you don't know the population mean, you have to use the sample mean in your calculation—and using the sample mean makes the sample seem less variable than it really is. When you divide by the number of cases minus one, you compensate for the smaller variability that you observe in the sample. ■■■

Large values for the variance tell you that the values are quite spread out. Small values indicate that the responses are pretty similar. In fact, a value of zero means that all of the values are exactly equal. For Figure 8.2, the variance for the Dean's List students is .44, while for the students on probation it is 36.44. This supports our observation that there is more variability in TV watching for students on probation.

The Standard Deviation

Since you calculate the variance by squaring differences from the mean, the unit of measurement that it is expressed in is things like squared hours, squared children, and so on. To express the variability in the same units as the observations, you can just take the square root of the variance. This is called the **standard deviation.** The standard deviation is expressed in the same units as the original data.

For the Dean's List students in Figure 8.1, the standard deviation is the square root of .44, or .66. For the students on probation, it is the square root of 36.44, or 6.04.

Computing the Variance with SPSS^x

Although it's good to know how to compute the different measures of variability so you can interpret them, you don't have to worry about doing the actual math. Just type

```
FILE HANDLE GSS / (system-specific information)
GET FILE=GSS
FREQUENCIES VARIABLES=AGE
 / STATISTICS MINIMUM MAXIMUM RANGE VARIANCE STDDEV
```

and you will obtain the measures of variability for the AGE variable. They are shown in Figure 8.6.

The youngest person in the sample is 18 and the oldest is 89, resulting in a range of 89 minus 18, or 71. The variance of AGE is 317 squared years. Its square root, the standard deviation, is 17.8 years.

Figure 8.6 Measures of variability from SPSS^x

STD DEV	17.811	VARIANCE	317.220	RANGE	71.000
MINIMUM	18.000	MAXIMUM	89.000		

| VALID CASES | 1467 | MISSING CASES | 6 | | |

> *What's this? Nobody in the General Social Survey sample was 90 years old or older?* Actually, this is just a quirk in the way ages were coded. For obscure historical reasons, the General Social Survey assigned an age of 89 to everyone with an age of 89 or older. Because not many people are that old, this quirk has very little effect on analysis of AGE. Still, it's completely unnecessary. When you design *your* study, leave room for ages of 100 or more.　■ ■ ■

MORE ABOUT THE FREQUENCIES PROCEDURE

You can use the SPSS[X] FREQUENCIES procedure to make frequency tables and bar charts. These are described in Chapter 7. You can also use FREQUENCIES to make histograms and to calculate:

- The mean, median, and mode.
- The minimum, maximum, and range.
- The variance and standard deviation.
- Percentiles.

The Simplest Way

If you just want to calculate the mean, standard deviation, minimum, and maximum, as well as a frequency table, type

```
FREQUENCIES VARIABLES=AGE / STATISTICS
```

Replace AGE with the names of the variables for which you want the statistics. The keyword STATISTICS tells SPSS[X] to calculate the mean, standard deviation, minimum, and maximum.

No Frequency Table

If you want to calculate the basic statistics but don't want a frequency table, type:

```
FREQUENCIES VARIABLES=AGE / FORMAT NOTABLE / STATISTICS
```

The variable(s) for which you want statistics must be listed first. It doesn't matter in what order you give the remaining instructions.

A Histogram without a Frequency Table

When a variable such as age, weight, or income can have many different values, you may want to make a histogram to see what the distribution of the variable looks like. However, you don't want to make a frequency table since it would be very large and not very useful. Type:

```
FREQUENCIES VARIABLES=AGE / FORMAT = NOTABLE / HISTOGRAM
```

Additional Statistics

If you want to calculate all of the descriptive statistics available in the FREQUENCIES procedure, type:

FREQUENCIES VARIABLES=AGE / STATISTICS ALL

This will give you the mean, median, mode, standard deviation, variance, range, minimum, maximum, and the sum. It will also give you some additional statistics we haven't discussed, such as skewness and kurtosis. (These statistics will be discussed in Chapter 14.) You can calculate any of these statistics individually by typing their keywords after the STATISTICS subcommand. The following statistics keywords are available in FREQUENCIES:

KURTOSIS	kurtosis	SEKURT	standard error of kurtosis
MAXIMUM	maximum	SEMEAN	standard error of the mean
MEAN	mean	SESKEW	standard error of skewness
MEDIAN	median	SKEWNESS	skewness
MINIMUM	minimum	STDDEV	standard deviation
MODE	mode	SUM	sum
RANGE	range	VARIANCE	variance

If you just type STATISTICS by itself, you get the mean, standard deviation, minimum, and maximum.

Percentiles

To get the 25th, 50th, and 75th percentiles for a variable, type:

FREQUENCIES VARIABLES=AGE / PERCENTILES 25 50 75

If you want both percentiles and descriptive statistics but no frequency table, type:

FREQUENCIES VARIABLES=AGE / STATISTICS
/ PERCENTILES 25 50 75 / FORMAT NOTABLE

If you want percentiles other than 25, 50, and 75, list their numbers after the word PERCENTILES. To get the 33d and 66th percentiles, type:

FREQUENCIES VARIABLES=AGE / STATISTICS
/ PERCENTILES 33 66 / FORMAT NOTABLE

WHAT'S NEXT?

This chapter was about summarizing your data. The next chapter shows you how to look at two or more variables at the same time. This will be your first look at the very important topic of relationships between variables.

Summary

How else, other than by making a frequency table, can you summarize the responses to a question?

The mode, or most frequently occurring value, is an appropriate summary for any variable, but is most appropriate for nominal variables, when the categories do not have any particular order.

The median, or middle value, is appropriate for ordinal, interval, or ratio variables.

The mean, or average, is appropriate for interval or ratio variables.

For interval or ratio variables, the mean makes more use of the available information than the median, but the median is less influenced by the presence of extreme values.

Bar charts display a frequency distribution graphically and are best suited to nominal or ordinal variables with few categories.

Histograms display the shape of a distribution and should be used for interval and ratio variables.

The variance and its square root, the standard deviation, measure the extent to which a distribution spreads out from its mean.

EXERCISES

Syntax

1 The weight losses, in pounds, of five students during finals week are 0, 2, 1, 5, and 3. Write the complete SPSS^X job, including data definition, to compute descriptive statistics and a frequency table for the weight-loss variable.

2 Modify your previous job to get a histogram, as well as the frequency table and descriptive statistics.

3 How would you change the FREQUENCIES command if you didn't want a frequency table?

4 Correct the following commands:

   a. FREQUENCIES VAR=WEIGHT / NOTABLE / BARCHART

   b. FREQUENCIES VAR=WEIGHT / FORMAT HISTOGRAM

   c. FREQUENCIES VAR=WEIGHT / HIST AND STATISTICS

Statistical Concepts

1 A sample consists of 5 consumers who are not satisfied with a new product (coded as 0), 21 consumers who are somewhat satisfied (coded as 1), and 10 consumers who are completely satisfied (coded as 2). Does it make sense to calculate the following statistics? If so, compute them.

   a. modal satisfaction
   b. median satisfaction
   c. mean satisfaction
   d. variance of satisfaction

2 A sample consists of 11 graduates of the University of Texas (coded 1), 10 graduates of the University of Michigan (coded 2) and 10 graduates of the University of Hawaii (coded 3). Which of the following statistics are appropriate for describing these data? Calculate the statistic if you think it is interpretable.

   a. modal college attended
   b. median college attended
   c. mean college attended

3 A sample contains 5 families who own no car (coded 0), 20 families who own 1 car (coded 1), and 10 families who own 2 cars (coded 2). Indicate which of the following statistics are appropriate and then calculate them.

   a. modal number of cars owned
   b. median number of cars owned
   c. mean number of cars owned

4 If a sample has 237 observations ranked from largest to smallest, which observation is the median? What if the observations are ranked from smallest to largest?

5 If you calculate the mean for a variable which has two categories coded as 0 and 1, what, if anything, does the mean tell you? For example, if the "average sex" of a sample is .75, (males are coded as 0 and females as 1), what does this mean?

6 In a corporation, a very small group of employees has extremely high salaries, while the majority of employees receive much lower salaries. If you were the bargaining agent for the employees, what statistic would you calculate to illustrate the low pay level, and why? If you were the employer, what statistic would you use to demonstrate a higher pay level, and why?

7 The number of dogs owned by 10 families are as follows: 0, 1, 1, 1, 2, 2, 2, 2, 2, 4. Fill in the following table based on these values.

MEAN		MEDIAN		MODE	
STD DEV	1.059	VARIANCE		RANGE	
MINIMUM		MAXIMUM			

8 Compute the missing entries in the following table:

   a.

VARIABLE	STD DEV	VARIANCE	VALID N
VARA	6.529		10

   b.

VARIABLE	RANGE	MINIMUM	MAXIMUM	VALID N
VARB		.000	19.000	10

   c.

VARIABLE	MEAN	SUM	VALID N
VARC		85.000	10

9 An absent-minded instructor calculated the following statistics for an examination: mean=50; range=50; number of cases=99, minimum=20; and maximum=70. She then found an additional examination with a score of 50. Recalculate the statistics, including the additional exam score.

10 The following data represent the number of periodicals read by 25 college students: 1, 1, 1, 1, 1, 1, 2, 2, 2, 3, 3, 3, 3, 3, 3, 4, 4, 5, 5, 5, 5, 8, 9, 9, 10.

a. Using these data, fill in the following histogram:

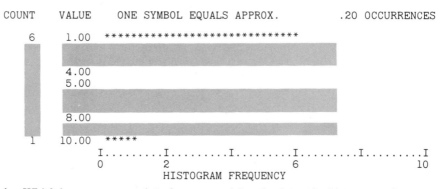

```
COUNT     VALUE     ONE SYMBOL EQUALS APPROX.          .20 OCCURRENCES

   6      1.00    ******************************

          4.00
          5.00

          8.00

   1     10.00    *****
                 I.........I.........I.........I.........I.........I
                 0         2                   6                  10
                          HISTOGRAM FREQUENCY
```

b. Which is more appropriate for summarizing the data, the histogram above, or the bar chart in Chapter 7, question 3 (Statistical Concepts exercises).

11 Which measures of central tendency are appropriate for each of the following variables? If several can be calculated, indicate which makes most use of the available information.

a. number of siblings
b. political party affiliation
c. satisfaction with family
d. vacation days per year
e. type of car driven
f. weight of father

12 For each of the variables in the previous question, would you make a bar chart or a histogram?

13 The number of pairs of shoes owned by 7 college freshmen are 1, 2, 2, 3, 4, 4, and 5.

a. Compute the mean, median, mode, range and standard deviation.
b. An eighth student, the heir to a shoe empire, is added to the sample. This student owns 50 pairs of shoes. Recompute the statistics in part (a).
c. Which of the statistics are not much affected by the inclusion of an observation which is far removed from the rest?

Data Analysis

Use the GSS file for the following questions.

1 AGEWED (age at first marriage), SATJOB (satisfaction with job or housework), and RACE (respondent's race) are all variables which characterize the respondents in the GSS.

a. Determine the level of measurement of each of these variables.

    b. Calculate appropriate descriptive statistics for each of the variables. Make histograms or bar charts as needed.

    c. For each of the variables compare the values of the different measures of central tendency. Indicate why and when you would prefer one measure over another.

    d. Based on your previous analysis, write a brief paragraph describing the participants in the GSS.

2 Consider the variable for total family income (INCOME82).

    a. Get a frequency table for the variable.

    b. Examine the coding scheme used to report the income value. Using this scheme, is INCOME82 a nominal, ordinal, interval, or ratio variable?

    c. What descriptive statistics are appropriate for describing this variable and why? Does it make sense to compute a mean?

    d. Discuss the advantages and disadvantages of recording income in this manner. Would you record income in the same way if you were doing a study? Describe some other ways of recording income.

3 Below are data for 10 cases from a study of heart disease in male workers. For each case we have recorded the number of cigarettes smoked per day in 1958 (CIG58), whether there is a history of heart disease (HISTORY 0=no, 1=yes), and the average diastolic pressure in 1958 (DBP58). Write an SPSS^X job which will read the data and compute appropriate descriptive statistics for each of the variables. Make sure to include variable labels and value labels in your data definition commands. Write a paragraph describing your results.

CASEID	CGT58	HISTORY	DBP58
13	0	1	70
30	60	0	87
53	0	0	89
84	15	1	105
89	25	0	110
102	30	0	88
117	0	0	70
132	30	0	79
151	0	0	102
153	10	1	99

9 Counting Responses for Combinations of Variables

How can you study the relationship between responses to two questions that have a small number of possible answers?

- Why is a frequency table not enough?
- How can you make a table that displays the responses to the two questions together?
- What kinds of percentages can you compute for a table, and how do you choose among them?
- Can one of the variables be considered a dependent variable?
- What if you want to examine more than two variables together?

In Chapter 7, we established that about 47% of our sample found life exciting. From the frequency table, we can tell nothing more. We can't tell whether the men found life more exciting than the women, or whether the single people were more excited than the people who were married or widowed, or whether those who believed in an afterlife were more likely to be excited by *this* life. We'd like to be able to explore these questions, and more like them.

TWO FREQUENCY TABLES

Frequency tables, bar charts, and histograms aren't of much help in answering questions like these—questions that involve relations among several variables—since they look at variables one at a time. From Figure 9.1, the frequency table for the exciting-routine-dull variable, and Figure 9.2, the frequency table for the sex variable, we still can't say whether the men found life more exciting than the women.

```
FILE HANDLE GSS / (system-specific information)
GET FILE=GSS
FREQUENCIES VARIABLES=LIFE, SEX
```

Figure 9.1 Frequency table for LIFE

FILE: 1984 General Social Survey

LIFE   Is life exciting or dull?

VALUE LABEL	VALUE	FREQUENCY	PERCENT	VALID PERCENT	CUM PERCENT
Exciting	1	684	46.4	46.8	46.8
Pretty routine	2	704	47.8	48.2	95.0
Dull	3	73	5.0	5.0	100.0
Don't know	8	5	.3	MISSING	
No answer	9	7	.5	MISSING	
	TOTAL	1473	100.0	100.0	

VALID CASES   1461   MISSING CASES   12

Figure 9.2 Frequency table for SEX

```
FILE:      1984 General Social Survey

SEX        Respondent's sex

                                                    VALID      CUM
    VALUE LABEL              VALUE   FREQUENCY   PERCENT   PERCENT   PERCENT
Male                          1          598       40.6      40.6      40.6
Female                        2          875       59.4      59.4     100.0
                                     _____   _____  _____
                           TOTAL        1473      100.0     100.0

VALID CASES      1473    MISSING CASES       0
```

What we need to do is take each line of the LIFE frequency table and *subdivide* it into the number of males and females.

CROSS-CLASSIFICATION TABLES

We want to know how many of the 684 people who found life exciting were men and how many were women. Of the 704 people who found life pretty routine, how many were men and how many were women? Similarly, how many of the 73 people who found life dull were men and how many were women?

No problem. Just type a CROSSTABS command into your command file:

```
FILE HANDLE GSS / (system-specific information)
GET FILE=GSS
CROSSTABS TABLES = LIFE BY SEX
```

The last command makes a table showing LIFE BY SEX: the categories of the variable before BY become the rows, and the categories of the variable after BY become the columns. Look at the results in Figure 9.3. The 1,461 people who answered the question about excitement are subdivided by whether they are males or females. The little boxes in Figure 9.3 are called **cells,** and they are arranged in rows and columns. Labels at the left and the top of the table describe what's in each of the rows and columns. To the right and at the bottom of the table are totals—often called **marginal totals** because they are in the table's margins.

Because the categories of the two variables are "crossed" with each other, this kind of table is called a **cross-classification table** or simply a **crosstabulation.** A cross-classification table shows a cell for every combination of categories of the two variables. Inside the cell is a number showing how many people gave that combination of responses. The table

Figure 9.3 A cross-classification table

```
FILE:     1984 General Social Survey
- - - - - - - - - -    C R O S S T A B U L A T I O N   O F   - - - - - - - - -
    LIFE      Is life exciting or dull?
BY  SEX       Respondent's sex
- - - - - - - - - - - - - - - - - - - - - - - - - - - -  PAGE  1 OF  1

                     SEX
           COUNT  |
                  |Male      Female      ROW
                  |                      TOTAL
                  |      1|       2|
LIFE       -------+-------+--------+
               1  |  300  |   384  |     684
   Exciting      |       |        |    46.8
                  +-------+--------+
               2  |  267  |   437  |     704
 Pretty routine  |       |        |    48.2
                  +-------+--------+
               3  |   29  |    44  |      73
   Dull          |       |        |     5.0
                  +-------+--------+
           COLUMN    596      865        1461
           TOTAL    40.8     59.2      100.0

NUMBER OF MISSING OBSERVATIONS =       12
```

is a very efficient way to present a lot of numbers. When you get used to it, it's quite easy to read. Let's look at what's in the cells.

The number in the first cell of the table, 300, tells you that 300 males found life exciting. The next number is in the column labeled Female, and it tells you that 384 females found life exciting. The sum of these two numbers—684—is shown in the margin. This is the same number that appears in Figure 9.1 for the total number of people who found life exciting. Each line of the figure tells you the number of men and the number of women who gave a particular answer about the excitement of their life.

The margins of the table show the same information as the frequency tables, in Figures 9.1 and 9.2. In the right-hand margin, labeled ROW TOTAL, you have the total number of people who gave the responses Exciting, Pretty routine, and Dull. The right-hand margin also shows what percentages those counts are of the total sample. In the bottom margin, labeled COLUMN TOTAL, you have the total number of males and of females, and what percentage each of *those* groups is of the sample. So a cross-classification table contains a lot of information. Besides telling you the number of males and females who gave each of the responses, it has little frequency tables in the margins.

Percentages

More women gave the answer Exciting than did men: 384 women compared to 300 men. The answer is clear. More women than men found life exciting. Wait—is that really what you want to know? From the column totals of Figure 9.3, you see that a lot more women than men were in the sample. Almost 60% of the sample were women. That difference makes it hard to compare just the counts in the cells. Even if men and women find life equally exciting, you would expect to see more women in the Exciting cell simply because more women were in the sample.

Figuring the Percentages

To compare the excitement rates among men and women, you need percentages. You need to figure out how many men would say they find life exciting if your sample had 100 men, and similarly how many women would say they find life exciting if your sample had 100 women. Then you can compare these two percentages. To get SPSS^X to compute the percentages for you, type:

```
FILE HANDLE GSS / (system-specific information)
GET FILE=GSS
CROSSTABS TABLES=LIFE BY SEX
OPTIONS 4
```

OPTIONS 4 tells SPSS^X to calculate the percentages so that the column totals are 100. That's what we want in order to compare 100 men to 100 women.

What kind of command is OPTIONS 4? Some SPSS^X procedures, like CROSSTABS, use numbers as instructions for what you want them to compute. Numbers aren't as easy to remember as words like TABLES, but some of the procedures that were put together a long time ago still use them. A list of the "magic numbers" for CROSSTABS is later in this chapter, in the section "More about the CROSSTABS Procedure." Other chapters have similar lists for other procedures. ■ ■ ■

The table with the percentages is shown in Figure 9.4. Each cell of the table now contains two numbers: the count of the cases in the cell and the percentage (called a **column percentage**) that the count is of the column total. A **directory** of all of the numbers in a cell appears in the upper left-hand corner of the table. The directory shows that each cell contains a count (COUNT) above a column percentage (COL PCT).

Results of Percentaging

Looking at the percentages in the table, you see that 50.3% of the men reported their life as exciting, but only 44.4% of the women reported the same thing. These percentages are just the opposite of what the counts show. It's easy to mislead yourself if you compare just the counts in the cells of a cross-classification table. Turn the counts into percentages. Percentages eliminate the differences that show up when you have more people in one group than in another.

Figure 9.4 The cross-classification table with column percentages

```
FILE:    1984 General Social Survey

- - - - - - - - -   C R O S S T A B U L A T I O N   O F   - - - - - - - - -
    LIFE      Is life exciting or dull?
BY  SEX       Respondent's sex
- - - - - - - - - - - - - - - - - - - - - - - - - - - -   PAGE  1 OF  1

                      SEX
            COUNT  |
            COL PCT|Male      Female      ROW
                   |                      TOTAL
                   |       1|        2|
    LIFE      -----+--------+--------+
               1   |   300  |   384  |    684
    Exciting       |  50.3  |  44.4  |   46.8
                   +--------+--------+
               2   |   267  |   437  |    704
    Pretty routine |  44.8  |  50.5  |   48.2
                   +--------+--------+
               3   |    29  |    44  |     73
    Dull           |   4.9  |   5.1  |    5.0
                   +--------+--------+
            COLUMN     596      865      1461
            TOTAL     40.8     59.2    100.0

NUMBER OF MISSING OBSERVATIONS =        12
```

Column Percentages and Row Percentages

If you add up the percentages in the Male column in Figure 9.3, they sum to 100. The percentages in the Female column also add to 100. That's what we wanted. We wanted to be able to compare the responses to the excitement variable as if there were 100 men and 100 women in the sample. (Don't be confused by the percentages in the margins of the table. They are always for the frequency tables printed in the margins. We are talking here about percentages *inside* the cells of the table.)

There's another way you could have computed percentages for the same table. If 100 people give the answer Exciting, how many of these are men and how many are women? The calculations are pretty easy. Of the 684 people who said life is exciting, 300 are men, which makes 43.9% men. (300 divided by 684 is .439, or 43.9%.) The 384 women made up the other 56.1% of the people who said life is exciting. Because these percentages are based on a row total (684), they are called **row percentages.**

What do these numbers tell you? They tell you how likely it was that a person who considered life exciting was a male or a female. But you're probably interested in knowing how likely it was that a male or female found life exciting—and the row percentages don't tell you that. It's usually true in a cross-classification table that either row percentages or column percentages answer your question. Deciding to use one or the other is often based on whether you consider one variable dependent and the other, independent.

DEPENDENT AND INDEPENDENT VARIABLES

Sometimes you look at two variables together because you think that one influences the other. In our example, the sex of the respondent may have influenced his or her perception of life. We know that the influence can't go in the other direction—your sex is determined much earlier than your views on how exciting life is. The variable doing the influencing is called the **independent variable**, and the variable being influenced is called the **dependent variable**.

How can you remember which variable is called independent, and which is called dependent? Those are important terms, which you'll run into again and again. Actually, it's easy to remember which is which:

- The *dependent* variable *depends* on the other one.
- The *independent* variable doesn't depend on the other one; it goes its own way, *independently*.

With a moment's thought, you should always be able to figure out whether to consider a variable dependent or independent. ■ ■ ■

If you can identify one of your variables as independent and the other as dependent, then you should compute percentages so that they sum to 100 for each category of the *independent* variable. If the values of the independent variable are at the heads of the columns, use column percentages.

Until you're comfortable with these ideas, you can use this system:

1 Figure out which variable is dependent on the other.

2 Type CROSSTABS TABLES = (dependent variable) BY (independent variable).

3 Use Option 4 for column percentages.

If you find that you've calculated your percentages the wrong way, go back and do it right. If you exploit your computer and have SPSS^X compute them *both* ways, figure out which way is the one you want, and then take a pencil and cross out the ones you don't want.

AN EXAMPLE: IS MARRIAGE EXCITING?

We've seen that the men were somewhat more likely to find life exciting than the women were. How about married people? Were they more likely to feel that life is routine than those who were still exploring? If you were

Figure 9.5 Excitement and marriage

```
FILE:     1984 General Social Survey
- - - - - - - - - -   C R O S S T A B U L A T I O N   O F   - - - - - - - - -
   LIFE      Is life exciting or dull?
BY  MARITAL   Marital status
- - - - - - - - - - - - - - - - - - - - - - - -   PAGE  1 OF  1
```

	COUNT COL PCT	MARITAL Married	Widowed	Divorced	Separated	Never married	ROW TOTAL
		1	2	3	4	5	
LIFE							
Exciting	1	392 47.6	51 33.8	77 46.7	18 42.9	146 52.3	684 46.8
Pretty routine	2	401 48.7	82 54.3	77 46.7	20 47.6	124 44.4	704 48.2
Dull	3	31 3.8	18 11.9	11 6.7	4 9.5	9 3.2	73 5.0
	COLUMN TOTAL	824 56.4	151 10.3	165 11.3	42 2.9	279 19.1	1461 100.0

NUMBER OF MISSING OBSERVATIONS =   12

analyzing your data without a computer, each question you wanted to look at would require someone going through all the forms again and counting. *With* a computer, all you have to do is set up a command file like this:

```
FILE HANDLE GSS / (system-specific information)
GET FILE=GSS
CROSSTABS TABLES=LIFE BY MARITAL
OPTIONS 4
```

Here, MARITAL is the independent variable, so we put it second on the CROSSTABS command. (People got married sometime before the interview; they're excited or bored during the interview. The marital condition is surely the independent variable.) We wanted to see how many people in each condition of marriage found life exciting or routine, so we calculated percentages to make it look as if there were 100 people in each condition of marriage. Since marital status is the independent variable and is in the columns, we asked for column percentages with Option 4. When you run this job, a table like that shown in Figure 9.5 appears on your screen or comes from a printer.

You should have no trouble reading the table. About 48% of the married people found life exciting. How does this compare to the other categories? There doesn't appear to be much of a difference between those who were married and those who were divorced. Almost 47% of the divorced people thought that life was exciting. People who hadn't ever been married were the most likely to find life exciting: 52% of them said so. Only 34% of the widowed reported that their lives were exciting. The percentage for separated people—43%—was between the percentages for the widowed and the married.

MORE THAN TWO VARIABLES

The popular press often reports that marriage is good for men and not as good for women. Married men even have much lower death rates than their single counterparts. Let's see whether the differences we've observed among the marital groups were similar for men and women. The simplest way to begin exploring this question is to type

```
FILE HANDLE GSS / (system-specific information)
GET FILE=GSS
CROSSTABS TABLES=LIFE BY MARITAL BY SEX
OPTIONS 4
```

Instead of getting a single table, you now get two partial tables or **subtables,** as shown in Figure 9.6. One of the subtables is for men, and the other is for women. The subtables show some interesting differences. The divorced men found life a lot less exciting than the men who were married or never married. Of the married men, about 51% described their lives as exciting, and of the never-married men, 54%. Of the divorced men, only 42% reported life exciting. In contrast, divorced *women* and women who had never been married were *more* likely to report life exciting than their married counterparts. Only 45% of the married women classified their lives as exciting, but 51% of the never-married women and 49% of the divorced women thought that life was exciting.

Both men and women who were widowed were less likely to report life exciting than were any of the other marital groups. There were not very many separated people, so you have to be careful in what you say about them.

Control Variables

When we split up a table in this way, into a separate subtable for each category of a third variable, we say that we **control** for the third variable. In the example, we controlled for SEX. Controlling for variables is a very important concept in data analysis. Here it meant that we were mainly interested in the LIFE BY MARITAL relationship, but we suspected that another variable (SEX) might influence the relationship between LIFE and MARITAL. We controlled this influence in the crosstabulation by simply producing a separate subtable of the main relationship (LIFE BY MARITAL) for each category of the control variable (SEX). Even if SEX affects the main relationship, it certainly doesn't affect it in the subtables —because everybody in a subtable has the *same* sex.

Figure 9.6 Is marriage good for men?

```
FILE:    1984 General Social Survey

- - - - - - - - - -   C R O S S T A B U L A T I O N   O F   - - - - - - - - - -
    LIFE       Is life exciting or dull?
BY  MARITAL    Marital status
CONTROLLING FOR..
    SEX        Respondent's sex
                                          =        1.  Male
- - - - - - - - - - - - - - - - - - - - - - - - - - - - -  PAGE  1 OF  1

                        MARITAL
            COUNT
            COL PCT |Married Widowed Divorced Separa- Never      ROW
                    |                         ted    married    TOTAL
                    |    1|     2|      3|      4|      5|
LIFE        --------+------+------+------+------+------+
            1       |  182     6     22     10     80      300
  Exciting          | 51.1   30.0   41.5   55.6   53.7     50.3
                    +------+------+------+------+------+
            2       |  161    11     27      7     61      267
  Pretty routine    | 45.2   55.0   50.9   38.9   40.9     44.8
                    +------+------+------+------+------+
            3       |   13     3      4      1      8       29
  Dull              |  3.7   15.0    7.5    5.6    5.4      4.9
                    +------+------+------+------+------+
            COLUMN      356    20     53     18    149      596
            TOTAL      59.7    3.4    8.9    3.0   25.0    100.0
```

```
FILE:    1984 General Social Survey

- - - - - - - - - -   C R O S S T A B U L A T I O N   O F   - - - - - - - - - -
    LIFE       Is life exciting or dull?
BY  MARITAL    Marital status
CONTROLLING FOR..
    SEX        Respondent's sex
                                          =        2.  Female
- - - - - - - - - - - - - - - - - - - - - - - - - - - - -  PAGE  1 OF  1

                        MARITAL
            COUNT
            COL PCT |Married Widowed Divorced Separa- Never      ROW
                    |                         ted    married    TOTAL
                    |    1|     2|      3|      4|      5|
LIFE        --------+------+------+------+------+------+
            1       |  210    45     55      8     66      384
  Exciting          | 44.9   34.4   49.1   33.3   50.8     44.4
                    +------+------+------+------+------+
            2       |  240    71     50     13     63      437
  Pretty routine    | 51.3   54.2   44.6   54.2   48.5     50.5
                    +------+------+------+------+------+
            3       |   18    15      7      3      1       44
  Dull              |  3.8   11.5    6.3   12.5    .8       5.1
                    +------+------+------+------+------+
            COLUMN      468   131    112     24    130      865
            TOTAL      54.1   15.1   12.9    2.8   15.0    100.0

NUMBER OF MISSING OBSERVATIONS =      12
```

You could subdivide your sample on the basis of all kinds of different things. You could build a table that classifies cases on the basis of sex, health, belief in the afterlife, and job satisfaction, in addition to the question about life being exciting. Such a large table would be difficult to read and interpret, especially since most of the cells would have few cases. You can have as many as 10 of these classifications, but whenever you include another classification, you are dividing up the same number of cases into more and more cells. Building tables is most useful when you have a *small* number of variables that you want to examine together.

MORE ABOUT THE CROSSTABS PROCEDURE

You use the CROSSTABS procedure to count the number of times different combinations of values for two or more variables occur in the data. You can get:

- Cross-classification tables for two or more variables.
- Row percentages.
- Column percentages.

Making the Table

If you want to tabulate the number of males and females who belong to various religions, type:

```
CROSSTABS TABLES=SEX BY RELIGION
```

The first variable forms the rows of the table. The second variable forms the columns. The word BY separates the variables. If you want to make religion the row variable, just reverse the order of the variable names:

```
CROSSTABS TABLES=RELIGION BY SEX
```

If you have several variables that you want to crosstabulate with SEX, list them before the word BY and separate them with commas or blanks:

```
CROSSTABS TABLES=RELIGION JOB LIFE BY SEX
```

More than Two Variables in a Table

To calculate separate tables of religion and sex for several regions of the country, type:

```
CROSSTABS TABLES=RELIGION BY SEX BY REGION
```

A separate table of religion by sex is printed for each region. To include additional variables in the table, list each of them after a BY. For example, to make a table of religion by sex for different regions and occupations within each region, type:

```
CROSSTABS TABLES=RELIGION BY SEX BY REGION BY OCCUP
```

Calculating Percentages

If you want to see the number of cases in each cell, and you also want the number in the cell as a percentage of all cases in the row or column, you must use the OPTIONS specification. The word OPTIONS must follow the CROSSTABS command. It must start in column 1. Following the word OPTIONS, type the number 3 to get row percentages. The command

```
CROSSTABS TABLES=RELIGION BY SEX
OPTIONS 3
```

gives you a crosstabulation that contains the number of males and females in each of the religions. The different religions are the rows of the table. OPTIONS 3 indicates that row percentages are to be computed. For each religion, the percentage of men and the percentage of women members are calculated.

If you type

```
CROSSTABS TABLES=RELIGION BY SEX
OPTIONS 4
```

you get column percentages. For each cell, the percentage of all men or women who are members of a particular religion is calculated.

Options for CROSSTABS

Here is a complete list of the numbers used on the OPTIONS command following a CROSSTABS command.

1	Include missing values	10	Write cell count for nonempty cells
2	Suppress labels	12	Suppress tables
3	Add row percentages	13	Suppress cell counts
4	Add column percentages	14	Add expected frequencies
5	Add total percentages	15	Add residuals
6	Suppress value labels	16	Add standardized residuals
8	Order rows by descending value	17	Add adjusted standardized residuals
9	Print index of tables	18	Include all cell information

You can also use a STATISTICS command after CROSSTABS, to request statistics pertaining to the table. The numbers for the individual statistics are given at the end of Chapter 19, where the statistics are discussed. Additional features of the CROSSTABS procedure are discussed in Chapters 17 and 19.

WHAT'S NEXT?

A crosstabulation is a very effective way of displaying the values of two or more variables at the same time. However, a crosstabulation becomes large and difficult to use when a variable has many categories. In the next chapter you will learn how to change the way your variables are coded, to solve this and similar problems.

Summary

How can you study the relationship between responses to two questions which have a small number of possible answers?

A crosstabulation shows the numbers of cases that have particular combinations of responses to two or more questions.

The number of cases in each cell of a crosstabulation can be expressed as the percentage of all cases in that row (the row percentage) or the percentage of all cases in that column (the column percentage).

The variable that is thought to influence the values of another variable is called the *independent* variable.

The variable that is influenced is called the *dependent* variable.

If there is an independent variable, percentages should be calculated so that they sum to 100 for each category of the independent variable.

When you have more than two variables, you can make separate crosstabulations for each of the combinations of the other variables.

EXERCISES

Syntax

1 For the two variables called RACE and SATJOB, write the SPSS^X command to produce:
   a. a crosstabulation table with RACE as the row variable and SATJOB as the column variable.
   b. a crosstabulation table with RACE as the column variable and SATJOB as the row variable.
   c. the table in (a) with row percents.
   d. the table in (b) with column percents.
   e. the table in (b) with row and column percents.

2 Correct the error in the following SPSS^X commands:
   a. CROSSTABULATION TABLES=ROW BY COLUMN
   b. CROSSTABS zodiac by life
   c. CROSSTABS TABLES=ZODIAC BY LIFE / OPTION 3
   d. CROSSTABS TABLES ZODIAC BY LIFE FOR MARITAL

3 Write the commands that produced the following crosstabulation.

```
FILE:      1984 General Social Survey

- - - - - - - - - -  C R O S S T A B U L A T I O N   O F  - - - - - - - - - -
    LIFE       Is life exciting or dull?
BY  SEX        Respondent's sex
- - - - - - - - - - - - - - - - - - - - - - - - - - - - -  PAGE  1 OF  1

                       SEX
            COUNT
            ROW PCT |Male     Female     ROW
            COL PCT |                    TOTAL
                    |     1|      2|
    LIFE    --------+-------+-------+
                1   |  300  |  384  |   684
    Exciting        | 43.9  | 56.1  |  46.8
                    | 50.3  | 44.4  |
                    +-------+-------+
                2   |  267  |  437  |   704
    Pretty routine  | 37.9  | 62.1  |  48.2
                    | 44.8  | 50.5  |
                    +-------+-------+
                3   |   29  |   44  |    73
    Dull            | 39.7  | 60.3  |   5.0
                    |  4.9  |  5.1  |
                    +-------+-------+
            COLUMN     596     865     1461
            TOTAL     40.8    59.2    100.0

NUMBER OF MISSING OBSERVATIONS =        12
```

Statistical Concepts

1 The following table indicates whether each of twenty people owns or rents a home (1=own, 2=rents), and how satisfied they are with city services (1=not satisfied; 2=satisfied; 3=very satisfied).

Person	Owner	Satisfied
1	1	1
2	1	1
3	1	1
4	1	1
5	1	1
6	1	2
7	1	3
8	1	3
9	2	2
10	2	2
11	2	3
12	2	3
13	2	3
14	2	3
15	2	3
16	2	3
17	2	3
18	2	3
19	2	3
20	2	3

a. Summarize the data by filling in the values for the cell counts and marginals of the following crosstabulation.

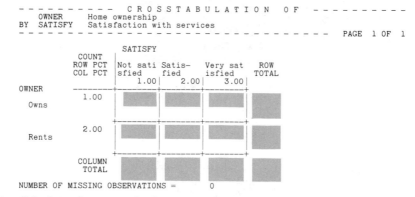

```
- - - - - - - - - - - -    C R O S S T A B U L A T I O N   O F   - - - - - - - - - -
    OWNER      Home ownership
BY  SATISFY    Satisfaction with services
- - - - - - - - - - - - - - - - - - - - - - - - - - - - - -    PAGE  1 OF  1
```

b. Calculate the row and column percentages.

c. What percent of the sample are homeowners?

d. What percent of the sample are very satisfied with city services?

e. What percent of homeowners are very satisfied with city services? Of non-owners?

2 Identify the dependent and independent variables, if possible, for each of the following pairs of variables:

a. satisfaction with job and race.

b. belief in life after death and sex.

c. astrological sign and excitement with life.

d. mother's highest degree and daughter's highest degree.

e. happiness with one's marriage and belief in life after death.

3 If you construct a crosstabulation for each of the pairs of variables in the previous question, with the first variable forming the rows of the table and the second variable forming the columns, should you calculate row or column percentages? Answer for all five pairs.

4 A study to determine the effect of grade-point average on performance on a test resulted in the following table:

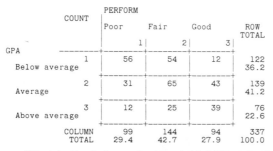

COUNT	PERFORM			
	Poor	Fair	Good	ROW TOTAL
	1		2		3		
GPA				
1 Below average	56	54	12	122 36.2
2 Average	31	65	43	139 41.2
3 Above average	12	25	39	76 22.6
COLUMN TOTAL	99 29.4	144 42.7	94 27.9	337 100.0

a. What is the independent variable? What is the dependent variable?

b. Would you look at row percentages or column percentages to see whether the independent variable seems to affect the dependent variable?

5 Fill in the missing information in the following table:

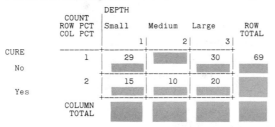

COUNT ROW PCT COL PCT	DEPTH			ROW TOTAL
	Small 1|	Medium 2|	Large 3|	
CURE No 1	29		30	69
Yes 2	15	10	20	
COLUMN TOTAL				

6 Your local newspaper's Sunday supplement contains an article on job satisfaction and marital status. The article contains the following table. The authors conclude that marriage makes people more satisfied with their jobs, since 63 percent of the very satisfied people are married, while only 14 percent have never been married. Comment on the conclusions from the study.

```
- - - - - - - - - -   C R O S S T A B U L A T I O N   O F   - - - - - - - - -
    MARITAL    Marital status
BY  SATJOB     Satisfaction with job or housework
- - - - - - - - - - - - - - - - - - - - - - - - - - - - -   PAGE  1 OF  1
```

COUNT COL PCT	SATJOB				ROW TOTAL
	Very sat isfied 1|	Modratly satisfi 2|	A little dissati 3|	Very dis satisfie 4|	
MARITAL					
Married 1	351 63.2	242 57.2	73 50.0	36 42.9	702 58.1
Widowed 2	44 7.9	31 7.3	7 4.8	5 6.0	87 7.2
Divorced 3	68 12.3	55 13.0	16 11.0	13 15.5	152 12.6
Separated 4	15 2.7	12 2.8	5 3.4	6 7.1	38 3.1
Never married 5	77 13.9	83 19.6	45 30.8	24 28.6	229 19.0
COLUMN TOTAL	555 45.9	423 35.0	146 12.1	84 7.0	1208 100.0

NUMBER OF MISSING OBSERVATIONS =   265

7 Below is a crosstabulation of belief in life after death and highest degree achieved. Calculate the appropriate percentages, and write a few sentences summarizing the table.

FILE: 1984 General Social Survey

```
- - - - - - - - - -   C R O S S T A B U L A T I O N   O F   - - - - - - - - -
    POSTLIFE   Belief in life after death
BY  DEGREE     Highest degree received
- - - - - - - - - - - - - - - - - - - - - - - - - - - - -   PAGE  1 OF  1
```

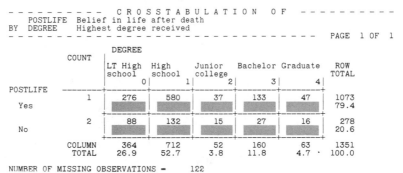

COUNT	DEGREE					ROW TOTAL
	LT High school 0|	High school 1|	Junior college 2|	Bachelor 3|	Graduate 4|	
POSTLIFE						
Yes 1	276	580	37	133	47	1073 79.4
No 2	88	132	15	27	16	278 20.6
COLUMN TOTAL	364 26.9	712 52.7	52 3.8	160 11.8	63 4.7	1351 100.0

NUMBER OF MISSING OBSERVATIONS = 122

8 For which of the following pairs of variables do you think a crosstabulation would be appropriate?
   a. weight in pounds and daily intake in calories
   b. number of cars and highest degree achieved
   c. body temperature in degrees and survival after an operation
   d. eye color and undergraduate grade-point average

Data Analysis

1 You're interested in examining the relationship between the happiness of a person's marriage and whether they find life to be exciting, routine, or dull. Generate the SPSS^X output that you need to investigate the question.

2 Discuss whether row or column percentages tell you what you want to know and why.

3 Write a brief paragraph summarizing your results.

4 Write the SPSS^X job to interchange the rows and columns of your table. That is, if in your previous table, HAPMAR was the row variable, make it the column variable.

5 Would you still look at the same percentages?

6 Write a brief paragraph summarizing the relationship between a person's job satisfaction (SATJOB) and whether he or she perceives life to be exciting.

10 Changing the Coding Scheme

How can you change the way your variables are coded?

- How can you switch the code numbers that stand for particular responses?
- How can you combine groups of codes into a smaller, more convenient number of codes?
- Can you preserve the original variable and make a new, recoded version, too?
- What happens to value labels when you recode the values?
- What happens to missing-value declarations when you recode the values?

A variable like AGE has too many categories to use in a crosstabulation. The table would contain hundreds of cells, and most of them would be empty or nearly empty. If the sample has only seven men who are exactly 53 years old, there's not much point in looking to see how many of them are excited by life. To use a variable like AGE in a crosstabulation, you need to create broader categories from the original data. The RECODE command lets you combine values into a single new code. This is sometimes called **collapsing** the codes. For example, you can group people's ages into decades or perhaps just into Young, Middle-aged, and Old categories. Then you can make a crosstabulation comparing excitement among people in the different age groups. You can also use RECODE simply to rearrange a coding scheme.

THE RECODE COMMAND

The RECODE command works in a straightforward manner. You enter specifications that say, "If the value is now this, make it equal to that." Recoding is useful in several circumstances.

Changing Individual Values

Remember that LIFE has three valid responses, coded 1–3:

1   Exciting
2   Pretty routine
3   Dull

Suppose you want to change the order to go from least excitement to most excitement:

1   Dull
2   Pretty routine
3   Exciting

In effect, you want to swap the values 1 and 3. You can do this easily by typing:

RECODE LIFE (1 = 3) (3 = 1)

Before the swap, the frequency table for LIFE looks like Figure 10.1, which by now should be familiar. After the swap, all the original 1s for

Figure 10.1 The LIFE frequency table before recoding

```
FILE:      1984 General Social Survey

LIFE       Is life exciting or dull?
```

| | | | | VALID | CUM |
VALUE LABEL	VALUE	FREQUENCY	PERCENT	PERCENT	PERCENT
Exciting	1	684	46.4	46.8	46.8
Pretty routine	2	704	47.8	48.2	95.0
Dull	3	73	5.0	5.0	100.0
Don't know	8	5	.3	MISSING	
No answer	9	7	.5	MISSING	
		_____	_____	_____	
	TOTAL	1473	100.0	100.0	

```
VALID CASES    1461    MISSING CASES    12
```

Figure 10.2 The LIFE frequency table after recoding

| | | | | VALID | CUM |
VALUE LABEL	VALUE	FREQUENCY	PERCENT	PERCENT	PERCENT
Dull	1	73	5.0	5.0	5.0
Pretty routine	2	704	47.8	48.2	53.2
Exciting	3	684	46.4	46.8	100.0
Don't know	8	5	.3	MISSING	
No answer	9	7	.5	MISSING	
		_____	_____	_____	
	TOTAL	1473	100.0	100.0	

```
VALID CASES    1461    MISSING CASES    12
```

Figure 10.3 The AGE frequency table after recoding

```
FILE:      1984 General Social Survey

AGE        Age collapsed into categories
```

| | | | | VALID | CUM |
VALUE LABEL	VALUE	FREQUENCY	PERCENT	PERCENT	PERCENT
18 – 29 years	1	393	26.7	26.8	26.8
30 – 45 years	2	476	32.3	32.4	59.2
46 – 59 years	3	253	17.2	17.2	76.5
60 or more years	4	345	23.4	23.5	100.0
	9	6	.4	MISSING	
		_____	_____	_____	
	TOTAL	1473	100.0	100.0	

```
VALID CASES    1467    MISSING CASES     6
```

LIFE have changed to 3s, and the original 3s have changed to 1s. However, the value labels are still the same. Code 1, which now stands for the Dull category, still has the label Exciting—a confusing situation. When you tinker with the way a variable is coded, you don't affect the variable label or value labels you may have given it. You can fix this problem easily, though, just by issuing a new VALUE LABELS command (and VARIABLE LABELS, if you want to) along with your RECODE command:

```
RECODE LIFE (1 = 3) (3 = 1)
VALUE LABELS LIFE  1 'Dull'  2 'Pretty routine'  3 'Exciting'
                   8 "Don't know"  9 'No answer'
```

Now a frequency table showing the recoded variable, LIFE, will have the right assignment of labels. The new frequency table is in Figure 10.2. Compare it to Figure 10.1, especially in the way that the CUM PERCENT column has changed. Also, if you list out the actual values in the file (see Chapter 6), you'll see that cases which had value 1 for LIFE have value 3 instead, and vice-versa.

Collapsing Values

Although the General Social Survey is large, you still wouldn't want to look at each age individually. Instead, you can collapse the variable AGE (the respondent's age at the time of the interview) into a small number of categories.

? *Where did that variable come from? The questionnaire asked for year of birth, not age.* It's quite easy to use SPSS^X to calculate age from the year of birth—we'll see how in Chapter 12. In fact, though, this calculation is done even before the General Social Survey data are released. ■■■

Let's create age categories representing different age groups. You can do this easily with the RECODE command:

```
RECODE AGE (18 THRU 29=1) (30 THRU 45=2)
   (46 THRU 59=3) (60 THRU 89=4) (ELSE=9)
VARIABLE LABELS AGE 'Age collapsed into categories'
VALUE LABELS AGE 1 '18 – 29 years' 2 '30 – 45 years'
                3 '46 – 59 years' 4 '60 or more years'
MISSING VALUES AGE (9)
```

This RECODE command combines the values 18 through 29 into a single category with the code of 1; it combines 30 through 45 into a category with the code of 2; 46 through 59 into a category with the code of 3; and 60 through 89 into a category with the code of 4. Everyone ELSE is assigned a code of 9.

? *What about people younger than 18 or older than 89? Is that who "everyone else" is?* There aren't any valid ages less than 18 or more than 89. The General Social Survey doesn't include anyone younger than 18, and it reports an age of 89 for people 90 or over. In the RECODE command, AGE values that aren't in the range 18–89 are recoded to 9, and then 9 is declared missing. So "everyone else" simply means people with missing values for AGE. ■■■

Without recoding, the frequency table for AGE would be pretty long, containing one line for every age between 18 and 89—72 lines in all. But after the recoding (and a new VALUE LABELS command for clarification), the frequency table is more compact and easier to interpret. It looks like Figure 10.3.

How Does It Work?

The RECODE command operates on one case at a time. It takes a case's value on the variable you are recoding and then starts searching through the recode specifications. If it finds a specification telling it what to do with the value, it makes the switch and stops processing the RECODE command for that case. This means that a RECODE command never changes the value of a case twice. The command

RECODE LIFE (1 = 3) (3 = 1)

changes the 1s to 3s and leaves them there. It doesn't recode them a second time, back to 1s. Only the cases that were originally 3 for the LIFE variable get recoded to 1.

Another important point to remember is that if you don't recode a value, the value doesn't change. In the example above, cases for which the variable LIFE doesn't equal 1 or 3 are totally unaffected by the RECODE command.

SPECIFYING THE RECODE COMMAND

The RECODE command is easy to read. The examples so far have had the following general form:

RECODE variable name (current codes = new code)
                     (current codes = new code)
            . . .

RECODE works on one variable before it starts on any others. You put the variable name after the word RECODE and then enter as many recode specifications as you want—each enclosed in parentheses. A **recode specification** is a current code (or a list of current codes), followed by an equals sign (=), followed by the single new code that you want the current one(s) changed to. If you have a list of codes, you can enter each of them separately:

RECODE AGE   (18 19 20 21 22 23 24 25 26 27 28 29 = 1)
  (30 31 32 33 34 35 36 37 38 39 40 41 42 43 44 45 = 2)
  ...and so on.

You can also enter them as a range of codes, like the earlier example:

RECODE AGE (18 THRU 29 = 1) (30 THRU 45 = 2) ...and so on.

Or you can mix the two styles. RECODE is very flexible that way:

RECODE AGE (18 19 20 21 22 23 24 25 26 27 28 29 = 1)
  (30 THRU 45 = 2) (46 47 48 49 THRU 59 = 3)
  ...and so on.

AGE AND EXCITEMENT WITH LIFE

Now that AGE is in a usable form for crosstabulations, we'd like to know whether young, middle-aged, and older people in the sample had different feelings about how exciting life is.

We'll group the men and the women into categories based on age and then make a cross-classification table of age categories and excitement categories:

```
FILE HANDLE GSS / (system-specific information)
GET FILE=GSS
RECODE AGE (18 THRU 29=1) (30 THRU 45=2)
          (46 THRU 59=3) (60 THRU 89=4) (ELSE=9)
VARIABLE LABELS AGE 'Age collapsed into categories'
VALUE LABELS    AGE 1 '18 - 29 years' 2 '30 - 45 years'
                3 '46 - 59 years' 4 '60 or more years'
MISSING VALUES  AGE (9)
CROSSTABS TABLES=LIFE BY AGE
OPTIONS 4
```

The results are in Figure 10.4, and they are as you might expect. Of the young people, aged 18-29, 54% found life exciting; but of the old people, aged 60 or over, only 37% did.

Let's introduce SEX as a control variable again, as in Chapter 9. That way, we can tell whether the pattern of declining excitement is the same for both men and women.

Figure 10.4 Age and life's excitement

```
FILE:   1984 General Social Survey

- - - - - - - - - - C R O S S T A B U L A T I O N   O F  - - - - - - - - -
    LIFE    Is life exciting or dull?
BY AGE      Age collapsed into categories
- - - - - - - - - - - - - - - - - - - - - - - - - - - -  PAGE  1 OF  1

                    AGE
           COUNT
           COL PCT  18 - 29  30 - 45  46 - 59  60 or mo   ROW
                    years    years    years    re years   TOTAL
                          1|       2|       3|       4|
LIFE       --------+--------+--------+--------+--------+
               1  |   211  |   219  |   125  |   128  |   683
    Exciting      |  54.1  |  46.3  |  49.6  |  37.5  |  46.9
           -------+--------+--------+--------+--------+
               2  |   168  |   237  |   115  |   180  |   700
    Pretty routine|  43.1  |  50.1  |  45.6  |  52.8  |  48.1
           -------+--------+--------+--------+--------+
               3  |    11  |    17  |    12  |    33  |    73
    Dull          |   2.8  |   3.6  |   4.8  |   9.7  |   5.0
           -------+--------+--------+--------+--------+
           COLUMN    390      473      252      341     1456
           TOTAL    26.8     32.5     17.3     23.4    100.0

NUMBER OF MISSING OBSERVATIONS =      17
```

```
FILE HANDLE GSS / (system-specific information)
GET FILE=GSS
RECODE AGE (18 THRU 29=1) (30 THRU 45=2)
           (46 THRU 59=3) (60 THRU 89=4) (ELSE=9)
VARIABLE LABELS AGE 'Age collapsed into categories'
VALUE LABELS    AGE 1 '18 - 29 years' 2 '30 - 45 years'
                    3 '46 - 59 years' 4 '60 or more years'
MISSING VALUES  AGE (9)
CROSSTABS TABLES = LIFE BY AGE BY SEX
OPTIONS 4
```

The separate cross-classification tables for men and women are shown in Figure 10.5. The men's enthusiasm for life doesn't seem to decline until age 60 or so. In both of the age groups 18-29 and 30-45, 52% of the men reported that life was exciting. The percentage actually increases somewhat in the age group 46-59. However, only 42% of those over 60 reported being excited with their lives.

The pattern for women is different. In the age group 18-29, 56% of the women reported being excited by life. In the age group 30-45 only 42% still classified their lives as exciting. This is a drop of 14%. Of the women over 60, only 35% were excited by life. For the younger age groups, age appears to have dampened the women's enthusiasm for life, but not the men's.

You can offer many explanations for this finding. Women may be discriminated against in the work force and rapidly lose their youthful enthusiasm. Women in the intermediate age group 30-45, especially those with children, may have greater demands on their time and therefore feel less enthusiastic than their younger counterparts (or less industrious husbands).

In any event, we couldn't have found this difference between men and women without entering all three variables (LIFE, AGE, and SEX) into the analysis at once.

MORE ABOUT RECODE

Now that you've seen an application of the RECODE command, here is some more information about how you can use it.

Recoding Several Variables

If you have more than one variable to recode, you can do one of two things. Either enter a RECODE command for each variable; or just put a slash after the specifications for the first one, and then enter the name and specifications for the next:

```
RECODE LIFE (1 = 3) (3 = 1) /
       AGE  (18 THRU 29=1) (30 THRU 45=2)
            (46 THRU 59=3) (60 THRU 89=4) (ELSE=9)
```

Figure 10.5 Controlling for sex

FILE: 1984 General Social Survey

```
- - - - - - - - - -  C R O S S T A B U L A T I O N   O F  - - - - - - - - -
    LIFE       Is life exciting or dull?
BY  AGE        Age collapsed into categories
CONTROLLING FOR..
    SEX        Respondent's sex
                                          =        1.  Male
- - - - - - - - - - - - - - - - - - - - - - - - - - -      PAGE  1 OF  1
```

```
                       AGE
             COUNT  |
             COL PCT |18 - 29  30 - 45  46 - 59  60 or mo   ROW
                     |years    years    years    re years   TOTAL
                     |      1|       2|       3|       4|
LIFE         -------+--------+--------+--------+--------+
           1 |     89 |    102 |     58 |     51 |    300
  Exciting    |   51.7 |   52.0 |   54.2 |   42.1 |   50.3
             +--------+--------+--------+--------+
           2 |     76 |     87 |     45 |     59 |    267
Pretty routine|  44.2 |   44.4 |   42.1 |   48.8 |   44.8
             +--------+--------+--------+--------+
           3 |      7 |      7 |      4 |     11 |     29
  Dull        |    4.1 |    3.6 |    3.7 |    9.1 |    4.9
             +--------+--------+--------+--------+
       COLUMN     172      196      107      121       596
       TOTAL     28.9     32.9     18.0     20.3     100.0
                                                          PAGE    3
```

FILE: 1984 General Social Survey

```
- - - - - - - - - -  C R O S S T A B U L A T I O N   O F  - - - - - - - - -
    LIFE       Is life exciting or dull?
BY  AGE        Age collapsed into categories
CONTROLLING FOR..
    SEX        Respondent's sex
                                          =        2.  Female
- - - - - - - - - - - - - - - - - - - - - - - - - - -      PAGE  1 OF  1
```

```
                       AGE
             COUNT  |
             COL PCT |18 - 29  30 - 45  46 - 59  60 or mo   ROW
                     |years    years    years    re years   TOTAL
                     |      1|       2|       3|       4|
LIFE         -------+--------+--------+--------+--------+
           1 |    122 |    117 |     67 |     77 |    383
  Exciting    |   56.0 |   42.2 |   46.2 |   35.0 |   44.5
             +--------+--------+--------+--------+
           2 |     92 |    150 |     70 |    121 |    433
Pretty routine|  42.2 |   54.2 |   48.3 |   55.0 |   50.3
             +--------+--------+--------+--------+
           3 |      4 |     10 |      8 |     22 |     44
  Dull        |    1.8 |    3.6 |    5.5 |   10.0 |    5.1
             +--------+--------+--------+--------+
       COLUMN     218      277      145      220       860
       TOTAL     25.3     32.2     16.9     25.6     100.0

NUMBER OF MISSING OBSERVATIONS =     17
```

If you want to recode several variables in the same way, you can simply list the names of all of them before the recode specifications. The next example recodes four variables representing the education of the respondent, spouse, father, and mother. We want to recode all four in the same way:

```
RECODE EDUC SPEDUC PAEDUC MAEDUC (0 THRU 6 = 1)
    (7 THRU 9 = 2) (10 THRU 12 = 3)
    (13 THRU 16 = 4) (17 THRU 20 = 5) (97,98,99 = 9)
```

What Happens to the Original Data?

When you recode a variable, you change its values to new ones. For the rest of the SPSS^X job, your data will contain the new values.

? *If you collapse the values of* AGE *as in the earlier example, have you lost the original codes forever?* Certainly not—they're still out there in the data file you read with DATA LIST or in the system file you read with GET. *You have* lost them for the duration of the SPSS^X job. RECODE really does change the data in your active file—but not in the data file or in the system file it read to create the active file. ■ ■ ■

If you want to have both versions of a variable, say AGE, then you can use RECODE to create a new, recoded variable, leaving your original AGE values alone. Let's say you want to call the new variable AGECAT, for AGE CATegories:

```
RECODE AGE (18 THRU 29=1) (30 THRU 45=2)
    (46 THRU 59=3) (60 THRU 89=4) (ELSE=9) INTO AGECAT
VARIABLE LABELS AGECAT 'Age collapsed into categories'
VALUE LABELS    AGECAT 1 '18 - 29 years' 2 '30 - 45 years'
                       3 '46 - 59 years' 4 '60 or more years'
MISSING VALUES AGECAT (9)
```

By typing INTO AGECAT at the end of the RECODE command, you create a new variable named AGECAT, which is a recoded version of AGE. AGE itself is unchanged.

What ELSE?

Suppose you have 50 numeric state codes, and you want to recode New York (code 36) to code 1, California (code 6) to code 2, Texas (code 48) to code 3, and the other 47 states to code 4. Do you have to list all 47 state codes in one enormous recode specification? You could, but there's an easier way:

```
RECODE STATE (36=1) (6=2) (48=3) (ELSE=4)
VALUE LABELS STATE 1 'New York' 2 'California' 3 'Texas' 4 'Other'
```

The handy keyword ELSE means just what it ought to mean. Anything *else*—anything that hasn't been recoded by a previous specification in this RECODE command—gets caught up and put into the new code 4.

Missing Values

One common way to use ELSE is to recode all the values you're interested in, and toss the rest into the system-missing value. (System-missing values are explained in Chapter 6.)

```
RECODE STATE (36=1) (6=2) (48=3) (ELSE=SYSMIS)
VALUE LABELS STATE 1 'New York' 2 'California' 3 'Texas'
```

ELSE catches everything that hasn't been recoded yet, including the values you've declared missing and the system-missing values. So be careful when you use ELSE.

The keyword SYSMIS (for SYSTEM-MISsing) also works in the opposite direction. For example, if you left blanks in your data file for a variable named SALES when there were no sales, the cases with blanks will turn up as system-missing. You may decide later that you want to use those cases in your analysis, with the understanding that their sales are zero. You can use RECODE to turn SYSMIS into the zero value you want:

```
RECODE SALES (SYSMIS=0)
```

The RECODE command never affects which values are defined as user-missing. Thus the command above does not make zero a missing value. If zero was already a user-missing value it remains one, however. For user-missing rather than system-missing values, use RECODE just as you would for any other values.

```
RECODE LIFE (8 = 2)
VALUE LABELS LIFE 1 'Exciting' 2 "Routine, don't know" 3 'Dull'
```

Even though code 8, Don't know, was originally declared missing, the above command recodes it to 2. Because RECODE doesn't affect the definition of missing values, 8 is still missing (although no cases have the value 8 after the recode); and 2 is not missing.

To recode *both* system-missing and user-missing values, you can use the keyword MISSING. You can only recode from MISSING to some other code (not the reverse):

```
RECODE STATE (36=1) (6=2) (48=3) (MISSING=0) (ELSE=4)
VALUE LABELS STATE 1 'New York' 2 'California' 3 'Texas' 4 'Other'
MISSING VALUES STATE (0)
```

Lowest and Highest Values

Two useful shortcuts for the RECODE command are the keywords LOWEST and HIGHEST. You use them in a range of values to mean just what they say—the lowest and highest values in your data, whatever those values are. Use the keywords like this:

```
RECODE INCOME (MISSING=0) (LOWEST THRU 10000=1)
    (10000 THRU 30000=2) (30000 THRU HIGHEST=3)
VALUE LABELS  INCOME  1 'Low'  2 'Moderate'  3 'High'
MISSING VALUES INCOME (0)
```

LOWEST and HIGHEST stand for current codes that will be changed into new ones. You can't use these keywords to refer to new codes.

Overlapping Values

You may have noticed in the last example that the values in the recode specifications overlap. The values for $10,000 and $30,000 each occur twice. Why should this be? A value of exactly $10,000 is recoded by the *first* specification to include that value—in this example, it is recoded to 1. But consider what happens if someone's income is $10,000.01. As the example is written, that person's income is recoded to 2. If the values in the specifications did *not* overlap, and the second specification were (10001 THRU 30000=2), the income of $10,000.01 wouldn't be recoded at all. Because of this type of problem, it's often a good idea to have overlapping values in the specifications.

SUMMARY OF KEYWORDS USED IN RECODE

The keywords you can use are:

SYSMIS   Refers to system-missing values. You can recode to or from SYSMIS (that is, it can be on either side of the equals sign).

MISSING   Refers to *all* missing values, whether user-missing or system-missing. You can only recode from MISSING to some other code, as shown above.

LOWEST   Refers to the lowest value in your data (including user-missing values but not system-missing values). LOWEST is normally used in a range of codes. You cannot recode values into LOWEST. It's an input specification only.

HIGHEST   Refers to the highest value in your data (including user-missing values but not system-missing values). HIGHEST is normally used in a range of codes. You cannot recode values into HIGHEST. It's an input specification only.

ELSE   Refers to any value not yet recoded by the RECODE command.

Notice that ELSE must be the last specification on a RECODE command. Specifications are checked in order, and ELSE grabs all values that are left unrecoded, so there's no point in having further specifications. They won't ever be used.

In fact, when you use more than one of these keywords, you should almost always use them in the order in which they're listed above: SYSMIS, then MISSING, then ordinary values (perhaps including LOWEST and HIGHEST), and last of all ELSE.

WHAT'S NEXT?

To use AGE in a crosstabulation, we had to combine its codes into a manageable number of categories. That worked fine, but we did lose some information about people's exact ages. In the next chapter, we'll compare the *average* ages of the people who said their lives were exciting, routine, or dull.

Summary

How can you change the way your variables are coded?

You can use the RECODE command to switch or combine the codes for any of your variables. RECODE takes values, lists of values, or ranges of values, and assigns them to new values according to your specifications.

RECODE changes the values for the remainder of your SPSS^X job. It doesn't change the data file or the system file from which you read the data. You can use the keyword INTO on the RECODE command to create a new variable, leaving the original unchanged.

You must reassign value labels and missing values if your recoding makes the existing ones inappropriate.

EXERCISES

Syntax

1 Correct the syntax errors in the following RECODE commands:

  a. `RECODE LIFE '1 = 3' '3 = 1'`

  b. `RECODE SEX ('M' = 1) ('F' = 2)`

  c. `RECODE EDUC (0 - 8 = 1)(9 - 12 = 2)(13 - 16 = 3)(16 - 20 = 4)`

  d. `RECODE AGE INTO AGECAT (18 THRU 29 = 1) (30 THRU 45 = 2)`
     `(46 THRU 59 = 3)(60 THRU 89 = 4) (ELSE = 9)`

2 Explain whether this command:

`RECODE LIFE (1 = 3) (3 = 1)`

does or does not have the same effect as these two commands:

```
RECODE LIFE (1 = 3)
RECODE LIFE (3 = 1)
```

3 The following RECODE commands are syntactically correct. Describe their effect, including their effect upon missing values.

  a. `RECODE SCORE (LOWEST THRU 50 = 1)(51 THRU HIGHEST = 2)`

  b. `RECODE OPINION (3 = 1) (ELSE = 2) (MISSING = 9)`

4 Why do the following commands not make sense? Don't just state a rule; show why the commands request something impossible.

  a. `RECODE AGECAT (1 = 18 THRU 29) (2 = 30 THRU 45)`
     `(3 = 46 THRU 59)(4 = 60 THRU 89) (9 = 99) INTO AGE`

  b. `RECODE SALES (LOWEST THRU 1000 = 1)(1000 THRU 4000 = 2)`
     `(4000 THRU HIGHEST = 3) (SYSMIS = MISSING)`

  c. `RECODE INCOME (0 = LOWEST) (1 = 4000) (2 = 8000) (3 = 12000)`
     `(4 = 16000) (5 = 20000) (6 = 30000) (7 = HIGHEST)`

Looking at Means

How can you summarize the relationship between two variables when one is measured on an interval or ratio scale and the other has a limited number of distinct categories?

- Why can't you make a table showing the number of times each combination of responses occurs?
- What are good summary measures for a variable measured on an interval scale?
- How can you display separate summary statistics for each of the different categories?

I n the previous chapter, we used a cross-classification table to look at the relation between age and excitement with life. People were assigned to one of four age categories based on their actual ages. It's always possible to group the values of variables like age into a smaller number of categories. But the grouping ignores some of the available information. All cases with values in the same range are treated as the same. In our sample, people who were 30 years old were grouped into the same category as people who were 45. Using *individual* ages in the cross-classification would've been cumbersome because there were so many different ones.

You can look at the relation between age and excitement in another way that still produces compact tables but is based on each person's actual age. What you can do is compute means. You can look at the average ages for people in each of the excitement categories.

COMPARING AVERAGES

To find out about the relation between the AGE variable and the LIFE variable, you can use SPSS^X to compute the average age of the people in each of the categories Exciting, Pretty routine, and Dull. That should give you some idea of whether the average ages in the excitement categories are different. You should also look at the standard deviation (see Chapter 8) for each category. That way, you'll have some idea of the spread of the age values. Just type:

```
FILE HANDLE GSS / (system-specific information)
GET FILE=GSS
BREAKDOWN TABLES = AGE BY LIFE
```

BREAKDOWN calculates means for the variable before the BY for each of the categories of the variable after the BY. (The second variable shouldn't have too many categories.) For this example, you get the results shown in Figure 11.1.

? *Break down? What kind of an instruction is that to give a computer?* Don't be alarmed. The procedure will harm neither you nor the computer. It's called BREAKDOWN because it "breaks down" the cases into groups and then calculates the group means.

You'll soon learn not to be alarmed at the words you must use to make a computer work. You may or may not stop thinking they're funny.

■ ■ ■

Figure 11.1 Breakdown of AGE by LIFE

```
FILE:      1984 General Social Survey

- - - -  D E S C R I P T I O N   O F   S U B P O P U L A T I O N S   - - - - -

CRITERION VARIABLE    AGE       Age of respondent
    BROKEN DOWN BY    LIFE      Is life exciting or dull?

- - - - - - - - - - - - - - - - - - - - - - - - - - - - - - - - - - - - - - -

VARIABLE        VALUE  LABEL                  MEAN     STD DEV    CASES

FOR ENTIRE POPULATION                        43.9760  17.7752    1456

LIFE              1    Exciting               41.9473  16.8140     683
LIFE              2    Pretty routine         45.0300  18.1265     700
LIFE              3    Dull                   52.8493  19.6869      73

   TOTAL CASES =      1473
MISSING CASES =        17 OR    1.2 PCT.
```

On the output, the variable whose means you're calculating, AGE, is called the CRITERION VARIABLE. The variable that determines the groups for which the means are calculated, LIFE, is listed where it says BROKEN DOWN BY.

The first line of Figure 11.1, labeled FOR ENTIRE POPULATION, gives the mean and standard deviation of the age variable for all of the cases in the sample. (Since we haven't included our entire population in the study, this line describes our entire sample, not the population.) These are the sample values you've seen in the results from the FREQUENCIES procedure (see Chapter 7). The average age of 1,456 cases in the sample was 44 years, and the standard deviation, almost 18. Now what about the ages of the people who found life exciting, routine, and dull?

The average age of 683 people who found life exciting was about 42. The people who found life pretty routine were older. Their average age was close to 45. The 73 people who found life dull were by far the oldest. Their average age was almost 53. The variability in the groups, as measured by the standard deviation, is pretty similar. The bored people had the largest standard deviation, close to 20.

From this table, you can see that, on the average, the younger people found life more exciting than the older people. There was over a 10-year difference in average ages between the people who found life exciting and those who found it dull. Is this true for both men and women? Let's see. Type:

```
FILE HANDLE GSS / (system-specific information)
GET FILE=GSS
BREAKDOWN TABLES = AGE BY LIFE BY SEX
```

This gives you Figure 11.2. As a result of adding BY SEX to the BREAKDOWN command, each of the categories in Figure 11.1 is now subdivided into two smaller categories: males and females. (The maximum number of BY keywords allowed is five.)

Figure 11.2 Breakdown of AGE by LIFE by SEX

```
FILE:      1984 General Social Survey

- - - -   D E S C R I P T I O N   O F   S U B P O P U L A T I O N S   - - - - -

CRITERION VARIABLE    AGE       Age of respondent
     BROKEN DOWN BY   LIFE      Is life exciting or dull?
                 BY   SEX       Respondent's sex


- - - - - - - - - - - - - - - - - - - - - - - - - - - - - - - - - - -

VARIABLE          VALUE  LABEL                 MEAN    STD DEV   CASES

FOR ENTIRE POPULATION                        43.9760  17.7752    1456

LIFE                1    Exciting            41.9473  16.8140     683
  SEX               1    Male                41.4033  16.0691     300
  SEX               2    Female              42.3734  17.3841     383

LIFE                2    Pretty routine      45.0300  18.1265     700
  SEX               1    Male                43.3408  17.6493     267
  SEX               2    Female              46.0716  18.3574     433

LIFE                3    Dull                52.8493  19.6869      73
  SEX               1    Male                47.7586  19.8794      29
  SEX               2    Female              56.2045  19.0429      44

   TOTAL CASES =    1473
 MISSING CASES =       17 OR    1.2 PCT.
```

The first line in Figure 11.2, after the values for the whole sample, gives the average age (and the standard deviation) for all the people who found life exciting. This line is exactly the same as the corresponding line in Figure 11.1. The next two lines divide the excited people into men and women. The men who found life exciting had an average age of 41.4; the women who found life exciting had an average age of 42.4. The men who found life routine had an average age of 43.3, while the women who found life routine had an average age of 46.1.

This table has the information you're after. But you can improve its layout to compare the numbers more easily.

A Different Table Format

To get a table that's easier to read for the example, type:

```
FILE HANDLE GSS / (system-specific information)
GET FILE=GSS
BREAKDOWN VARIABLES = AGE(LO,HI) LIFE(1,3) SEX (1,2)
   / CROSSBREAK = AGE BY LIFE BY SEX
```

You have to tell SPSS^X the lowest and highest values for your variables. As shown above, you do this with a VARIABLES subcommand followed by each variable name and then, in parentheses, each variable's range of values. (You can use LOWEST and HIGHEST for the first variable.) You also use the subcommand CROSSBREAK instead of TABLES.

The output is in Figure 11.3. The table looks very much like the cross-classification tables of Chapter 9. But it's not. Each of these cells

Figure 11.3 The CROSSBREAK table

```
FILE:     1984 General Social Survey

- - - - - - - - - -   C R O S S - - - B R E A K D O W N   O F   - - - - - - - - -

    LIFE        Is life exciting or dull?
BY  SEX         Respondent's sex

VARIABLE AVERAGED...    AGE       Age of respondent

- - - - - - - - - - - - - - - - - - - - - - - - - - - -   PAGE  1 OF  1
```

		SEX		
MEAN COUNT STD DEV		Male	Female	ROW TOTAL
		1	2	
LIFE				
Exciting	1	41.40 300 16.07	42.37 383 17.38	41.95 683 16.81
Pretty routine	2	43.34 267 17.65	46.07 433 18.36	45.03 700 18.13
Dull	3	47.76 29 19.88	56.20 44 19.04	52.85 73 19.69
COLUMN TOTAL		42.58 596 17.03	44.94 860 18.22	43.98 1456 17.78

```
NUMBER OF MISSING OBSERVATIONS =      17
```

contains not only the number of cases that fall into it but also the average age and the standard deviation for those cases. The directory for the cell contents is, once again, in the upper left-hand corner of the table.

The first cell is for the men who found life exciting. Their average age was 41.4. The next entry in the cell is the number of cases, 300. The last entry, 16.07, is the standard deviation.

Looking at this table, you can compare cells easily. In the margins, you can find the average ages for all the men and all the women, and the average ages for each of the categories of excitement. One of the first things to notice is that, on the average, the women in the sample were slightly older than the men. (Look at the numbers in the bottom margin of the table.) The average age of the women was almost 45, while the average age of the men was about 42½. This shouldn't be surprising. Women live longer than men.

For both the men and the women, the average age of the excited people was less than the average age of the bored people. There's a 14-year age difference between Exciting and Dull for the women and a 6-year difference for the men.

Since the women in the sample were older than the men, we can't really compare the average ages for the men and the women in each of the categories of excitement. We can see that the bored women were older than the bored men, but this doesn't necessarily mean that the women became bored later in life than the men. It could mean that the men and the women became bored at the same age, but the bored women continued growing older while the bored men died. Pleasant thought, isn't it!

SIMPLE SOLUTIONS

The last several chapters weren't meant to explain a problem as complex as "Why are some people excited by life and others not?" You can try some explanations on your own. These chapters just show you that using *simple* procedures—such as making tables of frequencies, percentages, and means—can help you look for answers. Don't think that for a complicated problem you always need some exotic statistical analysis. You might. But your first step should always be to look at the data carefully with simple but powerful methods. Make tables and look at them carefully. Think about the problem. No statistical procedure can substitute for thought. And always start simply.

MORE ABOUT THE BREAKDOWN PROCEDURE

You can use BREAKDOWN to:

- Compute means of a variable for each of the categories of one or more other variables.

- Arrange the means in a table format that you choose.

Order of Variables

The order of the variables you name on the TABLES subcommand determines their order on the output. The first variable is always the one for which the means are computed. If you type

BREAKDOWN TABLES = AGE BY **SEX BY LIFE**

you'll get a line for males, a line for females, and after each of these lines, the output will show lines for the three categories of LIFE. That arrangement is different from what you see in Figure 11.2, which was produced by:

BREAKDOWN TABLES = AGE BY **LIFE BY SEX**

More Than One Table

If you have more than one variable before the first BY on the TABLES subcommand, you'll get a separate table of means for each variable. If you type

BREAKDOWN TABLES = **AGE EDUC BY LIFE BY SEX**

you'll get one table for AGE BY LIFE BY SEX and another table for EDUC BY LIFE BY SEX.

Options for BREAKDOWN

You can use the OPTIONS command with BREAKDOWN to control some of the features of a table and the statistics it shows. To do so, type the word OPTIONS starting in the first column, and type one or more Option numbers after the word. Here is a list of the Option numbers and what they mean. (In the list, *independent variable* refers to a variable other than the criterion.)

1	Include missing values	7	Suppress cell standard deviations
2	Exclude missing for criterion only	8	Suppress value labels
3	Suppress variable and value labels	9	Suppress independent variable names
4	Tree format	10	Suppress independent variable values
5	Suppress cell frequencies	11	Suppress mean
6	Print cell sums	12	Print variance

You can also use a STATISTICS command after BREAKDOWN. Statistic 1 gives you an *analysis of variance*, the type of statistical procedure described in Chapter 18.

WHAT'S NEXT?

You've already seen how to use RECODE to change your original data. Chapter 12 describes some additional ways to do so. It's best to start simply, but sometimes you have to transform the original data to find out what you want to know.

Summary

How can you summarize the relationship between two variables when one is measured on an interval or ratio scale and the other has a limited number of distinct categories?

If cases are classified into several groups, you can study the relationship between the variables that form the groups and other variables.

For each of the groups, you can compute descriptive statistics such as the mean and standard deviation of a variable of interest.

By examining how the means and standard deviations vary among the groups, you can study the relationships among the variables.

In SPSS[X], the desriptive statistics for each of the groups can be displayed in a table.

EXERCISES

Syntax

1 Write the command to calculate average incomes (variable INCOME) for people who have different degrees of job satisfaction (SATJOB).

2 You want to calculate the average number of years of education (EDUC) for people who believe in life after death and those who don't (POSTLIFE). You type in

```
BREAKDOWN POSTLIFE BY EDUC
```

Describe the results this will produce.

3 An investigator is studying the relationship between systolic blood pressure (SYSTBP), smoking (SMOKE, coded 0=no, 1=yes), and drinking more than 4 oz. per day of alcohol (DRINK, coded 0=no, 1=yes). How would you instruct SPSS^X to calculate the average blood pressure for people who don't smoke and don't drink much; don't smoke but drink much; smoke but don't drink much; and smoke and drink much?

4 How would you change the previous instruction if the investigator wanted to obtain the means of the four smoking-drinking groups separately for females and for males (variable SEX)?

5 Correct the mistakes, if any, in the following commands, and describe the tables produced.

    a. BREAKDOWN INCOME BY AGECAT

    b. BREAKDOWN TABLES INCOME AGE BY SEX

    c. BREAKDOWN INCOME BY AGECAT BY SEX

    d. BREAKDOWN TABLES=SEX BY AGECAT BY INCOME

6 Which of the BREAKDOWN commands below produced the following table?

```
- - - -  D E S C R I P T I O N   O F   S U B P O P U L A T I O N S  - - - - -
CRITERION VARIABLE    SALNOW      CURRENT SALARY
   BROKEN DOWN BY     MINORITY    MINORITY CLASSIFICATION
           BY         SEX         SEX OF EMPLOYEE
- - - - - - - - - - - - - - - - - - - - - - - - - - - - - - - - - - - - - - -

VARIABLE          VALUE  LABEL                 MEAN       STD DEV    CASES

FOR ENTIRE POPULATION                       13767.8270   6830.2646    474

MINORITY            0    WHITE              14409.3243   7217.6382    370
   SEX              0    MALES              17790.1649   8132.2646    194
   SEX              1    FEMALES            10682.7159   3204.7575    176

MINORITY            1    NONWHITE           11485.5769   4568.6551    104
   SEX              0    MALES              12898.4375   5223.9525     64
   SEX              1    FEMALES             9225.0000   1588.9474     40

   TOTAL CASES =     474
```

    a. BREAKDOWN TABLES=SALNOW BY SEX MINORITY

    b. BREAKDOWN TABLES=SALNOW BY MINORITY BY SEX

    c. BREAKDOWN TABLES=MINORITY BY SALNOW BY SEX

Statistical Concepts

1 Indicate whether you would use procedure FREQUENCIES, CROSSTABS, or BREAKDOWN to find the following:

a. The average age for members of different political parties.

b. The number of married, single, widowed, divorced, and never married people in each of the political parties.

c. The number of members in each of the political parties.

d. The average age of men and women in each political party.

e. The number of men and women in each of the marital states within each of the political parties.

2 A market research company is trying to decide what color to make a new brand of breath mints. They ask 100 consumers to choose among the colors white, yellow, green striped, and red striped. A research analyst assigns the codes 1 through 4 to the possible choices and uses procedure BREAKDOWN to find average color preferences for men and women in each of 4 income categories. How would you interpret the resulting table?

3 Below is a BREAKDOWN table which shows the average ages of men and women who believe in life after death and those who don't or are uncertain.

```
FILE:      1984 General Social Survey

- - - - - - - - - -  C R O S S - - - B R E A K D O W N   O F  - - - - - - - - -

     SEX        Respondent's sex
BY   POSTLIFE   Belief in life after death

VARIABLE AVERAGED...    AGE     Age of respondent

- - - - - - - - - - - - - - - - - - - - - - - - - - - - - - - - - PAGE  1 OF  1

                        POSTLIFE
              MEAN
              COUNT     Yes         No or       ROW
              STD DEV               unsure      TOTAL
                          1  |        2  |
     SEX       --------+-----------+-----------+
                1       |  42.03    |  43.84    |   42.60
     Male               |   410     |   185     |    595
                        |  16.89    |  17.31    |   17.03
                        +-----------+-----------+
                2       |  45.33    |  43.54    |   44.91
     Female             |   662     |           |    864
                        |  18.25    |  18.26    |   18.26
                        +-----------+-----------+
     COLUMN TOTAL       |  44.07    |  43.68    |
                        |           |   387     |   1459
                        |  17.81    |  17.79    |   17.80

NUMBER OF MISSING OBSERVATIONS =          14
```

a. Fill in the missing information.

b. Based on the previous table what is the average age of people who believe in life after death?

c. What is the average age of men who don't believe in life after death?

d. From the table can you tell what the average age is of all men?

4 How is a table produced by the BREAKDOWN procedure (with the CROSSBREAK subcommand) similar to a CROSSTABS table, and how is it different?

5 You are interested in studying the relationship between highest degree received by a person in school, the person's marital status, and several other variables. Describe how you might investigate the relationship of these two variables and

a. the number of hours of television watched per week.

b. religious affiliation.

   c. job satisfaction.

   d. number of siblings.

   e. zodiac sign.

6 Two students are investigating the relationship between college grade point average and the number of cars owned five years after graduation. The first student plans to use the SPSS^X RECODE command to recode the actual grade point averages into the A range, the B range, the C range, and the D and lower range. He then plans to obtain a crosstabulation of the number of cars by recoded grade point average. The second student plans to calculate the mean grade point average for people who have different numbers of cars. How are these two approaches similar and how do they differ?

Data Analysis

1 You want to examine the relationship between the happiness of a person's marriage and their years of education. Run the appropriate SPSS^X analyses. (Use the EDUC variable which tells you the number of years of education a person has, and HAPMAR, which tells the happiness of the marriage.)

2 Summarize your results.

3 Rerun your analysis including an additional variable, the respondent's sex. Do there appear to be differences between men and women?

4 Make a crosstabulation of the highest degree received (DEGREE) and the happiness of a marriage (HAPMAR). Summarize your results.

5 For each of the categories of the DEGREE variable, find the average years of father's education (PAEDUC). Does there appear to be a relationship between a person's highest degree and the amount of education the person's father has?

Modifying Data Values

How can you use SPSS^X and the computer to create new variables and to change the values of the ones you have?

- How can you create a new variable for all the cases?

- How can you perform calculations using the values of your variables?

- How can you tell the computer to make decisions about whether to carry out a calculation, based on the values of your variables?

- What happens if a case has a missing value for one of the variables involved in a calculation?

- What happens if a case has a missing value for one of the variables involved in a decision about whether to carry out a calculation?

- Does it matter in what order transformation commands are entered?

- In what ways can you choose a smaller group of cases from your file for analysis?

Before you can even begin to analyze your data, you may have to switch them around somehow. You asked for the respondent's year of birth, but you want to analyze age. You asked for years of education in two separate questions, but you want to combine them into a single variable. Perhaps you want to take the two variables for the education of the respondent and the respondent's spouse and then make two variables that always contain husband's education and wife's education.

Changes like these are called **transformations.** SPSS^X lets you do them easily with a few commands. In Chapter 10, you saw how to use the RECODE command to change the way your data are coded. In this chapter, you'll look at some commands that do transformations you can't do with RECODE.

To ease into this subject, we'll start off with a simple example that's typical of what you can do by transforming your data. Then we'll look more closely at the specific commands you use. Another important subject we'll have to look at is what happens when you transform data in a file that has missing values.

AN EXAMPLE: COMPUTING AGE

Back in Chapter 3, you saw that the General Social Survey asks for date of birth rather than age. Most of the time, though, you want to use a person's age in your analysis. Determining age from year of birth seems simple enough: subtract the birth year from the current year, which was 1984 when the question was asked. With SPSS^X, that's just what you can do, using the COMPUTE command. The following command creates a new variable named AGE:

```
COMPUTE AGE = 1984 - BYEAR
```

After SPSS^X executes this command, each case in the file has a new variable, AGE, that didn't exist before. You can use this variable like any other variable. It's a part of the active file (see Chapter 6), and if you save the file, AGE is saved with the other variables.

? *Why ignore the actual month and day of birth?* AGE doesn't need to be precise within a fraction of a year. If you do want to know an exact age, or if you want to know the exact interval of time between any two dates, you can use the YRMODA function explained in "More about Transformations," at the end of this chapter. ∎ ∎ ∎

147

Now that you've seen an example of using a data transformation, let's look at it a little more carefully. We're not going to try to cover everything you can do with the SPSS^X transformation language, But you'll get an idea of how to do transformations that are often helpful in common research problems.

THE COMPUTE COMMAND

This is the general form of the COMPUTE command:

```
COMPUTE variable name = instructions
```

It includes:

- The word COMPUTE.
- A variable name for a variable you've already defined or for a brand-new variable.
- An equals sign.
- Instructions telling SPSS^X what you want to compute.

What kind of instructions can you use? You can add, subtract, multiply, divide, or do a lot of other things. You can do these things to variables in your file or to numbers. To add or subtract, use the plus sign or the minus sign, + or −. To multiply, use an asterisk, *. To divide, use a slash, /. You can also use **functions** that are built into the SPSS^X language and perform useful calculations automatically—such as taking the maximum of a set of values or taking a square root. Here are some examples that show COMPUTE used in various ways:

```
COMPUTE ZERO = 0
COMPUTE ONEVAR = ANOTHER
COMPUTE WHOLE = PART1 + PART2 + PART3 + PART4 + PART5 + 100
COMPUTE RECEIPTS = NUMSOLD * (COST + MARKUP)
COMPUTE PREDICT = .7204 * EDUC + .0937 * AGE + 16.25
COMPUTE EDUC = MAX(YRSEDUC,YRSCOLL)
```

How Does It Work?

When you use a COMPUTE command, it is executed on every case. For each case, SPSS^X first computes whatever you instructed it to compute (whatever's on the *right* side of the equals sign). It then sets the variable named on the *left* side of the equals sign to the results of the computation. If this variable is a new one, SPSS^X adds it to the list of variables in your file, and you have one more variable than you had before. If the variable to the left of the equals sign already exists, SPSS^X forgets the value that the variable had before the COMPUTE command and gives it the new value.

Let's look again at the examples in the previous list and see how COMPUTE works for all of them.

Neither of the following examples involves actual computation:

```
COMPUTE ZERO = 0
COMPUTE ONEVAR = ANOTHER
```

The variable ZERO is set to zero for every case, and the variable ONEVAR becomes a copy of the variable ANOTHER for every case.

A calculation for COMPUTE can involve several different parts:

```
COMPUTE WHOLE = PART1 + PART2 + PART3 + PART4 + PART5 + 100
```

This command just adds up each PART and then adds 100.

The next examples show how things can start to get complicated:

```
COMPUTE RECEIPTS = NUMSOLD * (COST + MARKUP)
COMPUTE PREDICT = .7204 * EDUC + .0937 * AGE + 16.25
```

The first of these commands computes RECEIPTS as NUMSOLD times the sum of COST and MARKUP. The second command multiplies EDUC by the number .7204, then multiplies AGE by the number .0937, then adds those two products to the number 16.25. These commands illustrate some basic rules:

- When the instructions include parentheses, SPSS[X] performs the part inside the parentheses first. Remember that you can always use parentheses to specify operations in the order that you want.
- When parentheses don't specify the order, SPSS[X] performs multiplications and divisions before it performs additions and subtractions. In a series of multiplications and divisions, SPSS[X] works from left to right.

The next example uses the built-in function MAX:

```
COMPUTE EDUC = MAX(YRSEDUC,YRSCOLL)
```

This function gives the maximum value of the variables named inside the parentheses. The command takes the two variables YRSEDUC and YRSCOLL from the questionnaire in Chapter 3 and computes EDUC as the maximum value of the two for each case. The variable names in parentheses are called the **arguments** of the function. You can use either numbers or variable names as arguments. When a variable name is an argument, SPSS[X] does not use missing values for that variable in figuring the value of the function.

Missing Values and COMPUTE

Missing values are always important to consider when you transform data. SPSS[X] does not use missing values in carrying out a COMPUTE command. If any variable used in a computation has a missing value, the variable being computed is set to the system-missing value. This happens when the computation runs into a system-missing value and when it runs into a user-missing value. In the command

```
COMPUTE RECEIPTS = NUMSOLD * (COST + MARKUP)
```

RECEIPTS is set to system-missing if NUMSOLD, COST, or MARKUP has a system-missing or a user-missing value.

Recovering User-Missing Values

When you compute one variable equal to another, the copy you get isn't completely exact; user-missing values are converted into system-missing. Usually this is a good thing, because you may not have declared those values missing for the new variable. However, if you want to preserve the user-missing values, include the VALUE function, like this:

```
COMPUTE YEARBORN = VALUE(BYEAR)
```

If 9999 is a user-missing value for BYEAR, then cases coded 9999 for BYEAR are also coded 9999 for YEARBORN. The VALUE function still does not make 9999 a missing value for YEARBORN. If you want to do that, enter a MISSING VALUES command.

THE IF COMMAND

The COMPUTE command works on every case. Sometimes, though, you want to treat different cases in different ways. If you need a variable containing the husband's education for every married respondent in the General Social Survey, you want to take respondent's education for male respondents but spouse's education for female respondents. You want a missing value for respondents who aren't married. You must check the value of the two variables SEX and MARITAL to see what action is required for each case. The IF command lets you do this.

An IF command looks much like a COMPUTE command, except that in place of the word COMPUTE, you have the word IF followed by the condition under which the calculation should be performed. You put parentheses around the condition. It all reads very naturally. (Actually the parentheses are not required, but most people find they make the command easier to read.) The general form of the command is:

```
IF ( something is true ) variable name = instructions
```

The new part of this command is the **condition,** which determines whether or not the instructions should be computed and stored in the variable that's named. A condition is a logical expression, something that is either true or false. Some examples of conditions are:

- IF the variable SEX equals 1.
- IF the string variable STATE equals 'TENNESSEE'. (Remember, the values of string variables should always be in quotes.)

- IF the variable LIFE equals 1 and the variable EDUC is greater than the variable PAEDUC.
- IF the sum of the variables TEENS and ADULTS is greater than 4.

Table 12.1 Abbreviations in IF conditions

EQ	or	=	means	EQual to
GT	or	>	means	Greater Than
LT	or	<	means	Less Than
NE	or	<> or ⌐=	means	Not Equal to
GE	or	>=	means	Greater than or Equal to
LE	or	<=	means	Less than or Equal to

When you're stating conditions like this, use the abbreviations shown in Table 12.1. You can use either a two-letter form or a symbolic form, whichever one you feel more comfortable with. When there's more than one condition, you can use the keywords AND and OR to combine them. With these abbreviations and keywords, you can state the above conditions like this:

```
IF (SEX EQ 1)
IF (STATE = 'TENNESSEE')
IF (LIFE = 1 AND EDUC > PAEDUC)
IF (TEENS + ADULTS > 4)
```

To make a complete SPSS^X command, of course, you include the variable name, the equals sign, and the instructions, just as on a COMPUTE command. For example,

```
IF (SEX EQ 1) SALARY = .59 * SALARY
```

Anything you can put after the word COMPUTE on a COMPUTE command is also legal after the parentheses on an IF command.

How Does It Work?

An IF command, like a COMPUTE command, is executed for every case—or at least it *starts* to be executed for every case. The difference is that IF commands come in two parts: a condition followed by a computation. If the condition is false, the command is not completed, and the case is not changed. Like a COMPUTE command, an IF command can also create an entirely new variable.

Let's create HUSED (husband's education) out of EDUC (respondent's education) and SPEDUC (spouse's education):

```
IF (MARITAL = 1 AND SEX = 1) HUSED = EDUC
IF (MARITAL = 1 AND SEX = 2) HUSED = SPEDUC
VARIABLE LABELS HUSED "Husband's education"
```

- As each case is processed, the first IF command checks whether the respondent is married and the value of SEX is 1. If so, the new variable HUSED is set equal to EDUC. If not, HUSED is undefined, or system-missing. (Every variable must have a value. When you create a new variable, SPSS^X initializes it to system-missing. It stays system-missing unless a valid value is assigned.)

- The second IF command similarly checks whether the respondent is married and SEX is 2; and if so, it sets HUSED equal to SPEDUC.

- For respondents not currently married, HUSED remains system-missing, which is what you want. If there were people with other values for SEX (there aren't in the General Social Survey), they also would remain system-missing.

- Finally, the VARIABLE LABELS command assigns a label to HUSED for clarity.

Missing Values and IF

In the second part of an IF, which actually computes something if the condition is true, missing values work just as they do in the COMPUTE command. But missing values in the condition itself are a new problem.

Can you test whether a condition involving a missing value is true? You cannot. Missing values in a condition are simply missing. You can't test them like ordinary values. You can't say that a missing value equals something, and you can't say that it doesn't equal something. When you're writing an IF command, remember that when a missing value turns up in a condition, the computation following the condition will not be executed. This happens both with system-missing values (where there really *isn't* any value) and with user-missing values (where there is a value but you instructed SPSS^X to treat it as missing).

The following job attempts to convert missing values for the exciting-routine-dull variable to Pretty routine:

```
DATA LIST FILE=GSSDATA / LIFE 19
MISSING VALUES LIFE (8, 9)
VARIABLE LABELS LIFE 'Is life exciting'
VALUE LABELS LIFE 1 'Exciting' 2 'Pretty routine' 3 'Dull'
   8 "Don't know" 9 'No answer'
IF (LIFE GT 7) LIFE=2
```

What does the IF command do? It tries to catch the 8s and 9s—the codes that are greater than 7—and set LIFE equal to 2 for those cases. But 8 and 9 are declared as missing. If the value of LIFE is missing (keep reading, this isn't a philosophy class), then it is *not* true that the value of LIFE is greater than 7. So the IF command won't work. Cases with the missing values 8 and 9 will keep the missing values 8 and 9.

One way to do what this example attempted is to use the VALUE function explained above to recover any values that are user-missing.

```
IF ( VALUE(LIFE) GT 7 ) LIFE=2
```

When IFs Multiply

The IF command is extremely flexible. Once you've learned how to use it, you'll see that you can do all sorts of things with it. Soon you'll find yourself doing things like the following, to divide up the new years-of-education variable into five convenient categories:

```
COMPUTE EDUC = MAX(YRSEDUC, YRSCOLL)
IF (EDUC LE 6)                      EDUC = 1
IF (EDUC GT 6 AND EDUC LE 9)        EDUC = 2
IF (EDUC GT 9 AND EDUC LE 12)       EDUC = 3
IF (EDUC GT 12 AND EDUC LE 16)      EDUC = 4
IF (EDUC GT 16 AND EDUC LE 20)      EDUC = 5
IF ( VALUE(EDUC) EQ 98 )            EDUC = 9
VALUE LABELS EDUC 1 "Elementary" 2 "Junior high" 3 "High school"
     4 "College" 5 "Graduate school" 9 "Don't know"
MISSING VALUES EDUC(9)
```

These are a lot of IF commands. They work just fine, but they are tedious to type—they waste your valuable time. They also waste the computer's valuable time. There's an easier way. When you find that you have a lot of IF commands that just use one variable, try to use the RECODE command instead (see Chapter 10). That's what RECODE is designed for. When you can use it, it's easier to type than a lot of IF commands, and it's more efficient for the computer too.

THE ORDER OF TRANSFORMATION COMMANDS

Commands are executed one at a time, in the order you enter them. This sounds obvious enough, but let's look again at the previous example of the IF command. Suppose the commands had been entered in reversed order:

```
IF (EDUC GT 16 AND EDUC LE 20)      EDUC = 5
IF (EDUC GT 12 AND EDUC LE 16)      EDUC = 4
IF (EDUC GT 9 AND EDUC LE 12)       EDUC = 3
IF (EDUC GT 6 AND EDUC LE 9)        EDUC = 2
IF (EDUC LE 6)                      EDUC = 1
```

Look what the last IF command does. It takes all the values of 5, 4, 3, and 2 that the first four commands created, and assigns them—along with everybody else—to code 1. All the nonmissing values in the file end up coded 1 for EDUC. (Notice that this sort of problem doesn't arise when you use a RECODE command. A RECODE command never changes the value of a case more than once.)

The moral here is pretty obvious. When you have a series of transformation commands, take the time to step through them to make sure you know how they're going to work. Try them with missing values, too.

Labeling New Variables

As with RECODE (see Chapter 10), you'll often need to change the variable labels and value labels for variables you've tinkered with by using COMPUTE or IF. Simply enter VARIABLE LABELS and VALUE LABELS commands when you want them to take effect. Remember, you can't label a variable that doesn't exist. If you're *creating* a new variable on one of these transformation commands, wait until after you create it to assign labels to it.

? *Do these transformation commands permanently change the data? What if I need the original values again sometime?* You can always read your original data again, whether you used DATA LIST to read a data file or GET to read a system file. The transformation commands don't affect any of your disk files. They affect your active file, the file you're using in your current SPSS[X] run. Similarly, VARIABLE LABELS and VALUE LABELS commands affect only your active file.

Of course, you can always SAVE a new system file after making transformations. If you save a file that's been transformed with RECODE, COMPUTE, or IF commands, the transformed values will be the ones saved. If you've changed the labels, the new labels will also be saved.

■■■

SELECTING AND SAMPLING CASES

Sometimes you don't want to process all of the cases that you have. There are two ways to select some of them. One is to select certain cases yourself by telling SPSS[X] which ones to use. The other is just to tell SPSS[X] how many cases you want to use and let it take a sample for you.

The SELECT IF Command

SELECT IF means just what says. It tells SPSS[X] to SELECT cases for processing IF they satisfy some condition. You specify a condition just like the condition for the IF command, and you may want to put the condition in parentheses to make it clearer. Cases that are not selected (because the condition is not true) are discarded. They're no longer available to you during the SPSS[X] job. Of course, they are still in your input file, and you can read them again with another DATA LIST or GET command.

Here's an example of how you might use SELECT IF to process only people in their thirties:

```
SELECT IF (AGE GE 30 AND AGE LE 39)
```

You can also use SELECT IF with string variables—just remember to put the values in quotes.

```
SELECT IF (CITY = 'CHICAGO')
```

The SAMPLE Command

With the SELECT IF command, you tell SPSS[X] which cases to process. Sometimes you don't want to say *which* cases to select, but you just want to cut down the number of cases. Maybe you've got a file with a thousand or more cases, and you want to make a plot (see Chapter 20). Plots are more readable if they don't show too many cases. In SPSS^X, it's easy to cut down the number of cases. Use the SAMPLE command, and give it a decimal fraction telling it what proportion of the cases in the file to use. The following command takes a random sample of about 10% (.1) of the cases in your file:

```
SAMPLE .1
```

If you know how many cases you have in all, you can also sample an exact number of them. Say you have 2,391 cases in your file, and you want to take a random sample of 100 cases. You can do it this way:

```
SAMPLE 100 OF 2391
```

MORE ABOUT TRANSFORMATIONS

Although the commands in this chapter are enough for most of the situations you'll encounter, the SPSS^X transformation language has many features that are more advanced. We'll discuss just a few of these: string variables, temporary transformations, and functions.

String Variables

The important things to remember about string variables are:

- Enclose the values of string variables in apostrophes or quotation marks.
- Specify quoted values *exactly* the way they appear in your data: with upper-case or lower-case letters or both, and with the same number of blanks in the same positions.

You don't need to specify blank spaces at the end of a quoted value; for example, 'A   ' is the same as 'A'.

A string variable has a definite length—the length you specified on the DATA LIST command (see Chapter 6). You can't change that length, but if you need a string variable of a different length, you can use the STRING command. You specify a new variable (with a new name), followed by parentheses containing the letter A and the new variable's length:

```
STRING STATENAM (A15)
RECODE STATE ('AK' = 'Alaska') ('AL' = 'Alabama') ('AR' = 'Arkansas')
    . . .
    ('WY = 'Wyoming) INTO STATENAM
```

This STRING command defines a new string variable STATENAM with a length of 15. You can then recode the two-character values of STATE to longer names in STATENAM.

Temporary Transformations

Normally, a transformation makes a permanent change to your active file. When you transform a variable, it remains transformed until you define a new active file with a DATA LIST or GET command. But the TEMPORARY command lets you make transformations that are—you guessed it—temporary. Any transformation command after the TEMPORARY command affects only the next time SPSS^X uses your data. Any further procedures you carry out use the data as they were before the temporary transformation.

The TEMPORARY command is particularly useful with SELECT IF and SAMPLE. You can reduce the number of cases, perform one procedure, and then continue with all your cases as before:

```
TEMPORARY
SELECT IF (AGE LT 35)
CROSSTABS TABLES = LIFE BY MARITAL
TEMPORARY
SELECT IF (AGE GE 35)
CROSSTABS TABLES = LIFE BY MARITAL
```

Without the first TEMPORARY command in this example, the second SELECT IF would have no cases to select.

Functions

SPSS^X provides dozens of functions you can use in transforming your data. You supply to a function one or more arguments in parentheses. The arguments are numbers or variable names that SPSS^X uses to evaluate the function.

Here are some of the more useful functions. As you see them here, *arg* stands for a single number or variable name, and *arg list* stands for one or more numbers or variable names separated by commas.

ABS(arg)	*Absolute value.* The value converted, if necessary, to a positive number.
RND(arg)	*Round.* The value rounded to an integer.
TRUNC(arg)	*Truncate.* The value with any fractional part stripped off.
SUM(arg list)	*Sum.* The total of the values in the argument list.
MEAN(arg list)	*Mean.* The average of the values in the argument list.
MIN(arg list)	*Minimum.* The smallest of the values in the argument list.
MAX(arg list)	*Maximum.* The largest of the values in the argument list.
VALUE(arg)	*Numeric value.* A variable's numeric value, even if that value is declared user-missing. System-missing if the value is system-missing.
MISSING(arg)	*Test for missing.* A true or false value telling whether or not the argument has a missing value. Use this function in the condition of an IF or SELECT IF command.

SYSMIS(arg)   *Test of system-missing.* A true or false value telling whether or not the argument has a system-missing value. Use this function in the condition of an IF or SELECT IF command.

YRMODA(yr,mo,da)   *Day number.* The number of days since October 15, 1582. The three arguments are either variables or integer constants representing year, month, and day. By subtracting two such day numbers, you can calculate time intervals in days, as shown below.

This example uses the YRMODA function to calculate the number of days between the date stored in YEAR1, MONTH1, DAY1 and the date stored in YEAR2, MONTH2, DAY2.

```
COMPUTE PERIOD = YRMODA(YEAR2,MONTH2,DAY2)
               - YRMODA(YEAR1,MONTH1,DAY1)
VARIABLE LABELS PERIOD 'Number of days from date 1 to date 2'
```

WHAT'S NEXT?

You've learned a lot about using SPSS^X, describing your data, and transforming it when you need to. In the next chapters, you'll see how to analyze data in new ways.

Summary

How can you use SPSS^X and the computer to create new variables and to change the values of the ones you have?

You can use the COMPUTE command to create or modify variables by calculating their values. The calculation can simply involve making a copy of an existing variable.

You can use the IF command to test the values of your variables and decide whether to carry out a calculation.

Calculations involving missing values result in the system-missing value for a case.

Calculations are not carried out if they depend on a test that involves missing values.

Transformation commands (COMPUTE and IF) are carried out in the order in which you enter them. You must consider the order when planning a series of related commands.

You can use the SELECT IF command to choose a group of cases for processing based on a logical decision, or the SAMPLE command to choose a group randomly.

EXERCISES

Syntax

1 Correct the syntax errors in the following commands:

a. `SCORE = PART1 + PART2 + PART3`

b. `COMPUTE PROFIT1 = SALES1 - EXPENSE1`
   `    /   PROFIT2 = SALES2 - EXPENSE2`

c. `IF (YEAR = 1980) COMPUTE ADJUSTED = WAGE / 1.73`

d. `COMPUTE COMPOSIT = VERBAL PLUS MATH`

e. `COMP X = A + B`

2 A specification on the RECODE command says, roughly, "If the value is this, set it equal to that." It's often possible, therefore, to replace a RECODE by a series of IF commands, or to replace a series of IF commands by a RECODE.

a. Which form is shorter?

b. Can you replace the commands

```
IF (AGE LT 40) AGECAT = 1
IF (AGE GE 40) AGECAT = 2
IF (MISSING(AGE)) AGECAT = 9
```

with a single RECODE command? If so, show the command. If not, explain why this is not possible.

c. Can you replace the commands

```
IF (SEX EQ 1) HUSED = EDUC
IF (SEX EQ 2) HUSED = SPEDUC
```

with a single RECODE command? If so, show the command. If not, explain why this is not possible.

Concepts

1 On a COMPUTE command which uses several operations, you can use parentheses to specify the order in which these operations should be performed. If you don't, SPSS^X performs multiplications and divisions before it performs additions and subtractions. In a series of multiplications and divisions, SPSS^X works from left to right. In which of these examples would the answer be different if SPSS^X worked from left to right?

a. `COMPUTE ANSWER = A * B * C`

b. `COMPUTE ANSWER = A / B / C`

c. `COMPUTE ANSWER = A * B / C`

d. `COMPUTE ANSWER = A / B * C`

Hint: try these out. Make up values for A, B, and C (perhaps 2, 3, and 4). Work first from the left: 2 times 3 is 6, times 4 is 24. Now from the right: 4 times 3 is 12, times 2....

PART 3   **CHAPTERS 13-18**

13 Means from Samples

What can you say about the mean of a population, based on the results observed in a sample?

- Will the results from a sample be identical to the results you would get if you examined the entire population?

- How does the size of your sample affect what you can say about the population?

- How does the variability in the population affect your sample results?

- Do means computed from different samples from the same population differ?

- What determines how much sample means vary from sample to sample?

- What is a statistic, and what is a parameter?

- What is the distribution of a statistic?

In previous chapters, we've tried to answer questions like: "What percentage of the sample thought that life is exciting?" or "What was the average age of the people who said life is dull?" or "In this study, what percentage of married people and what percentage of single people thought that life is exciting?" The emphasis was always on reporting just the results of the survey. We looked at the data and described the sample. Nothing more.

In this chapter, we'll begin to look at the problems we face when drawing conclusions about a whole population on the basis of what's observed in a sample.

FROM SAMPLE TO POPULATION

In our sample, the men were more likely than the women to find life exciting. No doubt about it: 50% of the men but only 44% of the women called life exciting. Unless an error was made somewhere in entering the data into the file, the results are crisp and clear. We can speak about the sample with confidence. We know, or can figure out, anything we want to about the sample—assuming that we asked the right questions and had the data entered correctly into the file.

But talking about a sample is usually not enough. We don't want conclusions about the 1,473 people in the General Social Survey sample; we want conclusions about the population that this sample represents. We want to be able to say things like: "American men are more excited about life than American women" or "As Americans age, their enthusiasm for life diminishes" or "People who have never been married find life more exciting than people who have." Based on the results in the sample, we want to speak about the population from which the sample was selected.

That may not seem like a big deal. Why not just assume that whatever is true for the sample is also true for the population? If the men in the sample found life more exciting than the women did, why not claim that the same must be true in the population? Let's just conclude that American men are more enthusiastic about life than American women. That would certainly be simple. But would it always be correct?

Problems in Generalizing

Suppose you had a sample of two men and two women, and you found that one of the men but neither of the women was excited by life? Would you be willing to draw the conclusion that, in general, men are more excited by life than are women? The numbers, especially if you don't think about them, suggest the headline, "Amazing new research shows that half of all men but no women at all are excited by life!" It doesn't take much statistical know-how to find fault with this headline. Generalizing from a tiny sample of two men and two women to the whole U.S. population is laughable. If you sampled another two men and two women, you'd probably get completely different results. But you couldn't generalize from those results, either. You can't conclude much at all about the whole population from a sample of four people.

What if the sample were larger, say 200 men and 200 women? Conclusions from a study with this sample size would certainly be more believable than those from a four-person study. It's easier to believe that the results observed in the larger sample hold true for the population. But if you found that 50% of all the men and 49% of all the women in the larger sample said their lives were exciting, would you be willing to conclude that in the population, men are more likely than women to find life exciting? What if the difference were larger, say 50% of the men compared to 40% of the women?

Sampling Variability

You get different results from different samples. Consequently, it takes some thought to sort out what you can reasonably say about the population, based on the results from a sample. If you and I each look at samples of 400 people from the same population, we're not going to get exactly the same answers when we analyze our own data. Our samples will undoubtedly include different people, and our results will differ. With any luck, the results will be similar, but it's very unlikely that they'll be identical to the last decimal place. Even if they are, they probably won't be the values we'd obtain if we questioned the whole population.

How much the results from different samples vary from one to another depends not only on the size of the samples but also on how often the various responses occur in the population. (Statisticians call this the distribution of responses in the population.) If everybody in the United States plans to vote for the same candidate for President—say, the one you've been working for—any old sample will lead to the same answer to the question, "What percentage of the vote will my candidate receive?" The answers wouldn't vary from person to person, and they wouldn't vary from survey to survey. Any survey would tell you that 100% of the voters plan to vote for your candidate.

On the other hand, if only half of the voters plan to vote for your candidate, there would be more variability in the samples. One sample might show that 60% of the vote will go to your candidate, and another sample might show that your candidate will get 45% of the vote. If 1,000 researchers took random samples of 400 voters each, there would be a lot of different percentages. Some would be close to the correct figure of 50%, while others would be higher or lower.

A COMPUTER MODEL

We can use the computer to actually do what we've been talking about. With the proper instructions, it can set up a population in which half of the people say they'll vote for your candidate, and half say they won't.

We can instruct the computer to conduct a hypothetical survey by randomly selecting 400 cases from this population. Then we can tell the computer to calculate from this sample the percentage of the cases that endorse your candidate. We can have the computer repeat this kind of survey as many times as we want. Each time, it will select a new random sample of 400 hypothetical people and compute the percentage planning to vote for your candidate. (This is called a simulated survey.)

Let's have the computer do the survey 1,000 times. We then have 1,000 results, one for each time the survey was simulated. We can tell how much these results vary from simulated survey to simulated survey, and how different the results are from the "true" value of 50%. This kind of information will help us decide what can be said about the population based on the survey.

Building 1,000 Samples

For the examples that follow, a computer did exactly what was just described. It set up a population in which half the people agree with the statement about planning to vote for your candidate, and the other half disagree. Then it selected a random sample of 400 cases from the population and calculated the percentage that agreed with the statement. It went on to conduct 1,000 such surveys, each with 400 cases.

The results of the 1,000 simulated surveys were stored in a variable named VOTE. Each case corresponds to the results from a survey of 400 people. A value for the vote variable is the percentage of people who plan to vote for the candidate.

Comparing the Results

Now that we have results from 1,000 surveys, we can see how close the results come to the population value (which we know to be 50% for these simulations).

Figure 13.1 Responses to 1,000 hypothetical surveys

```
FILE:     Means from hypothetical samples of 400; population mean = 50

VOTE      Percent who will vote for my candidate
```

VALUE	FREQ	PCT	CUM PCT	VALUE	FREQ	PCT	CUM PCT	VALUE	FREQ	PCT	CUM PCT
42.50	1	0	0	48.00	27	3	22	53.25	14	1	89
42.75	2	0	0	48.25	38	4	25	53.50	18	2	90
43.00	2	0	0	48.50	36	4	29	53.75	15	1	92
43.25	1	0	1	48.75	42	4	33	54.00	9	1	93
43.50	1	0	1	49.00	33	3	36	54.25	17	2	94
43.75	2	0	1	49.25	35	3	40	54.50	10	1	95
44.00	2	0	1	49.50	46	5	45	54.75	7	1	96
44.25	1	0	1	49.75	38	4	48	55.00	9	1	97
44.75	4	0	2	50.00	46	5	53	55.25	5	0	98
45.00	6	1	2	50.25	31	3	56	55.50	4	0	98
45.25	2	0	2	50.50	28	3	59	55.75	3	0	98
45.50	5	0	3	50.75	30	3	62	56.00	2	0	98
45.75	7	1	4	51.00	33	3	65	56.50	1	0	99
46.00	14	1	5	51.25	43	4	69	56.75	2	0	99
46.25	17	2	7	51.50	32	3	73	57.00	1	0	99
46.50	16	2	8	51.75	28	3	75	57.25	4	0	99
46.75	14	1	10	52.00	30	3	78	57.50	2	0	99
47.00	22	2	12	52.25	22	2	81	57.75	3	0	100
47.25	19	2	14	52.50	25	2	83	59.25	1	0	100
47.50	27	3	16	52.75	25	2	86	59.75	1	0	100
47.75	24	2	19	53.00	15	1	87				

How can we summarize the data from the 1,000 surveys? We can start with a frequency table. Many different results from the surveys are possible, so the table could be large. A condensed frequency table will be easier to read, and a histogram and some descriptive statistics will also be helpful:

```
FREQUENCIES VARIABLES = VOTE /
    FORMAT = CONDENSE /
    HISTOGRAM /
    STATISTICS = MEAN MEDIAN MODE STDDEV MIN MAX
```

The frequency table is shown in Figure 13.1. Each entry in a column labeled VALUE is a percentage from at least one of the samples—the percentage that endorsed the candidate. About 5% of the samples (46 out of 1,000) got the true population value of 50 on the nose. The remaining 954 samples didn't. So it doesn't seem very likely that sample results are identical to the population value. However, all is not lost. Most of the values are *around* 50. Some are a little larger, some a little smaller. The smallest value is 42.50; the largest is 59.75.

Look at the histogram of the results, in Figure 13.2. You can see that most of the samples do have values bunched around 50. Not very many samples are far off the mark. In fact, the farther away you move from 50 (the true value in the hypothetical population), the smaller the number of samples with those values. Of the 1,000 samples, 60% are concentrated in the range of 48 to 52.

Figure 13.2 Histogram for the hypothetical surveys

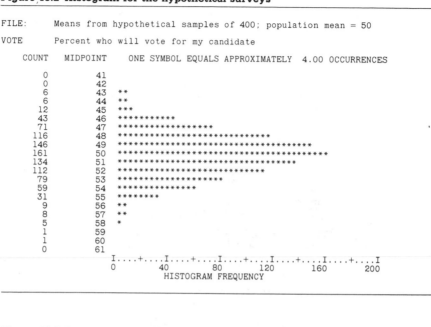

```
FILE:      Means from hypothetical samples of 400; population mean = 50

VOTE       Percent who will vote for my candidate

   COUNT    MIDPOINT    ONE SYMBOL EQUALS APPROXIMATELY  4.00 OCCURRENCES

      0        41
      0        42
      6        43    **
      6        44    **
     12        45    ***
     43        46    **********
     71        47    *****************
    116        48    *****************************
    146        49    *************************************
    161        50    ****************************************
    134        51    **********************************
    112        52    ****************************
     79        53    *********************
     59        54    ***************
     31        55    ********
      9        56    **
      8        57    **
      5        58    *
      1        59
      1        60
      0        61
             I....+....I....+....I....+....I....+....I....+....I
             0        40        80       120       160       200
                         HISTOGRAM FREQUENCY
```

Figure 13.3 Statistics for the hypothetical surveys

```
MEAN          50.129     MEDIAN      50.000     MODE       49.500
STD DEV        2.615     MINIMUM     42.500     MAXIMUM    59.750

VALID CASES    1000      MISSING CASES    0
```

Consider the descriptive statistics in Figure 13.3. The mean, median, and mode for the cases are very similar; they are equal or close to 50. The average of all 1,000 samples is pretty much on target. The standard deviation of the sample percentages is 2.62, not a very large number. That's because most of the values are close to 50.

? *What is a statistic?* A statistic is nothing more than some characteristic of a sample. The average height of the people in a sample is a statistic. So is the standard deviation or the variance of the heights. The term *statistic* is used only to describe sample values. The term *parameter* is used to describe characteristics of the population. If you could measure the height of all the people in the United States and calculate their average height, the result would be a parameter, since it would be the value for the population. Most of the time, population values, or parameters, are not known. You must estimate them based on statistics calculated from samples. ■ ■ ■

What you've seen here is true in general. It doesn't just happen in hypothetical surveys inside computers. It happens in real-life surveys and experiments. *The average value of the results from many samples is fairly close to the population value.*

The Effect of Sample Size

What if we take smaller samples, say 50 people in each survey instead of 400? Would the smaller samples change the results or how much they differ from one another? These questions are simple enough to answer. A computer ran the simulations again but this time included 50 people in each survey instead of 400. Everything else was done the same way.

The histogram and descriptive statistics for the new hypothetical surveys are shown in Figure 13.4. The values still bunch around 50, but they show a lot more spread. Only 24% of the samples have results between 48 and 52. That's less than half as many as before. The standard deviation is 6.9, a fairly big increase from the 2.6 for the 400-case samples. Of the 1,000 50-case surveys, 15 show results in the low 30s, and 4 show results in the 70s. Among the 400-case surveys, the smallest value was 42.50, and the largest was 59.75. A basic fact to remember is that *results from large samples do not vary as much as results from small samples.*

The overall average for the 400-case samples was 50.13. For the 50-case surveys, it's 50.40. Both of these values are fairly close to the

Figure 13.4 Results of 1,000 smaller hypothetical surveys

```
  COUNT    MIDPOINT    ONE SYMBOL EQUALS APPROXIMATELY  4.00 OCCURRENCES

      3        31    *
      7        33    **
      5        35    *
     17        37    ****
     21        39    *****
     28        41    *******
     51        43    *************
     81        45    ********************
     91        47    ***********************
    110        49    *****************************
    135        51    **********************************
     98        53    *************************
     99        55    *************************
     87        57    **********************
     63        59    ****************
     48        61    ************
     22        63    ******
     14        65    ****
     12        67    ***
      4        69    *
      4        71    *
                     I....+....I....+....I....+....I....+....I....+....I
                     0        40       80      120      160      200
                              HISTOGRAM FREQUENCY

  MEAN        50.390    MEDIAN     50.000    MODE       50.000
  STD DEV      6.912    MINIMUM    30.000    MAXIMUM    72.000

  VALID CASES   1000    MISSING CASES     0
```

true value of 50. If the number of samples were increased from 1,000 to 100,000—a lot of simulations—the overall average would be even closer to the population value.

THE EFFECT OF POPULATION VARIABILITY

In the previous examples, half of the voting population correctly appreciated the candidate you were working for. The other half remained unenlightened. What if there is more agreement in the population? What if 90% of the voters plan to vote for your candidate. Will the results from different surveys vary as much as they do when only half of the population are in your camp?

Again, the tireless computer can perform 1,000 hypothetical surveys, each with 400 respondents. With a flick of a finger at the text editor, we change the simulations so that 90% of the population of voters will vote for your candidate. What do the simulations report now?

Figure 13.5 shows the histogram and descriptive statistics for the new simulations. As you'd expect, the average value over the 1,000

Figure 13.5 Hypothetical surveys from a more uniform population

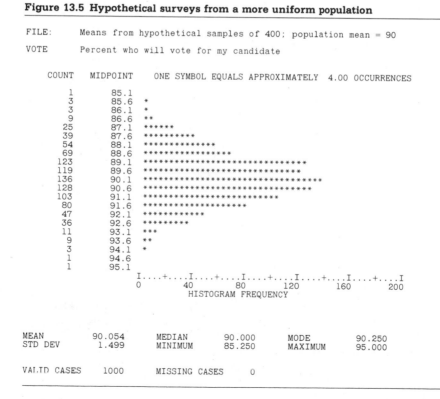

```
FILE:       Means from hypothetical samples of 400; population mean = 90

VOTE        Percent who will vote for my candidate

    COUNT   MIDPOINT   ONE SYMBOL EQUALS APPROXIMATELY  4.00 OCCURRENCES

        1     85.1
        3     85.6   *
        3     86.1   *
        9     86.6   **
       25     87.1   ******
       39     87.6   **********
       54     88.1   **************
       69     88.6   *****************
      123     89.1   *******************************
      119     89.6   ******************************
      136     90.1   **********************************
      128     90.6   ********************************
      103     91.1   **************************
       80     91.6   ********************
       47     92.1   ***********
       36     92.6   *********
       11     93.1   ***
        9     93.6   **
        3     94.1   *
        1     94.6
        1     95.1
                     I....+....I....+....I....+....I....+....I....+....I
                     0       40       80      120      160      200
                          HISTOGRAM FREQUENCY


    MEAN       90.054   MEDIAN    90.000   MODE       90.250
    STD DEV     1.499   MINIMUM   85.250   MAXIMUM    95.000

    VALID CASES  1000    MISSING CASES    0
```

surveys, 90.05, is very close to 90%, the "true" value. Do the results vary from hypothetical survey to hypothetical survey as much as they did when 50% of the population was in agreement? No. The standard deviation of the sample percentages is only 1.5, as compared with 2.6 from the 50-50 samples. Again, this makes sense. If most people are in agreement with each other about an issue, it's much harder to come up with unusual samples. Most samples will result in fairly similar results. In this example, the smallest result from a sample is 85.25, and the largest is 95.00. All sample values are closer to the true value than before.

These last simulations give us another rule about variability among samples: *The less a characteristic varies in the population, the less estimates of it vary from sample to sample.*

Other Statistics

Although we examined the percentage of people planning to vote for a candidate, we could have looked at some other characteristic, such as mean weight, mean number of pencils owned, or mean income. The procedure would have been the same. For each of the random samples from a population, we would have calculated the mean. Then we would have seen how much the mean values varied from sample to sample. The results would have been very similar to what we've seen, and the same basic rules would have applied. After all, percentages agreeing with a statement are equivalent to means.

? *How can a percentage be the same thing as a mean?* For a variable that can have only two possible values (such as Yes or No, Agree or Disagree, Cured or Not cured), you can code one of the responses as zero and the other response as one. If you add up the values for all of the cases, divide by the number of cases, and then multiply by 100, you'll obtain the percentage of cases giving the response coded as 1.

Let's consider a simple example. You ask five people whether they approve of the President's performance. Three say they do, and two say they don't. If you code Approve as 1, you have the values 1, 1, 1, 0, 0. The mean of these values is 3/5 = .6. To get the percentage agreeing with the statement, just multiply the mean by 100. In this survey, 60% of the people approved of the President's performance. ■ ■ ■

DISTRIBUTIONS OF STATISTICS

You can now see that both variables and statistics have distributions. Think about that. You can make a histogram of the actual ages of all the cases in a sample. This is fairly easy to visualize. You just count the number of cases that have ages within particular intervals. Using such histograms, you can answer questions like, "What percentage of the sample are older than 50?" and "What percentage of the cases are in their thirties?" The distribution of a variable like age tells you about the individual cases in the sample.

The *mean* age calculated from a sample of, say, 100 cases also has a distribution. The distribution of mean age describes how often the different mean age values are expected to occur if the same survey is repeated over and over, using the same population and a sample of the same size.

The distribution of a statistic (like the mean or the percentage) is used to answer questions like, "How often would I get a sample value of 60% or more with a sample size of 100 cases if the true population value is 50%?" "How often would I get a mean income of $13,000 or more with a sample size of 100 if the mean income in the population is $12,000?" The distribution tells you about a particular statistic for *samples* of a particular number of cases, rather than about the *individual* cases.

WHAT'S NEXT?

When you conduct a survey, you calculate one mean or one percentage for each item. From this sample result, you want to draw conclusions about the population. You can figure out (with mathematics) what the distribution of sample values looks like, based on the results from just a single sample. That's how you can determine what you're able to say about your whole population. The next chapter will explain how this is done.

Summary

What can you say about the mean of a population, based on the results observed in a sample?

When you take a sample from a population and compute the sample mean, it will not be identical to the mean you would have gotten if you'd observed the entire population.

Different samples result in different means.

The distribution of all possible values of the mean, for samples of a particular size, is called the *sampling distribution of the mean*.

The variability of the distribution of sample means depends on how large your sample is and on how much variability there is in the population from which the samples are taken.

As the size of the sample increases, the variability of the sample means decreases.

As variability in a population increases, so does the variability of the sample means.

EXERCISES

Statistical Concepts

1 Let's assume that our population of interest consists of five creatures who were found on Mars. The number of limbs on each of the creatures is: 10, 12, 14, 16, and 50.

    a. List all possible samples of size 2 from this population. (There are ten different samples you can take. The same creature cannot be included more than once in any sample.)

    b. Calculate the mean for each of the ten samples.

    c. Calculate the mean of the means in part (b). How does this compare to the value that you get when you find the mean for the original five creatures?

2 Repeat question (1) taking all possible samples of size 3. Look at the variability of the means for samples of size 2 and samples of size 3. Which appears to be smaller, and why?

3 Suppose you're interested in estimating the average IQ of all people who have come to see the Wednesday matinee of *Attack of the Killer Tomatoes* at a Selected Theater near you. All 200 people in the theater audience at the time are your population. In the audience there are 5 brilliant college professors attempting to evade their students, 30 students attempting to avoid studying, 25 farmers who think this is an agricultural movie, and 140 average folks looking for cheap thrills.

    a. If you take a random sample of 5 people, discuss what sorts of samples it's possible to obtain. That is, describe possible mixes of people in the sample.

    b. If you take a random sample of 50 people, discuss what sorts of samples it's possible to obtain. Can you get the same types of samples as when you were taking samples of five people?

    c. Would samples of size 5 or size 50 be more variable?

4 In a large university there is a proposal to drop statistics as a requirement for graduation. Each of the 500 deans at the university commissions a survey to gauge student support for the proposal. Each survey contains a random sample of 50 students. The histogram below shows the distribution of the results of the surveys.

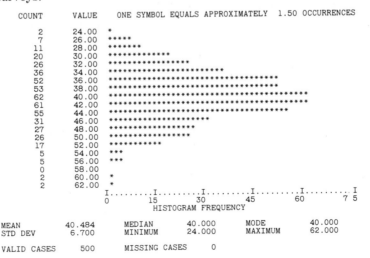

```
        COUNT     VALUE    ONE SYMBOL EQUALS APPROXIMATELY  1.50 OCCURRENCES

           2      24.00    *
           7      26.00    *****
          11      28.00    *******
          20      30.00    *************
          26      32.00    *****************
          36      34.00    ************************
          52      36.00    ***********************************
          53      38.00    ************************************
          62      40.00    *****************************************
          61      42.00    ****************************************
          55      44.00    *************************************
          31      46.00    ********************
          27      48.00    ******************
          26      50.00    *****************
          17      52.00    ***********
           5      54.00    ***
           5      56.00    ***
           0      58.00
           2      60.00    *
           2      62.00    *
                           I.........I.........I.........I.........I.........I
                           0        15        30        45        60       7 5
                                         HISTOGRAM FREQUENCY

        MEAN      40.484   MEDIAN    40.000   MODE       40.000
        STD DEV    6.700   MINIMUM   24.000   MAXIMUM    62.000

        VALID CASES  500   MISSING CASES   0
```

Based on the histogram and summary statistics:

a. What is your best guess for the percentage of students favoring the proposal?

b. When all 500 Deans presented their results to the President, she was aghast that the results of all of the surveys were not similar. She is considering censuring the Deans whose polls were far removed from the average value. She thinks that they "rigged" their polls to support their own viewpoints. How would you defend the Deans at their censure hearing?

c. Based on the histogram, if the true percentage favoring the the proposal is 40%, what's the probability that a poll will estimate the value to be 25% or greater? 55% or greater? Less than 35%?

5 Explain why you agree or disagree with each of the following statements:

a. It's better to include a small number of subjects in a study than a large number.

b. All samples from the same population give the same results.

c. How much means vary from sample to sample depends on both the size of the sample and the variability in the population.

d. Both variables and statistics have distributions.

14 Working with the Normal Distribution

What is the normal distribution, and why is it important for data analysis?

- What does a normal distribution look like?
- Within a normal distribution, what percentage of the observations fall where?
- What is the relationship of the mean, median, and mode in a normal distribution?
- What are standard scores, and how are they computed?
- Is a sample from a normal population exactly normal?
- What is the Central Limit Theorem, and what does it tell you about the distribution of sample means?
- What is a confidence interval?

You may have noticed that the shapes of all the histograms in the previous chapter were similar. The histograms looked like bells. Most of the values were bunched in the center. As you looked farther and farther from the center, you found fewer and fewer observations.

In the general population, many variables—such as height, weight, blood pressure, and scores on IQ tests—turn out to have distributions that are bell-shaped. There is a particular type of bell-shaped distribution, called the **normal distribution,** which describes them well. The normal distribution is very important in data analysis, as you'll see throughout the rest of this book. In this chapter, you'll look more closely at some characteristics of the normal distribution.

THE NORMAL DISTRIBUTION

A mathematical equation defines the normal distribution exactly. For a particular mean and standard deviation, this equation determines what percentage of the observations fall where. Figure 14.1 is a picture of a normal distribution with a mean of 100 and a standard deviation of 15. As you can see, the distribution is symmetric. If you folded it in the center, the two sides would match; they're identical. The center of the distribution is at the mean. The mean of a normal distribution is also the most

Figure 14.1 A normal distribution

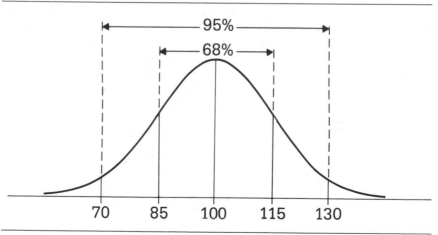

frequently occurring value (the mode), and it's the value that splits the distribution into two equal parts (the median). In any normal distribution, the mean, median, and mode all have the same value.

Areas in the Normal Distribution

For a normal distribution, the percentage of values falling within any interval can be calculated exactly. For example, in a normal distribution with a mean of 100 and a standard deviation of 15 (as in Figure 14.1), 68% of all values fall between 85 (one standard deviation less than the mean) and 115 (one standard deviation more than the mean). And 95% of all values fall in the range 70 to 130, within two standard deviations from the mean.

A normal distribution can have any mean and standard deviation. However, the percentage of cases falling within a particular number of standard deviations from the mean is always the same. The shape of a normal distribution doesn't change. Most of the observations are near the average, and a mathematical function describes how many observations are at any given distance (measured in standard deviations) from the mean. Means and standard deviations differ from variable to variable. But the percentage of cases within specific intervals is always the same in a true normal distribution.

It turns out that many variables you can measure have a distribution close to the mathematical ideal of a normal distribution. We say these variables are "normally distributed," even though their distributions are not exactly normal. Usually when we say this, we mean that the histograms look like Figure 14.1. For example, we say that IQ scores are normally distributed with a mean of 100 and a standard deviation of 15. Heights of adult males or females are also said to be normally distributed.

? *Serious questions have been raised about interpreting these so-called intelligence tests. Do they really tell you anything, or are they culturally biased?* That's a question for another book. The only important thing about IQ in this book is that scores from an IQ test administered to the adult population are found to follow a normal distribution with a mean of 100 and a standard deviation of 15. IQ scores are used here simply as an example of a normally distributed variable with a standard deviation that's known.   ■ ■ ■

STANDARD SCORES

If I tell you that I own 250 books, you probably won't be able to make very much of this information. You won't know how my library compares to that of the average college professor. And you won't know how unusual I am compared to them (based only on books!). Wouldn't it be much more informative if I told you that I own the average number of books, or that I am two standard deviations above the average? Then, if you know that the number of books owned by college professors is normally distributed, you could calculate exactly what percentage of my colleagues have more books than I do.

To describe my library better in this way, you can calculate what's called a **standard score.** It describes the location of a particular case in a distribution: whether it's above average or below average and how much above or below. The computation is simple:

1 Take the value and subtract the mean from it. If the difference is positive, you know the case is above the mean. If it's negative, the case is below the mean.

2 Divide the difference by the standard deviation. This tells you how many standard-deviation units a score is above or below the average.

For example, if book ownership among college professors is normally distributed with a mean of 150 and a standard deviation of 50, you can calculate my standard score for the 250 books I own like this:

Step 1:

$$\begin{array}{l} 250 \text{ (my books)} \\ -\ 150 \text{ (average number of books)} \\ \hline 100 \text{ (I own 100 books more than the average professor.)} \end{array}$$

Step 2:

$$\frac{100 \text{ (difference from step 1)}}{50 \text{ (standard deviation of books)}} = 2 \text{ (standard score)}$$

My standard score is 2. Since its sign is positive, it indicates that I have more books than average. The number 2 indicates that I am 2 standard-deviation units above the mean. In a normal distribution, 95% of all cases are *within* 2 standard deviations of the mean. Therefore, you know that my library is remarkable.

In a sample, the average of the standard scores for a variable is always 0, and the standard deviation is always 1. Suppose you ask 15 people on the street how many hamburgers they consume in a week. If you calculate the mean and standard deviation for the number of hamburgers eaten by these 15 people and then compute a standard score for each person, you'll get 15 standard scores. The average of the scores will be 0, and their standard deviation will be 1.

When you use standard scores, you can compare values for a case on *different* variables. If you have standard scores of 2.9 for number of books, −1.2 for metabolic rate, and 0.0 for weight, then you know:

- You have many more books than average.
- You have a slower metabolism than average.
- Your weight is exactly the average.

You couldn't meaningfully compare the original numbers since they all have different means and standard deviations. Owning 20 cars is much more extraordinary than owning 20 shirts.

A SAMPLE FROM THE NORMAL DISTRIBUTION

Even if a variable is normally distributed in the population, a sample from the population doesn't necessarily have a distribution that's exactly normal. Samples vary, so the distributions for individual samples vary as well. However, if a sample is reasonably large and it comes from a normal population, its distribution should look more or less normal.

Consider Figure 14.2, a histogram for a normally distributed variable, like IQ, for a sample of 400 cases. In the population, the variable has a mean of 100 and a standard deviation of 15. The histogram for the sample looks about normal. SPSS^X can help you imagine what a true normal distribution for the variable would look like. If you type

```
FREQUENCIES VARIABLES = YOURVAR
     / HISTOGRAM = NORMAL
```

SPSS^X places colons and dots on the histogram to show a true normal distribution. The colons and dots indicate how many cases would be expected in the intervals if the distribution were exactly normal with the same mean and standard deviation as the sample. A colon instead of a star appears on the output if the normal distribution falls inside the histogram. A dot appears if the normal distribution falls outside the histogram. You can see that the observed numbers of cases don't always match the numbers expected on the basis of the normal distribution. That's all right. Overall, the observed distribution doesn't differ much from the expected normal distribution.

Distributions that Aren't Normal

The normal distribution is often used as a reference for describing other distributions. A distribution is called **skewed** if it isn't symmetric but has more cases, more of a "tail," toward one end of the distribution than the other. If the long tail is toward larger values, the distribution is called positively skewed, or skewed to the right. If the tail is toward smaller values, the distribution is negatively skewed, or skewed to the left. A variable like income has a positively skewed distribution. That's because some incomes are very much above average and make a long tail to the right. Since incomes are rarely less than zero, the tail to the left is not so long.

Figure 14.2 A histogram for a normally distributed variable

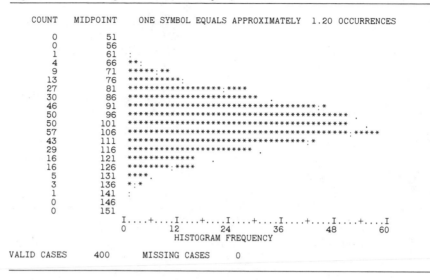

```
  COUNT    MIDPOINT    ONE SYMBOL EQUALS APPROXIMATELY  1.20 OCCURRENCES

     0        51
     0        56
     1        61   :
     4        66   **:
     9        71   *****:**
    13        76   *********:
    27        81   *****************:****
    30        86   ************************  .
    46        91   **********************************:*
    50        96   ********************************************  .
    50       101   ******************************************
    57       106   ***********************************:*****
    43       111   ************************************:*
    29       116   ***********************  .
    16       121   ************  .
    16       126   ********:****
     5       131   ****.
     3       136   *:*
     1       141   :
     0       146
     0       151
                   I....+....I....+....I....+....I....+....I....+....I
                   0        12        24        36        48        60
                             HISTOGRAM FREQUENCY

VALID CASES    400      MISSING CASES    0
```

Figure 14.3 Skewness and kurtosis

```
MEAN          100.319    STD DEV    14.403    KURTOSIS    -.169
SKEWNESS         .004


VALID CASES     400      MISSING CASES    0
```

If a larger proportion of cases falls into the tails of a distribution than into those of a normal distribution, the distribution has positive **kurtosis.** If fewer cases fall into the tails, the distribution has negative kurtosis.

You can compute statistics that measure how much skewness and kurtosis there is in a distribution, in comparison to a normal distribution. These statistics are zero if the observed distribution is exactly normal. Positive values for kurtosis indicate that a distribution has heavier tails than a normal distribution. Negative values indicate that a distribution has lighter tails than a normal distribution. Of course, the measures of skewness and kurtosis for samples from a normal distribution will not be exactly zero. Because of variation from sample to sample, they will fluctuate around zero.

To calculate these statistics, just type:

```
FREQUENCIES VARIABLES = YOURVAR
  / FORMAT = NOTABLE
  / STATISTICS = MEAN STDDEV SKEWNESS KURTOSIS
```

Figure 14.3 gives the statistics for the distribution shown earlier, in Figure 14.2. Both the value for skewness and the value for kurtosis are small. The distribution is close to normal.

MORE ON THE DISTRIBUTION OF THE MEANS

It's understandable that variables like height and weight have distributions that are approximately normal. We know that most of the world is pretty close to average and that the farther we move from average, the fewer people we find. But why did the distributions of sample *means* in the last chapter look normal?

Let's look again at the histogram for samples of size 400 from a hypothetical population in which half of the people agree to vote for a candidate (see Figure 14.4). The observed frequencies are very close to those expected if the distribution is normal. That's surprising, in a way. The distribution of the sampled responses wasn't even close to normal. It had equal proportions of ones (agree) and zeros (disagree).

The Central Limit Theorem

This remarkable fact is explained by the Central Limit Theorem. The Central Limit Theorem says that for samples of a sufficiently large size, the real distribution of means is almost always approximately normal. The original variable can have any kind of distribution. It doesn't have to be bell-shaped in the least. ("Real" distribution means the one you'd get if you took an infinite number of random samples. The "real" distribution is a mathematical concept. You can get a pretty good idea of what the "real" distribution looks like by taking a lot of samples and examining plots of their values—as we've been doing.)

? *Sufficiently large size? What kind of language is that for a mathematical theorem?* Actually, there are several vague parts of our paraphrase of the Central Limit Theorem. You have to say what you're willing to consider "approximately normal" before you know what size sample is "sufficiently large." How large a sample you need depends on the way the variable itself is distributed. The important point is that the distribution of means gets closer and closer to normal as the sample size gets larger and larger—regardless of what the distribution of the original variable looks like. ■ ■ ■

Let's suppose that the number of books that professors own ranges from 0 to 300 and that all values from 0 to 300 are equally likely, making the distribution **uniform.** Figure 14.5 shows a histogram of this uniform distribution. All of the lines representing intervals from 0 to 300 are of approximately equal length.

What happens if we take a sample of 10 professors, calculate the average number of books they own, and do this sampling and calculating again and again? What will the distribution of the average values look like? To answer this question, we can use another computer model. Each

Figure 14.4 The histogram for the hypothetical surveys

```
FILE:      Means from hypothetical samples of 400; population mean = 50

VOTE       Percent who will vote for my candidate

      COUNT    MIDPOINT    ONE SYMBOL EQUALS APPROXIMATELY  4.00 OCCURRENCES

          0       41
          0       42
          6       43    :*
          6       44    **.
         12       45    ***  .
         43       46    **********:
         71       47    *****************.
        116       48    **************************:**
        146       49    ************************************:**
        161       50    **************************************:.**
        134       51    **********************************    .
        112       52    ****************************.
         79       53    ******************.
         59       54    *************:**
         31       55    ******:*
          9       56    **.
          8       57    :*
          5       58    *
          1       59
          1       60
          0       61
                        I....+....I....+....I....+....I....+....I....+....I
                        0        40       80      120      160      200
                                         HISTOGRAM FREQUENCY
```

Figure 14.5 A uniform distribution

```
      COUNT    MIDPOINT    ONE SYMBOL EQUALS APPROXIMATELY 16.00 OCCURRENCES

        677      10.00    *****************************************
        663      30.00    *****************************************
        690      50.00    ******************************************
        651      70.00    ****************************************
        673      90.00    *****************************************
        670     110.00    *****************************************
        637     130.00    ****************************************
        666     150.00    *****************************************
        621     170.00    **************************************
        686     190.00    ******************************************
        691     210.00    ******************************************
        694     230.00    ******************************************
        647     250.00    ****************************************
        642     270.00    ***************************************
        692     290.00    ******************************************
```
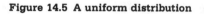
```
                        I....+....I....+....I....+....I....+....I....+....I
                        0       160      320      480      640      800
                                         HISTOGRAM FREQUENCY
```

MEAN	149.994	STD ERR	.869	MEDIAN	150.792
MODE	.005	STD DEV	86.861	VARIANCE	7544.783
KURTOSIS	-1.210	S E KURT	.049	SKEWNESS	-.002
S E SKEW	.024	RANGE	299.966	MINIMUM	.005
MAXIMUM	299.971	SUM	1499936.41		

VALID CASES   10000   MISSING CASES   0

Figure 14.6 The distribution of means from the uniform distribution

```
MEAN

   COUNT    MIDPOINT    ONE SYMBOL EQUALS APPROXIMATELY  4.00 OCCURRENCES

       0      60.00
       6      70.00    :*
       3      80.00    *.
      17      90.00    ***:
      37     100.00    ******:**
      48     110.00    ************.
      67     120.00    ****************   .
     121     130.00    ****************************:**
     126     140.00    *******************************.
     153     150.00    **************************************:***
     131     160.00    *********************************:
      95     170.00    ***********************
      92     180.00    *********************:***
      56     190.00    *************:*
      25     200.00    ******.
      12     210.00    ***.
       9     220.00    *:
       2     230.00    :
       0     240.00
                       I....+....I....+....I....+....I....+....I....+....I
                       0        40       80       120      160      200
                                     HISTOGRAM FREQUENCY
```

simulation will compute the average of 10 observations from the uniform distribution. Figure 14.6 shows the results of 1,000 such simulations.

The means from these simulations have a distribution that's not at all like the uniform distribution of the individual observations. The distribution of means is approximately normal. *That's* why the normal distribution is so important in data analysis. Your *variable* doesn't have to be normally distributed. Means that you calculate from samples will be normally distributed, anyway. If the variable you're studying actually does have a normal distribution, then the distribution of means will be normal for samples of any size. The further from normal your variable is, the larger the samples have to be for the distribution of the means to be approximately normal.

MORE ABOUT MEANS OF MEANS

We've seen that for a sufficiently large sample size, the distribution of means is normal. That tells us a lot about how likely different means are, but only if we know what the mean and standard deviation of the distribution are. The mean of the "real" distribution of means is the population mean.

? *The mean of the means is the mean? What does that mean?* It means (one step at a time, now): Suppose you could take an infinite number of samples and calculate the average for each one. Suppose you could then calculate the average of your averages. What you'd get is the same number as if you just went ahead and took the average of the whole population. That really isn't surprising at all. ■ ■ ■

For example, if 50% of all the people in a population agree with a statement, then

- The true population mean is 50%. (We just said that: 50% of all the people in a population agree.)
- The mean of the distribution of sample means from that population is 50%, too.

Similarly, if the average IQ in the population is 100, then the mean of the distribution of means from the population is also 100. It doesn't matter how large the samples are, whether you have 10-case samples or 10,000-case samples. Nor does it matter whether IQ itself is normally distributed. The mean of the distribution of means is the population mean.

THE STANDARD ERROR OF THE MEAN

If the mean of the distribution of sample means is the population mean, what's the standard deviation of the distribution of sample means? Is it also just the standard deviation of the population? No! In Chapter 13, you saw that the standard deviation of the means depends on two things:

1 How large a sample you take. When we looked at samples of 400 cases, most of the means were pretty close to the population value. When we looked at smaller samples of size 50, the means had more spread. Larger samples meant a smaller standard deviation for the sample means.

2 How much variability there is in the population. When only 50% of our population agreed with a statement, there was more variability in the means than when 90% of the population agreed with the statement. Less variability in the samples also meant a smaller standard deviation for the sample means.

To calculate the exact standard deviation of the distribution of sample means, you must know:

- The standard deviation in the population.
- The number of cases in the sample.

All you have to do is divide the standard deviation by the square root of the sample size. The result, the standard deviation of the distribution of sample means, is called the **standard error of the mean.** Although it has an impressive name, it's still just a standard deviation—the standard deviation of the sample means.

Think about the formula for computing the standard error of the mean: take the standard deviation of the variable and divide by the square root of the sample size. Suppose the standard deviation of number of books owned is 50, and the sample size is four cases. Then the standard error is 50 divided by the square root of 4, or 25. If the sample size is *increased* to 9, the standard error decreases to: 50 divided by the square root of 9, or 16.7. If the sample size is *increased* to 100, the standard error is only 5. The larger the sample size, the less variability there is in the sample means.

CALCULATING A CONFIDENCE INTERVAL

You've spent a lot of time reading about sample means and how they vary. You've actually seen what their distribution looks like. You have to understand these things in order to use statistics for testing hypotheses about the population. If you know how much the means vary from sample to sample, you can draw conclusions about the population by looking at just a single sample. Watch.

Let's take a well-defined population: the audience at a matinee performance of the classic film *Attack of the Killer Tomatoes*. Suppose that you want to estimate the average IQ of the people in the audience. You go to the theater, randomly select 25 patrons, and give them an IQ test. The average IQ of these 25 lovers of the cinema turns out to be 112, and the standard deviation of their IQ scores is close to 15, the value for the population. Based on this sample, what can you conclude about *all* of the patrons in the theater?

The sample you selected is one of many possible samples. So the mean you calculated is one of many possible means. In particular, it's one of the means in the distribution of means for samples of size 25. The problem is that you don't know where your sample falls in the distribution of means. Is it close to the true population value? Is it one of the extreme means? Since you don't know the true value for the IQ of people at the movie, you can't tell if your sample value is too high, too low, or right on target. You *never* know the true value in the population, because if you did you wouldn't do the study!

You don't know the population mean, and therefore you don't know the mean of the distribution of sample means. Nevertheless, you can estimate the standard error of the mean from your observed standard deviation. Remember, the standard error of the mean is the standard deviation of the distribution of sample means. The estimated standard error is the standard deviation (15) divided by the square root of the sample size (25), which makes 15 divided by 5, or 3. Using this piece of information, you can visualize the sampling distribution of means, as shown in Figure 14.7.

Based on the Central Limit Theorem, you can assume that the distribution is normal. That's what the Central Limit Theorem says: for a sufficiently large sample size, sample means are normally distributed, whether the original variable, IQ in this case, is normally distributed or

Figure 14.7 The sampling distribution of means

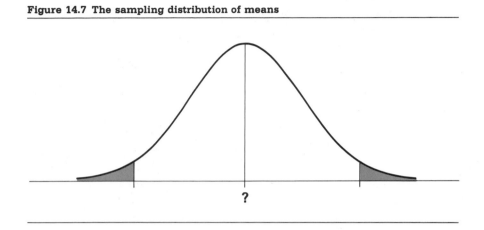

?

not. Since you don't know the mean IQ for the population in the theater, it's labeled with a question mark in the figure. Because the distribution is normal, you know that 95% of all sample means should fall within two standard errors of the mean. The standard error of the mean was found to equal 3. So 95% of all sample means should fall within 6 of the question mark. The values falling outside of this interval are shaded in the figure.

Where is your sample mean in this distribution? Sorry—you can't figure that out. If you knew the population value (at the question mark), then you could mark the location of the mean; but, of course, you don't.

Based on this picture, what can you say about the value of the population mean? Although you can't give an exact value, you can calculate a range of values—an interval—that should include the population mean 95% of the time. You calculate the lower limit of this interval by subtracting two times the standard error from your mean. The lower limit is 112 − 6 = 106. You calculate the upper limit by adding two times the standard error to your mean. This is 112 + 6 = 118. The interval is from 106 to 118. Now you have what's known as a **confidence interval,** extending from two standard errors below the sample mean to two standard errors above the sample mean.

Think of what the diagram shows. You can imagine your sample mean somewhere in the distribution and see what happens. Figure 14.8 shows the sample mean at 1.5 standard errors above the population mean (the question mark). The confidence interval is marked off. Does the interval include the unknown population value? Sure—because it reaches out 2 standard errors, and the difference between your sample mean and the population mean is only 1.5 standard errors.

Figure 14.8 The sample mean 1.5 standard errors above the population mean

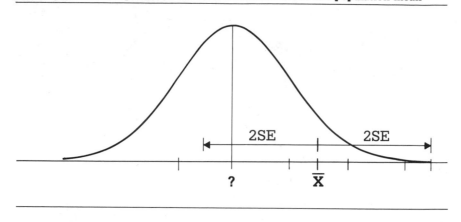

Figure 14.9 The sample mean 1 standard error below the population mean

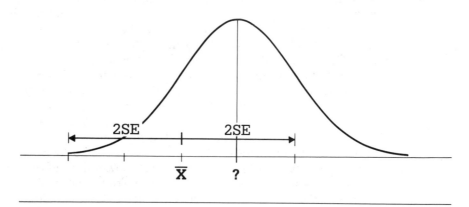

Now imagine your sample value at 1 standard-error unit below the mean, as in Figure 14.9. Does the confidence interval still include the population value? Yes. Once again, your sample mean is within 2 standard errors of the population mean, so the population mean lies within the confidence interval.

The only time your interval wouldn't include the population value is when your sample mean falls in the shaded region of Figure 14.7. The shaded region corresponds to the 5% of the distribution that is more than two standard-error units from the population mean.

You don't know the exact value for the population mean. But as shown here, you can calculate an interval around your sample mean that will include the true, unknown population mean 95% of the time. This is called a *95%* confidence interval. Of course, you can never tell whether your particular sample mean is one of the unlikely ones in the shaded region. All you can do is calculate the interval and hope that you have one of the 95-out-of-a-100 times that the interval includes the population value.

Smarter than Average?

You calculated a mean IQ of 112 for a sample of 25 patrons at the movie. This is 12 points higher than 100, which is supposedly the average value for people in general. Is it reasonable to conclude that these moviegoers (the people in the audience at *Killer Tomatoes* that night) are different, on average, from people in general? You know that sample means vary, so you don't expect the value observed in a sample to be exactly the same as the population value.

? *Where did the population come in here? We were just looking at people in the theater, right?* Yes. In this rather improbable study, the "population" is just the people who were in the theater that night. For them, the "population value" of average IQ is the value you'd get if you gave tests to everybody in the theater and took the average. Any time you're talking about statistics, the word "population" has a special meaning. It's the people (or animals or things) you're trying to draw conclusions about. In this study, it's the movie audience.   ■ ■ ■

What you have to figure out from your sample of moviegoers is this: How likely is this sample mean of 112 if the population mean (for everybody at the theater) is 100?

Use a picture again. Figure 14.10 is the distribution of means for samples of size 25 when the population value is 100 and the standard deviation is 15. It looks a lot like some of the previous diagrams. The difference is that instead of the question mark, you see the value 100, the mean for people in general. You can now locate the observed sample mean on the distribution. It doesn't fit well, since the value 112 is 4 standard error units above the mean.

This result indicates that it's very unlikely to observe a sample mean as large as 112 in a sample of size 25 when the true population value is

Figure 14.10 The distribution of means for samples of size 25

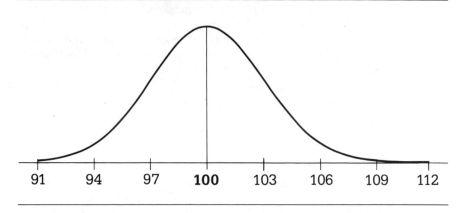

100. Only about .006% of the cases in a normal distribution have values as much as 4 standard deviations away from the mean. So it appears highly unlikely that the movie patrons have the same mean IQ as the general population. On the other hand, if you'd observed a mean IQ of 103 in your sample, you couldn't say with confidence that the patrons were smarter than average, since a sample mean of 103 is perfectly reasonable for a population value of 100.

WHAT'S NEXT?

In this chapter, you saw how to use distributions of the mean to calculate confidence intervals for the population mean. You also saw how to use them to evaluate hypotheses about a population mean. We'll spend the rest of the book using ideas from this chapter to evaluate hypotheses of many kinds.

Summary

What is the normal distribution, and why is it important for data analysis?

A normal distribution is bell-shaped. It is a symmetric distribution in which the mean, median, and mode all coincide. In the population, many variables, such as height and weight, have distributions that are approximately normal.

Although normal distributions can have different means and variances, the distribution of the cases about the mean is always the same.

You use standard scores to locate an observation within a distribution. The mean of standard scores is 0, and the standard deviation is 1.

The Central Limit Theorem states that for samples of a sufficiently large size, the distribution of sample means is approximately normal. (That's why the normal distribution is so important for data analysis.)

A confidence interval provides a range of values that, with a designated likelihood, contains the population mean.

EXERCISES

Statistical Concepts

1 If I tell you that in the population of adults in the United States, nostril width is normally distributed with a mean of .9 inches and a standard deviation of .2 inches, list all the facts about nostril width that you can deduce from my statement.

2 If grades on an examination are approximately normally distributed with an average of 70 and a standard deviation of 10, what percentage of the students:
   a. Received grades less than 70?
   b. Received grades greater than 70?
   c. Received grades less than 60?
   d. Received grades less than 50?
   e. Received grades less than 50 or greater than 90?
   f. Received grades less than the median?

3 Based on the previous problem, what is the standard score for a student who received a grade of
   a. 70?
   b. 75?
   c. 60?
   d. 55?
   e. 90?

4 For a second examination, scores are normally distributed with a mean of 75 and a standard deviation of 15. If a student received a grade of 80 on the first exam and a grade of 90 on the second exam, on which exam did he perform better? Explain your answer.

5 Two researchers are studying the effect of positive thinking on recovery time after surgery. Both take a sample of 25 persons about to undergo surgery, teach them how to think positively, and then examine how long they stay in the hospital.

   a. The first researcher calculates the average stay to be 12 days, and the standard deviation to be 3 days. He reports these results in the *Journal of Positive Living*. The second researcher calculates the average stay to be 12.5 days. He reports the standard error of the mean to be .6 days. When he submits his results to the same journal, the editors question his findings. They want to know why his measure of variability is so much less than the first researcher's. Explain to the editors of the journal the difference between the two statistics. Indicate the relationship of the two statistics as well.

   b. What would be the standard error of the mean if the standard deviation remained at 3, but the sample size was increased to 50? What if it was decreased to 10?

6 You read in the newspaper that the average person watches 4 hours of television per night. The 95 percent confidence interval for the number of hours watched is reported as 3 hours to 5 hours. Do you agree or disagree with each of the following statements? Give your reasons:

   a. Ninety-five percent of all people watch between 3 and 5 hours of television per night.

   b. You can't tell whether this particular interval does or doesn't include the true population value for hours of television watched per night.

   c. The purpose of a confidence interval is to provide a range of values which are thought to include the sample mean.

   d. When you do a study you want your 95% confidence interval to be as wide as possible, since it will then include more values.

   e. The size of a confidence interval depends on the number of cases in the sample and the standard deviation.

7 You take a sample of 100 hamburgers and find their average weight to be .15 pounds. If the standard deviation of hamburger weights is known to be .05 pounds, calculate a 95% confidence interval for the unknown population value.

8 A macaroni manufacturer claims that the weight of one-pound boxes of his macaroni is normally distributed with a mean of 1 and a standard deviation of .02 pounds. You take a random sample of 16 boxes of the macaroni and find their average weight to be .90 pounds. What is the probability that you would obtain a sample mean of .90 or less if the manufacturer's claim is correct? Do you believe the manufacturer's claim?

15 Testing Hypotheses about Two Independent Means

Based on the means observed in two independent samples, how can you test the hypothesis that two population means are equal?

- What does a distribution of the differences between two sample means look like?

- How can you figure out whether the difference you have observed between two sample means is unlikely or likely, if the two population means are equal?

- How can you use statistical methods to test a hypothesis?

- What is the null hypothesis?

- What is the observed significance level?

- What are Type 1 and Type 2 errors, and when do you make them?

- What is a *t*-test?

- What is the difference between a one-tailed and a two-tailed significance level?

- What assumptions about your data are necessary in order to use the *t*-test?

A few chapters back, you looked at excitement with life and how it related to several other characteristics, such as age, sex, and marital status. All that you did was to describe a sample. That was all you could do when you didn't understand very much about the relationships of samples and populations. Now you can do more.

You can look in the sample at the percentage of people who found life exciting and relate that information back to the population. You know you have one of many possible samples and that the chances are pretty slim for the value calculated from the sample to be identical to the population value. However, you know that the General Social Survey sample is very large, 1,473, so the variability of the sample means is probably not very much. You can calculate the standard error for the percentage who found life exciting (it's .013) and use that number to calculate a 95% confidence interval for the population value. The interval is from 44.2% to 49.4%.

Although you never know if the particular interval you calculated contains the population value (it either does or it doesn't), you know that the interval will include the population value 95 times out of 100.

The confidence interval from 44.2% to 49.4% is narrow. That's good, since you want to pinpoint the population value as much as possible. You don't know where within a confidence interval the population value might be. It's much more useful, then, to know that the 95% confidence interval is from 44 to 49 than to know that it's from 20 to 80. When you conduct a survey or experiment, look at both the mean and its confidence interval. If the interval is wide, you have only a very rough estimate of the population mean.

IS THE DIFFERENCE REAL?

Usually when you conduct a study, you have some ideas that you want to explore. These ideas, often called *hypotheses*, typically involve comparisons of several groups: "Do men and women find life equally exciting?" "Does income differ between people who find life exciting and those who don't?" "Are excited people more educated than those who find life dull?"

If you look at the results in your sample for the groups of interest, you'll probably find that they do differ. For example, people who said life is exciting had, on the average, 14.2 years of education, compared to 13.1 for people who said life is routine or dull. What can you make of this difference? You can say that the excited people in your sample had more education than those who were unexcited. But is that true for the population?

You've seen that different samples from the same population give different results. Even if the education levels are the same for the excited and the unexcited groups in the population, their sample means will differ. The real issue is, how much will they differ? How can you decide whether a difference in sample means can be attributed to their natural variability or to a real difference between groups in the population?

Review of the Distribution of Means

The question about sample means isn't terribly hard. Look at Figure 15.1, which you've seen in previous chapters. It shows the distribution of sample means for an agree/disagree item. These means are for 400-person samples from a population in which 50% agree and 50% disagree.

The histogram in the figure gives you a pretty good idea of the real mathematical distribution of the sample values. What if a sample value is 52? It falls near the other cases in the distribution. This would lead you to believe that the observed sample may well be from a population in which 50% agree. You certainly wouldn't have much reason to doubt that. On the other hand, what if a sample value is 70? That's certainly far removed from the other cases. It seems unlikely that you'd get a sample value of 70 based on a sample of 400 cases if the population value is 50. It's so unlikely that you'd doubt the hypothesis that the sample actually comes from a population with a value of 50.

Differences between Means

We can extend these ideas to differences between two means. Let's say we want to compare the mean IQ of students on the Dean's List to the mean IQ of students on academic probation. We have a sample of 20 students from each group. What we'll need to find out is how likely various differences in means are if the two groups have the same mean IQ in the population. We'll look at the distribution of differences between pairs of means. This will give us some idea of how much variability between means to expect when both samples are from the same population.

Let's do this by building a computer model again. We'll take two samples of 20 cases each from a normal population with a mean of 100 and a standard deviation of 15. Then we'll calculate the means for the two samples, and find the difference between the two means. We'll have to keep repeating this again and again to get an idea of what the real distribution looks like. Figure 15.2 is a histogram of 1,000 such differences. The Central Limit Theorem works not just for means but for differences of means as well, so the distribution looks normal. The mean of the distribution is close to zero. That's because the samples are from the same population. If you had taken one of the samples from a

Figure 15.1 Means from samples of size 400

```
FILE:      Means from hypothetical samples of 400; population mean = 50

VOTE       Percent who will vote for my candidate

    COUNT   MIDPOINT    ONE SYMBOL EQUALS APPROXIMATELY  4.00 OCCURRENCES

       0       41
       0       42
       6       43    **
       6       44    **
      12       45    ***
      43       46    ***********
      71       47    ******************
     116       48    *****************************
     146       49    *************************************
     161       50    *****************************************
     134       51    **********************************
     112       52    ****************************
      79       53    ********************
      59       54    ***************
      31       55    ********
       9       56    **
       8       57    **
       5       58    *
       1       59
       1       60
       0       61
                     I....+....I....+....I....+....I....+....I....+....I
                     0       40       80      120      160      200
                              HISTOGRAM FREQUENCY
```

Figure 15.2 Differences between two means

```
DIFF       Difference between two means

    COUNT   MIDPOINT    ONE SYMBOL EQUALS APPROXIMATELY  4.00 OCCURRENCES

       1      -15.0
       3      -13.5    :
       2      -12.0    :
      11      -10.5    **:
      21       -9.0    ****:
      30       -7.5    ********.
      51       -6.0    ************.
      94       -4.5    ******************:****
     100       -3.0    ***********************:
     118       -1.5    *****************************:
     129        .0     *******************************:
     108       1.5     **************************
     106       3.0     **************************:*
      88       4.5     *********************:*
      59       6.0     *************:
      27       7.5     ******* .
      30       9.0     ****:***
      12      10.5     **:
       7      12.0     :*
       1      13.5     .
       2      15.0     *
                     I....+....I....+....I....+....I....+....I....+....I
                     0       40       80      120      160      200
                              HISTOGRAM FREQUENCY
```

MEAN	.135	STD ERR	.149	MEDIAN	.083
MODE	-15.159	STD DEV	4.719	VARIANCE	22.270
KURTOSIS	-.052	S E KURT	.155	SKEWNESS	.061
S E SKEW	.077	RANGE	30.421	MINIMUM	-15.159
MAXIMUM	15.262	SUM	134.611		

VALID CASES	1000	MISSING CASES	0

population with a mean IQ of 120 and the other sample from a population with a mean IQ of 110, the average difference for all pairs of samples would be 10. Sample means from the smarter population would be, on average, 10 points higher than means from the other population—just as you'd expect.

Looking at the histogram in Figure 15.2, you see that there's quite a bit of variability among the differences. Differences greater than 4 points are not unusual. However, differences of more than 10 points are infrequent.

To compare the mean IQ of a sample of 20 students on the Dean's List and the mean of a sample of 20 students on academic probation, you need to see where the observed difference between the means falls in the distribution of differences. If you observe a difference of 10 points or more, you may not be willing to believe that the difference is due to the natural variability of means from the same population. You wouldn't often see a difference this large when two population means are equal. You may think that a more likely explanation for this large a difference is that two population means really are not equal.

Evaluating a Difference between Means

How can you decide when a difference between two means is big enough for you to believe that the two samples are from a population with different means? It depends on how willing you are to be wrong.

Look at Figure 15.3, which is the real distribution of differences for samples of size 20 from a distribution with a standard deviation of 15. (You can calculate the standard deviation of the distribution of differences. It's called the **standard error of the difference.**) Since the distribution is normal, you can find out what percentage of the samples falls into each of the intervals.

The scale on the distribution is marked with the actual values and with "standardized" values, which are computed by dividing the differences by the standard error. Looking at standardized distances is convenient, since the percentage of cases within a standardized distance from the mean is always the same. For example, 34% of all samples are between 0 and 1 standardized unit greater than the mean, and another 34% are between 0 and 1 standardized unit less than the mean. If you always express your distances in standardized units, you can use the same normal distribution for evaluating the likelihood of a particular difference.

Suppose the Dean's List students in your sample had a mean IQ of 112, and the academic probation students had a mean IQ of 105. The difference is 7. For samples of size 20 from a population with a standard deviation of 15, the standard error of the difference is 4.74. (Don't worry now about the calculations.) Since you observed a difference of 7 between your two groups, the standardized difference is simply 7 divided by 4.74,

Figure 15.3 Theoretical distribution of differences of means

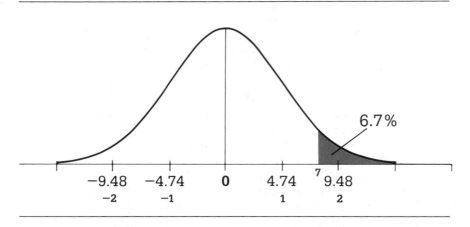

or 1.48. That is, your observed difference of 7 is about one and a half standard errors above the mean.

From Figure 15.3, you can see that about 13% of the time, you'd expect to have at least a 7-point IQ difference in the sample means when two population means are equal. Why? You just found out that the 7-point difference is 1.5 standard errors. Look on the figure to see what percentage of the differences are that big. You should look at the area to the right of +1.5 and the area to the left of −1.5. Since the distribution is symmetric, the two areas are equal. Each one is about 6.7% of the total, and together they make up a little over 13% of the total. So about 13% of differences in means are going to be as big as 1.5 standard errors (or 7 points of IQ score) if the real difference in means is zero.

Why the Entire Area?

You may wonder why you don't find the probability of getting a difference of just 7. Think of the following analogy. You're tired of being a poor student and have decided that the quickest (legal) way to upgrade your status is to marry rich. You settle on a definition of rich. Perhaps you need an income of $250,000 a year. Now you want to see how likely it is that you can achieve your goal. You go to the university library and ask the reference librarian to find some facts. Would you ask her to find just the number of eligible singles with incomes of $250,000? No, you'd ask for incomes of $250,000 or more, since they all satisfy your criterion of being rich. In evaluating your chances of marrying rich, you'd include all incomes of $250,000 or more. Similarly, when you're trying to decide whether 7 is a likely outcome for a difference, your interest is not just on the number 7 but on all differences that are at least that large.

The example referred to differences that were not only larger than +7 but also less than −7—differences at both sides of the distribution in Figure 15.3. Why include the area less than −7? The reason is that when you did your study, you had no idea of which of the two groups of students should have the higher mean IQ. It's certainly possible that brighter students may goof off more than average ones and increase their chances of winding up on probation. Or, of course, it's possible that brighter students may find making the Dean's List easier, so it's more likely that you'll find them there. You had no idea of the direction in which the difference might go.

Since both outcomes were possible, when you evaluate the chances of seeing a difference at least as large as 7 points, you have to look in both directions. Both of the extreme regions of the distribution are atypical.

Sometimes, though, you can look in just one direction. It really depends on how you stated your initial hypothesis. If you hypothesized that students on the Dean's List have higher scores than students on probation, you look at only one side of the distribution in Figure 15.3. This type of test is called a **one-tailed test.** The only possibility that would concern you is that Dean's List students do score higher. But if their scores turn out to be lower in your sample, you're out of luck. You can't switch sides and apply the one-tailed test for a difference that's in the other direction. Use a one-tailed test only if you definitely expect one specific group to be higher. Otherwise, use a **two-tailed test,** and look at both sides of the distribution.

Drawing a Conclusion

In the previous example, you saw that when there is no difference between the two population means, you expect to see sample differences bigger than +7 or less than -7 about 13% of the time. Generally, 5% or less is considered unusual. So the observed results aren't all that unlikely. They don't make it hard to believe the hypothesis that in the population, the mean IQ values of the two groups are equal.

? *Now that I've seen how to use the standard error of a difference in means, how do I compute it?* You take the square root of the variance of the difference. How do you get the variance of the difference? When you have two means from independent samples, the variance of their difference equals the sum of their variances. This neat little fact would take too long to prove here, but you can see how it's used. The example above had two means from independent samples of size 20, taken from a population whose standard deviation was 15. You calculate the standard error of the difference by following these steps:

1 As explained in Chapter 14, the standard error of each mean equals 15 (the standard deviation) divided by the square root of 20 (the sample size).

2 The variance of each mean is just the square of that fraction: 15 squared divided by 20. That's 225 divided by 20, or 11.25.

3 The variance of the difference between the means is the sum of the variances of each mean. That's 11.25 plus 11.25, or 22.5.

4 The standard error of the difference between the means is therefore the square root of 22.5, or 4.74.   ■ ■ ■

MORE ON HYPOTHESIS TESTING

In the previous example, you performed a statistical test of a hypothesis. You tested whether students on the Dean's List and students on academic probation have the same average IQ scores in the population. This was the basic procedure:

1 You wanted to draw conclusions about the population of students on the Dean's List or on probation. But you couldn't include all possible students, so you had to base your conclusions about the population on the results from the sample.

2 You calculated how likely it is that a difference as large as the one you observed would occur *if* there is no difference between the two means in the population.

3 Since there was a 13% chance that you could see a difference as large as the one you observed when there is no difference between the population means, the evidence was too skimpy to reject the hypothesis of no difference.

Why Is That So Complicated?

You're probably wondering why an admirably clear book like this has suddenly become garbled. Just listen to that last part again: "The evidence was too skimpy to reject the hypothesis of no difference." Why are we going around in circles? Why do we have to assume that there's no difference between the means in the population and then figure out how likely the observed results are if there is no difference? Why not just calculate the probability that there *is* a difference? That's what we really want to know, isn't it?

Although it sounds like a good idea, in this situation there's no way that you can calculate the probability that there is no difference. There either is a difference or there isn't a difference. If we have two *sample* means, say 11 and 12, what do they tell us about whether it's true that the two means in the population are different? Not much. The probability of getting two sample means that differ by at least 1 depends on how much of a difference there is in the population. It depends on whether the true difference is 0, 1, 2, 4, 100, or whatever. A difference of 1 may be very unlikely if the true difference is 100 but perfectly likely if the true difference is 0 or 2. But we don't know what the true difference is! We can only consider the likelihood of a value of 1 or more in relation to some hypothetical situation, such as a true difference of 0 or a true difference of 100. We can't assign the difference some overall probability.

What if you found that the two sample means were 11 and 11? Would you claim that it's certain the two means are exactly equal in the population? Would you be willing to forget the possibility that the population means might be 11 and 11.1? Of course not (I hope). You've seen that there's variability from sample to sample and that it's most unlikely for two sample means to be exactly equal even if the two means are equal in the population.

You simply can't figure out the probability that two population means are equal or unequal. You can, however, estimate the probability that you'd see a difference of at least 2 (or some other value) in the sample when there is no difference in the population (or when there is a difference of a particular size.) In the previous example, you saw the calculations for the probability that the means from two samples would differ by at least 7 when there is no difference in the population.

To test a hypothesis, you do the following:

1 State the hypothesis of interest. This is what you think is really true for the population. (Dean's List students and probation students differ in average IQ score. Excited people and unexcited people differ in average income and education.)

2 Determine the frame of reference you'll use to evaluate your hypothesis. This is what's true in the population if your hypothesis is wrong. This "frame of reference" is called the **null hypothesis,** since it describes the population when the hypothesis you're interested in is not true, when it's null. One null hypothesis is that Dean's List students and probation students have the same average IQ. Another is that excited and unexcited people do not differ in their average income and education.

3 Calculate the probability that you'd see a difference at least as large as the one you observed in your sample if the null hypothesis is true.

4 If this probability (called the **observed significance level**) is small, say less than .05, reject the null hypothesis.

5 If the observed significance level is large, do not reject the null hypothesis. This doesn't mean that you accept the null hypothesis. You simply do not reject it. You remain uncertain.

You must state the null hypothesis in such a way that you can calculate the distribution of sample means when it's true. You can't use a null hypothesis that says the population means are unequal, since there's no single distribution of sample means for that statement. But you can have a null hypothesis that says the difference between two population means is 5 or some other particular number. The null hypothesis must provide the reference point for calculating the probability of the observed results. You calculate the probability of the observed results *if* the null hypothesis is true.

T-TESTS

Let's consider another example of testing a hypothesis. Let's see if there's a difference in the average years of education for people who find life exciting and those who don't.

To simplify things while getting started, we'll just compare two groups. We'll combine the people who say that life is pretty routine with those who say it's dull and call them the *Not excited* group, in contrast with the *Excited* group. The SPSS^X jobs in the rest of this chapter will use this collapsed version of the variable LIFE.

Think of how we'd test the hypothesis that the two groups (Excited and Not excited) differ in the years of education they've had. In previous chapters, we've seen that age seems to be related to the way people feel about life. If we find that excited people are better educated than unexcited people, we'll have some difficulty in interpreting the results. In the United States today, people in their thirties have more education than people in their sixties. If excited people are better educated than unexcited people, that difference may just be due to a difference in age. (In this example, age may be an **intervening variable,** since it may come between the variables we're actually interested in, education and excitement. Age may explain a difference in education between the two excitement groups.)

We can minimize this problem by restricting the comparison to people in a particular age group. If we take people in their thirties and compare the years of education for the two excitement groups, we'll be controlling for age. That is, age will no longer affect the comparison as much. The results will be much easier to interpret.

The null hypothesis is that the excited people have the same average number of years of education as the unexcited people. The hypothesis of interest (sometimes called the **alternative hypothesis**) is that excited and unexcited people differ in average years of education.

Figure 15.4 contains the means and standard deviations for years of education in the two groups. (Later on, you'll see the job that produced these numbers.) There were 161 people in the age range 30–39 who found life exciting (labeled Group 1 in the figure). The average education for Group 1 is 14.17 years. The standard deviation is 2.76. Since the sample size is fairly large, the standard error is small, .22. (The 95% confidence interval for average years of education in Group 1 is from 13.8 to 14.6.) For Group 2, the people who found life routine or dull, the average education is 13.1 years. (The 95% confidence interval is 12.7 to 13.5.) The difference between the two averages is 1.07 years.

Figure 15.4 Statistics for the Excited and Not excited groups

```
FILE:      1984 General Social Survey

- - - - - - - - - - - - - - - T - T E S T- - - - - - - - - - - - - - - -

GROUP 1 - LIFE    EQ       1.
GROUP 2 - LIFE    EQ       2.


VARIABLE          NUMBER            STANDARD   STANDARD
                  OF CASES   MEAN   DEVIATION  ERROR
─────────────────────────────────────────────────────
EDUC      Highest year of school completed
          GROUP 1    161    14.1739    2.758    0.217

          GROUP 2    171    13.1053    2.718    0.208
─────────────────────────────────────────────────────
```

Using the *t*-Distribution

Now we have to answer the question, "How often would we expect to see a difference of 1.07 years in the sample when there's no difference between the two groups in the population?"

In Chapter 14, we always knew or pretended to know the standard deviation in the population. In fact, though, it usually must be estimated from the sample. When this is necessary—when we use the same sample both to test the hypothesis and to estimate the standard deviation in the population—we have to use the *t*-distribution instead of the normal distribution.

The *t*-distribution is very much like the normal distribution. It just shifts the area in the normal distribution to adjust for the fact that we don't know what the standard deviations really are. (When sample sizes are large, the *t*-distribution looks very much like the normal distribution.)

As always, we compute the difference between the two means, find its standard error, and then calculate how improbable the observed difference is. For example, our difference is 1.07 years, and its standard error is .30. By dividing the difference by its standard error, we compute its standardized score, 3.55. Then we calculate how often a standardized score of 3.55 or greater occurs when there is no difference between the two groups in the population.

Of course, we don't actually have to do any of the computations. Just type:

```
FILE HANDLE GSS  /  (system-specific information)
GET FILE = GSS
SELECT IF (AGE GE 30 AND AGE LE 39)
RECODE LIFE (3 = 2)
T-TEST GROUPS = LIFE(1, 2)  /  VARIABLES = EDUC
```

This generates the output shown in Figures 15.4 and 15.5.

Figure 15.5 A *t*-test for the difference between two means

FILE: 1984 General Social Survey

- - - - - - - - - - - - - - - T - T E S T- - - - - - - - - - - - - - - -

GROUP 1 - LIFE   EQ   1.
GROUP 2 - LIFE   EQ   2.

VARIABLE	NUMBER OF CASES	MEAN	STANDARD DEVIATION	STANDARD ERROR
EDUC Highest year of school completed				
GROUP 1	161	14.1739	2.758	0.217
GROUP 2	171	13.1053	2.718	0.208

		* POOLED VARIANCE ESTIMATE		* SEPARATE VARIANCE ESTIMATE		
F VALUE	2-TAIL PROB.	T VALUE	DEGREES OF FREEDOM	2-TAIL PROB.	T VALUE	DEGREES OF FREEDOM	2-TAIL PROB.
1.03	0.851	3.55	330	0.000	3.55	328.15	0.000

The first part of the output in Figure 15.5 should be familiar; it just shows statistics we've already seen. The numbers at the bottom, where it says POOLED VARIANCE ESTIMATE, contain the information we're after. In the column labeled T VALUE is the standardized score, 3.55, that was described above. The entry in the column labeled DEGREES OF FREEDOM is based on the number of observations in each of the two groups. (It's just the total number of observations minus two.) The **degrees of freedom** are used together with the *t*-value to determine how likely it is to get a score as big as 3.55 (or as small as -3.55) if the mean value of education for the two groups is the same in the population. You see this probability in the column labeled 2-TAIL PROB.

The probability given is 0.000. Does this show that the probability is zero? No. It means that the probability is less than 0.0005. In this procedure, SPSS[X] prints probabilities to only three decimal places. Anything less than 0.0005 is printed as 0.000.

This probability, the **observed significance level,** is very small. It therefore appears unlikely that the excited people in the population have the same amount of education as the unexcited people. We qualified this conclusion with "appears unlikely" not to be wishy-washy but because we can't be absolutely sure. It's possible, though very unlikely, that this sample came from a population in which there really is no difference. The probability that it did is less than 0.0005.

Two Types of Errors

There are two types of mistakes that you can make when testing a hypothesis about two means. You can claim that the two means are *not* equal in the population when in fact they are. Or you can fail to say that there's a difference when there really is one. Statisticians, being very methodical people, have given these two types of errors particularly descriptive, easy-to-remember names. They call the first error (claiming that two means are not equal when in fact they are) a *Type 1* error. No doubt you've deduced what to call the second type of error (not finding a difference when there is one): a *Type 2* error.

? *It may be easy to remember that you call the two kinds of error Type 1 and Type 2, but how do you remember which is which?* Perhaps you can remember it this way. The Type 1 error is the error you're tempted to make. When you say, proudly, "There *is* a difference. Something is happening here. I have found a relationship," you are taking the chance of making a Type 1 error.

If you can remember what the Type 1 error is, then it's pretty easy to figure out that the Type 2 error is the one you're not tempted to make, saying "Nothing is happening here" when there really is a difference in the population. ∎∎∎

Table 15.1 shows what can happen when testing a hypothesis. There may or may not be a difference in the population, and you may or may not find it. When you detect a difference that exists in the population, you're doing fine. When there is no difference in the population and you conclude, based on your sample, that there is no difference, all is well. The problems are in the remaining two cells of the table. We'll talk more about that later.

Table 15.1 What can happen when testing a hypothesis

		The real world:	
		The null hypothesis is really...	
		True	False
Your conclusion:			
You say the null	True	No problem	Type 2 error
hypothesis is...			
	False	Type 1 error	No problem

Output from the T-TEST Procedure

The computation of the *t*-test differs depending on whether you assume that in the population the two groups have the same variances or not. If you can assume that the two variances are equal, use the numbers in the columns labeled POOLED VARIANCE ESTIMATE. If you cannot assume that the two variances are equal, use the *t*-test labeled SEPARATE VARIANCE ESTIMATE.

The ratio of the variances in the two samples is shown in the column labeled F VALUE. It is 1.03. If this number is close to 1, the sample variances are similar. The larger the number, the more dissimilar the sample variances.

Next to the *F* value of 1.03, SPSS^X prints the probability that you would see a difference at least as large as the one observed in the sample if the variances are equal in the population and if the distribution of the variable is normal. (The *F*-test for equality of variances is quite sensitive to departures from normality, while the *t*-test is not. If the data are not from normal populations, the observed significance level for the *F* statistic may be unreliable.) If the observed significance level is large, there's little reason to worry about your variances. If the number is small, you should use the *t*-test marked SEPARATE VARIANCE ESTIMATE. In Figure 15.5, the probability of an *F* as large as 1.03—assuming equal variances in the population—is .851. So there is no reason to suspect that the population variances are different, and you can use the pooled-variance calculations for the *t*-test.

In general, it's a good idea to use the separate-variance *t*-test whenever you suspect that the variances are unequal.

INTERPRETING A T-TEST

Now that you have an idea of what happens when you test a hypothesis about two means, let's test one more hypothesis. Is there a difference in the average size of the households for excited people and unexcited people? Again, since older people often live in smaller households than people who are raising families, let's restrict the comparison to people in their thirties. The null hypothesis is that average household size for people who are excited by life is the same as that for people who are not. The alternative hypothesis is that average household size differs between the two groups.

The variable name in the General Social Survey for the question that asks how many people live in the household is HOMPOP. Type

```
FILE HANDLE GSS / (system-specific information)
GET FILE=GSS
SELECT IF (AGE GE 30 AND AGE LE 39)
RECODE LIFE (3 = 2)
T-TEST GROUPS = LIFE (1,2) / VARIABLES = HOMPOP
```

and you get the output shown in Figure 15.6.

Figure 15.6 Do excited people live in larger or smaller households?

```
FILE:    1984 General Social Survey
- - - - - - - - - - - - - - - -T - T E S T- - - - - - - - - - - - - - - -
GROUP 1 - LIFE     EQ      1.
GROUP 2 - LIFE     EQ      2.
```

VARIABLE	NUMBER OF CASES	MEAN	STANDARD DEVIATION	STANDARD ERROR
HOMPOP Number of people in household				
GROUP 1	161	3.2298	1.530	0.121
GROUP 2	171	3.3801	1.519	0.116

		* POOLED VARIANCE ESTIMATE			* SEPARATE VARIANCE ESTIMATE		
F VALUE	2-TAIL PROB.	* T VALUE	DEGREES OF FREEDOM	2-TAIL PROB.	* T VALUE	DEGREES OF FREEDOM	2-TAIL PROB.
1.01	0.926	-0.90	330	0.370	-0.90	328.50	0.370

The respondents who found life exciting (Group 1) had an average household size of 3.23 people, while the average household size for those who found life unexciting was 3.38. How likely is it to see a difference of this magnitude if, in fact, there is no difference in household size between the two groups in the population? Look at the pooled-variance t-test. The observed significance level associated with a t-value of $-.90$ is .37. This says that 37% of the time a difference of at least this size would occur when the two population means are equal. There doesn't seem to be much reason to believe that the means differ in the population.

You've probably noticed the hesitancy in this and the other conclusions. This one doesn't say that the two means are equal in the population. It hedges. It says there's no reason to doubt that the means are equal. There's a reason for being conclusion-shy. It's *impossible* to prove, based on samples, that two population means are exactly equal. What if the excited people in the population have a mean household size of 3.2500, and the unexcited people have a mean household size of 3.2501? Since sample means differ, and the statistical procedures for evaluating differences between means must allow for variability from sample to sample, we'll never be able to detect such a small difference in the population.

What does happen, instead, is that we take two samples, compute a t-test, and find a large observed significance level. Perhaps we find a probability of .50 that the t-value could be observed in a population with no difference. This large observed significance level doesn't tell us that the means are exactly equal. It just indicates that the results would not be "far out" if the two means are equal in the population. So instead of embracing the null hypothesis and claiming that it's true, we just say that we have no evidence to believe that it's not true. We can't *prove* the null hypothesis.

An Analogy: Coin Flips

Suppose someone comes up to you, hands you a coin, and says, "Tell me if this is a fair coin—a coin in which heads and tails are equally likely." If you had nothing better to do, you'd probably start flipping the coin and counting the number of times heads and tails occur.

You're no longer naive. You know that if you flip a fair coin 10 times, it's not often that you'll get exactly 5 heads and 5 tails. All sorts of outcomes are possible. There's even a reasonable chance that with a fair coin you'll get 8 tails and 2 heads, or 8 heads and 2 tails. The first histogram in Chapter 13 gives you an idea of the probability that you'd get an unusually high proportion of heads (or tails) in 400 flips of a fair coin. If the coin is really way off (say, it has 2 heads or 2 tails) you should be able to figure that out with 10 flips. The probability that you get all heads or all tails on 10 flips of a fair coin is 2/1024. So, if it always comes up the same, you can be pretty sure that it's rigged.

As the coin becomes less and less unfair, it gets harder and harder for you detect the difference. If the true probability of a head on the coin is 0.4999 instead of 0.5000, you'd never figure that out unless you're willing to spend the rest of your life coin flipping. Any combination of flips that you come up with will appear perfectly reasonable if the coin is fair or if it's minutely biased. Although you can disprove with a certain degree of confidence that a coin is fair, it's an impossible task to prove that it's exactly fair.

That's why we couldn't say we proved the average household sizes are the same in the two groups. All we could say is that there wasn't evidence to disprove it.

Observed Significance Levels

When your observed significance level is small, its interpretation is fairly straightforward: the two means seem to be unequal in the population. The observed significance level tells you the probability that the observed difference could be due to chance. The observed significance level is the probability that your sample could show a difference at least as large as the one that you observed, if the means are really equal.

? *So what is a small significance level?* Most of the time, significance levels are considered small if they're less than .05; sometimes, if they're less than .01. Rather than just rejecting or not rejecting the null hypothesis, look at the actual significance level as well. An observed significance level of .06 is not the same as an observed significance level of .92, though both may not be statistically significant. When reporting your results, give the exact observed significance level. It will help the reader evaluate your results. Treat the observed significance level as a guide to whether or not the difference could be due to chance alone.   ■ ■ ■

If your observed significance level is too large to reject the hypothesis that the means are equal, more than one explanation is possible.

The first explanation is that there may be no difference between the two means, or it may be so small that you just can't detect it. If the true difference is very small, it may not matter that you can't find it. Who really cares about a difference in household size of .001 or a difference in annual income of $10? Little, if anything, is lost by your failure to establish such tiny differences.

The second explanation is more troublesome: There is an important difference, and you can't find it. This can occur if the sample size is small. If you flip a coin only twice, you'll never be able to establish whether it's fair. A fair coin has a 50% chance of coming up heads twice or tails twice in two flips and a 50% chance of coming up with one of each. Any outcome that you see is consistent with the coin's being fair. As the number of flips increases, so does your ability to detect differences.

In the previous chapters, you saw how the distribution of means has less variability as sample size increases. To detect a small difference, you need a big sample so that the difference would clearly be outside the expected amount of sample variation.

The variability of the responses (in the population) also affects your ability to detect differences. If there's a lot of variability in the observations, the sample means will vary a lot as well. Even large differences in observed means can be attributed to variability among the samples.

To wrap up all of this: if you don't find evidence to reject the hypothesis that two means are equal in the population, one of two possibilities is true:

1 The means are equal or very similar.

2 The means are unequal, but you aren't able to detect the difference because of small sample size, large variability, or both.

Tails and Significance Tests

An observed significance level printed on the SPSS[X] *t*-test output is labeled 2-TAIL PROB., standing for *two-tailed probability*. This value tells you the probability that you'd see in *either direction* a difference at least as large as the one you observed when there's no difference in the population. Either the first group has a mean larger than the second group by at least the observed size, or the second group has a mean larger than the first group by at least the observed size.

If you don't know which of the two groups should have the larger mean, that's what you have to ask. It isn't obvious how household size, or even education, might be related to a feeling that life is exciting. There's no reason to believe that excited people should come from larger households than unexcited people. Similarly, the excited people need not be better educated than the unexcited people. It's perfectly reasonable to think that too much education may wear you down and make it harder to find life exciting. Or, of course, the opposite may be true. Differences in either direction cast doubt on the null hypothesis that in the population the two groups have the same means.

If you do know in advance which group will have the larger mean if they differ, then you use a one-tailed significance level.

Suppose you know that a new drug for insomnia will either leave the amount of time you need to fall asleep unchanged, or the drug will decrease it. You take two random samples of people and perform an experiment. One group gets the drug, and the other gets a placebo (a fake drug just to make the subjects think they're being treated). Then you find the average time it takes each group to fall asleep. You calculate the difference between the two means, along with its standard error. To find out how often you'd get a difference of this magnitude by chance when the drug and placebo are equally effective, you need only calculate the probability that you see a decrease at least as large as the one observed. You're confident that people treated with the drug won't take longer to fall asleep, so you decide in advance not even to test for that possibility.

Think back to the coin analogy. Suppose your friend tells you, as he is handing you the coin, that he suspects the coin is biased. Perhaps his wife always used it to settle disputes, and she always bet heads and won. You've got a pretty good suspicion that the coin is biased in favor of heads, and no reason at all to suspect bias in favor of tails. If you toss the coin 10 times, and it comes up all heads, you just want to know what the probability is that a fair coin comes up 10 heads out of 10 flips. You don't worry that it might have come up with 10 tails, since the only situations that will cause you to doubt your coin are excesses of heads.

If you know in advance which of two means should be larger, you can convert the two-tailed significance level to a one-tailed level. All you do is divide the two-tailed probability by two. The result tells you the percentage of the t-distribution in one of the tails.

THE HYPOTHESIS-TESTING PROCESS

In the previous example, we used a statistical technique called the t-test to test the hypothesis that two groups have the same mean in the population. We did the following:

1 For each of the groups, we calculated the mean of the variable we were interested in comparing.

2 We subtracted one mean from the other to determine the difference between the two.

3 We calculated a t statistic by dividing the difference of the two sample means by its standard error.

4 We calculated the observed significance level. This told us how often we'd expect to see a difference as large as the one we observed if there was no difference between the groups in the population.

5 If the observed significance level was small (less than .05), we rejected the hypothesis that the two means are equal in the population.

6 Otherwise, we didn't reject the null hypothesis, and we didn't accept it either. We remained undecided. That's because we didn't know whether there really was no difference in the means or whether our sample was simply too small to detect the difference.

This procedure is the same for tests of most hypotheses:

1 You formulate a null hypothesis and its alternative.

2 You calculate the probability of observing a difference of a particular magnitude in the sample when the null hypothesis is true.

3 If this probability (the observed significance level) is small enough, you reject the null hypothesis.

4 If the probability is not small enough, you remain undecided.

The only part of this ritual that changes for different situations is the actual statistic used to evaluate the probability of the observed difference. In the chapters that follow, we'll use different types of statistics to test these kinds of hypotheses:

- Variables are independent.
- Several groups have the same means.
- There is no linear relationship between several variables.

If you make sure now that you understand the way hypothesis testing works, the rest of this book will be easy.

Assumptions Needed

To perform a statistical test of a hypothesis, you must make certain assumptions about the data. The particular assumptions you must make depend on the statistical test you are using. Some procedures require stricter assumptions than others.

The assumptions are needed so that you (or your computer) can figure out what the distribution of the statistic is. Unless you know the distribution, you can't determine the correct significance levels. For the pooled-variance t-test, you need to assume that you have two random samples with the same population variance. You also need to assume that the distribution of the means is approximately normal, which can happen one of two ways. The variable itself is normally distributed, so the means will automatically be normally distributed. Or the sample size must be large enough so you can rely on the Central Limit Theorem to make sure the means are distributed normally.

Of course, some assumptions are more important than others. Moderate violation of some of them may not have very serious consequences. Therefore, it's important to know for each statistical procedure, not only what assumptions are needed but also how severely their violation may influence the results. We'll talk about these things when we discuss the different statistical procedures. For example, the F-test for equality of variances is quite sensitive to departures from normality. The t-test for equality of means is less so. (We talked about the F-test briefly above, and it will turn up again in Chapter 18.)

You should include tests of the assumptions as part of your hypothesis-testing procedure. Whenever possible, SPSS^X provides such tests.

MORE ABOUT THE T-TEST PROCEDURE

Using the SPSS^X T-TEST procedure, you can test the hypothesis that in the population, two independent groups have the same mean. You obtain:

- The number of cases, the mean, the standard deviation, and the standard error for each of the two groups.
- Two t-statistics for testing the hypothesis that two population means are equal, as well as their two-tailed observed significance levels. SPSS^X calculates one test based on the assumption that the two population variances are equal (the pooled-variance t-test) and the other test based on the assumption that the population variances are not equal (the separate-variance t-test).

To calculate a t-test for the hypothesis that the average age of men is the same as that of women, type:

```
T-TEST GROUPS = SEX(1,2) / VARIABLES = AGE
```

Following the keyword GROUPS, you give the name of the variable that's used to classify the cases into the two groups. The actual codes assigned to the two groups are given in parentheses. The specification GROUPS= SEX(1,2) tells the computer that the cases are to be split into two groups according to the values of the SEX variable. Cases with values of 1 for SEX go into one group, while cases with values of 2 go into the other. If there are cases with other values for the SEX variable, they're excluded from the analysis.

You can give only two distinct codes for the variable that's used to determine the groups. The codes can be any integers. For example, in the unlikely event that you had coded males as 10 and females as 8, you would type:

```
T-TEST GROUPS = SEX (8,10) / VARIABLES = AGE
```

After the word VARIABLES, give the name of the variable whose means are being compared. In the above example, the means of the AGE variable are compared for the groups coded 8 and 10 on SEX. If you want to compare the means of several variables, follow the word VARIABLES with a list of all of them. This variable list must follow the GROUPS subcommand.

WHAT'S NEXT?

This chapter explained the logic of hypothesis testing by discussing *t*-tests. But all the *t*-tests we looked at involved cases from completely separate groups. We compared the mean for one group of people against the mean for another group of people. Sometimes, though, we want to compare means that aren't independent in this way. The next chapter shows how you can use *t*-tests for the new type of comparison.

Summary

Based on the means observed in two independent samples, how can you test the hypothesis that two population means are equal?

To test the null hypothesis that two population mean are equal, you must calculate the probability of seeing a difference at least as large as the one you've observed in your two samples, if there is no difference in the population.

The hypothesis that there is no difference between the two population means is called the *null hypothesis*.

The probability of seeing a difference at least as large as the one you've observed, when the null hypothesis is true, is called the *observed significance level*.

If the observed significance level is small, usually less than .05, you reject the null hypothesis.

If you reject the null hypothesis when it's true, you make a Type 1 error. If you don't reject the null hypothesis when it's false, you make a Type 2 error.

The *t*-test is used to test the hypothesis that two population means are equal.

EXERCISES

Syntax

1 You type in the command

```
T-TEST VARIABLES=WEIGHT/GROUPS=SEX(1,2)
```

and get the following error message:

```
>ERROR  11820  LINE   3, COLUMN 17, TEXT: =
>An illegal keyword is used on the T-TEST command.  Valid keywords are  GROUPS,
>VARIABLES, and PAIRS.
>THIS COMMAND NOT EXECUTED.
```

Explain what caused this error and write the correct command.

2 You want to see whether there is a difference in the weight of infants whose mothers received a new type of vitamin and those whose mothers did not. The old-vitamin receivers are coded 0 and the new-vitamin receivers are coded 1. The variable name for the weight in grams is WEIGHT. Write the command to perform a t-test to test the hypothesis that there is no difference in weight between the two groups.

3 What if the two groups were coded 1 and 2? How would your command change?

4 What if you were giving two dosages of both the old and new vitamin so that you have four codes for the variable TREAT: 1=old vitamin, low dose; 2=old vitamin, high dose; 3=new vitamin, low dose; 4=new vitamin, high dose. Write the commands necessary to perform a t-test for a comparison of the new vitamin (both doses combined) to the old vitamin (both doses combined).

5 Correct the following commands if necessary:

    a. `TEST groups=sales(0,1)/var=income`

    b. `T-TEST groups=employ(7,9)/ dep=age`

    c. `T-TEST gr=employ(7,9,8)/va=children`

    d. `T-TEST variable=eggs/groups=Feed(12,19)`

    e. `T-TEST groups=sex(1,2) race (1,4)/var=reslengt`

Statistical Concepts

1 You think that Republicans earn more money than Democrats. To test this you take a random sample of 100 Democrats and 100 Republicans and record their earned income.

    a. What is the null hypothesis that you want to test?

    b. What is the alternative hypothesis?

2 You run a two-sample t-test using the SPSS^X T-TEST procedure. The output is shown below. Write a short paragraph summarizing your conclusions. (Group 1 is Democrats, Group 2 is Republicans.)

```
- - - - - - - - - - - - - - - - T - T E S T- - - - - - - - - - - - - - - - - -

GROUP 1 - PARTYID   EQ        1.
GROUP 2 - PARTYID   EQ        2.

VARIABLE           NUMBER                STANDARD   STANDARD
                   OF CASES     MEAN     DEVIATION    ERROR
------------------------------------------------------------------------
INCOME    Family income in thousands
      GROUP 1      100       23.8300      20.396      2.040

      GROUP 2      100       31.2750      21.303      2.130


------------------------------------------------------------------------
                   * POOLED VARIANCE ESTIMATE * SEPARATE VARIANCE ESTIMATE
                   *                           *
     F    2-TAIL   *    T   DEGREES OF 2-TAIL  *   T   DEGREES OF 2-TAIL
   VALUE  PROB.    *  VALUE   FREEDOM   PROB.   * VALUE   FREEDOM   PROB.
------------------------------------------------------------------------
   1.09   0.666    * -2.52     198     0.012    * -2.52   197.63    0.012
------------------------------------------------------------------------
```

3 Answer the following questions based on the preceding output.

  a. Have you proved that in the population Democrats and Republicans have exactly the same income? Explain.

  b. Have you proved that in the population Democrats and Republicans don't have the same income? Explain.

  c. How often would you expect to see a difference at least as large as the one you observed if the null hypothesis is true?

4 What if you had obtained the following results? Summarize your conclusions.

```
- - - - - - - - - - - - - - - - T - T E S T- - - - - - - - - - - - - - - - - -

GROUP 1 - PARTYID   EQ        1.
GROUP 2 - PARTYID   EQ        2.

VARIABLE           NUMBER                STANDARD   STANDARD
                   OF CASES     MEAN     DEVIATION    ERROR
------------------------------------------------------------------------
INCOME    Family income in thousands
      GROUP 1      100       23.8300      20.396      2.040

      GROUP 2      100       27.2750      21.303      2.130


------------------------------------------------------------------------
                   * POOLED VARIANCE ESTIMATE * SEPARATE VARIANCE ESTIMATE
                   *                           *
     F    2-TAIL   *    T   DEGREES OF 2-TAIL  *   T   DEGREES OF 2-TAIL
   VALUE  PROB.    *  VALUE   FREEDOM   PROB.   * VALUE   FREEDOM   PROB.
------------------------------------------------------------------------
   1.09   0.666    * -1.17     198     0.244    * -1.17   197.63    0.244
------------------------------------------------------------------------
```

5 Discuss whether the following statement is true or false, and why: "The observed significance level tells you the probability that the null hypothesis is true."

6 Discuss whether the following statement is true or false, and why: "The observed significance level tells you the probability that the null hypothesis is false."

7 The following table is the output from an independent samples *t*-test. Fill in the missing information and interpret the results.

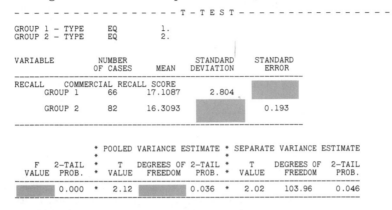

```
- - - - - - - - - - - - - - - - - T - T E S T - - - - - - - - - - - - - - - -

GROUP 1 - TYPE    EQ      1.
GROUP 2 - TYPE    EQ      2.


VARIABLE           NUMBER             STANDARD    STANDARD
                   OF CASES   MEAN    DEVIATION    ERROR
_____
RECALL    COMMERCIAL RECALL SCORE
       GROUP 1       66    17.1087    2.804

       GROUP 2       82    16.3093                 0.193
_____
```

```
                  * POOLED VARIANCE ESTIMATE * SEPARATE VARIANCE ESTIMATE
                  *                           *
     F    2-TAIL  *   T    DEGREES OF 2-TAIL  *   T    DEGREES OF 2-TAIL
  VALUE   PROB.   * VALUE   FREEDOM   PROB.   * VALUE   FREEDOM   PROB.
_____
          0.000   *  2.12              0.036  *  2.02   103.96   0.046
_____
```

8 Assume that the observed significance level for the test of the null hypothesis that two groups have the same alcohol intake is .0005. Is there a possibility that the two population means are really equal? Explain.

9 Assume for question 8 that the observed significance level is .75. Is there a possibility that the two population means are really unequal? Explain.

10 A market research analyst is studying whether men and women find the same types of cars desirable. He asks 150 men and 75 women to indicate which one of the following types of cars they would be most likely to buy: two-door with trunk; two-door with hatchback; convertible; four-door with trunk; four-door with hatchback; or station wagon. Each of the possible responses is assigned a code number. The analyst runs a t-test and finds that the average value for males and females appears to differ (p=.008). He doesn't know how to interpret his output, so he comes to you for advice. Explain to him what his results mean.

11 You are interested in whether average family income differs for people who find life exciting and for those who don't. You take a sample of people at a local museum on Sunday afternoon and find that there is a $5,000 difference in income between the two groups. You do a t-test and find the observed significance level to be .03.

    Your friend is also studying the same problem. She takes a sample of people in a department store on Saturday afternoon. She finds a $10,000 difference in family income between the two groups. But when she does a t-test, and finds an observed significance level of .2.

    Discuss these studies, their shortcomings, and possible reasons for the contradictory results.

12 You're doing a door-to-door survey. Some people won't let you in. Others are not at home. You don't let this bother you; all you do is go to more houses to get the total sample size you want. Discuss possible problems with your approach and ways you might overcome them.

Data Analysis

1 You think that people who believe in life after death have less education than people who do not.

  a. State the null hypothesis that you will be testing.

  b. Perform the appropriate statistical analysis to test the null hypothesis.

  c. Write a brief paragraph summarizing your results.

2 Make a crosstabulation of the highest degree received by a person and whether the person believes in an afterlife or not. Be sure to calculate the appropriate percentages. How do the results of this analysis compare to those you obtained in question 1?

3 Using the SELECT IF command described in Chapter 12, make histograms of years of education for people who do believe in life after death and those who don't. Compare the two distributions.

4 Test the null hypothesis that the average age in the population is the same for people who believe in life after death and for people who don't. Write a paragraph summarizing your results.

5 Test the null hypothesis that the average age at which males and females get married is the same. Summarize your results.

16 Testing Hypotheses about Two Dependent Means

Based on the means observed in two related samples, how can you test the null hypothesis that in the population there is no difference between the means?

- What are paired experimental designs, and what are their advantages?
- What types of problems can occur when you use paired designs?
- How must you arrange the data file for a paired design?
- What is a paired t-test?
- What assumptions do you need to use the paired t-test?
- If a difference is statistically significant, does that mean it is important?

In the previous chapter, you looked at tests of two null hypotheses: people who find life exciting have the same amount of education, on average, as people who find life routine or dull, and these two groups come from households that are the same average size. Testing the hypotheses involved two distinct groups of cases: those with responses of Exciting and those with responses of Pretty routine or Dull. A case was a member of either one group or the other. It couldn't belong to both. In such situations, the two groups are called **independent,** and the t-tests you calculate are sometimes called **independent-sample** t-tests, since they are used only when there is no relationship between the cases in the two groups.

But sometimes the groups you want to compare are related in some important way. There is a special way of dealing with these situations statistically.

PAIRED DESIGNS

Suppose you're studying whether a new treatment for insomnia is effective. You record how long it takes subjects to fall asleep when they're not taking the drug and again how long it takes the same subjects to fall asleep when they are taking the drug. Or you may be studying father-and-son pairs and want to find out whether the fathers' caloric intake differs from the sons'. Or you may want to know whether there is a difference between husbands and wives in average hours worked around the house.

All of these study designs involve *pairs* of observations. In the insomnia study, a pair consists of the same case before and after treatment. In the math study, a pair consists of father and son. In the comparison of hours of work, a pair consists of husband and wife.

Designs in which the same subject is observed under two different conditions or the members of two groups are matched in some way are called **paired-sample** or **correlated-sample** designs. Each subject in one group has a corresponding subject in the other group. Often, the corresponding subject is the very same person. In any event, the members of the groups form pairs.

Advantages of Comparing Subjects in Pairs

You might wonder why anyone would want to use designs like these. Why not take two groups of subjects, give one the drug and the other the placebo, and see if the means are significantly different? Instead of studying couples, why not just take a sample of married men and married women and not worry about who's married to whom? To answer that question, think about possible explanations for why two sample means can be unequal. One obvious reason is that there is a difference between the population means. Another possible reason is just that the people in the two samples are different.

For example, people suffer from insomnia in varying degrees. One person may take two hours to fall asleep without a drug, and another person may have to toss and turn for five hours before falling asleep. When you select two random samples of insomniacs with the intention of giving placebos to one group and the new drug to the other, you have no assurance that the two groups are comparable. They might differ in severity of insomnia or suggestibility. If your placebo group happens to contain the more severe sufferers, the drug may appear to have an effect even though it's actually no more effective than the placebo. Why? Because the people who received the drug were better off to start with.

How can you make your two groups as similar as possible so that observed differences are more likely due to the treatment rather than the random variation between the two groups? One possibility is to use the same individual twice. You can give each person the placebo one time and the new drug another time. That way, you eliminate some of the differences between people from your comparison. You *control* for variables such as severity of insomnia, suggestibility, sex, age, and so on. The placebo and the treatment groups are as similar as possible: they're the same people!

Consider the study comparing caloric intake in fathers and sons. Suppose you select two independent groups of men: men who are fathers of high school students and men who are high school students themselves. You don't match fathers and sons, you just have a bunch of fathers and a bunch of sons. If you find differences between the two groups, there are many possible explanations. Suppose one group is richer than the other, and socioeconomic level is related to caloric intake. You'll find differences between the groups that have nothing to do with the father-son distinction you're interested in.

If you select father-son pairs, on the other hand, then you can eliminate some of the differences. For example, a father and son will probably be of the same socioeconomic level. Some possible explanations for the observed differences will be eliminated or at least minimized.

? *When comparing two treatments in an experiment, is it always better to form pairs of similar subjects (or to observe the same subject under both conditions) than to use two independent groups?* No. Paired experimental designs are only useful when you can form pairs on the basis of a variable that's related to the one you're studying. If you pair your subjects based on shoe size when you're studying responses to a new drug, the paired design actually makes it *less* likely that you can identify a true difference when it exists. The two members of a pair are not alike in any way that matters. In this case, using a paired *t*-test makes it more difficult, statistically, to detect true differences than just treating the two groups as independent samples.   ■ ■ ■

Some Possible Problems

A paired design is a good way to eliminate some of the differences between subjects in two groups, so you can focus on the particular difference that you're testing. But you need to keep some things in mind:

- If the effect of a treatment does not wear off quickly, you must make sure that enough time passes between treatments so that one wears off before another begins. Otherwise, you won't know whether the first or the second treatment is causing the results during the second observation.
- You should also be aware of the learning effect. You encounter it when a subject's response improves merely by doing the same thing again. For example, if you give subjects the same test twice, they may do better the second time, regardless of what else has happened.

You must pay attention to both the timing and the sequence of administering the treatments. You may also want to include a control group for which you obtain measurements but that doesn't receive any treatment at all.

Paired Data and the Computer

When you have paired samples, information from both members of each pair must be together in the data file. The case is the pair of responses, not the individual person. For example, if you're comparing husbands' with wives' education, you have two variables, one for the husbands and one for the wives. The variables have different variable names, such as HUSED and WIFED. If each subject gets two treatments, you have two variables for each subject, say PLACEBO for the length of time to fall asleep when the placebo is administered and NEWTREAT for the length of time to fall asleep when the drug is administered. Your paired data might look like this:

PLACEBO   NEWTREAT
2.4   1.0
1.8   4.6

This arrangement differs from a design using independent groups. You still have two variables for each case, but one variable contains the response, and the other identifies the group to which each case belongs. Suppose you have two groups of subjects: one received the placebo, and the other received the new treatment. The variable you measured might be called TIME, representing the length of time it took for the subject to fall asleep. You would also have a variable called, say, GROUP, which might be coded 1 if the subject received the placebo and 2 if the subject received the new treatment. Each person is represented only once in the file, because each received either the drug or the placebo, not both. The data for the independent groups design might look like this:

GROUP	TIME
1	2.4
2	1.0
1	1.8
2	4.6

? *Why do you have to set up the file differently just because your subjects are paired? Couldn't the people who designed SPSS^X have let you use the same setup either way?* Actually, the way it's done makes sense. In a paired design, you have to know for each individual:

1 Which group the individual is in.

2 The other member of the pair.

3 The value of the variable or score you're comparing.

If you set up a file with each individual as a separate case, you'd need three variables to keep track of these things. By setting up a file with cases representing the pairs, you need only half as many cases, and you need only two variables. There's no magic here. In a file of pairs, the two variable names tell you which value goes with which "group," and they're paired with one another simply by being part of the same case. That's just a better way of representing the same information. ■ ■ ■

ANALYZING PAIRED DESIGNS

When you have paired data, you test hypotheses basically in the same way as when you have two independent groups. The only thing that changes is how you compute the t statistic. For each pair, you find the difference between the two values. Then you analyze these differences.

The Paired *t*-Test

The General Social Survey contains information about years of education for both the person interviewed and his or her spouse. Let's test the null hypothesis that there is no difference in years of education between husbands and wives. This is a paired-samples design, since we have husbands and wives that match (or at least matched themselves). In the data file, we have to construct two variables that describe each couple. We have to set up the HUSED and WIFED variables ourselves, since sometimes the husband was the respondent, and sometimes he was the spouse. It wouldn't make a lot of sense to test respondent's education versus spouse's education; one of the two was chosen randomly to be the respondent.

To do a paired *t*-test using SPSS^X, type:

```
FILE HANDLE GSS / (system-specific information)
GET FILE=GSS
COMMENT Now set up HUSED and WIFED according to sex of respondent
IF (SEX EQ 1) HUSED=EDUC
IF (SEX EQ 1) WIFED=SPEDUC
IF (SEX EQ 2) WIFED=EDUC
IF (SEX EQ 2) HUSED=SPEDUC
VARIABLE LABELS HUSED "Husband's education"
               WIFED "Wife's education"
T-TEST PAIRS=HUSED WIFED
```

The COMMENT command is followed by any explanation you want; it doesn't affect the job at all. The PAIRS subcommand tells SPSS^X that you have a paired design. The names of the two variables that contain the information for each pair follow the keyword PAIRS.

Look at Figure 16.1, which shows the output from this *t*-test. You can see that the wives had an average of 12.42 years of education, while the husbands had an average of 12.53. On the average, these husbands had about .11 more years of education than their mates. This is shown in the column labeled (DIFFERENCE) MEAN. The standard deviation of the 822 differences is 2.669. The standard error of the difference is .093. The *t* value, printed in the last set of columns, is obtained by dividing the difference between the two means by its standard error: −.1095 divided

Figure 16.1 Paired *t*-test for years of education

FILE: 1984 General Social Survey

- - - - - - - - - - - - - - - - T - T E S T- - - - - - - - - - - - - - - - -

VARIABLE	NUMBER OF CASES	MEAN	STANDARD DEVIATION	STANDARD ERROR
WIFED	Wife's education			
	822	12.4197	2.679	0.093
	822	12.5292	3.417	0.119
HUSED	Husband's education			

(DIFFERENCE) MEAN	STANDARD DEVIATION	STANDARD ERROR	* CORR.	2-TAIL * PROB. *	T VALUE	DEGREES OF FREEDOM	2-TAIL PROB.
−0.1095	2.669	0.093	* 0.641	0.000 *	−1.18	821	0.240

by .093 equals −1.18. The degrees of freedom used in calculating the observed significance level are just the number of *pairs* of cases minus one.

In this specific example, you see that the probability is .240 of obtaining a difference as large as this one if you took a sample of 822 pairs from a population in which there was no difference. Since this probability, the observed significance level, is fairly large, you don't have enough evidence to reject the null hypothesis.

The Confidence Interval for a Difference

As explained in the last few chapters, it's a good idea to calculate confidence intervals for means and differences of means. Confidence intervals give you an idea of the range of values within which the population value may fall. The 95% confidence interval for the average difference in years of education between husbands and wives is from −.29 to +.07.

Where did those numbers come from? They don't appear on the output, but you can calculate them easily, as shown in Chapter 14. To refresh your memory, here's how it works:

- The mean is −.11.
- The standard error is .09, so twice the standard error is .18. Remember that 95% of the time, the sample mean will be within two standard errors of the population mean.
- Therefore, the bottom end of the confidence interval is −.11 − .18 = −.29, and the top end of the confidence interval is −.11 + .18 = +.07.

That's all there is to it.   ■ ■ ■

The confidence interval includes 0. This tells you the same thing that the hypothesis test did. Namely, it's not unlikely that the true value for the difference is zero. There's a close relationship between hypothesis tests and confidence intervals:

- If you take any value within a 95% confidence interval and test the null hypothesis that it is the population value, you will not reject the null hypothesis. Your observed significance level will be greater than .05.
- If a value is outside of the 95% confidence interval, then your hypothesis test will find it to be an unlikely value as well. You will reject the null hypothesis that it's likely to be the population value. The observed significance level will be less than .05.

When you don't know the population standard deviation and your sample sizes are small (less than 30), you must use a value from the t-distribution instead of just multiplying the standard error by 2 to get the confidence interval.

Assumptions

Remember that in the independent-samples t-test output, there were two different tests. You used the pooled-variance test when it was reasonable to assume that the variances were the same for the two groups. You used the separate-variance test when you had reason to doubt that the groups had the same variances.

For the paired t-test, you don't have to make any assumptions about the variances of the original variables. For each pair, you compute the difference between the husband's and wife's education. It doesn't matter what the standard deviations of the original variables are, because you analyze just the differences.

For the paired-samples t-test, just as for the independent-samples t-test, it's essential for the observations to be a random sample from the population. It's also a good idea to look at the distribution of the differences. If the distribution looks more or less normal, you don't have to worry about anything. However, if the sample size is small, and the distribution is very far from normal, the t-test may not be a good way to test the hypothesis you're interested in.

Remember, if the variables are normal, their means and the differences of their means will be normally distributed. If the variables are not normal, you have to rely on the Central Limit Theorem, and that may require larger samples. If you have a small sample *and* the distribution of the variables isn't normal, you may have to use a **nonparametric test.** That's a type of test that doesn't require assumptions about the form of the distribution. SPSS^X provides nonparametric tests, but this book doesn't cover them.

Figure 16.2 is a histogram of the differences between husbands' and wives' average years of education. The distribution looks fairly symmetric, but it has a very large peak at 0. Why? Most men and women in the sample were high school graduates. It's quite likely that their spouses were high school graduates as well. There were also a lot of couples in which both the husband and the wife were college graduates. So there were a *lot* of cases in which the years of education matched perfectly. Since the sample size is large, and the distribution differs from normal only in having a very high peak, you can be pretty confident that the distribution of sample means is approximately normal.

Figure 16.2 Histogram for differences in education

```
DIFF
      COUNT     VALUE    ONE SYMBOL EQUALS APPROXIMATELY  8.00 OCCURRENCES

          1    -12.00
          1    -11.00
          1    -10.00
          1     -9.00
          3     -8.00
          5     -7.00    *
         11     -6.00    *
         11     -5.00    *
         37     -4.00    *****
         40     -3.00    *****
         68     -2.00    *********
         90     -1.00    **********
        258       .00    ********************************
         71      1.00    *********
         93      2.00    ***********
         50      3.00    ******
         46      4.00    ******
         12      5.00    **
         13      6.00    **
          3      7.00
          7      8.00    *
                         I........I........I........I........I........I
                         0        80      160      240      320      400
                                       HISTOGRAM FREQUENCY

VALID CASES    822     MISSING CASES    651
```

Education and Excitement

Although there is no overall difference in the average years of education for husbands and wives, let's see if this is true both for people who find life exciting and for those who find life routine or dull. Perhaps unexcited people differ from their spouses in some important way.

Since men and women may differ in their responses, we'll take that into consideration as well. Let's first look at men who classify their lives as exciting and see how they compare in education to their wives. Figure 16.3 shows a test of the hypothesis that men who find life exciting have the same average number of years of education as their wives. The following commands produced the test:

```
FILE HANDLE GSS / (system-specific information)
GET FILE=GSS
SELECT IF (LIFE EQ 1 AND SEX EQ 1)
COMMENT    Simplify calculation here, since we have selected men
           only.
COMPUTE HUSED = EDUC
COMPUTE WIFED = SPEDUC
VARIABLE LABELS HUSED "Husband's education"
                WIFED "Wife's education"
T-TEST PAIRS = WIFED HUSED
```

Figure 16.3 Paired *t*-test for men excited by life

```
FILE:      1984 General Social Survey

- - - - - - - - - - - - - - - T - T E S T- - - - - - - - - - - - - - - -

VARIABLE    NUMBER                 STANDARD    STANDARD
            OF CASES      MEAN     DEVIATION   ERROR

WIFED       Wife's education
               182       12.6484     2.767      0.205

               182       13.1429     3.693      0.274
HUSED       Husband's education
```

(DIFFERENCE) MEAN	STANDARD DEVIATION	STANDARD ERROR	* *	2-TAIL CORR. PROB.	* *	T VALUE	DEGREES OF FREEDOM	2-TAIL PROB.
−0.4945	2.627	0.195	*	0.704 0.000	*	−2.54	181	0.012

The average years of education for the wives was 12.65, while for their husbands it was 13.14. On the average, men who characterized their lives as exciting had about half a year of education more than their wives. The observed significance level for the test of the hypothesis that there is no difference is .012. We can reject the null hypothesis that men who find life exciting have the same average level of education as their wives. It looks as if these men are married to somewhat less educated women, although the difference is not very large.

Let's see if the same holds true for men who are not excited by life. These results are shown in Figure 16.4, and they were produced by the following commands:

```
FILE HANDLE GSS  /  (system-specific information)
GET FILE=GSS
SELECT IF (LIFE GE 2 AND SEX EQ 1)
COMMENT   Simplify calculation here, since we have selected men
only.
COMPUTE HUSED = EDUC
COMPUTE WIFED = SPEDUC
VARIABLE LABELS HUSED "Husband's education"
                WIFED "Wife's education"
T-TEST PAIRS = WIFED HUSED
```

The wives had an average of 12.11 years of education. The husbands had an average of 12.00 years of education. The observed significance level associated with this difference is .602, so we don't reject the null hypothesis that men who find life routine or dull have the same average level of education as their wives.

Figure 16.4 Paired *t*-test for men unexcited by life

```
FILE:     1984 General Social Survey

- - - - - - - - - - - - - - - - T - T E S T - - - - - - - - - - - - - - - - -

VARIABLE    NUMBER                STANDARD   STANDARD
            OF CASES     MEAN     DEVIATION    ERROR
------------------------------------------------------------
WIFED       Wife's education
               173      12.1098     2.792     0.212

               173      12.0000     3.331     0.253
HUSED       Husband's education
------------------------------------------------------------


(DIFFERENCE) STANDARD   STANDARD   *   2-TAIL  *    T     DEGREES OF  2-TAIL
   MEAN      DEVIATION    ERROR    * CORR. PROB. * VALUE    FREEDOM    PROB.
------------------------------------------------------------------------------
   0.1098     2.763       0.210    * 0.605 0.000 *  0.52      172      0.602
------------------------------------------------------------------------------
```

Looking at the means in the previous analyses, you see what you've seen before. The biggest difference between any of the means is for the actual years of education of married men who found life exciting, compared to those who didn't. Married men who found life exciting had an average of 13.14 years of education, while married men who found life unexciting had an average of 12.00.

SIGNIFICANCE VERSUS IMPORTANCE

What does it mean if you reject the null hypothesis that two population means are equal? Does it mean that there's an important difference between the two groups? Not necessarily. Whether a difference of half a year of education between two groups is found to be statistically significant or not depends on several factors. It depends on the variability in the two groups, and it depends on the sample sizes.

A difference can be statistically significant with a sample size of 100, while the same difference would not be significant with a sample size of 50. The difference between the two sample means is the same, half a year, but its statistical interpretation differs. For large sample sizes, small differences between groups may be statistically significant, while for small sample sizes, even large differences may not be.

What can you make of this? Finding that a difference is *statistically significant* does not mean that the difference is *large*, nor does it mean that the difference is *important* from a research point of view.

For sufficiently large sample sizes, you might find that a difference of even a month in education between excited men and unexcited men is statistically significant. That doesn't mean that the difference is of any practical importance. We all know that on the average, an extra month of education won't do much for you. It's unlikely to alter your perception of the world. It probably does little to enhance your ability to explain why some people find life exciting and others don't.

On the other hand, if the sample sizes in the two groups are small, even a difference of four years of education may not appear to be statistically significant. In this case, you don't want to rule out education as an important variable. Instead, you must worry about the fact that with small sample sizes you can miss important differences. You must allow yourself the possibility that there might be a big difference, because your ability to find it is poor.

(The probability of detecting a difference of a particular magnitude when it exists is called the **power** of a test. You can estimate in advance how big a sample you need to detect a difference that you consider really important. Discussion of how that's done is a little beyond this book.)

In summary, remember that even though two groups are statistically found to be different, their difference is not necessarily of practical importance. Evaluate the difference on its own merits.

MORE ABOUT PAIRED T-TESTS

You can use T-TEST to compare two means from:

- Independent groups, as discussed in Chapter 15.
- Paired data, as discussed in this chapter.

A typical application of a paired-samples test is the comparison of scores before and after an experimental procedure. To obtain a paired-samples *t*-test, use the PAIRS subcommand to indicate the two variables being compared, as in:

```
T-TEST PAIRS = BEFORE AFTER
```

More than Two Variables

If you list more than two variables on the PAIRS subcommand, each variable is compared with every other variable. For example, if you specify

```
T-TEST PAIRS = SON DAD MOM
```

the following are compared: SON with DAD, SON with MOM, and DAD with MOM.

If you have several variables that you've measured at two times, for example before and after a treatment, you can use the keyword WITH and Option 5 to request that each variable before the WITH be compared with the corresponding variable after the WITH. The commands

```
T-TEST PAIRS = WEIGHT1 BP1 ANXIETY1 WITH WEIGHT2 BP2 ANXIETY2
OPTIONS 5
```

compare WEIGHT1 with WEIGHT2, BP1 with BP2, and ANXIETY1 with ANXIETY2. If you use the WITH keyword without Option 5, each variable before the WITH is compared with each variable after the WITH. In the previous example, that would be nine comparisons in all.

Options for T-TEST

The following options are available in the T-TEST procedure:

1 Include user-missing values in the analysis
2 Exclude cases that have missing values
3 Suppress variable labels
4 Print output with an 80-character width
5 Compare variables before and after WITH pairwise

WHAT'S NEXT?

In the two previous chapters, we've discussed ways to test the null hypothesis that two population means are equal. In the next chapter, we'll look at variables that have a limited number of categories, and we'll consider how to test whether the two variables are independent.

Summary

Based on the means observed in two related samples, how can you test the null hypothesis that in the population there is no difference between the means?

In a paired design, the same subject is observed under two conditions, or data are obtained from a pair of subjects that have been matched on some basis.

Paired designs help to make the two groups being compared more similar. Some of the differences between subjects are eliminated.

If you observe the same subject under two conditions, you must make sure that the effect of one treatment has worn off before the other one is given.

In your data file, you must record the values for both members of a pair in the same case

You can compare two related means using a paired-sample *t*-test.

A statistically significant difference need not be large or important.

EXERCISES

Syntax

1 You've done a study in which you measured learning time in rats before and after administration of a memory improvement drug. Each of the rats ran through the maze twice: before and after the drug was administered. How would you arrange your data in the file? What values would you record for each case?

a. Write the DATA LIST command for your file.

b. Write the appropriate T-TEST command for the test of the hypothesis that there is no difference in learning times.

2 Suppose that instead of studying the same rats under two conditions, you had two groups of rats. One received the agent, and the other did not. How would you arrange your data file? How does this arrangement differ from that in question 1? Write the appropriate T-TEST command to test the null hypothesis that the new agent has no effect.

3 You run the following command to perform a paired t-test:

```
T-TEST  VARIABLES=BEFORE AFTER
```

You receive this error message:

```
>ERROR  11820  LINE   4, COLUMN 18, TEXT: =
>An illegal keyword is used on the T-TEST command.  Valid keywords are GROUPS,
>VARIABLES, and PAIRS.
>THIS COMMAND NOT EXECUTED.
```

Identify and correct the problem.

4 Where necessary, correct the following commands:

a. TTEST GROUPS = BEFORE AFTER

b. TTEST PAIRS = BEFORE

c. T-TEST GROUPS = SEX(0,1) / PAIRS = BEFORE AFTER

d. T-TEST VARS = TREAT1 TREAT2 / GROUPS = EDUC(1,2)

Statistical Concepts

1 For the following experimental designs, indicate whether an independent-samples or paired t-test is appropriate:

a. Weight is obtained for each subject before and after Dr. Nogani's new treatment. The hypothesis to be tested is that the treatment has no effect on weight loss.

b. The Jenkins Activity Survey is administered to 20 couples. The hypothesis to be tested is that husbands' and wives' scores do not differ.

c. Elephants are randomly selected from a jungle and Trunkgro1 is administered to one group of elephants and Trunkgro2 to the other. The hypothesis to be tested is that both agents are equally effective in promoting trunk growth.

d. Subjects are asked their height and then a measurement of height is obtained. The hypothesis to be tested is that self-reported and actual heights do not differ.

e. Two sleeping pills (Drugs A and B) are given to a sample of insomniacs. The subjects take Drug A during the first week of the study and Drug B during the second week. The total amount of time before falling asleep is recorded for each subject for each week.

2 Assume that the following output is obtained from the study of the memory drug (see question 1 in Syntax exercises):

```
- - - - - - - - - - - - - - - - - T - T E S T- - - - - - - - - - - - - - - - -
```

VARIABLE	NUMBER OF CASES	MEAN	STANDARD DEVIATION	STANDARD ERROR
BEFORE	Learning time without memory drug			
	356	12.5787	3.560	0.189
	356	12.3820	2.785	0.148
AFTER	Learning time with memory drug			

(DIFFERENCE) MEAN	STANDARD DEVIATION	STANDARD ERROR	*	2-TAIL * CORR. PROB. *	T VALUE	DEGREES OF FREEDOM	2-TAIL PROB.
0.1966	2.704	0.143	*	0.661 0.000 *	1.37	355	0.171

a. State your null hypothesis.

b. State the alternate hypothesis.

c. What can you conclude on the basis of the t-test?

d. Interpret the observed significance level.

3 For the memory problem, when would you be justified in doing a one-tailed t-test instead of a two-tailed t-test?

4 How can you calculate the one-tailed observed significance level based on the two-tailed level printed on the output?

5 An investigator wishes to test the hypothesis that children who drink orange juice before class will be more attentive than children who drink milk. He selects a classroom of children and obtains an alphabetic list of the students. He assigns the first child to orange juice therapy, the next to milk therapy, and so on down the list. He wants to analyze the experiment using the paired t-test since he has formed pairs of children based on the alphabetic list. Suggest to him how he might analyze his data. Do you think this is a paired experiment? If not, give an example of a paired design for this question.

6 Studies sometimes use twins who have been raised separately in order to investigate questions like, "What are the roles of parental influence and genetic heritage on children's intellectual development?" Discuss the advantages and disadvantages that you see in using twins for studies of this nature.

7 Discuss any problems you see in the following experiments:

a. Anxiety often affects performance on tests. A psychologist has formulated a new method for reducing stress during statistics exams. To evaluate the new method he tests each of 50 students under two conditions. He gives each student the final exam before administration of the stress reduction training, and then again after the training. He wishes to compare the two scores.

b. A market researcher wishes to study consumer preferences for five brands of pizza. He invites 250 people to a "pizza party." Each person is instructed to make sure that throughout the course of the evening he or she eats a piece of all five brands. As they are leaving, each participant fills out a questionnaire evaluating the five brands of pizza.

   c. A drug company is interested in studying the effectiveness of a new drug for headache relief. They advertise in the newspaper for "headache sufferers" who wish to participate in their study. At the beginning of the study they question each participant about the frequency and duration of headaches. Then they send the sufferers home with a week's supply of the new medicine. Upon returning a week later, each participant is again asked the same questions about headaches.

   d. You wish to compare two methods for weight reduction. You recruit 123 people who are interested in losing weight. You instruct everyone to use the first method until they have lost ten pounds, and then the second method until they have lost ten more. You then compare the length of time it takes to lose the first 10 pounds to the length of time it takes to lose the next 10 pounds.

Data Analysis

1 Test the null hypothesis that the average years of education are the same for a person's mother and father. Summarize your results.

2 Using COMPUTE, calculate a new variable that is the difference between mother's and father's years of education. Using the FREQUENCIES procedure, calculate descriptive statistics for the difference variable. How can you calculate the paired t-test based on the FREQUENCIES output?

3 Test the null hypothesis that there is no difference between the average years of education for respondents in the survey and their fathers. Write a paragraph summarizing your results.

4 Repeat the previous test for respondents and their mothers.

17 Testing Hypotheses about Independence

How can you test the null hypothesis that two percentages are equal in the population? How can you test the null hypothesis that two variables are independent?

- What are observed and expected frequencies, and how are they calculated?
- What is the chi-square statistic, and how is it used to compare two proportions?
- What does it mean to say that two variables are independent?
- What are the degrees of freedom of a crosstabulation?
- How can you use the chi-square test to test the null hypothesis that two variables are independent?
- How does sample size affect the value of the chi-square test for independence?

In the previous chapters, you saw how to test hypotheses about two population means. This works fine for variables such as age, education, and income since the mean is a good descriptive measure for them. But how about variables that aren't measured on an interval or ratio scale? If you want to test whether people's marital status or health or belief in an afterlife is related to whether or not they perceive life as exciting, you can't use a t-test. The mean is not an appropriate summary measure for variables like these. In fact, anytime you're using a variable that's nominal, calculating its mean doesn't make sense, and therefore, performing a t-test doesn't make sense. For example, it's not reasonable to test whether the mean marital status is the same for those who find life exciting and those who don't. What's a "mean" marital status?

All is not lost. To deal with variables like these, you can calculate chi-square tests. That's what this chapter is all about.

CROSSTABULATION AGAIN

In Chapter 9, we saw that 50.3% of all the men and 44.4% of all the women in the General Social Survey sample described life as exciting. Is this sufficient evidence for us to believe that the percentages of men and women who find life exciting differ in the population? Or can the observed difference just be attributed to variability among samples?

Figure 17.1 is a table from the CROSSTABS procedure. It was produced by the following commands:

```
FILE HANDLE GSS / (system-specific information)
GET FILE=GSS
COMMENT Combine Pretty routine (3) and Dull (2)
        into single category.
RECODE LIFE (3 = 2)
VALUE LABELS LIFE 1 'Excited' 2 'Not excited'
CROSSTABS TABLES = LIFE BY SEX
OPTIONS 4
```

The table tells us how many men and how many women in the sample found life exciting and how many did not. It contains column percentages, showing that 50.3% of all the men and 44.4% of all the women found life exciting. The row totals tell us that overall, 46.8% of the sample found life exciting. How can we use these numbers to test whether there are differences in the population between men's and women's outlooks?

Figure 17.1 Crosstabulation of SEX and LIFE

```
FILE:     1984 General Social Survey
- - - - - - - - - -   C R O S S T A B U L A T I O N   O F   - - - - - - - - -
   LIFE        Is life exciting or dull?
BY SEX         Respondent's sex
- - - - - - - - - - - - - - - - - - - - - - - - - -   PAGE  1 OF  1

                       SEX
            COUNT   |
            COL PCT |Male     Female    ROW
                    |                   TOTAL
                    |      1|        2|
LIFE        --------+--------+--------+
                 1  |   300  |   384  |  684
     Excited        |  50.3  |  44.4  | 46.8
                    +--------+--------+
                 2  |   296  |   481  |  777
     Not excited    |  49.7  |  55.6  | 53.2
                    +--------+--------+
            COLUMN      596     865     1461
            TOTAL      40.8    59.2    100.0

NUMBER OF MISSING OBSERVATIONS =        12
```

First of all, let's consider the hypotheses:

- The null hypothesis is that men and women are equally likely to find life exciting.
- The alternative hypothesis is that they are *not* equally likely to find life exciting.

Another way of phrasing the null hypothesis is to say that excitement and sex are *independent*, meaning there's no relationship between a person's sex and whether the person finds life exciting. We'll talk more about independence later.

THE NULL HYPOTHESIS FOR A CROSSTABULATION

As with the *t*-test, we must first figure out what results to expect if the null hypothesis is true. Remember that in Chapter 15, we followed these steps:

1 Assume that the null hypothesis is true.
2 Figure out what the distribution of means would look like on the basis of that assumption.
3 Estimate how often we'd expect to see a difference as large as the one observed if the null hypothesis is true.

Would we expect the same number of men and women in the sample to find life exciting if the null hypothesis is true? No, because there were different numbers of men and women in the sample. Instead, we'd expect that the same *percentage* of men and women would find life exciting, and the same *percentage* of both sexes would find life unexciting.

We need estimates of what these percentages should be. The only information we have is from the sample. Reasonable estimates based on the null hypothesis are the percentage of people in the sample who found life exciting and the percentage who did not. These are the row percentages given in the right margin of Figure 17.1. If the null hypothesis is true, we'd expect that 46.8% of the men and 46.8% of the women would have said that they find life exciting. Similarly, we'd expect that 53.2% of both the men and the women would have described life as unexciting.

Expected Frequencies

Let's convert these percentages to the actual number of cases we expect to find in each of the cells of the table. In the sample, there were 596 men, so we'd expect

$$596 \times 46.8\% = 279 \text{ men}$$

who found life exciting. The number who found life routine or dull should be:

$$596 \times 53.2\% = 317.$$

Similarly, if the null hypothesis is true, we'd expect

$$865 \times 46.8\% = 405 \text{ women}$$

who found life exciting, and we'd expect that the remaining 460 found life unexciting. Notice that the expected frequencies for men add up to the total number of men in the sample, and the expected frequencies for women add up to the total number of women. The expected frequencies for excited people also add up to the total number of excited people, and the expected frequencies for the unexcited add up to the number of unexcited people.

Comparing Observed and Expected Frequencies

Now we must compare the observed number of cases in each of the cells to the number that would be expected if the null hypothesis is true. These two sets of numbers are called the **observed frequencies** and the **expected frequencies.** Based on differences between the observed and expected frequencies, we'll be able to estimate the likelihood of seeing a difference at least as large as the one observed in the sample if the null hypothesis is true. As in the *t*-test, we know that even if there's no difference between the sexes in the population, the sample percentages won't be exactly equal. We expect to see variability from sample to sample.

THE CHI-SQUARE STATISTIC

When comparing two sample means, you use the t-distribution to figure how likely the observed difference between the means would be if the null hypothesis is true. You use a similar procedure with crosstabulations.

When you want to evaluate the discrepancy between a set of observed frequencies and a set of expected frequencies, you use the **chi-square statistic.** It's simple to compute. For each cell,

1 Find the difference between the observed frequency and the expected frequency.

2 Square this difference.

3 Then divide the squared difference by the expected frequency.

Repeat this three-step procedure for each of the cells in your table. Then add up all of these numbers. The sum is the chi-square statistic for the table.

Think of our current example. Figure 17.2 shows a table that contains in each cell the observed frequency, the expected frequency, and the difference between the two. (The directory in the upper left-hand corner always explains the numbers in a table.) Each difference is called a **residual,** and it's obtained in step 1 in the above procedure. Look at the first cell. It shows that 300 men found life exciting. If the null hypothesis is true, we'd expect 279 men in this cell. The residual, 21, is the difference between these two numbers. A residual with a positive sign indicates that more cases were observed than are expected if the null hypothesis is true. A negative residual indicates that fewer cases were observed than expected.

Figure 17.2 Expected frequencies and residuals

```
FILE:     1984 General Social Survey

- - - - - - - - -    C R O S S T A B U L A T I O N    O F   - - - - - - - - -
    LIFE       Is life exciting or dull?
BY  SEX        Respondent's sex
- - - - - - - - - - - - - - - - - - - - - - - - - - -    PAGE  1 OF  1

                     SEX
            COUNT |
            EXP VAL |Male    Female    ROW
            RESIDUAL|                  TOTAL
                    |    1|       2|
LIFE      ----------+--------+--------+
              1 |  300 |   384 |    684
    Excited     |  279.0 |  405.0 |  46.8%
                |   21.0 |  -21.0 |
                +--------+--------+
              2 |  296 |   481 |    777
   Not excited  |  317.0 |  460.0 |  53.2%
                |  -21.0 |   21.0 |
                +--------+--------+
            COLUMN   596     865     1461
            TOTAL   40.8%   59.2%   100.0%

NUMBER OF MISSING OBSERVATIONS =      12
```

This is how you calculate the chi-square statistic for the table:

1 For each cell, subtract the expected frequency from the observed frequency. The differences are the residuals: 21, −21, −21, and 21. (Don't be distracted by the fact that these numbers are all plus or minus the same value. This always happens when both variables have just two categories but not when either one has more.)

2 Square the differences. All four squared residuals equal 441.

3 Divide by the expected frequencies. For cell 1, 441 divided by 279 equals 1.58. For cell 2, 441 divided by 405 equals 1.09. For cell 3, 441 divided by 317 equals 1.39. For cell 4, 441 divided by 460 equals .96.

Now add up the parts: $1.58 + 1.09 + 1.39 + .96 = 5.0$.

If there's no difference in the population between men's and women's descriptions of life, the observed and expected frequencies should be fairly close. When this is true, the chi-square statistic is not very large. On the other hand, if the discrepancies between the observed and expected frequencies are big, the chi-square statistic will also be big. In general, large chi-square values occur when the sample results differ from those predicted by the null hypothesis.

Just as with the t statistic, you can calculate how often you would obtain a value of the chi-square statistic at least as large as the one you observed for your table if the null hypothesis is true. If the null hypothesis is true, the observed significance level for the chi-square statistic can be obtained from the **chi-square distribution.** You can use the chi-square distribution to find out how often you'd expect to observe various values of the chi-square statistic in samples when the null hypothesis is true.

USING SPSS^X TO CALCULATE CHI-SQUARE

You don't have to bother to do the calculations for chi-square yourself. SPSS^X will do them for you if you type:

```
FILE HANDLE GSS / (system-specific information)
GET FILE=GSS
RECODE LIFE (3 = 2)
VALUE LABELS LIFE 1 'Excited' 2 'Not excited'
CROSSTABS TABLES = LIFE BY SEX
OPTIONS 14 15
STATISTICS 1
```

The Option numbers tell SPSS^X to calculate the expected cell frequencies and the residuals. Option 14 is for expected cell frequencies, and Option 15 is for residuals. Those Option numbers were also used for Figure 17.2. Statistic 1 tells SPSS^X to compute the chi-square test. You can request several statistics on the STATISTICS command after CROSSTABS. The others are discussed in Chapter 19. At the end of that chapter is a list of all the available statistics and their numbers.

Results of the Test

The results are shown in Figure 17.3. SPSS^X prints two versions of the chi-square statistic, which you can see below the crosstabulation. The standard one, labeled BEFORE YATES CORRECTION, equals 5.005. (We'll consider the other version below.) The observed significance level for a chi-square of 5.005 with a table that has two rows and two columns is .025. A discrepancy this large between the observed and expected frequencies would only occur 2.5% of the time if, in the population, men and women are equally excited with their lives. Since the observed significance level is quite small, we reject the null hypothesis that men and women find life equally exciting.

If some of the *expected* values in a table are less than 5, the observed significance level based on the chi-square distribution may not be correct. On the output, you should look at the column labeled MIN. E.F. (minimum expected frequency) to see what the smallest expected frequency is for your table. In this example, the smallest expected frequency is 279, which certainly isn't less than 5, so you have nothing to worry about. If there are cells with expected frequencies less than five, the number of such cells is shown in the column labeled CELLS WITH E.F. < 5. In general, you should not use the chi-square test if more than 20% of the cells have expected values less than 5. You should also make sure that none of the expected values are less than 1.

Figure 17.3 A chi-square test

```
FILE:      1984 General Social Survey

 _ _ _ _ _ _ _ _ _ _ _       C R O S S T A B U L A T I O N   O F   _ _ _ _ _ _ _ _ _ _
     LIFE       Is life exciting or dull?
BY   SEX        Respondent's sex
 _ _ _ _ _ _ _ _ _ _ _ _ _ _ _ _ _ _ _ _ _ _ _ _ _ _ _ _ _     PAGE  1 OF  1

                         SEX
            COUNT
            EXP VAL |Male     Female   ROW
            RESIDUAL|                  TOTAL
                    |      1|       2|
LIFE        --------+-------+--------+
             1      |  300  |   384  |  684
   Excited          | 279.0 |  405.0 | 46.8%
                    |  21.0 |  -21.0 |
                    +-------+--------+
             2      |  296  |   481  |  777
   Not excited      | 317.0 |  460.0 | 53.2%
                    | -21.0 |   21.0 |
                    +-------+--------+
            COLUMN     596      865     1461
            TOTAL     40.8%    59.2%   100.0%


  CHI-SQUARE      D.F.      SIGNIFICANCE      MIN E.F.      CELLS WITH E.F.| 5
  ----------      ----      ------------      --------      ------------------

   4.76884         1          0.0290          279.031           NONE
   5.00462         1          0.0253       ( BEFORE YATES CORRECTION )

  NUMBER OF MISSING OBSERVATIONS =        12
```

If the number of cases in your table is less than 30, and you have a table with just two rows and two columns, SPSS^X automatically performs a different test, called **Fisher's exact test,** instead of the chi-square test. Fisher's exact test evaluates the same hypothesis as the chi-square test, and it's suitable for tables having two rows and two columns with small expected frequencies.

Yates' Correction

For a table with two rows and two columns, an adjustment to the chi-square statistic is sometimes made. The adjustment is intended to improve the estimate of the observed significance level. It's called **Yates' correction,** and you can see it in the SPSS^X output in Figure 17.3. For this table, Yates' corrected chi-square equals 4.769. Statisticians aren't in agreement as to whether this correction is really necessary. Yates' correction makes the observed chi-square value smaller.

RELATIONSHIPS BETWEEN VARIABLES

The chi-square test helps us decide whether two variables are related in the population. In the previous examples, the two variables were LIFE (Excited versus Not excited) and SEX (Male versus Female). It's time to look more closely at the concept of a relationship between variables. What do we mean when we say that the two variables forming the rows and columns of a crosstabulation are *related?*

Let's back into that question by first considering what it means to say that variables are *not* related. Sex is not related to voting preference if men and women have the same preferences among the candidates. Hair color is not related to having fun if the same percentage of people with every hair color have fun. If these variables are unrelated, then knowing your hair color tells me nothing about the likelihood of your having fun, and knowing that you're enjoying yourself tells me nothing about your hair color. When this is true, hair color and fun are described as statistically *independent*, which is a statistical way of saying *unrelated.*

Two values are **independent** whenever knowing the value of one variable tells you nothing about the value of the other variable. If you toss a die while your friend flips a coin, your getting a 1 on the die has no effect on whether the coin comes up heads or tails. The two events are completely unrelated, or independent.

What Is a Relationship?

When do we say that two variables are related? For example, it's an old superstition among college faculty that the number of hours students study for a class is related to their final grades. It's more widely believed that your eating habits are related to your weight. Or that your anxiety level is related to your ability to perform well on a test.

In all of these situations, the word *related* means that the two variables have something in common. They are in some way connected to each other. Up to a point, the more hours you study, the better your grade should be. The more between-meal snacks and high-calorie foods you consume, the heavier you should be. Anxiety and performance are thought to be related in a more complex way. Moderate anxiety levels can be helpful for doing well on an exam. Very severe anxiety—or no anxiety at all—can get in the way.

When two variables are related, knowing the value of one variable is helpful in *predicting* the value of the other variable. If you tell me that you got an *A* on the statistics exam, I would predict that you studied a lot. I may well be wrong; perhaps you understand statistics without much effort at all. But on the average, I expect that students who studied hard did well, and students who did well studied hard. (Those two statements are not the same. Think how one of them could be true and the other one false.)

The existence of a relationship between two variables does *not* mean that one causes the other. A famous study found that the number of storks in an area was related to the local birth rate. Areas with many storks had a high birth rate, while areas with few storks had a lower birth rate. Well, storks don't bring babies. It turns out that storks live mostly in rural areas and that rural areas have higher birth rates than the storkless urban areas.

We'll discuss this more in Chapter 21.

Testing Independence

So how do we test whether two variables are independent? We've already done it! The chi-square test we used to see whether men and women find life equally exciting is the same as a test of whether sex is independent of perception of life. That's because the expected values we used in calculating chi-square are literally the values that would be expected if the two variables are independent.

CHI-SQUARE IN LARGER TABLES

The procedure described for the previous example can be extended to test whether any two variables in a crosstabulation are independent. For example, you can test whether hair color is related to education or whether the size of the car people drive is related to belief in life after death or whether health is related to perception of life as exciting. Look

Figure 17.4 Health and excitement with life

```
FILE:     1984 General Social Survey

- - - - - - - - - -   C R O S S T A B U L A T I O N   O F   - - - - - - - - -
    LIFE      Is life exciting or dull?
BY  HEALTH    Condition of health
- - - - - - - - - - - - - - - - - - - - - - - - - -   PAGE  1 OF  1

                        HEALTH
            COUNT  |
            COL PCT|Excel-   Good    Fair    Poor     ROW
                   |lent                             TOTAL
                   |     1|      2|      3|      4|
LIFE        -------+-------+-------+-------+-------+
               1   |   249 |   320 |    95 |    16 |   680
    Exciting       |  57.6 |  46.0 |  37.3 |  23.2 |  46.9
                   +-------+-------+-------+-------+
               2   |   175 |   350 |   137 |    36 |   698
 Pretty routine    |  40.5 |  50.4 |  53.7 |  52.2 |  48.1
                   +-------+-------+-------+-------+
               3   |     8 |    25 |    23 |    17 |    73
    Dull           |   1.9 |   3.6 |   9.0 |  24.6 |   5.0
                   +-------+-------+-------+-------+
            COLUMN     432     695     255      69    1451
            TOTAL     29.8    47.9    17.6     4.8   100.0

NUMBER OF MISSING OBSERVATIONS =      22
```

at Figure 17.4, a crosstabulation of health and perception of life. It was produced by these commands:

```
FILE HANDLE GSS / (system-specific information)
GET FILE=GSS
CROSSTABS TABLES = LIFE BY HEALTH
OPTIONS 4
```

From the column percentages, you can see that almost 58% of the people who claimed to be in excellent health found life exciting, 46% of those in good health, 37% of those in fair health, and only 23% of those in poor health. These percentages tell us that in the sample, there is a relationship between health and finding life exciting.

As before, however, our primary interest is in the population that the sample represents. Do we have sufficient evidence to suggest that there's a relationship between the two variables—health and excitement —in the population? How often would you expect to see differences as large as the ones observed in the sample if the two variables aren't related in the population (that is, if the two variables are independent)?

CHI-SQUARE TEST OF A RELATIONSHIP

We'll use the chi-square statistic to compare the observed frequencies to those that would be expected if the two variables are independent.

First, let's consider how to calculate the expected frequencies. Look at Figure 17.4 again. From the row totals (at the right-hand side of the table), you see that 46.9% of the sample found life exciting, 48.1% found life routine, and 5.0% found life dull. If health and excitement are independent, you'd expect that the same percentage of the people in each of the health categories would've found life exciting, that the same percentage in each category would've found life routine, and that the same percentage in each category would've found life dull. That's what it means for variables to be independent. Thus, 46.9% of the 432 people in excellent health should've found life exciting, 48.1% should've found it routine, and 5% should've found it dull. Exactly the same should have been true for the people in the other health categories.

Expected Frequencies and Chi-Square

For the chi-square test, we must convert the expected percentages to actual numbers. This is simple enough. Just multiply the expected percentages by the number of people in each of the categories. There were 432 people in excellent health, so we'd expect 46.9% of 432, or 202.5, to be excited by life. In exactly the same way, we'd expect 48.1% of 432, or 207.8, to find life routine, and we'd expect 5% of 432, or 21.7, to find life dull. You calculate the chi-square statistic exactly as before. For each cell:

1 Compute the difference between the observed number of cases and the number expected if the two variables are independent.

2 Square the difference.

3 Divide by the expected count.

Then add up the results of this process for all the cells.

You can have SPSS^X do these calculations by typing the following commands:

```
FILE HANDLE GSS / (system-specific information)
GET FILE=GSS
CROSSTABS TABLES = LIFE BY HEALTH
OPTIONS 14 15
STATISTICS 1
```

Figure 17.5 contains the observed frequencies, the expected frequencies, and the residuals (the differences between the observed and expected frequencies), as well as the chi-square statistic. Remember: *expected* values are what you'd expect if the two variables are independent. If the variables are independent, then the observed and expected frequencies should be close to each other, and the value of the chi-square statistic should be small.

The residual for the first cell of Figure 17.5 is 46.5. This means that there were many more people in Excellent health who found life exciting than you'd expect if the two variables are independent. For the rest of the Exciting row, the residuals are negative. This means that there were fewer excited people than you'd expect. The residuals are large for the Fair and Poor health categories. For any particular row or column, the

Figure 17.5 Chi-square test for health and excitement

```
FILE:    1984 General Social Survey

- - - - - - - - - -   C R O S S T A B U L A T I O N   O F   - - - - - - - - -
     LIFE     Is life exciting or dull?
BY  HEALTH    Condition of health
- - - - - - - - - - - - - - - - - - - - - - - - - - - - - -   PAGE  1 OF  1

                        HEALTH
            COUNT  |
            EXP VAL|Excel-   Good     Fair     Poor      ROW
            RESIDUAL lent                                TOTAL
                   |     1|      2|      3|      4|
LIFE        -------+-------+-------+-------+-------+
                1  |   249     320      95      16      680
    Exciting      | 202.5   325.7   119.5    32.3     46.9%
                   |  46.5    -5.7   -24.5   -16.3
                   +-------+-------+-------+-------+
                2  |   175     350     137      36      698
Pretty routine    | 207.8   334.3   122.7    33.2     48.1%
                   | -32.8    15.7    14.3     2.8
                   +-------+-------+-------+-------+
                3  |     8      25      23      17       73
    Dull          |  21.7    35.0    12.8     3.5      5.0%
                   | -13.7   -10.0    10.2    13.5
                   +-------+-------+-------+-------+
            COLUMN     432     695     255      69     1451
            TOTAL    29.8%   47.9%   17.6%    4.8%   100.0%


CHI-SQUARE     D.F.      SIGNIFICANCE       MIN E.F.      CELLS WITH E.F.| 5
----------     ----      ------------       --------      -------------------

104.21250       6          0.0000            3.471        1 OF    12 ( 8.3%)

NUMBER OF MISSING OBSERVATIONS =       22
```

sum of the residuals is zero. The value of the chi-square statistic is 104.213.

Degrees of Freedom

It may occur to you, if you think about it, that a big table (one with lots of rows and columns) is likely to produce a big chi-square statistic. You do the three-step calculation for each cell in the table and then add up all the results. This makes it seem that the bigger your table, the more likely you are to get a big value for chi-square.

In fact, this is true—so we account for it. To calculate the observed significance level, we also use the number of degrees of freedom in the table. The number of degrees of freedom in a table is a way of accounting for how many different cells could each contribute their part when you add up the pieces to get chi-square. To calculate the degrees of freedom:

1 Subtract 1 from the number of rows.

2 Subtract 1 from the number of columns.

3 Multiply these two numbers together.

The product is the number of degrees of freedom. As you can see, the degrees of freedom are based on the number of observed and expected frequencies being compared and their arrangement in a table.

In the example above, we had three rows and four columns. The number of rows minus one is two, and the number of columns minus one is three. Multiply two times three, and you find that the table has six degrees of freedom.

Interpreting the Chi-Square Test

The observed significance depends both on the degrees of freedom and on the value of the chi-square statistic. For this table, the observed significance level is less than .00005.

? *Where did this .00005 come from—the output says the probability is zero?* As with *t*-tests, the probability isn't really zero. It's less than .00005, and SPSS^X prints it as zero. If it weren't less than .00005, it would've been rounded up. ■■■

The very low probability indicates that it's quite unlikely the two variables are independent in the population. The chances are less than 5 in 100,000 that we'd get sample results like the ones we've seen if the variables are independent in the population. That's sufficient for us to reject the null hypothesis of independence. From the figure, you can see that one cell has an expected value of less than 5. However, the expected value, 3.5, is bigger than 1, and only one cell out of 12 has this problem. So you can be pretty confident about using the chi-square statistic in this situation.

SAMPLE SIZE AND THE CHI-SQUARE STATISTIC

In previous chapters, we considered how the number of cases included in a study affects whether or not you can reject the null hypothesis. If the sample is too small, we won't be able to detect even large differences. On the other hand, if the sample size is very large, even small differences can be statistically significant. Let's consider another example so we can observe how this works with the chi-square test.

We've identified several variables that are related to whether life is perceived as exciting—age, sex, and condition of health. How about race? Is there any reason to believe that members of minorities respond to life differently? Let's crosstabulate RACE with LIFE. To keep the cell sizes from getting too small, we'll collapse the races coded 2 (Black) and 3 (Other) into a new code 2 (Black & Other):

```
FILE HANDLE GSS / (system-specific information)
GET FILE=GSS
RECODE RACE (3 = 2)
VALUE LABELS RACE 1 'White' 2 'Black & Other'
CROSSTABS TABLES = LIFE BY RACE
OPTIONS 14 15
STATISTICS 1
```

Figure 17.6 Race and excitement about life

```
FILE:     1984 General Social Survey

- - - - - - - - - -   C R O S S T A B U L A T I O N   O F   - - - - - - - - -
     LIFE       Is life exciting or dull?
BY   RACE       Respondent's race
- - - - - - - - - - - - - - - - - - - - - - - - - - - - -   PAGE   1 OF  1

                          RACE
               COUNT
               EXP VAL  White    Black &   ROW
               RESIDUAL           Other    TOTAL
                              1|        2|
LIFE         -------+--------+--------+
               1  |   584   |   100   |   684
  Exciting       | 581.5   | 102.5   |  46.8%
                 |   2.5   |  -2.5   |
             +--------+--------+
               2  |   599   |   105   |   704
  Pretty routine | 598.5   | 105.5   |  48.2%
                 |    .5   |   -.5   |
             +--------+--------+
               3  |    59   |    14   |    73
  Dull           |  62.1   |  10.9   |   5.0%
                 |  -3.1   |   3.1   |
             +--------+--------+
           COLUMN    1242      219      1461
           TOTAL    85.0%    15.0%    100.0%


CHI-SQUARE    D.F.     SIGNIFICANCE      MIN E.F.    CELLS WITH E.F.| 5
----------    ----     ------------      --------    ------------------

  1.08148       2        0.5823           10.943        NONE
NUMBER OF MISSING OBSERVATIONS =        12
```

Figure 17.6 is a crosstabulation of race and perception of life. Look at the residuals. All are close to zero. This suggests that there's not much relationship between race and excitement with life. As expected, the value of the chi-square statistic is small, 1.081, and the observed significance level is large, .582. What can we conclude from this? We can conclude it's unlikely that race and excitement are related in the population. We can't reject the null hypothesis that the two variables are independent.

But what would happen if we multiplied all the observed counts in Figure 17.6 by 10. That is, we increase our sample size tenfold, but we don't change the pattern of the data. The percentage of cases in each of the cells remains exactly the same. The new table is shown in Figure 17.7.

As a result of multiplying the sample size by a factor of 10, we've multiplied all of the entries in the table by 10. That is, for each cell, the observed frequency is now 10 times as large as before. Therefore, the expected frequency is 10 times as large, and so is the residual. Since everything we use in calculating the chi-square statistic is 10 times as large, the value of the chi-square statistic for the table also is multiplied by 10. The chi-square value is now 10.81.

Figure 17.7 Race and excitement, with 10 times the cases

```
FILE:      1985 General Social Survey (weighted by 10)

- - - - - - - - -  C R O S S T A B U L A T I O N   O F  - - - - - - - - -
      LIFE      Is life exciting or dull?
BY    RACE      Respondent's race
- - - - - - - - - - - - - - - - - - - - - - - - - - - - -  PAGE  1 OF  1

                       RACE
              COUNT  |
              EXP VAL|White     Black &    ROW
              RESIDUAL|         Other      TOTAL
                      |     1|        2|
    LIFE      --------+-------+--------+
                 1    | 5840  | 1000   | 6840
    Exciting         |5814.7 |1025.3  | 46.8%
                      | 25.3  |-25.3   |
                      +-------+--------+
                 2    | 5990  | 1050   | 7040
    Pretty routine   |5984.7 |1055.3  | 48.2%
                      |  5.3  | -5.3   |
                      +-------+--------+
                 3    |  590  |  140   | 730
    Dull             | 620.6 | 109.4  | 5.0%
                      |-30.6  | 30.6   |
                      +-------+--------+
              COLUMN  12420    2190     14610
              TOTAL   85.0%    15.0%    100.0%


CHI-SQUARE    D.F.      SIGNIFICANCE      MIN E.F.    CELLS WITH E.F.| 5
----------    ----     ------------      --------    ------------------

 10.81476      2         0.0045           109.425        NONE

NUMBER OF MISSING OBSERVATIONS =     120
```

Look at the observed significance level associated with this chi-square value. It's very small, .0045. The conclusion we'd now draw is that there *is* a relationship between the variables. That's completely different from before. We haven't changed the type of relationship in the data. We've just increased the sample size.

There's no mystery in this. It happens for the same reasons we've discussed earlier. If you've got a large sample size, even a very small difference between two groups (or a very small departure from independence between two variables) may turn out to be statistically significant. You must look at the actual percentages in the table to determine whether the observed differences are of any practical importance.

WHAT'S NEXT?

In the last few chapters, you've seen several types of statistical hypothesis testing: for means from independent groups, for means from paired samples, and now for independence of the two variables in a crosstabulation. The next chapter will expand our discussion of hypothesis testing with a test for equality of several means. The technique will build on what we've already discussed. When it comes to hypothesis testing, it's always the same but always new.

Summary

How can you test the null hypothesis that two percentages are equal in the population? How can you test the null hypothesis that two variables are independent?

Observed frequencies are simply the numbers of cases with specific combinations of values.

Expected frequencies are the numbers of cases that would have specific combinations of values if the null hypothesis were true.

The chi-square statistic is based on a comparison of observed frequencies with expected frequencies. From it, you can obtain an observed significance level for the hypothesis that two proportions are equal.

Two variables are independent if knowing the value of one variable tells you nothing about the value of the other.

The degrees of freedom of a crosstabulation reflect the number of cells in the table that are free to vary. You compute them by taking the number of rows minus one and multiplying that by the number of columns minus one.

From the chi-square statistic and the degrees of freedom in a crosstabulation, you can calculate the observed significance level for the null hypothesis that the two variables are unrelated.

Chi-square increases in direct proportion to sample size, if the strength of the relationship stays the same. If you double the number of cases in each cell of a crosstabulation, chi-square is doubled.

EXERCISES

Syntax

1 You want to study whether there is a relationship between the highest degree a person's father received (PADEG) and the highest degree the person received (DEGREE). Write the SPSS^x command to make a crosstabulation with the father's degree as the column variable and the child's degree as the row variable. Make sure the command will produce the appropriate percentages and calculate the chi-square test of independence.

2 You type in the following command

```
CROSSTABS VAR=EYECOLOR, CARCOLOR
STATISTICS 1
```

and receive the following error message:

```
>ERROR   10367
>Error in CROSSTABS command.  Perhaps a table request specified only one
>dimension.  Perhaps the 'BY' keyword is left out of a tables request.  The
>form should be VARA BY VARB.  Perhaps ranges were omitted for INTEGER MODE.
>Check the VARIABLES = subcommand, if INTEGER MODE intended.
>THIS COMMAND NOT EXECUTED.
```

Correct the command.

3 Correct the errors in the following commands:

   a. `CROSSTABS TABLES=VAR1 VAR2`

   b. `CROSSTABS TABLES=A BY B / OPTIONS 3 / STATISTICS 1`

   c. `CROSSTABS TABLES=A BY C`
      `STATISTICS1`

   d. `CROSSTABS TABLES A BY C`
      `STA 1`

4 You are studying the relationship between obesity in children and obesity in parents. For each child in your study you have the actual weight and height of the child (WEIGHT, HEIGHT) and of the parents (PAWEIGHT, PAHEIGHT, MAWEIGHT, MAHEIGHT). Using a special formula which relates height and sex to ideal body weight, you have created additional variables which contain the ideal body weight for the child and both parents (IDEAL, PAIDEAL, MAIDEAL). Write an SPSS^X job to

   a. Compute the ratio of actual weight to ideal weight for the child and each parent. Make up any names you like for these ratios.

   b. Create a new set of variables (OBESE, PAOBESE, MAOBESE) which have the value 1 if the ratio of actual weight to ideal weight is greater than or equal to 1.3. (That is, see if each of the people exceeds their ideal body weight by more than 30%.) If the ratio is less than 1.3, the variable should be set to 0.

   c. Crosstabulate OBESE with PAOBESE and MAOBESE. Also calculate the chi-square test of independence.

Statistical Concepts

1 Which pairs of variables do you think are independent, and which are dependent?

   a. Zodiac sign and number of hamburgers consumed per week.

   b. Severity of a disease and prognosis.

   c. Shoe size and glove size.

   d. Color of car and highest degree received.

   e. Husband's highest degree and wife's highest degree.

2 Consider the following table:

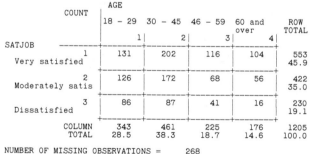

```
                        AGE
            COUNT   |
                    |18 - 29  30 - 45  46 - 59  60 and    ROW
                    |                           over      TOTAL
                    |      1|       2|       3|       4|
   SATJOB    -------+-------+-------+-------+-------+
                  1 |  131     202     116     104       553
   Very satisfied  |                                     45.9
                    +-------+-------+-------+-------+
                  2 |  126     172      68      56       422
   Moderately satis |                                     35.0
                    +-------+-------+-------+-------+
                  3 |   86      87      41      16       230
   Dissatisfied     |                                     19.1
                    +-------+-------+-------+-------+
            COLUMN     343     461     225     176      1205
            TOTAL     28.5    38.3    18.7    14.6     100.0

NUMBER OF MISSING OBSERVATIONS =      268
```

   a. Calculate the number of cases you would expect in each cell if the two variables are independent.

   b. For each cell, calculate the difference between the observed and the expected number of cases.

    c. Calculate the chi-square statistic for the table.

    d. What are the degrees of freedom for the table?

    e. What null hypothesis are you testing with the chi-square statistic you computed?

3 The observed significance level for a chi-square value of 7.83753 with 3 degrees of freedom is .0495.

    a. What conclusion would you draw about the relationship between the two variables based on the observed significance level?

    b. How often would you expect to see a chi-square value at least as large as the one you observed if the two variables are independent?

    c. If you reject the null hypothesis that the two variables are independent, can you conclude that one of the variables causes the other?

4 The following table is a crosstabulation of respondent's sex and satisfaction with family life:

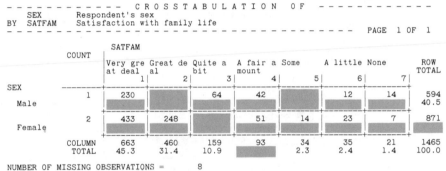

```
- - - - - - - - - - -  C R O S S T A B U L A T I O N   O F  - - - - - - - - - - -
   SEX     Respondent's sex
BY SATFAM  Satisfaction with family life
- - - - - - - - - - - - - - - - - - - - - - - - - - - - - - -  PAGE  1 OF  1
```

	COUNT	Very gre at deal 1	Great de al 2	Quite a bit 3	A fair a mount 4	Some 5	A little 6	None 7	ROW TOTAL
SEX									
Male	1	230		64	42		12	14	594 / 40.5
Female	2	433	248		51	14	23	7	871
	COLUMN TOTAL	663 / 45.3	460 / 31.4	159 / 10.9	93	34 / 2.3	35 / 2.4	21 / 1.4	1465 / 100.0

NUMBER OF MISSING OBSERVATIONS = 8

    a. Fill in the missing entries. Be sure to fill in the appropriate percentages.

    b. Write a few sentences summarizing the table. What can you conclude about the relationship between the two variables?

5 Suppose a random sample of size 100 resulted in Table 1 below, while another random sample of size 500 resulted in Table 2. If you know that the chi-square value for Table 1 is 9.09, can you find the chi-square value for Table 2 without doing any chi-square calculations involving the data in Table 2?

Table 1

	COUNT	VARB COUGH 1	NO COUGH 2	ROW TOTAL
VARA				
SMOKER	1	30	20	50 / 50.0
NONSMOKER	2	15	35	50 / 50.0
	COLUMN TOTAL	45 / 45.0	55 / 55.0	100 / 100.0

Table 2

	COUNT	VARB COUGH 1	NO COUGH 2	ROW TOTAL
VARA				
SMOKER	1	150	100	250 / 50.0
NONSMOKER	2	75	175	250 / 50.0
	COLUMN TOTAL	225 / 45.0	275 / 55.0	500 / 100.0

6 The following table is a crosstabulation of belief in life after death and excitement with life.

```
- - - - - - - - - -  C R O S S T A B U L A T I O N   O F  - - - - - - - - - -
    POSTLIFE  Belief in life after death
 BY LIFE      Is life exciting or dull?
- - - - - - - - - - - - - - - - - - - - - - - - - -  PAGE  1 OF  1

                        LIFE
              COUNT
                     |Exciting Pretty r Dull      ROW
                     |         outine             TOTAL
                     |     1|       2|       3|
      POSTLIFE  -----+--------+--------+--------+
                  1  |  531   |░░░░░░░░|   50   |   1070
         Yes         |        |        |        |   79.5
                     +--------+--------+--------+
                  2  |░░░░░░░░|  157   |░░░░░░░░|   276
         No          |        |        |        |
                     +--------+--------+--------+
              COLUMN     635      646       65      1346
              TOTAL   ░░░░░░░░ ░░░░░░░░    4.8     100.0

NUMBER OF MISSING OBSERVATIONS =      127
```

a. Fill in the missing entries in the table.

b. Calculate the value of the chi-square statistic.

c. Summarize your results.

7 You do a study looking at the relationship between severity of a disease at diagnosis and whether someone lives for five years. (Severity of a disease is objectively coded as 1=mild; 2=moderate; and 3=severe.) You compute a chi-square test of independence and find the observed significance level to be .35. Another investigator does a similar study using the same criteria for determining severity of a disease. He calculates a chi-square test of independence and obtains an observed significance level of .002. You examine his results and notice that the percentage of cases in each of the severity categories that survive five years is almost identical to the percentages that you observed. You conclude that he doesn't know how to correctly calculate a chi-square value. Give another explanation for why his chi-square could differ from yours.

8 Looking at the residuals—the differences between the observed and expected frequencies—is helpful in locating which cells don't fit the independence model well.

a. What does a negative residual mean?

b. What does a positive residual mean?

c. What does a zero residual mean?

d. What is the sum of the residuals for any row of a table?

e. What is the sum of the residuals for any column of a table?

f. Is it possible for a table to have only positive or negative residuals?

g. If all of the residuals for a table are zero, what is the value of the chi-square statistic?

Data Analysis

1 You wonder whether the same percentage of men and women believe in life after death.

    a. Make a crosstabulation of POSTLIFE and SEX. Be sure to include the appropriate percentages.

    b. State the null hypothesis that you are testing.

    c. Obtain the appropriate statistical test to test the null hypothesis.

    d. Write a short paragraph summarizing your results.

2 Test the null hypothesis that perception of life as exciting, routine, or dull is independent of one's views on afterlife. Summarize the results of your analysis.

3 Look at the variables that are available in your copy of the GSS file. Select two pairs of categorical variables and test the two null hypotheses that the variables in each pair are independent. Write a summary of your results.

18 Comparing Several Means

How can you test the null hypothesis that several population means are equal?

- What is analysis of variance?
- What assumptions about the data are needed to use analysis of variance techniques?
- How can you test hypotheses about means by looking at the variability of the observations?
- What is within-groups variability?
- What is between-groups variability?
- How is an *F*-test computed, and how is it interpreted?
- What are multiple comparison procedures, and why do you need them?

To compare two means, you can use the two-sample *t*-test described previously. But what if you have more than two groups? For example, what if you want to compare the average years of education for people who find life exciting, those who find it routine, and those who find it dull? You need a special class of statistical techniques called *analysis of variance*. That's what this chapter is about.

DESCRIBING THE GROUPS

Before you worry about any type of statistical analysis, you should always look at the data first. Look at the means and standard deviations for each of the groups. You'll find out how different the observed means are and how much the observations in the groups vary. This is important information, since you know that even large differences between observed means are not statistically significant if there's a lot of variability in the groups. If you find that the differences are statistically significant, it's important to know how large they are.

The basic descriptive statistics for years of education for the three excitement groups are shown in Figure 18.1. (These statistics come from the SPSS^X ONEWAY procedure. The SPSS^X commands are given later in the chapter.) The excited people (labeled Grp 1) have the highest average years of education (13.0), while the bored people (Grp 3) have the smallest (9.5). The people who found life routine (Grp 2) fall in the middle, with an average of 12.0 years. The standard deviations in the first two groups are fairly similar, around 3. The last group has a somewhat higher standard deviation, 3.5.

The minimum value is zero for all three groups. It's interesting that at least one person in each group claimed to have no formal education. From the maximum values, you can see that at least one person in each group reported more than four years of college.

Figure 18.1 also has a column for standard error of the mean. (Remember that this is a measure of how much the sample means vary in repeated samples from the same population.) Since the first two groups in Figure 18.1 contain about 700 cases each, the standard error of the mean for each of these groups is fairly small: it is .12 for people who find life exciting and .11 for people who find life routine.

Figure 18.1 Descriptive statistics for years of education

GROUP	COUNT	MEAN	STANDARD DEVIATION	STANDARD ERROR	95 PCT CONF INT FOR MEAN		
Grp 1	684	13.0365	3.1789	.1215	12.7979	TO	13.2752
Grp 2	702	11.9929	2.9385	.1109	11.7751	TO	12.2106
Grp 3	73	9.5479	3.5002	.4097	8.7313	TO	10.3646
TOTAL	1459	12.3598	3.1884	.0835	12.1961	TO	12.5236

GROUP	MINIMUM	MAXIMUM
Grp 1	.0000	20.0000
Grp 2	.0000	20.0000
Grp 3	.0000	18.0000
TOTAL	.0000	20.0000

The confidence intervals are shown in the last columns of the figure. Recall what a confidence interval is. It's the range of values that, with a designated likelihood, contains the true population value. If you take repeated samples from the same population and calculate 95% confidence intervals, 95% of them should include the unknown population value. Because the standard errors for the first two groups in Figure 18.1 are fairly small, the 95% confidence intervals for these groups are fairly narrow. You can be 95% confident that, in the population, the average years of education for people who find life exciting is somewhere between 12.8 and 13.3; and for people who find life routine, between 11.8 and 12.2.

Only 73 people found life dull. There are fewer cases in this group than in the others, and the observed standard deviation is larger, so the standard error of the mean is also larger. Since the confidence interval depends on the standard error of the mean, the confidence interval for the bored people is wider than for the other two groups. You can be 95% confident that the true mean for the bored group is somewhere between 8.7 and 10.4, a range of almost two years.

After the statistics for the individual groups in Figure 18.1, SPSS[X] prints statistics for all of the cases combined, in the row labeled TOTAL. From these statistics, you can see that the overall average years of education is 12.4 with a standard deviation of 3.2.

The Distribution of the Responses

The means, standard deviations, and confidence intervals give you some idea about the years of education in each of the three groups. If you look at a histogram for the years of education, you can see even more detail.

You can also see whether the distribution looks approximately normal. This is important in many situations, since statistical hypothesis testing is often based on the assumption of normality. If the population from which you're taking a sample has a distribution that's approximately normal, even for small sample sizes the distribution of sample means will be normal. The three excitement groups may have different distributions, so it's important to look at them individually.

Figures 18.2, 18.3, and 18.4 show the histograms for years of education among the three groups. For people who found life exciting, the distribution has a very sharp peak at 12 years, the year of high school graduation. It has smaller peaks at 14 and 16 years. The majority of cases have 12 to 16 years of education. For people who found life routine, there's a single peak at 12 years, or high school graduation. The distribution is fairly symmetric about this peak.

For people who found life dull, the distribution is different. Although there's a peak at 12 years, it's not as marked as for the other two groups. Smaller peaks are at 8 and 10 years of education. Very few of the cases have values of more than 12 years.

Figure 18.2 Education: people who found life exciting

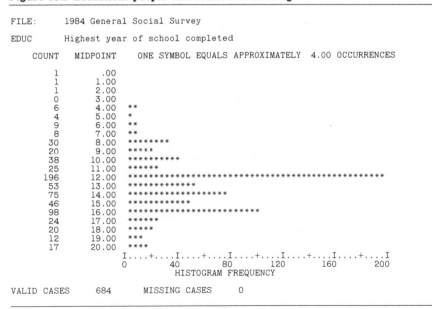

Figure 18.3 Education: people who found life routine

```
FILE:      1984 General Social Survey

EDUC       Highest year of school completed

    COUNT    MIDPOINT    ONE SYMBOL EQUALS APPROXIMATELY  8.00 OCCURRENCES

        1       .00
        0      1.00
        3      2.00
        8      3.00   *
        3      4.00
        5      5.00   *
        4      6.00   *
       16      7.00   **
       33      8.00   ****
       34      9.00   ****
       49     10.00   ******
       63     11.00   ********
      273     12.00   **********************************
       51     13.00   ******
       42     14.00   *****
       28     15.00   ****
       47     16.00   ******
       16     17.00   **
       10     18.00   *
        8     19.00   *
        8     20.00   *
                      I....+....I....+....I....+....I....+....I....+....I
                      0       80      160      240      320      400
                              HISTOGRAM FREQUENCY

VALID CASES     702     MISSING CASES     2
```

Figure 18.4 Education: people who found life dull

```
FILE:      1984 General Social Survey

EDUC       Highest year of school completed

    COUNT    MIDPOINT    ONE SYMBOL EQUALS APPROXIMATELY   .40 OCCURRENCES

        1       .00   ***
        2      1.00   *****
        0      2.00
        1      3.00   ***
        2      4.00   *****
        2      5.00   *****
        6      6.00   ***************
        2      7.00   *****
       12      8.00   ******************************
        4      9.00   **********
       11     10.00   ***************************
        3     11.00   ********
       17     12.00   *******************************************
        3     13.00   ********
        4     14.00   **********
        0     15.00
        2     16.00   *****
        0     17.00
        1     18.00   ***
        0     19.00
        0     20.00
                      I....+....I....+....I....+....I....+....I....+....I
                      0        4        8       12       16       20
                              HISTOGRAM FREQUENCY

VALID CASES      73     MISSING CASES     0
```

Are the Means Really Different?

The descriptive statistics as well as the histograms suggest that there are differences in years of education among the three excitement groups. Now we need to figure out whether the observed differences in the samples may be attributed to just the natural variability among sample means or whether there's reason to believe that the three groups have different means in the population.

The null hypothesis says that in the population, the means of the three groups are equal. That is, there's no difference in the average years of education for people who find life exciting, routine, or dull. The alternative hypothesis is that there is a difference. The alternative hypothesis doesn't say which groups differ from one another. It just says that the groups are not all the same; at least one of the groups differs from the others.

ANALYSIS OF VARIANCE

The statistical technique used to test the null hypothesis that several population means are equal is **analysis of variance.** It's called that because it examines the variability in the sample and, based on the variability, it determines whether there's reason to believe the population means are not equal. We'll be drawing conclusions about means by looking at variability.

SPSS^X contains several different procedures that can perform analysis of variance. In this chapter, we'll use the ONEWAY procedure. It's called **one-way analysis of variance** because cases fall into different groups based on their values for one variable. In our example, the variable is perception of life.

Necessary Assumptions

The data must meet two conditions for you to use analysis of variance:

1 Each of the groups must be a random sample from a normal population.

2 In the population, the variances in all groups must be equal.

You can visually check these conditions by making a histogram of the data for each group and seeing whether the data are approximately normal. To check whether the groups have the same variance in the population, you can examine the histograms as well as compute the variance for each of the groups and compare them.

In practice, analysis of variance gives good results even if the normality assumption doesn't quite hold. If the number of observations in each of the groups is fairly similar, the equal-variance assumption is also not too important. The assumption of random samples, however, is always important and cannot be relaxed.

Partitioning the Variability

In analysis of variance, the observed variability in the sample is divided, or **partitioned,** into two parts: variability of the observations *within* a group (around the group mean), and variability *between* the group means themselves.

? *Why are we talking about variability? Aren't we testing hypotheses about means?* In Chapter 14, we considered the relationship between variability of observations (in the population) and variability of sample means. If you know the standard deviation of the observations, you can estimate how much the sample means should vary.

In your data, you have several different groups—for example, people who found life exciting, people who found it routine, and people who found it dull. If the null hypothesis is true (that is, if all three groups have the same mean in the population), you can estimate how much the observed means should vary due to sampling variation alone. If the means you actually observe vary more than you'd expect from sampling variation, you have reason to believe that this extra variability is due to the fact that some of the groups don't have the same mean in the population.   ■ ■ ■

Within-Groups Variability

Let's look a little more closely now at the two types of variability we need to consider. **Within-groups variability** is a measure of how much the observations within a group vary. It's simply the variance of the observations within a group in your sample, and it's used to estimate the variance within a group in the population. (Remember, analysis of variance requires the assumption that all of the groups have the same variance in the population.) Since you don't know if all of the groups have the same mean, you can't just calculate the variance for all of the cases together. You must calculate the variance for each of the groups individually and then combine these into an "average" variance.

For example, suppose you have three groups of 20 cases each. All 20 cases in the first group have a value of 100, all 20 cases in the second group have a value of 50, and all 20 cases in the third group have a value of 0. Your best guess for the population variance within a group is 0. It appears from your sample that the values of the cases in any particular group don't vary at all. But if you'd computed the variance for all of the cases together, it wouldn't even be close to zero. You'd calculate the overall mean as 50, and cases in the first and third groups would all vary from this overall mean by 50. There would be plenty of variation.

Between-Groups Variability

Remember the discussion in Chapter 13. There's a relationship between the variability of the observations in a population and the variability of sample means from that population. If you divide the standard deviation of the observations by the square root of the number of observations, you have an estimate of the standard deviation of the sample means, also known as the standard error. So if you know what the standard error of the mean is, you can estimate what the standard deviation of the original observations must be. You just multiply the standard error by the square root of the number of cases to get an estimate of the standard deviation of the observations. You square this to get an estimate of the variance.

Let's see how this insight can give you an estimate of the variance based on **between-groups variability.** You have a sample mean for each of the groups, and you can compute how much these means vary. If the population mean is the same in all three groups, you can use the variability between the sample means (and the sizes of the sample groups) to estimate what the variability of the original observations is. Of course, this estimate depends on whether the population means really are the same in all three groups—which is the null hypothesis. If the null hypothesis is true, the between-groups estimate is correct. However, if the groups have different means in the population, then the between-groups estimate, the estimate of variability based on the group means, will be too large.

Back to the Examples

In the above example, the three sample means were 100, 50, and 0. Since they vary quite a bit, you'd expect the observations in the groups to vary even more. They didn't. In fact, all 20 observations in each group were equal. Your within-groups and between-groups estimates of variability were therefore quite different. This suggests that the differences you saw in the group means from the sample weren't attributable just to natural variability from sample to sample. The groups almost certainly do have different means in the population.

How does this apply to the question about education in the General Social Survey? Suppose the means of the three groups vary a lot, but the amount of education doesn't vary much for individuals within the excitement groups. (For example, most of the people who found life routine had no more than high school educations.) Then you have reason to suspect that the population means are not all equal for these groups.

In summary, with analysis of variance you compare the within-groups and between-groups estimates of variability. You compare them to see if there is reason to reject the null hypothesis that the population means are equal for the groups.

Analysis of Variance in SPSS^X ONEWAY

These are the commands you need for getting an analysis of variance from the SPSS^X procedure ONEWAY:

```
FILE HANDLE GSS / (system-specific information)
GET FILE=GSS
ONEWAY EDUC BY LIFE(1,3)
STATISTICS 1
```

The variable named after the command ONEWAY and before BY is the one whose means you want to test. The variable after BY defines the different groups, and the numbers following it in parentheses are the group variable's highest and lowest values. The output from this analysis of variance appears below, in Figure 18.5. Figure 18.1 shows the descriptive statistics produced by Statistic 1 in ONEWAY.

Computing Within-Groups Variability

Now let's see how the numbers in Figure 18.5 are computed. We use three steps to compute the estimate of how much the observations within a group vary. First, we calculate the **within-groups sum of squares.** Just take the variance in each of the groups (the square of the standard deviation), multiply it by one less than the number of cases in the group, and add all the results together.

For our example, the within-groups sum of squares is:

$$3.1789^2 \times 683 + 2.9385^2 \times 701 + 3.5002^2 \times 72 = 13{,}837$$

This number is shown in the second row of numbers in Figure 18.5, in the column labeled SUM OF SQUARES.

The second step of estimating the variability in the individual groups is to divide the previously computed sum of squares by its **degrees of freedom.** The degrees of freedom are easy to obtain. For each group, find the number of cases minus one, and add all the results together for all the groups. In our example, the degrees of freedom are

$$(684 - 1) + (702 - 1) + (73 - 1) = 1456$$

This number is shown on the WITHIN GROUPS line of Figure 18.5, in the column labeled D.F. (for Degrees of Freedom).

The third and final step is to divide the sum of squares by its degrees of freedom, to get what's called a **mean square.** This is an estimate of the average variability in the groups. It's really nothing more than an average of the variances in each of the groups, adjusted for the fact that the numbers of observations in the groups are unequal. As you can see in Figure 18.5, the WITHIN GROUPS mean square is 13,837 divided by 1,456, or 9.50.

Figure 18.5 Analysis of variance

```
FILE:     1984 General Social Survey

- - - - - - - - - - - - - - - - O N E W A Y - - - - - - - - - - - - - - - - - -

     Variable  EDUC      Highest year of school completed
  By Variable  LIFE      Is life exciting or dull?
                              ANALYSIS OF VARIANCE

                                 SUM OF        MEAN           F      F
          SOURCE        D.F.     SQUARES       SQUARES      RATIO   PROB.

BETWEEN GROUPS           2       984.9535      492.4768    51.8204  .0000

WITHIN GROUPS          1456    13837.1328        9.5035

TOTAL                 1458    14822.0864
```

Computing Between-Groups Variability

Now we must calculate another estimate of the variance, based on how much the means differ among themselves. Again the computations involve three steps. First we calculate the between-groups sum of squares, then the degrees of freedom, and finally the between-groups mean square.

To calculate the between-groups sum of squares, start by subtracting the overall mean (the mean of all the observations) from each group mean. Then square each difference, and multiply the square by the number of observations in its group. Finally, add all the results together. For our example, the between-groups sum of squares is:

$$684 \times (13.04 - 12.36)^2 + 702 \times (11.99 - 12.36)^2 + 73 \times (9.55 - 12.36)^2$$
$$= 984.95$$

To find the degrees of freedom for the between-groups sum of squares, subtract one from the number of groups. In this example, there are 3 groups, so there are 2 degrees of freedom.

The between-groups mean square is calculated just like the within-groups mean square. Divide the sum of squares by its degrees of freedom:

$$984.95 / 2 = 492.5$$

This number is found in the column labeled MEAN SQUARES in Figure 18.5.

Calculating the *F*-Ratio

You now have two estimates of the variability in the population: the *within-groups* mean square and the *between-groups* mean square. The within-groups mean square is based on how much the observations within each of the groups vary. The between-groups mean square is based on how much the group means vary among themselves. If the null hypothesis is true, the two numbers should be close to each other. If we divide one by the other the ratio should be close to one.

The statistical test for the null hypothesis that all of the groups have the same mean in the population is based on computing such a ratio. It's called an F statistic. You take the between-groups mean square and divide it by the within-groups mean square as shown in the following formula:

$$F = \frac{\text{between-groups mean square}}{\text{within-groups mean square}}$$

For our example,

$$F = \frac{492.5}{9.5} = 51.8$$

This number appears in Figure 18.5 below the label F RATIO. It certainly doesn't appear to be close to 1. What we need to do now is obtain the observed significance level. We want to know how often we'd expect to see a ratio of 51.8 or larger if the null hypothesis is true.

The observed significance level is obtained by comparing the calculated F value to the F-distribution, the distribution of the F statistic when the null hypothesis is true. (Like the normal distribution, the F-distribution is defined mathematically. SPSS^X can calculate it and compare your F value to it automatically.) The significance level is based on both the actual value of F you obtain and on the degrees of freedom for the two mean squares.

For our example, the observed significance level is shown in the column labeled F PROB. in Figure 18.5. Since a value of .0000 is printed, you know that the observed significance level is less than .00005. In other words, it's very unlikely that you'd see such a large F-ratio when the null hypothesis is true. You reject the null hypothesis that people who find life exciting, routine, or dull have the same number of years of education, in the population from which this sample was drawn.

MULTIPLE COMPARISON PROCEDURES

A significant F value only tells you that the population means are probably not all equal. It doesn't tell you *which* pairs of groups appear to have different means. You can reject the null hypothesis that all means are equal in several different situations. For example, people who find life exciting may differ in education from people who find life dull but not from people who find life routine. Or people who find life exciting may differ from both other groups. In most situations, you want to pinpoint exactly where the differences are. To do this, you must use **multiple comparison procedures.**

? *Why do you need yet another statistical technique? Why not just calculate t-tests for all possible pairs of means?* The reason for not using many t-tests is that when you make a lot of comparisons involving the same means, the probability that one out of the bunch will turn out to be statistically significant increases.

For example, if you have 5 groups and compare all pairs of means, you're making 10 comparisons. When the null hypothesis is true (that is, all of the means are equal in the population), the probability that at least one of the 10 observed significance levels will be less than .05 is about .29. If you keep looking, even unlikely events will happen. Therefore, when you're testing statistical significance, the more comparisons you make, the more likely it is that you'll find one or more pairs to be statistically different, even if all means are equal in the population.

Multiple comparison procedures protect you from calling too many differences significant. They adjust for the number of comparisons you're making. The more comparisons you're making, the larger the difference between pairs of means must be for a multiple comparison procedure to report a significant difference. So, you can get different results from multiple t-tests and from multiple comparison procedures. Differences that the t-tests find significant may not be significant based on multiple comparison procedures. When you use a multiple comparison procedure, you can be more confident that you're finding true differences. ■ ■ ■

There are several different procedures that can be used when making multiple comparisons. The procedures differ in how they adjust the observed significance level for the fact that many comparisons are being made. Some require larger differences between pairs of means than others. For further discussion of multiple comparisons, see R. Kirk's *Experimental Design* (1968).

Multiple Comparisons in ONEWAY

Multiple comparisons are simple to do in SPSS^X ONEWAY. A number of different methods are available; one of the most widely used is called the *Tukey-b* multiple comparison test. To calculate the Tukey-b test, type:

```
FILE HANDLE GSS / (system-specific information)
GET FILE=GSS
ONEWAY EDUC BY LIFE(1,3) / RANGES=TUKEYB
```

Figure 18.6 is the output you obtain. At the bottom of the output, all of the group means are ordered from smallest to largest in rows and columns. Pairs of means that are different at the .05 level are marked with an asterisk in the lower half of the little table. You can see that all of the groups differ from one another. Asterisks appear for Group 2 versus Group 3 and for Group 1 versus both Group 2 and Group 3. In other

Figure 18.6 Multiple comparisons from ONEWAY

```
FILE:     1984 General Social Survey

- - - - - - -  - - - - - - - - O N E W A Y - - - - - - - - - - - - - - - - -

         Variable  EDUC        Highest year of school completed
      By Variable  LIFE        Is life exciting or dull?


MULTIPLE RANGE TEST


TUKEY-B PROCEDURE
RANGES FOR THE 0.050 LEVEL -

         3.07   3.33

THE RANGES ABOVE ARE TABLE RANGES.
THE VALUE ACTUALLY COMPARED WITH MEAN(J)-MEAN(I) IS..
         2.1799 * RANGE * DSQRT(1/N(I) + 1/N(J))

      (*) DENOTES PAIRS OF GROUPS SIGNIFICANTLY DIFFERENT AT THE 0.050 LEVEL


                                  G G G
                                  r r r
                                  p p p

          Mean      Group        3 2 1

          9.5479    Grp 3
         11.9929    Grp 2        *
         13.0365    Grp 1        * *
```

words, people who find life routine (Group 2) differ in education from people who find life dull (Group 3), and people who find life exciting (Group 1) differ from both of the other groups.

Differences are marked only in the lower half of the table. If the significance level is not less than .05, an asterisk is not printed; the space is left blank. The formula above the table indicates how large an observed difference must be for the comparison procedure to call it significant. If no pairs are found to be significantly different, the table is not printed at all. Instead, a message is shown to tell you of that fact.

MORE COMPLICATED ANALYSIS OF VARIANCE DESIGNS

In this chapter, we've considered analysis of variance when one variable determines the groups. That is, our three groups were formed according to one variable, LIFE, whose values indicate whether a person finds life exciting, routine, or dull. But you can use analysis of variance techniques for more complicated designs as well.

Suppose you're interested in testing hypotheses about both view of life and the sex of the respondent. You would classify cases based on both of these variables. Since the sex variable has two values and the excitement variable has three, each case is classified into one of six groups (called **cells**, analogous to the cells in a crosstabulation). Using analysis of variance techniques, you could test whether men and women differ in average years of education, whether the three excitement groups differ in average years of education, and whether the relationship between excitement and years of education is the same for men and women. All of these tests would be included in a **two-way analysis of variance.** It's called that because it's based on two classification variables, in this example LIFE and SEX.

Interactions

Analysis of variance allows you to test not only for the effects of individual variables but also for their combinations. This is an important concern. As you've seen in previous chapters, combinations of variables sometimes have a different effect than you'd expect from each of the variables alone.

Think back to the crosstabulation relating excitement, marital status, and sex in Chapter 9. You saw that the relationship between marital status and excitement was different for men and women. Single women were much more likely to find life exciting than single men. The relationship between marital status and excitement differed for the two sexes. In statistical terms, we say that there was an **interaction effect** between sex and marital status, as they affect excitement. It's important to identify interaction effects, since it doesn't make sense to talk about the effect of marital status alone if the effect is quite different for men and women. If there is an interaction effect, you must talk about the effect of marital status separately for men and women.

Cases can also be classified on the basis of more than two variables. Then analysis of variance provides tests for the effects of the individual variables and all possible interactions of the variables. A discussion of interaction effects and of the many complicated relationships that analysis of variance can test for is beyond the scope of this book. If you're interested in knowing more, a good place to start is Kirk's *Experimental Design.*

MORE ABOUT THE ONEWAY PROCEDURE

You use the ONEWAY analysis of variance procedure to test the null hypothesis that several population means are equal. To test that there is no difference in average age for people who find life exciting, routine, and dull, specify

```
ONEWAY AGE BY LIFE(1,3)
```

The variable whose means are being compared is named before the BY keyword. The variable used to form the groups is indicated after the BY. Give the lowest and highest values for the variable which forms the groups in parentheses, separated by a comma. These values must be integers. You can use only one variable to designate the groups in ONEWAY.

If you have several variables you want to compare, list them all before the keyword BY, separated by commas or blanks. For example,

```
ONEWAY AGE EDUC SALARY BY LIFE(1,3)
```

produces separate analyses for age, education, and salary.

Obtaining Multiple Comparisons

To obtain multiple comparison tests, enter a slash, the RANGES keyword, and the name of the test after the previous specification. For example,

```
ONEWAY AGE BY LIFE(1,3) / RANGES=TUKEYB
```

The following keywords for designating tests are available:

LSD	Least Significant Difference
DUNCAN	Duncan's multiple range test
SNK	Student-Newman-Keul's test
TUKEYB	Tukey(b)
TUKEY	Tukey's honestly significant difference
LSDMOD	Modified least significant difference
SCHEFFE	Scheffe's test

For description of these tests, see Winer (1971).

Available Options

These options can be specified on the OPTIONS command:

1   Include cases with missing values
2   Exclude cases with missing values listwise
3   Don't print variable labels
6   Use value labels as group labels

Available Statistics

On the STATISTICS command, you can request descriptive statistics using Statistic 1. These include the number of cases, mean, standard deviation, standard error, minimum, maximum, and 95% confidence interval for each group.

WHAT'S NEXT?

In this part of the book, we have considered how to draw conclusions about the population based on results observed in a sample. We have also looked at several commonly used procedures for testing hypotheses about group means. In the next part of the book we'll continue to test various hypotheses, but the emphasis will change from studying whether groups differ to studying what the relationships are between pairs of variables. We'll consider how to describe the strength and nature of the relationships between variables. In Chapter 19 we look at how to describe a relationship between the variables in a crosstabulation.

Summary

How can you test the null hypothesis that several population means are equal?

Analysis of variance can be used to test the null hypothesis that several population means are equal.

To use analysis of variance, your groups must be random samples from normal populations with the same variance.

In analysis of variance, the observed variability in the samples is subdivided into two parts—variability of the observations within a group about the group mean (within-groups variation), and variability of the group means (between-groups variation).

The *F*-statistic is calculated as the ratio of the between-groups estimate of variance to the within-groups estimate of variance.

The analysis of variance *F*-test does not pinpoint which means are significantly different from each other.

Multiple comparison procedures, which protect you against calling too many differences significant, are used to identify pairs of means that appear to be different from each other.

EXERCISES

Syntax

1 You type in the following command:

ONEWAY WEIGHT BY INCOME

and get the following error message:

```
>ERROR   11404  LINE   4, (END OF COMMAND)
>The parenthesized range appears to be missing on the ONEWAY command.
>THIS COMMAND NOT EXECUTED.
```

Fix the command.

2   Correct the following commands (if necessary):

  a.   `ONEWAY INCOME BY RACE(4)`

  b.   `oneway temperature by region (1,4)`

  c.   `ONEWAY educ BY zodiac(1,12)`

  d.   `oneway EDUC by ZODIAC(1,12)`
       `options ranges tukeyb`

3   You wish to investigate the relationship between cholesterol levels (CHOL) and years of education (EDUC). You have education recorded in actual years. Use SPSS[X] to create four categories of people (8 or fewer years of education; 9-12 years; 13-16 years; and more than 16 years). Then write the ONEWAY command to test the hypothesis that there is no difference in average cholesterol levels for the different education categories.

4   Modify your previous commands to obtain multiple comparisons using the TUKEYB procedure.

5   Correct the following commands (if necessary):

  a.   `ONEWAY  VAR=BLP BY DISEASE(1,3) /`

  b.   `ONEWAY  VAR1 BY VAR2(1,3) VAR3(2,8)`

  c.   `ONEWAY VAR BY VAR2(2,9)`

  d.   `ONEWAY  WEIGHT HEIGHT TEMP BY REGION(1,4)`

Statistical Concepts

1   You are interested in comparing four methods of teaching. You randomly assign 20 students to each of the four methods and then administer a standardized test at the end of the study.

  a.   What null hypothesis are you interested in testing?

  b.   What statistical procedure might you use to test the hypothesis?

  c.   What assumptions are necessary for the statistical procedure you have selected?

2   You wish to test the null hypothesis that, in the population, there is no difference in the average age at marriage for people who find life exciting, routine, or dull. You run an analysis of variance and obtain the following table:

```
- - - - - - - - - - - - - - - - O N E W A Y - - - - - - - - - - - - - - - - - -


        Variable  AGEWED     Age of first marriage
        By Variable  LIFE      Is life exciting or dull?

                              ANALYSIS OF VARIANCE
```

SOURCE	D.F.	SUM OF SQUARES	MEAN SQUARES	F RATIO	F PROB.
BETWEEN GROUPS	2	46.6433	23.3216	1.0832	.3388
WITHIN GROUPS	1164	25060.5461	21.5297		
TOTAL	1166	25107.1894			

  a.   Is there sufficient evidence to reject the null hypothesis?

  b.   What conclusion can you draw from the table?

  c.   If you compute the average ages at marriage for each of the groups, would you expect the sample means to be similar or quite different?

d. Since people who have never been married are assigned a "missing" code for the AGEWED variable, do you think they are included in this analysis or not?

3 We've seen that there is a statistically significant difference in average years of education for people who find life exciting, routine, or dull. Now let's see whether there is a difference in their mothers' education levels.

a. The variable name for mother's education is MAEDUC. Write the SPSS^X command to obtain an analysis of variance table and Tukey's second multiple comparison test (TUKEYB).

b. What is the null hypothesis that you're testing?

c. The following table is the analysis of variance. What can you conclude from it?

```
- - - - - - -  - - - - - - - - O N E W A Y - - - - - - - - - - - - - - - - -


        Variable  MAEDUC      Mother's highest year of school
        By Variable  LIFE      Is life exciting or dull?

                            ANALYSIS OF VARIANCE


                              SUM OF        MEAN         F      F
        SOURCE        D.F.    SQUARES      SQUARES     RATIO  PROB.

  BETWEEN GROUPS       2     503.2386     251.6193    21.8666  .0000

  WITHIN GROUPS      1228   14130.5989     11.5070

  TOTAL              1230   14633.8375
```

d. The results of Tukey's multiple comparisons procedure is shown below. Which groups are significantly different from each other?

```
MULTIPLE RANGE TEST


TUKEY-B PROCEDURE
RANGES FOR THE 0.050 LEVEL -

      3.07   3.33

THE RANGES ABOVE ARE TABLE RANGES.
THE VALUE ACTUALLY COMPARED WITH MEAN(J)-MEAN(I) IS..
      2.3986 * RANGE * DSQRT(1/N(I) + 1/N(J))

  (*) DENOTES PAIRS OF GROUPS SIGNIFICANTLY DIFFERENT AT THE 0.050 LEVEL


                            G G G
                            r r r
                            p p p
     Mean       Group       3 2 1

     8.0204     Grp 3
     9.9537     Grp 2       *
    10.8464     Grp 1       * *
```

e. Write a brief paragraph summarizing the results of this analysis.

4 A market researcher wants to see whether people in four regions of a city buy the same brand of dishwashing detergent. He takes a random sample of people in the different areas and asks them which of 10 brands (coded from 1 to 10) they purchase most often. He enters the data into SPSS^X and runs the ONEWAY procedure. The observed significance level for his F-value is 0.00001.

a. Explain his results to him. What can he conclude?

b. How would you analyze these data?

Data Analysis

1 Using the RECODE command, modify the marital status variable (MARITAL) so it has three categories: 1=married; 2=widowed, divorced, or separated; and 3=never married.

 a. Test the null hypothesis that the average number of years of education is the same in all three groups.

 b. Using a multiple-comparison procedure, identify which groups are significantly different from each other.

 c. Summarize your results.

 d. Explain why you agree or disagree with the statement that people who are well-educated tend not to marry. Perform whatever analysis you may think is helpful to support your position. Consider other possible explanations for the results you obtain.

2 You're interested in seeing whether the number of siblings a person has (SIBS) is related to perception of life.

 a. State the null hypothesis.

 b. Perform the appropriate statistical analysis to test the hypothesis.

 c. Which groups have significantly different means?

 d. What explanations can you offer for the observed results?

3 We've seen that there is a relationship between education and perception of life. Investigate whether there is a relationship between the education of a person's parents and his or her perception of life. Write a paragraph summarizing your results.

4 For the General Social Survey data, formulate four hypotheses that can be tested using analysis of variance procedures. Explore two of these hypotheses with ONEWAY and write a short paper summarizing your results.

PART **4**   CHAPTERS 19-25

STUDYING
RELATIONSHIPS

19 Measuring Association

How can you measure the strength of the relationship between two categorical variables?

- What are measures of association, and why are they useful?
- Is there a single best measure of association?
- Why is the chi-square statistic not a good measure of association?
- How can the chi-square statistic be modified so it could be used to express the strength of the association between two variables?
- What is proportional reduction in error?
- When a measure of association equals zero, does that always mean the two variables are unrelated?
- For variables measured on an ordinal scale, how can the additional information about order be incorporated into a measure of association?
- What are concordant and discordant pairs, and how are they used in various measures of association?

One of the most frequently asked questions in any study is, "Are these two variables related?" Is education related to voting behavior? Is marital status related to happiness? Is ability to close a sale related to the experience of the salesperson? You usually want to know more than just *whether* the two variables are related. You also want to know the strength and nature of the relationship. If job satisfaction is related to perceiving life as exciting, how strongly is it related? And does the likelihood of perceiving life as exciting increase or decrease as job satisfaction increases?

THE STRENGTH OF A RELATIONSHIP

Many different statistical techniques are used to study the relationships among variables. We'll consider some of them in the chapters that follow. In this chapter, we'll look at techniques that are useful for measuring the strength and nature of associations when the two variables are categorical. These variables have a limited number of possible values, and their distribution can be examined with a crosstabulation table.

Why Not Chi-Square?

In Chapter 17, we used the chi-square test to test the null hypothesis that two categorical variables are independent. If you reject the null hypothesis of independence, what can you say about the two variables? Can you conclude anything about the strength or nature of their association on the basis of the actual chi-square value? Do large chi-square values indicate strong associations and small values indicate weak ones?

The actual value of the chi-square statistic provides you with little information about the strength and type of association between two variables. In Chapter 17, you saw how sample size influences the value of chi-square. If you take a particular crosstabulation and multiply all cell frequencies by 10, you also increase the value of the chi-square by 10. By increasing the frequency in each cell, you're not in any way changing the nature or strength of the association—that remains exactly the same. The value of the chi-square statistic depends on the sample size as well as the amount of departure from independence for the two variables. So you can't compare chi-square values from several studies with different sample sizes. This is one reason why the chi-square statistic isn't very useful as a measure of association.

Furthermore, since chi-square is based only on expected and observed frequencies, it's possible for many different types of tables to have the same value for the chi-square statistic. Different types of relationships between two variables can result in the same chi-square value. Knowing the chi-square tells you nothing about the nature of the association.

Measures of Association

Statistics that are used to quantify the strength and nature of the relationship between two variables in a crosstabulation are called **measures of association.** There are many different measures of association, since there are many different ways to define "association." The measures differ in how they can be interpreted and in how they define perfect and intermediate levels of association. They also differ in the level of measurement required for the variables. For example, if two variables are measured on an ordinal scale, it makes sense to talk about their values increasing or decreasing together. Such a statement would be meaningless for variables measured on a nominal scale.

No single measure of association is best for all situations. To choose the best one for a particular situation, you must consider the type of data and the way you want to define association. If a certain measure has a low value for a table, this doesn't necessarily mean that the two variables are unrelated. It can also mean that they're not related in the way that the measure can detect. But you shouldn't calculate a lot of measures and then report only the largest. Select the appropriate measures in advance. If you look at a enough different measures, you increase your chance of finding significant associations in the sample that do not exist in the population.

MEASURES OF ASSOCIATION FOR NOMINAL VARIABLES

When you have variables that are measured on a nominal scale, you're limited in what you can say about their relationship. You can't say that marital status increases as religious affiliation increases, or that automobile color decreases with increasing state of residence. You can't say anything about the direction of the association. If the categories of the variables don't have a meaningful order, it doesn't make sense to say they're associated in one direction or another. All you can do is try to measure the strength of the association. Two types of measures of association are useful for nominal variables: measures based on chi-square and measures of proportional reduction in error (called PRE measures). Let's look at each of these in turn.

Measures Based on Chi-Square

We just finished discussing why the chi-square statistic is not a good measure of association. And it isn't. However, since its use is common in tests of independence, people have tried to construct measures of association based on it. The measures based on chi-square attempt to modify it so it isn't influenced by sample size and so it falls in the range of 0 to 1. Without such adjustments, you can't compare chi-square values from tables with different sample sizes and different dimensions. (In the range from 0 to 1, a value of 0 corresponds to no association and a value of 1, to perfect association. Coefficients are often **normalized** to fall in this range.)

The Phi Coefficient. This is one of the simplest modifications of the chi-square statistic. To calculate a phi coefficient, just divide the chi-square value by the sample size and then take the square root. The formula is

$$\phi = \sqrt{\frac{\chi^2}{N}}$$

The maximum value of phi depends on the size of the table. If a table has more than two rows or two columns, the phi coefficient can be greater than 1—an undesirable feature.

The Coefficient of Contingency. This measure is always less than or equal to 1. It's often abbreviated with the letter C. It's calculated from the chi-square statistic using the following formula:

$$C = \sqrt{\frac{\chi^2}{\chi^2 + N}}$$

Although the value of C is always between 0 and 1, it can never get as high as 1, even for a table showing what seems to be a perfect relationship. The largest value it can have depends on the number of rows and columns in the table. For example, if you have a four-by-four table, the largest possible value of C is .87.

Cramér's V. This is a chi-square-based measure of association that *can* attain the value of 1 for tables of any dimension. Its formula is:

$$V = \sqrt{\frac{\chi^2}{N(k - 1)}}$$

where k is the smaller of the number of rows and columns. If the number of rows or columns is 2, Cramér's V is identical in value to phi.

Calculating Chi-Square-Based Measures

To make our discussion a little more concrete, let's compute Cramér's *V* and the contingency coefficient *C* for Figure 19.1. (This figure is the crosstabulation of marital status and excitement. It's from Chapter 9, with added statistics.) The commands for the crosstabulation and the statistics are:

```
FILE HANDLE GSS / (system-specific information)
GET FILE=GSS
CROSSTABS TABLES=LIFE BY MARITAL
OPTIONS 4
STATISTICS 1 2 3
```

Notice the STATISTICS command in this job. Statistic 1 gives us chi-square, Statistic 2 gives Cramér's *V*, and Statistic 3 gives the contingency coefficient.

Look at the chi-square value and its associated significance level printed at the bottom of the table. From these, you'd reject the null hypothesis that the two variables are independent. Now look at the two chi-square-based measures to see how marital status and excitement are

Figure 19.1 Chi-square-based measures of association

```
FILE:     1984 General Social Survey

- - - - - - - - - -   C R O S S T A B U L A T I O N   O F   - - - - - - - - -
    LIFE      Is life exciting or dull?
BY  MARITAL   Marital status
- - - - - - - - - - - - - - - - - - - - - - - - - - - - -   PAGE   1 OF   1
```

	COUNT COL PCT	MARITAL Married	Widowed	Divorced	Separated	Never married	ROW TOTAL
		1	2	3	4	5	
LIFE							
Exciting	1	392 47.6	51 33.8	77 46.7	18 42.9	146 52.3	684 46.8
Pretty routine	2	401 48.7	82 54.3	77 46.7	20 47.6	124 44.4	704 48.2
Dull	3	31 3.8	18 11.9	11 6.7	4 9.5	9 3.2	73 5.0
	COLUMN TOTAL	824 56.4	151 10.3	165 11.3	42 2.9	279 19.1	1461 100.0

CHI-SQUARE	D.F.	SIGNIFICANCE	MIN E.F.	CELLS WITH E.F.	5
31.04002	8	0.0001	2.099	1 OF	15 (6.7%)

STATISTIC	VALUE
CRAMER'S V	0.10307
CONTINGENCY COEFFICIENT	0.14424

NUMBER OF MISSING OBSERVATIONS =   12

related. Since marital status is a nominal variable, all you can do is measure the strength of the association between the two variables.

The value for Cramér's V is .103. It's the square root of the chi-square value divided by twice the sample size. You divide by twice the sample size because k, the smaller of the number of rows and columns, is 3, so $k-1$ is 2.

The contingency coefficient C is .144. It's the square root of the chi-square value divided by the sum of chi-square and the sample size.

Although the two measures of association aren't equal, they're of the same magnitude. On a scale of 0 to 1, neither number is particularly large. They're not large, even though the observed significance level for the chi-square statistic is quite small. That's because for large sample sizes, even small departures from independence are statistically significant.

The interpretation of these statistics, "not particularly large," isn't very satisfying. It would be helpful to have a more concrete interpretation, some way of putting into words what it means for two variables to have a Cramér's V of .103. Unfortunately, there is none. Chi-square-based measures are difficult to interpret. They can be used to compare the strength of association in different tables. However, the "strength of association" being compared isn't easily related to an intuitive concept of association.

Proportional Reduction in Error

Commonly used alternatives to the measures based on chi-square are coefficients based on the idea of **proportional reduction in error,** or PRE. Unlike chi-square-based measures, PRE coefficients have a clear interpretation. These measures are based on how well you can predict the value of a dependent variable when you know the value of the independent variable. The measures compare the errors in two different situations: one where you don't use the independent variable for prediction and one where you do.

Suppose you have a sample of married people. The dependent variable is whether life is seen as exciting, routine, or dull, and the independent variable is the happiness of a person's marriage.

- In the first situation, you try to predict how a person feels about life, knowing only what percentage of the sample falls into each of the excitement categories.
- In the second situation, you have an additional piece of information available—the happiness of a person's marriage.

The additional piece of information in the second situation improves your ability to predict correctly—if the two variables are related. If all happily married people find life exciting, all moderately happy people find life routine, and all unhappily married people find life boring, then knowing the condition of a person's marriage lets you predict perfectly whether they find life exciting, routine, or dull. There is a perfect relationship between the variables. If you know one, you know the other. Most of the time, though, a relationship is less than perfect.

Let's consider how you can compare the error rates in these two situations and calculate lambda, a commonly used PRE measure.

Calculating Lambda

Figure 19.2 is a crosstabulation of the happiness of people's marriages with the excitement they find in life. The entry in each cell is just the number of cases in that cell. The following commands produced the crosstabulation as well as lambda statistics (more on those soon):

```
FILE HANDLE GSS / (system-specific information)
GET FILE=GSS
CROSSTABS TABLES=LIFE BY HAPMAR
STATISTICS 4
```

Figure 19.2 Excitement by marital happiness

```
FILE:     1984 General Social Survey

- - - - - - - - - -   C R O S S T A B U L A T I O N   O F  - - - - - - - - - -
    LIFE      Is life exciting or dull?
BY  HAPMAR    Happiness of marriage
- - - - - - - - - - - - - - - - - - - - - - - - - -   PAGE  1 OF  1

                      HAPMAR
              COUNT |
                    |Very hap Pretty  Not too   ROW
                    |py       happy   happy     TOTAL
                    |      1|       2|       3|
LIFE         -------+--------+--------+--------+
                  1 |   302  |    83  |     6  |   391
    Exciting       |        |        |        |   47.6
                   +--------+--------+--------+
                  2 |   225  |   161  |    14  |   400
Pretty  routine    |        |        |        |   48.7
                   +--------+--------+--------+
                  3 |    11  |    14  |     5  |    30
    Dull           |        |        |        |   3.7
                   +--------+--------+--------+
              COLUMN    538      258       25      821
              TOTAL    65.5     31.4      3.0    100.0
```

If you had no information about how happy a person's marriage is, what would you predict that the person would say about how exciting life is? Since you're interested in making as few errors as possible, you should predict the excitement category that occurs most often in the sample. In this case, you should predict that the person finds life routine. More people said they find life routine than any other response, so that's the best guess when you don't know anything about a person. Now count the number of cases in the table that you'd misclassify if you guessed "routine" for everyone. Your prediction would be wrong for the 391 people who said life is exciting and for the 30 people who said life is dull.

The total number of misclassified people is the sum of these two numbers, 421. This is the error for the first situation, when you know nothing except the distribution of the dependent variable in the sample.

Let's take a look at the second situation. The rule is straightforward: for each category of the *independent* variable, predict the category of the *dependent* variable that occurs most frequently. If you know that someone is very happily married, the best guess for the excitement category is Exciting, because that's the most frequent choice of people who were very happily married. Using this rule, you'd incorrectly classify 236 people who said they're very happily married: 225 who found life routine and 11 who found life dull.

Applying the same rule, you'd predict Pretty routine for people who said their marriages were pretty happy. You'd be wrong in 97 cases. For people whose marriages were not too happy, you'd also predict Pretty routine. You'd be wrong for 11 of these people.

Now let's compare the errors. In the first situation, you incorrectly classified 421 people. In the second situation, you incorrectly classified 344 people. The **lambda** statistic measures how much your error rate decreases when you use the additional information about a person's marital happiness. Lambda (λ) is calculated as:

$$\frac{\text{Misclassified in situation 1} - \text{Misclassified in situation 2}}{\text{Misclassified in situation 1}}$$

That is, for this table,

$$\lambda = \frac{421 - 344}{421} = \frac{77}{421} = 0.183$$

By knowing how happy a person's marriage was, you reduced your error by 18%. Lambda tells you the proportion by which you can reduce your error in predicting the dependent variable if you know the independent variable. That's why it's called a *proportional reduction in error* measure.

The largest value that lambda can be is 1. You can see a table in which lambda is 1 in Figure 19.3. For each category of the independent variable, there is one cell with all of the cases. If you guess that value for all cases, you make no errors. The introduction of an additional variable lets you predict perfectly, and it results in a 100% reduction in error rate.

A value of zero for lambda means the independent variable is of no help in predicting the dependent variable. When two variables are statistically independent, lambda is zero; but a lambda of zero does not necessarily imply statistical independence. As with all measures of association, lambda measures association in a very specific way— reduction in error when values of one variable are used to predict values of the other. If this particular type of association is absent, lambda is

Figure 19.3 A table in which lambda equals 1

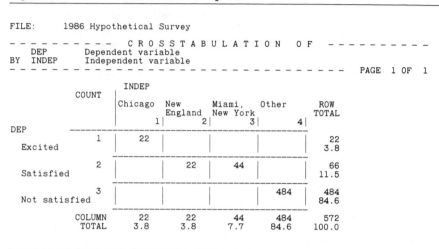

FILE: 1986 Hypothetical Survey

```
- - - - - - - - -      C R O S S T A B U L A T I O N    O F   - - - - - - - - -
     DEP        Dependent variable
BY   INDEP      Independent variable
- - - - - - - - - - - - - - - - - - - - - - - - - - - -     PAGE   1 OF   1

                       INDEP
              COUNT
                     |Chicago  New       Miami,    Other       ROW
                     |         England   New York              TOTAL
                     |      1|       2|       3|        4|
DEP           ----------------------------------------------------
              1      |   22   |       |        |         |      22
   Excited           |       |       |        |         |      3.8
                     --------------------------------------------
              2      |       |   22   |   44   |         |      66
   Satisfied         |       |       |        |         |      11.5
                     --------------------------------------------
              3      |       |       |        |   484    |     484
 Not satisfied       |       |       |        |         |      84.6
                     --------------------------------------------
              COLUMN     22      22       44      484        572
              TOTAL     3.8     3.8      7.7     84.6      100.0
```

Figure 19.4 Different versions of lambda

STATISTIC	SYMMETRIC	WITH LIFE DEPENDENT	WITH HAPMAR DEPENDENT
LAMBDA	0.11364	0.18290	0.01060

NUMBER OF MISSING OBSERVATIONS =   652

zero. Even when lambda is zero, other measures of association may find association of a different kind. No measure of association is sensitive to every type of association imaginable.

Two Different Lambdas

Lambda is not a symmetric measure. Its value depends on which variable you predict from which. Suppose that instead of predicting the excitement category based on marital happiness, you tried to predict the reverse—how happy a person's marriage was, based on how exciting the person found life to be. You'd get a different value for lambda. You'd get a value of .011. Both of these values are shown in Figure 19.4. The first is in the column labeled WITH LIFE DEPENDENT, and the second is in the column labeled WITH HAPMAR DEPENDENT.

The statistics in Figure 19.4 actually were produced by the same CROSSTABS job that produced the table in Figure 19.2. In the commands that produced the table, you can see that we asked for Statistic 4. Statistic 4 gives us both lambdas, as well as another one we're about to discuss.

Symmetric Lambda

Although in the previous example, we considered view of life as the dependent variable and happiness of the marriage as the independent variable, that need not be the case. It's certainly possible that a good marriage makes life exciting or that an exciting life makes for a happy marriage. If you have no reason to consider one of the variables dependent and the other independent, you can compute a *symmetric* lambda coefficient. You predict the first variable from the second and then the second variable from the first.

For example, if marital state is predicted without knowledge of the excitement category, you misclassify 283 people. With the addition of the excitement variable, you misclassify 280 people, not a big difference. From the calculation of lambda with excitement as dependent, you found that inclusion of marital status decreased the number misclassified from 421 to 344. The symmetric lambda is calculated as the sum of the two differences divided by the total number misclassified without additional information. In other words, you just add up the numerators for the two lambdas, then add up the denominators, then divide:

$$\text{Symmetric } \lambda = \frac{(421-344) + (283-280)}{421 + 283}$$

$$= \frac{77 + 3}{421 + 283} = 0.114$$

This number is printed under the column labeled SYMMETRIC in Figure 19.4.

? *Is it really possible for variables to be related and still have a lambda of zero? That doesn't sound right.* Actually, this can happen easily, depending on the distribution of the dependent variable. For example, consider Figure 19.5. The two variables are clearly associated, but value 2 of the dependent variable occurs most often in each category of the independent variable. You'd predict that value whether or not you knew the independent variable. Since knowing the independent variable doesn't help at all, lambda equals zero. You can see that SPSS^X reports a lambda of zero, when DEP is the dependent variable. Remember: a measure of association is sensitive to a particular kind of association. ■ ■ ■

Figure 19.5 A table in which lambda equals zero

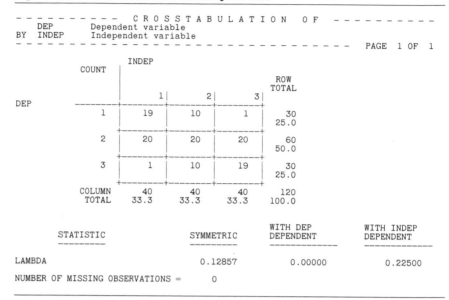

```
- - - - - - - - - -   C R O S S T A B U L A T I O N   O F   - - - - - - - - -
    DEP        Dependent variable
BY  INDEP      Independent variable
- - - - - - - - - - - - - - - - - - - - - - - - - - - -   PAGE  1 OF  1
                          INDEP
             COUNT  |
                    |                                    ROW
                    |                                    TOTAL
                    |      1|      2|      3|
DEP          -------+-------+-------+-------+
                 1  |   19  |   10  |    1  |    30
                    |       |       |       |    25.0
                    +-------+-------+-------+
                 2  |   20  |   20  |   20  |    60
                    |       |       |       |    50.0
                    +-------+-------+-------+
                 3  |    1  |   10  |   19  |    30
                    |       |       |       |    25.0
                    +-------+-------+-------+
             COLUMN    40      40      40      120
             TOTAL    33.3    33.3    33.3    100.0
```

STATISTIC	SYMMETRIC	WITH DEP DEPENDENT	WITH INDEP DEPENDENT
LAMBDA	0.12857	0.00000	0.22500

NUMBER OF MISSING OBSERVATIONS =   0

MEASURES OF ASSOCIATION FOR ORDINAL VARIABLES

Lambda can be used as a measure of association for variables measured on ordinal scales as well as for variables measured on nominal scales. In fact, both variables we used in the previous example, happiness of marriage and degree of excitement with life, are ordinal variables. The computation of lambda, however, didn't use the order information. We could have interchanged the order of the rows and columns in any way we wanted (for example, we could have put Not too happy before Very happy, or Pretty routine before Excited) and not changed the value of lambda at all.

There are measures of association that make use of the additional information available for ordinal variables. They tell us not only about the strength of the association but the direction as well. If the degree of excitement with life increases as the degree of happiness of marriage increases, we can say that the two variables have a **positive relationship.** If, on the other hand, the values of one variable increase while those of the other decrease, we can say the variables have a **negative relationship.** We can't make statements like these about nominal variables, since there's no order to the categories of the variables. Values can't increase or decrease unless they have an order.

Concordant and Discordant Pairs

Many ordinal measures of association are based on comparing pairs of cases. For example, look at Table 19.1, which contains a listing of the values of LIFE, the excitement variable, and HAPMAR, the marriage variable, for three cases.

Table 19.1 Values of LIFE and HAPMAR

	LIFE	HAPMAR
Case 1	1	2
Case 2	2	3
Case 3	3	2

Consider the pair of cases, Case 1 and Case 2. Both Case 2 values are larger than the corresponding values in Case 1. That is, the value for LIFE is larger for Case 2 than for Case 1, and the value for HAPMAR is larger for Case 2 than for Case 1. Such a pair of cases is called **concordant.** A pair of cases is concordant if the value of each variable is larger (or each is smaller) for one case than for the other case.

A pair of cases is **discordant** if the value of one variable for a case is larger than the value for the other case, but the direction is reversed for the second variable. For example, Case 2 and Case 3 are a discordant pair, since the value of LIFE for Case 3 is larger than for Case 2, but the value of HAPMAR is larger for Case 2 than for Case 3.

When two cases have identical values on one or both variables, they are said to be **tied.**

There are five possible outcomes when you compare two cases. They can be concordant, discordant, tied on the first variable, tied on the second variable, or tied on both variables. When data are arranged in a crosstabulation, it's easy to compute the number of concordant, discordant, and tied pairs, just by looking at the table and adding up cell frequencies.

If most of the pairs are concordant, the association is said to be positive. As values of one variable increase (or decrease), so do the values of the other variable. If most of the pairs are discordant, the association is negative. As values of one variable increase, those of the other tend to decrease. If concordant and discordant pairs are equally likely, we say there is no association.

Measures Based on Concordant and Discordant Pairs

The ordinal measures of association that we'll consider are all based on the difference between the number of concordant pairs (P) and the number of discordant pairs (Q), calculated for all *distinct* pairs of observations. Since we want our measures of association to fall within a known range for all tables we must standardize the difference, P−Q (if possible, from −1 to 1, where −1 indicates a perfect negative relationship, +1 indicates a perfect positive relationship, and 0 indicates no relationship). The measures differ in the way they attempt to standardize P−Q.

Goodman and Kruskal's Gamma

One way of standardizing the difference between the number of concordant and discordant pairs is to use Goodman and Kruskal's **gamma.** You calculate the difference between the number of concordant and discordant pairs, (P−Q), and then divide this difference by the sum of the number of concordant and discordant pairs (P+Q). Look at Figure 19.6, which contains the value of gamma for the LIFE by HAPMAR table. Commands for producing the table and gamma are:

```
FILE HANDLE GSS / (system-specific information)
GET FILE=GSS
CROSSTABS TABLES=LIFE BY HAPMAR
STATISTICS 8
```

Statistic 8 requests the value of gamma for the table.

Figure 19.6 Goodman and Kruskal's gamma

```
          STATISTIC              VALUE
          ---------              -----

GAMMA                           0.45929

NUMBER OF MISSING OBSERVATIONS =     652
```

Gamma is .459. What does this mean? A positive gamma tells you that there are more "like" (concordant) pairs of cases than "unlike" pairs. There is a positive relationship between happiness of marriage and degree of excitement. As happiness of marriage increases, so does excitement with life. A negative gamma would mean that as happiness in marriage increases, excitement with life decreases.

The absolute value of gamma has a proportional reduction in error interpretation. What you are trying to predict is whether a pair of cases is like or unlike. In the first situation, you classify pairs as like or unlike based on the flip of a fair coin. In the second situation, you base your decision rule on whether there are more concordant or discordant pairs. If most of the pairs are concordant you predict "like" for all pairs. If most of the pairs are discordant you predict "unlike." The absolute value of gamma (the numerical value, ignoring a minus sign if there is one) is the proportional reduction in error when the second rule is used instead of the first.

For example, if half of the pairs of cases are concordant and half are discordant, guessing randomly and classifying all cases as concordant leads to the same number of misclassified cases—one half. The value of gamma is then zero. If all the pairs are concordant, guessing "like" will result in correct classification of all pairs. Guessing randomly will classify only half of the pairs correctly. In this situation, the value of gamma is 1.

If two variables are independent, the value of gamma is zero. However, a gamma of zero does not necessarily mean independence. (If the table is two by two, though, a gamma of zero *does* mean that the variables are independent.)

Kendall's Tau-*b*

Gamma ignores all pairs of cases that involve ties. A measure that attempts to normalize P–Q by considering ties on each variable in a pair separately (but not ties on both variables) is **tau-b.** It's computed as

$$\tau_b = \frac{P - Q}{\sqrt{(P + Q + T_X)(P + Q + T_Y)}}$$

where T_X is the number of ties involving only the first variable, and T_Y is the number of ties involving only the second variable. Tau-*b* can have the value of +1 and −1 only for square tables. Since the denominator is complicated, there's no simple explanation in terms of proportional reduction of error. However, tau-*b* is a commonly used measure.

Tau-*c*

A measure that can attain, or nearly attain, the values of +1 and −1 for a table of any size is **tau-c.** It's computed as

$$\tau_c = \frac{2m(P - Q)}{N^2(m - 1)}$$

where m is the smaller of the number of rows and columns. Unfortunately, there is no simple proportional reduction of error interpretation of tau-*c* either.

Somers' *d*

Gamma, tau-*b*, and tau-*c* are all symmetric measures. It doesn't matter whether one of the variables is considered dependent. The value of the statistic is the same. Somers proposed an extension of gamma in which one of the variables is considered dependent. It differs from gamma only in that the denominator is the sum of all pairs of cases that are not tied on the independent variable. (In gamma, *all* cases involving ties are excluded from the denominator.)

MEASURES INVOLVING INTERVAL DATA

If the two variables are measured on an interval scale, you can calculate coefficients that make use of this additional information. The Pearson correlation coefficient, discussed in Chapter 21, measures the strength of what's called a *linear* association. The eta coefficient can be used when a dependent variable is measured on an interval scale, and the independent variable on a nominal or ordinal scale. When eta is squared, it can be interpreted as the proportion of the total variance in the dependent variable that can be accounted for by knowing the values of the independent variable.

TESTING HYPOTHESES

In addition to assessing the strength and nature of a relationship, you may want to test hypotheses about the various measures of association. For example, you may want to test the null hypothesis that the value of a measure is zero in the population. This doesn't involve anything new. You just have to calculate the probability that you'd obtain a value as large (in absolute value) as the one you observed if the value is zero in the population. SPSS^X prints the observed significance levels for some of the measures of association we've discussed in this chapter.

STATISTICS FOR CROSSTABS

Here is a complete list of the numbers used on the STATISTICS command following a CROSSTABS command. (The numbers for the OPTIONS command following CROSSTABS were given at the end of Chapter 9.)

1	Chi-square	6	Kendall's tau-b
2	Phi for 2 × 2 tables, Cramer's V otherwise	7	Kendall's tau-c
3	Contingency coefficient	8	Gamma
4	Lambda	9	Somers' d
5	Uncertainty coefficient	10	Eta
		11	Pearson's r

WHAT'S NEXT?

In this chapter, we considered how to measure the strength and nature of the relationship between two variables that have a limited number of distinct categories. What if we want to examine the relationship between two variables that are measured on an interval or ratio scale? That's what the remainder of the book is about.

Summary

How can you measure the strength of the relationship between two categorical variables?

Many measures of association can be used to measure the strength of the relationship between two categorical variables.

Measures of association differ in the way they define association.

You should select a measure to use based on the characteristics of the data and how you want to define association.

The chi-square statistic is not a good measure of association. Its value doesn't tell you anything about the strength of the relationship between two variables.

Measures of proportional reduction in error (PRE) compare the error you make when you predict values of one variable based on values of another, with the error when you predict them without information about the other variable.

Special measures of association are available for ordinal variables. They are based on counting the number of concordant pairs (as one variable increases, so does the other) and the number of discordant pairs (as one variable increases, the other decreases).

EXERCISES

Syntax

1 Write the commands to recode the AGE variable into decades and to obtain a crosstabulation of age in decades and satisfaction with job or housework (SATJOB). Include the appropriate percentages and measures of association.

2 Correct the errors in the following job:

```
RECODE SATJOB (1= 1,2) (2=3) (3=4)
VALUE LABELS SATJOB 1 VERY OR MODERATELY SATISFIED/
2 A LITTLE DISATISFIED/ 3 VERY DISSATISFIED
CROSSTABS SATJOB BY LIFE/STATISTICS ALL
```

3 Write the appropriate commands to obtain a crosstabulation of condition of health and belief in life after death. Obtain appropriate percentages and measures of association.

Statistical Concepts

1 Indicate whether you agree or disagree with each of the following statements, and why.

a. If one of the measures of association provided by CROSSTABS has a very small value, it is safe to assume that the other measures of association will also have small values.

    b. Chi-square-based measures of association are easier to interpret than PRE-based measures.

    c. A good measure of association for nominal variables indicates the strength of the association as well as the direction.

    d. Large values for the chi-square statistic indicate strong association between two variables.

2 For each of the following measures of association, indicate whether its value depends on which variable is specified as the row variable and which is specified as the column variable.

    a. Lambda.

    b. Symmetric lambda.

    c. Gamma.

    d. Somers' d.

    e. Cramer's V.

    f. Tau-b.

    g. Tau-c.

3 Which of the measures of association calculated by CROSSTABS are sensitive to all types of association?

4 What is the reason for normalizing measures of association to make their values fall within the range from −1 to +1, or from 0 to 1?

5 The following is a crosstabulation of condition of health and perception of life as exciting, routine, or dull:

```
- - - - - - - - - -  C R O S S T A B U L A T I O N   O F  - - - - - - - - - -
     LIFE      Is life exciting or dull?
BY  HEALTH    Condition of health
- - - - - - - - - - - - - - - - - - - - - - - - - - - -  PAGE  1 OF  1

                   HEALTH
           COUNT   |
           EXP VAL |Excellen Good     Fair      Poor      ROW
           COL PCT |t                                     TOTAL
                   |     1|      2|      3|      4|
   LIFE    --------+-------+-------+-------+-------+
             1     |   249     320      95      16       680
   Exciting        | 202.5   325.7   119.5    32.3      46.9%
                   | 57.6%   46.0%   37.3%    23.2%
                   +-------+-------+-------+-------+
             2     |   175     350     137      36       698
   Pretty routine  | 207.8   334.3   122.7    33.2      48.1%
                   | 40.5%   50.4%   53.7%    52.2%
                   +-------+-------+-------+-------+
             3     |     8      25      23      17        73
   Dull            |  21.7    35.0    12.8     3.5       5.0%
                   |  1.9%    3.6%    9.0%    24.6%
                   +-------+-------+-------+-------+
           COLUMN      432     695     255      69      1451
           TOTAL     29.8%   47.9%   17.6%    4.8%    100.0%


   CHI-SQUARE     D.F.    SIGNIFICANCE      MIN E.F.    CELLS WITH E.F.| 5
   ----------     ----    ------------      --------    ------------------

   104.21250        6       0.0000           3.471      1 OF   12 (  8.3%)

                                              WITH LIFE        WITH HEALTH
             STATISTIC         SYMMETRIC      DEPENDENT        DEPENDENT
             ---------         ---------      ---------        ---------

   LAMBDA                       0.04904        0.09827          0.00000

             STATISTIC           VALUE
             ---------           -----

   CRAMER'S V                  0.18950
   GAMMA                       0.30264

   NUMBER OF MISSING OBSERVATIONS =      22
```

a. Interpret all of the statistics printed.

b. Discuss the advantages and disadvantages of the various measures.

c. Show how lambda was computed.

6 The following table shows the relationship between depth of hypnosis and success in treatment of migraine headaches (Cedercreutz, 1978). Calculate the appropriate lambda statistic. How can you interpret this value?

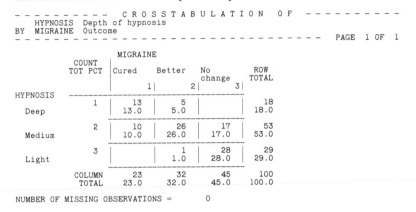

```
- - - - - - - - - -  C R O S S T A B U L A T I O N   O F  - - - - - - - - -
   HYPNOSIS  Depth of hypnosis
BY  MIGRAINE  Outcome
- - - - - - - - - - - - - - - - - - - - - - - - - - - - -  PAGE  1 OF  1

                      MIGRAINE
             COUNT
             TOT PCT  Cured    Better   No        ROW
                                        change    TOTAL
                        1|       2|         3|
HYPNOSIS     -------------------------------------
               1        13       5                  18
   Deep               13.0     5.0                18.0
             -------------------------------------
               2        10       26       17        53
   Medium             10.0     26.0     17.0      53.0
             -------------------------------------
               3                 1       28        29
   Light                        1.0     28.0      29.0
             -------------------------------------
             COLUMN     23       32       45       100
             TOTAL    23.0     32.0     45.0     100.0

NUMBER OF MISSING OBSERVATIONS =        0
```

7 Discuss the difference you would see in the gamma statistic if you coded job satisfaction from low to high and condition of health from good to poor, as compared to the value you would get if both job satisfaction and condition of health are coded in the same direction.

Data Analysis

1 We've seen that there is a relationship between perception of life and marital status. Compute the appropriate statistics to measure the strength of the association. Discuss why you selected those particular measures.

2 To see whether the strength of the association of marital status and perception of life is similar for males and for females, make two separate tables. Compute the measures of association you chose in the previous question for each of the two tables. What do you conclude about the strength of the relationship? Give some possible explanations for it.

3 Select four pairs of variables in the GSS file for which the gamma statistic would be an appropriate measure of association. Write and run the SPSS[X] job to compute it. Describe your results.

4 Select two nominal variables from the data file and compute appropriate measures of association. What can you conclude about the *direction* of the association?

20 Plotting Data

How can you display the relationship between two variables that are measured on an interval or ratio scale?

- What is a plot and why is it useful?
- What happens if several cases have the same or similar values for the variables you're plotting?
- How can a plot of two variables be modified to include information about an additional variable?
- How can a plot be used to identify unusual observations?

In the last chapter, you saw how to use various statistics to measure the strength of a relationship between two variables. The way you looked at the data depended on the information you wanted and on the characteristics of the variables. If you're interested in variables that have a limited number of categories—such as race, sex, or excitement with life—crosstabulations are effective ways to look at relationships.

However, you may want to study the relationship between two variables that are measured on an interval or ratio scale. If so, then counting the number of cases for each of the possible combinations of values may be awkward, and it may not tell you much. Think of all the possible combinations of salary and age if salary is measured in dollars and age in years. A crosstabulation of these variables would have a very large number of cells. Of course, you could group the values into smaller numbers of categories, such as salary ranges of $5,000 or $10,000. It's easy then to construct tables based on these grouped values, and this is often a convenient way to examine the patterns in the data. But the grouping does ignore some of the available information.

PLOTTING YOUR VARIABLES

A better way to display the data is to *plot* the values of the variables for all the cases. Look at Figure 20.1, a plot of father's education by mother's education for about 10% of the respondents in the General Social Survey. The commands used to produce this plot were these:

```
FILE HANDLE GSS / (system-specific information)
GET FILE=GSS
COMMENT The SAMPLE command takes a 10% sample of the cases.
SAMPLE .1
PLOT  HSIZE = 50 / VSIZE = 50/
   PLOT=PAEDUC WITH MAEDUC
```

The 10% sample of the large number of respondents makes the plots easier to read. The HSIZE and VSIZE subcommands are optional. They control the horizontal and vertical size of the plot. You can use them to produce a plot of the size you want. The variable before the WITH is displayed on the vertical axis, and the variable after WITH is displayed on the horizontal axis.

Figure 20.1 Plot of father's and mother's education

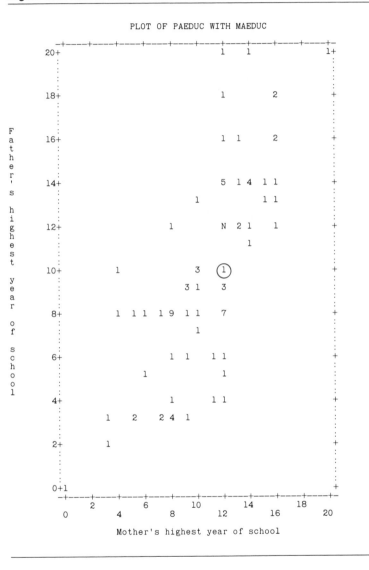

PLOT OF PAEDUC WITH MAEDUC

Mother's highest year of school

Each person in the survey was asked about the education of both of his or her parents. The plot displays the pairs of values—father's education and mother's education. The number of years of education for the mother is shown on the horizontal axis (also called the **X axis**), and the number of years of education for the father is shown on the vertical axis (the **Y axis**). Look at the circled point in Figure 20.1. Its value on the horizontal axis is 12 and on the vertical axis 10. This point represents a person whose mother had 12 years of education and whose father had 10.

You might wonder why the father's education is on the vertical axis and the mother's is on the horizontal axis. In this plot, there's no particular reason. These two variables could be interchanged. However, if one of the variables is considered a dependent variable and the other an independent variable, it's customary to plot the dependent variable on the vertical axis and the independent variable on the horizontal axis. For example, if salary is thought to depend on age, then it's customary to put salary on the vertical axis and age on the horizontal axis.

Interpreting a Plot

Looking at the plot in Figure 20.1, you see that a variety of different symbols are used to represent points. The number 1 is shown at the circled point, while the letter N appears above it. The symbol chosen by SPSS[X] to represent a point depends on the number of cases in the data that have the particular combination of values. Since there is only one case plotted for which the mother has 12 years of education and the father has 10, the symbol 1 is used. When there are two cases with a certain combination of values (for example, 16 years for both parents), the symbol 2 is used.

Figure 20.2 explains the meaning of each of the symbols. The number at the left of each dash indicates a possible number of cases that could coincide at a point on the plot, and the symbol following the dash represents that number of cases on the plot. For example, you can see

Figure 20.2 The table from PLOT showing symbols used

```
FILE:     1984 General Social Survey

* * * * * * * * * * * * * * * * *  P  L  O  T  * * * * * * * * * * * * * * * * *

Data    Information

        154 unweighted cases accepted.

Size of the plots

    Horizontal size is 50
    Vertical size is 50

Frequencies and symbols used (not applicable for control or overlay plots)

        1 - 1      11 - B      21 - L      31 - V
        2 - 2      12 - C      22 - M      32 - W
        3 - 3      13 - D      23 - N      33 - X
        4 - 4      14 - E      24 - O      34 - Y
        5 - 5      15 - F      25 - P      35 - Z
        6 - 6      16 - G      26 - Q      36 - *
        7 - 7      17 - H      27 - R
        8 - 8      18 - I      28 - S
        9 - 9      19 - J      29 - T
       10 - A      20 - K      30 - U
```

that the numerals 1 to 9 represent 1 to 9 cases. The symbol N is used to represent 23 cases. Looking at the plot again, you can see that for 23 cases, both parents are high school graduates.

What does the plot show? The points seem to be arranged in a band running from the bottom left to the top right. You can see the pattern: as one variable increases, so does the other. Most of the cases with low values for MAEDUC, also have low values for PAEDUC. Similarly, most of the cases with high values of one variable also have high values of the other. Looking at a plot is one of the best ways to examine relationships. You just look for patterns among the values of the two variables.

Cases with Similar Values

We specified a plot size of 50 by 50, and our variables are measured in whole years from 0 through 20, so each possible response has a different position along the axes—with some space in between.

What if both variables were salaries measured in dollars from $0 through $50,000? With just 50 positions available, SPSS^X would have to lump cases within each $1000 range into a single print position. Therefore, when you plot variables with many values and find a symbol indicating two or more cases at the same position, it's possible that those cases have close but not identical values.

USING A CONTROL VARIABLE ON A PLOT

Suppose you also want to know if father's and mother's education seem to make any difference in how the respondent perceives life. You could make three separate plots: one for people who found life exciting, one for people who found life routine, and one for people who found life dull. You could then compare the three plots and see whether the relationship between parents' education differs for the three groups. Another way to approach the problem, though, is to make a single plot in which individual points are identified as belonging to the different excitement categories. This **control plot** is easy to produce with SPSS^X:

```
FILE HANDLE GSS / (system-specific information)
GET FILE=GSS
SAMPLE .1
VALUE LABELS LIFE 1 'Exciting' 2 'Routine' 3 'Dull'
PLOT   HSIZE = 50 / VSIZE = 50/
   PLOT=PAEDUC WITH MAEDUC BY LIFE
```

The PLOT command looks like the one used before. The only change is the addition of the keyword BY and the variable LIFE. The keyword BY indicates that the points are to be identified by their values on an additional variable. The name of the variable, in this case LIFE, follows the keyword.

Figure 20.3 A control plot

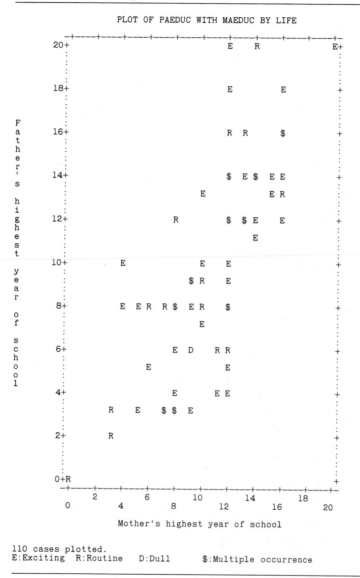

PLOT OF PAEDUC WITH MAEDUC BY LIFE

110 cases plotted.
E:Exciting R:Routine   D:Dull $:Multiple occurrence

Interpreting a Control Plot

Look at the plot in Figure 20.3. The symbols that represent the points no longer indicate the number of cases. Instead, they tell you whether the person found life exciting (E), routine (R), or dull (D). If cases with more than one excitement level overlap at the same point on the plot, a dollar sign is printed. The explanation of the symbols is printed below the plot.

> *How does SPSS^X know what symbols to print for people who found life exciting, routine, or dull?* It just takes the first character in each value label. If a control variable doesn't have value labels, the first character of the actual value is used. This is the only way SPSS^X can guess what symbol you want. Often, you'll want to supply new value labels before making a control plot—as we did here. You'll certainly need to do this if the value labels for more than one category begin with the same letter, or you won't be able to tell the categories apart. ■ ■ ■

If there's a relationship between excitement and mother's and father's education, you should be able to see it by studying the patterns of the symbols. For example, look at Figure 20.4, where you see a line that was drawn in to separate people whose mothers had more education from people whose fathers had more education. The people represented below the line are those whose mothers were better educated than their fathers. If people with better-educated mothers were more excited by life than people with better-educated fathers, you'd expect to find a higher proportion of Es below the line than above it.

USING REFERENCE LINES

In Figure 20.4, the diagonal line was drawn in by hand. If you want a vertical or horizontal line on a plot, the computer can print it for you. These lines are called **reference lines.** If you want to easily separate high school graduates from the parents of the other cases, you can instruct SPSS^X to draw reference lines at the value 12 for both of the axes. Just modify the job like this:

```
FILE HANDLE GSS / (system-specific information)
GET FILE=GSS
SAMPLE .1
VALUE LABELS LIFE 1 'Exciting' 2 'Routine' 3 'Dull'
PLOT  HSIZE = 50 / VSIZE = 50 /
    HORIZONTAL REFERENCE(12) / VERTICAL REFERENCE(12) /
    PLOT=PAEDUC WITH MAEDUC BY LIFE
```

Two additional instructions are included in this PLOT command. The instruction HORIZONTAL REFERENCE(12) tells SPSS^X to draw a line at the value of 12 on the horizontal axis. The instruction VERTICAL REFERENCE(12) does the same for the vertical axis.

You can see the plot produced by the above command in Figure 20.5. It differs from Figure 20.3 only in that two lines have been added. Now it's even easier to break up the plot into groups of people, because the groups are boxed in. For example, it looks as if people with both parents well educated (in the upper right part of the plot) were more likely to be excited by life than people with less-educated parents (in the lower left

Figure 20.4 Which parent was better educated?

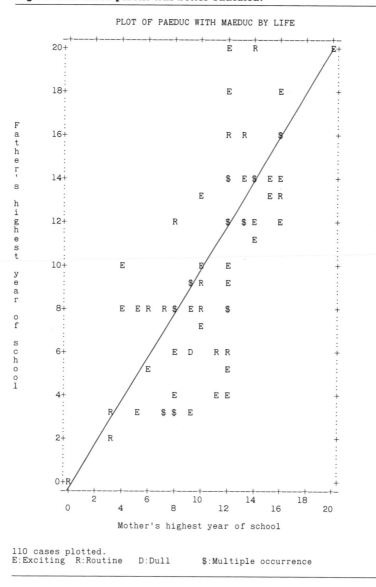

PLOT OF PAEDUC WITH MAEDUC BY LIFE

110 cases plotted.
E:Exciting   R:Routine   D:Dull $:Multiple occurrence

part). Few people in the sample had only one parent with a college education.

These conjectures might be a good starting point for further investigation. Reference lines on plots can make it easier to see the patterns that indicate relationships in the data.

Figure 20.5 A plot with reference lines

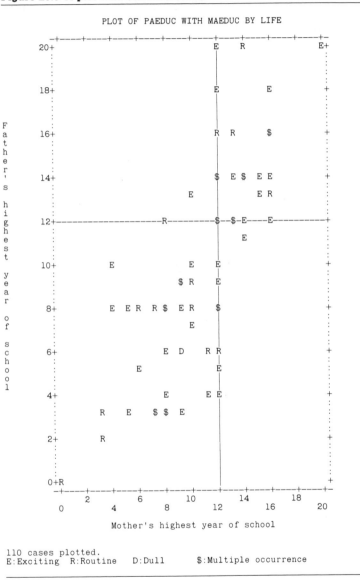

PLOT OF PAEDUC WITH MAEDUC BY LIFE

110 cases plotted.
E:Exciting R:Routine   D:Dull $:Multiple occurrence

WHY PLOT?

Plotting data is one of the best ways to look for relationships and patterns. A plot is simple to understand and conveys a lot of information about the data. In other chapters, we discuss methods of summarizing and describing relationships, but those methods are no substitute for plots. Whenever possible, you should plot the data *first*, and then think about appropriate methods for describing the plots.

A plot can also alert you to possible problems in the data. For example, if you're plotting salary and age, and you find a 22-year-old with a salary of $100,000, you have reason to be suspicious. Although there's a chance that the values are correct, it's much more likely that either the age or the salary was recorded or entered incorrectly. You wouldn't have been able to pick out this point as suspicious if you examined the variables individually. A salary of $100,000 is high but possible. An age of 22 is not usual. It's the combination of the values that leads you to suspect the point may be a mistake. Even if the point is correct, it's important to identify it early, since it may need special treatment in later analyses.

MORE ABOUT THE PLOT PROCEDURE

The minimum specification to obtain a plot is simply the PLOT subcommand:

```
PLOT PLOT=PAEDUC WITH MAEDUC
```

The first variable named (before WITH) goes on the vertical axis; the second goes on the horizontal axis. The PLOT procedure labels the axes according to the ranges of values it finds in the data, and according to the size of the plot. You can change the size of the plot, either for a more convenient size or for more convenient labels, by using the HSIZE (horizontal size) and VSIZE (vertical size) keywords. All additional specifications such as these must *precede* the PLOT subcommand.

```
PLOT  HSIZE = 40 / VSIZE = 40 /
   PLOT = PAEDUC WITH MAEDUC
```

The default plot size is 80 horizontal spaces by 40 vertical lines.

Reference Lines.   You can supply one or more reference lines crossing either the horizontal or the vertical axis. For reference lines at 12 and 16 years of mother's education, on the horizontal axis:

```
PLOT  HORIZONTAL REFERENCE(12,16) /
   PLOT = PAEDUC WITH MAEDUC
```

Note that lines crossing the horizontal axis are themselves vertical.

Control Plots.   To get a control plot, where each plotted point is labeled by the first letter of the value label from a third ("control") variable, specify:

```
PLOT PLOT=PAEDUC WITH MAEDUC BY LIFE
```

Regression Plots.   The specification FORMAT = REGRESSION places the letter R in the margins of the plot to show where the "best" line through the data points would fall. This line is discussed in more detail in Chapter 22.

Remember that you can use the SAMPLE or SELECT IF command to limit the number of cases. Always place the required PLOT subcommand last:

```
PLOT  HSIZE = 50 / VSIZE = 50 /
    HORIZONTAL REFERENCE(12,16) / VERTICAL REFERENCE(12,16) /
    FORMAT=REGRESSION /
  PLOT=PAEDUC WITH MAEDUC BY LIFE
```

WHAT'S NEXT?

Many important relationships look much like Figure 20.1. The values cluster around a straight line running through the plot. If the cases cluster tightly around a straight line, there is a strong relationship between the two variables. You can measure the strength of a linear relationship of this kind with a statistic, the correlation coefficient. We'll look at correlations in the next chapter.

Summary

How can you display the relationship between two variables that are measured on an interval or ratio scale?

A plot displays the values of two variables for each case.

By examining a plot, you can see what sort of relationship, if any, there is between two variables.

The points on a plot may be identified by their values on an additional variable (called a *control variable*). This lets you see whether the relationship between the two variables differs for the different categories of the control variable.

Points that have unusual combinations of values can be identified from a plot, since they will be far removed from the other cases.

EXERCISES

Syntax

1 Write the appropriate command to obtain a plot of INCOME and AGE. Put values of INCOME on the vertical axis.

2 How would you change the command in question 1 so that INCOME would be on the horizontal axis?

3 Write the command to identify each of the points on the INCOME and AGE plot as males or females (variable SEX).

4 Correct the errors in the following PLOT commands:

   a. PLOT SBP BY AGE

   b. PLOT SPB WITH AGE

   c. PLOT PLOT SBP WITH AGE BY SEX(1,2)

   d. PLOT PLOT AGE BY SEX WITH SBP

5 You run the PLOT procedure and obtain the following error messages. Explain the error messages and indicate how you would correct the mistake.

```
>ERROR   14104 LINE   4, COLUMN  6, TEXT: EDUC
>An illegal subcommand has been specified.  The valid subcommands are: MISSING,
>HSIZE, VSIZE, CUTPOINT, SYMBOL, TITLE, HORIZONTAL, VERTICAL, FORMAT and PLOT.
>THIS COMMAND NOT EXECUTED.


>ERROR   14102
>'PLOT' must be the last subcommand.
```

Statistical Concepts

1 Indicate whether you would use the CROSSTABS procedure, the BREAKDOWN procedure, or the PLOT procedure to display the relationship between the following pairs of variables:

   a. Job satisfaction and income measured in dollars.

   b. Race and marital status.

   c. Systolic blood pressure and age.

   d. Husband's highest degree and wife's highest degree.

   e. Hours studied for an examination and letter grade on the exam.

   f. Miles per gallon that a car gets and its weight in pounds.

2 Describe the relationships between the variables in the following plots:

   a.   b.

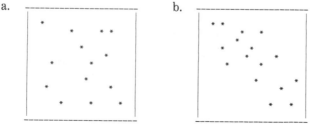

c.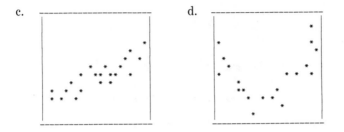

d.

3 The following table contains age at first marriage, years of education, and sex for five people. Plot these values, identifying whether each is for a male or female.

AGEWED	EDUC	SEX
18	12	Male
22	13	Female
30	16	Male
16	10	Male
25	18	Female

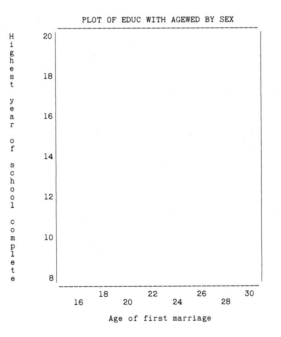

Data Analysis

1 Obtain a plot of the age at which a person first marries (AGEWED) and his or her years of education (EDUC). (To make the plot easier to read, take a random sample of 10% of the cases.) Describe the relationship that you see.

2 Repeat the plot in question 1, this time drawing reference axes corresponding to grammar school, high school, and college. Also identify the points as corresponding to males or females.

3 Suggest four pairs of variables in the GSS for which it makes sense to obtain plots. Draw plots for two of these pairs, and describe any relationship that you might see.

4 For men and women separately, obtain a plot of the age at which they were first married and the years of education of their mothers (MAEDUC). Describe the relationships that you see. Do they differ for the two sexes? Repeat using father's education (PAEDUC). Are the relationships similar?

21 Interpreting Correlation Coefficients

> ## *How can you summarize the strength of the linear relationship between two variables?*

- What is a linear relationship?
- What is a positive linear relationship, and what is a negative linear relationship?
- What is the Pearson correlation coefficient?
- What does a correlation coefficient of $+1$ or -1 indicate?
- Is it possible that two variables are related if the correlation coefficient is zero?
- How can you test the hypothesis that, in the population, two variables have a correlation coefficient of zero?
- Does correlation imply causation?
- When should you use a one-tailed significance level?
- What can happen if you test whether a large number of correlation coefficients are zero?
- What should you do if you have cases with missing information in your data file?

From a plot of the values of two variables, we can see if they appear to be related. What do we mean by "related" here? Nothing complicated. Two variables are **related** if knowing the value of one variable tells us something about the value of the other variable. Neither of the variables has to be considered dependent or independent; all we're interested in is how they behave together. In Chapter 20, we saw that father's education and mother's education appear to be related. As years of education for one parent increase, so do the years for the other.

In this chapter, we'll consider some different types of relationships between variables and how we can statistically measure the strength of the relationships. Our primary interest will be in **linear** relationships— those in which the values of the two variables cluster about a straight line on a plot.

TYPES OF RELATIONSHIPS

To get some idea of the types of relationships among variables, let's consider relationships between parents' and children's educational levels. We'll also include the age at which the children marry.

Relationships can be very complicated and can require many different complex analyses. However, a good place to start is by looking at the plots of the variables. Let's first look at a plot in which there doesn't appear to be any relationship. It'll serve as a good reference point for determining whether relationships are present.

Using a random sample of cases from the General Social Survey, Figure 21.1 is a plot of the age at which a respondent first married and the years of education of the respondent's mother. The SPSS^X commands that produced the plot are:

```
FILE HANDLE GSS / (system-specific information)
GET FILE=GSS
SAMPLE .1
PLOT  HSIZE = 55 / VSIZE = 50 /
  PLOT=MAEDUC WITH AGEWED
```

Figure 21.1 Mother's education with age at marriage

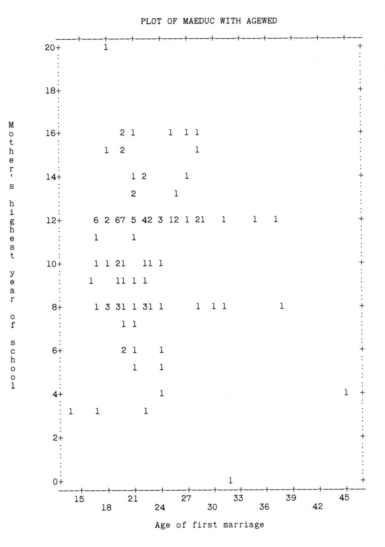

PLOT OF MAEDUC WITH AGEWED

Age of first marriage

110 cases plotted.

How would you characterize the relationship between the two variables? There doesn't appear to be any. The points are scattered all over the plot. Knowing the age at which a person was married tells you nothing about the education of the person's mother. Or if you're told the mother's education, you nothing about the age at which the person was married. There seems to be no association, or relationship, between the two variables.

Perfect Relationships

When there's no relationship between two variables, you can't see any kind of pattern on a plot. Points appear to be randomly distributed. If there's a perfect relationship between two variables, you should be able to see a distinct pattern. There are no perfect relationships in the General Social Survey, so we'll create one. Let's pretend that every father is twice as old as his child. If we know the father's age, we know the child's age, and vice-versa. We can use the following commands to create the fathers' ages we want and to plot the results:

```
FILE HANDLE GSS / (system-specific information)
GET FILE=GSS
SELECT IF (AGE < 50)
SAMPLE .1
COMPUTE DADSAGE = 2 * AGE
VARIABLE LABELS DADSAGE "Father's age"
PLOT HSIZE = 50 / VSIZE = 50 /
  PLOT = DADSAGE WITH AGE
```

The result is in Figure 21.2. The relationship is perfectly linear, since the points fall exactly on a straight line. The relationship is also positive, since as DADSAGE increases, so does AGE.

Now let's look at a perfect negative linear relationship. We need a variable that *decreases* as age increases. If everyone lived to a spry 100 years, we could calculate the remaining years of life for each case using:

```
FILE HANDLE GSS / (system-specific information)
GET FILE=GSS
SAMPLE .1
COMPUTE TIMELEFT = 100 - AGE
VARIABLE LABELS TIMELEFT "Years remaining"
PLOT HSIZE = 50 / VSIZE = 50 /
  PLOT = TIMELEFT WITH AGE
```

Figure 21.3 is a plot of actual age and remaining years. Again the points fall exactly on a straight line, but as the values of one variable increase, the values of the other variable decrease.

Figure 21.2 Perfect linear positive relationship

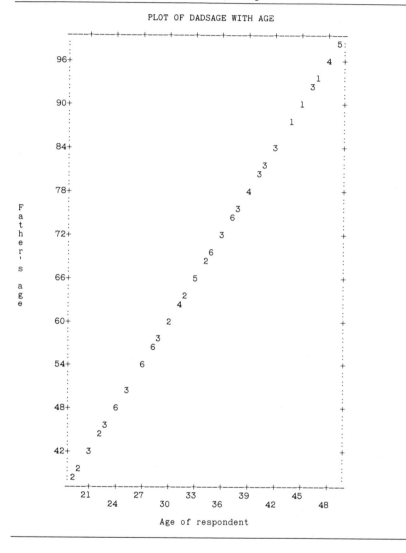

PLOT OF DADSAGE WITH AGE

Figure 21.3 Perfect linear negative relationship

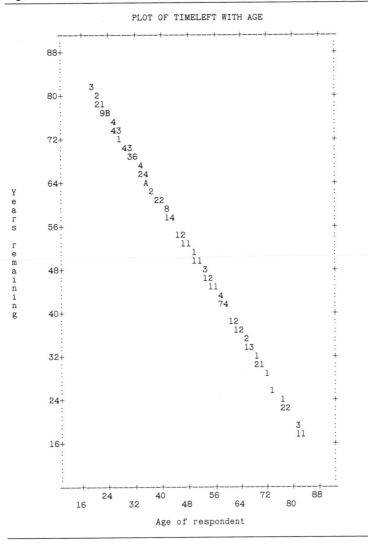

PLOT OF TIMELEFT WITH AGE

More about Linear Relationships

In real life, linear relationships look more like the plot of parental education in the last chapter. The plot is shown again in Figure 21.4, with a straight line drawn through the center of the points. The points are clustered around the line, but most of them don't fall exactly on it. To find out the best place to draw the line, put the subcommand FORMAT = REGRESSION on the PLOT command. SPSS^X puts the letter R at two positions on the frame of the plot, and the line connects those positions. (In Chapter 22, we'll find out how this works.)

```
PLOT  HSIZE = 55 / VSIZE = 50 /
   FORMAT=REGRESSION /
  PLOT=PAEDUC WITH MAEDUC
```

You can see that the points don't fall exactly on the line. Instead they are distributed around it. There's quite a bit of variability around the line, but most points are not too far removed. You can see that the relationship is *positive,* since as mother's education increases, so does father's.

A Weaker Linear Relationship

Although the relationship between father's and mother's education is not perfect, there's a fairly strong tendency for the points to cluster around a straight line. Figure 21.5 shows an example of a weaker linear relationship. It's a plot of the respondents' age and their fathers' education.

```
FILE HANDLE GSS / (system-specific information)
GET FILE=GSS
SAMPLE .1
PLOT  HSIZE = 50 / VSIZE = 50 /
   FORMAT=REGRESSION /
  PLOT=AGE WITH PAEDUC
```

We know that people's average education has increased substantially over the last several decades, so we would expect that older people have less education than young people. They would also have parents with less education than the parents of younger people. The plot supports this notion. A line through the Rs that SPSS^X puts in the border of the plot indicates that there is a negative relationship between age and father's education. As age increases, fathers' education decreases. However, you'll notice that the points are widely scattered around the line. The relationship does not appear to be as strong as that for mother's and father's education.

Figure 21.4 Father's education with mother's education

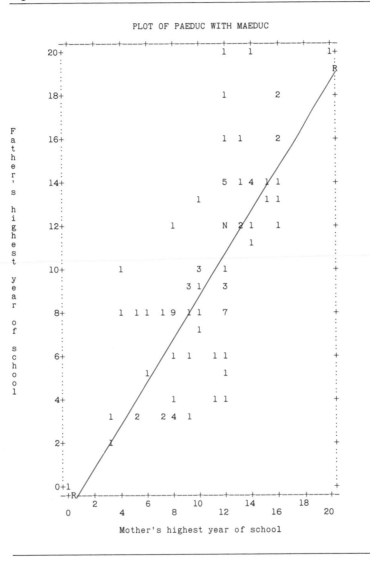

PLOT OF PAEDUC WITH MAEDUC

Figure 21.5 Age with father's education

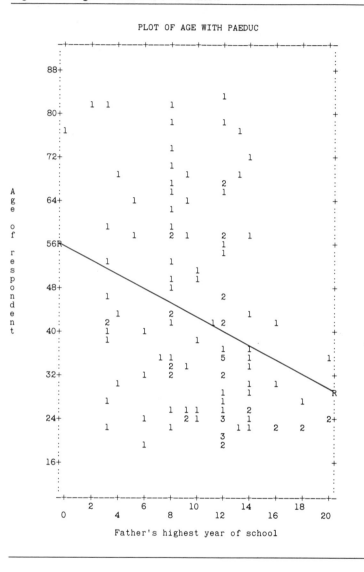

Father's highest year of school

CORRELATION

Although plots give you a pretty good idea of the strength of a linear association, they don't provide an objective summary measure that you could use to compare and summarize the relationships between pairs of variables. On the basis of the previous plots you could say that the relationship between parents' education *appears* to be stronger than the relationship between father's education and respondent's age. You can't really say how much stronger unless you have a summary measure that quantifies your visual impressions.

The Pearson Correlation Coefficient

The mostly commonly used measure is the **Pearson correlation coefficient,** which is abbreviated as **r.** (The statistic is named after Karl Pearson, an eminent statistician of the early twentieth century.) Let's consider some of its characteristics:

- If there is no linear relationship between two variables, the value of the coefficient is 0.
- If there is a *perfect positive linear* relationship, the value is +1.
- If there is a *perfect negative linear* relationship, the value is −1.

To summarize, the values of the coefficient can range from −1 to +1, with a value of 0 indicating no linear relationship. Positive values mean that there's a positive relationship between the variables. Negative values mean that there's a negative relationship. If one pair of variables has a correlation coefficient of +.8, while another pair has a coefficient of −.8, the strength of the relationship is the same for both. It's just the direction of the relationship that differs.

Let's find out what the correlation coefficients are for some of the plots that we've considered previously. (These are printed by the SPSS[X] PLOT procedure if you use the FORMAT = REGRESSION subcommand shown above.) The correlation coefficient for age at marriage and mother's education is −.077. This supports what we've said before, that there doesn't appear to be much of a relationship between the two variables. For mother's and father's education, the correlation coefficient is .75. This is a fairly large positive value, as you would expect. How about father's education and age of the respondent? From the plot, we saw that the relationship is negative so the sign of the correlation coefficient should also be negative. The relationship was not a very strong one, so the coefficient shouldn't be very large. In fact, it's −.32.

> ❓ *Does a correlation coefficient of zero mean that there is no relationship between two variables.* No! The Pearson correlation coefficient only measures the strength of a *linear* relationship. Two variables can have a correlation coefficient close to zero and yet have a very strong *nonlinear* relationship. Look at Figure 21.6, which is a plot of two hypothetical variables.
>
> You'll note that there is a strong relationship between the two variables. The value of the correlation coefficient, however, is close to zero. It's very important to always plot the values of the variables before you compute a correlation coefficient. This will allow you to detect non-linear relationships, for which the Pearson correlation coefficient is not a good summary measure. The Pearson correlation coefficient should only be used for linear relationships. ■ ■ ■

CALCULATING THE CORRELATION COEFFICIENT

There's a mathematical formula that tells you how to calculate the correlation coefficient for a pair of variables. It's

$$r = \frac{\sum_{i=1}^{N}(X_i - \bar{X})(Y_i - \bar{Y})}{(N-1)S_X S_Y}$$

where X and Y are the values of the two variables for a case, N is the number of cases, and S_X and S_Y are the standard deviations of the two variables. It doesn't matter which variable you take to be X and which to be Y in the formula, since the correlation coefficient will be the same.

The correlation coefficient is not expressed in any unit of measurement. The correlation coefficient between two variables will be the same regardless of how you measure them. For example, you'll get the same answer if you convert education from years to months. The correlation is an absolute number.

The SPSS^X PLOT procedure calculates Pearson's correlation coefficient, but SPSS^X also has a procedure specifically dedicated to computing correlations. To obtain correlations for the variables we've been discussing, type:

```
FILE HANDLE GSS / (system-specific information)
GET FILE=GSS
SAMPLE .1
PEARSON CORR EDUC PAEDUC MAEDUC AGE AGEWED
OPTION 3
```

Figure 21.6 Strong relationship but very low correlation

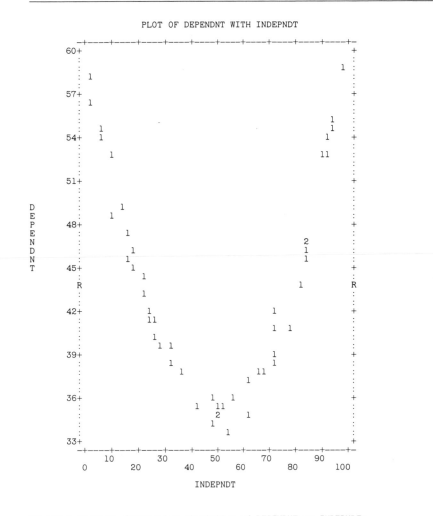

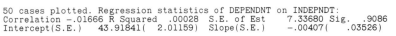

50 cases plotted. Regression statistics of DEPENDNT on INDEPNDT:
Correlation −.01666 R Squared   .00028 S.E. of Est   7.33680 Sig.   .9086
Intercept(S.E.)   43.91841(2.01159) Slope(S.E.)   −.00407(.03526)

Figure 21.7 Pearson correlation coefficients

FILE: 1984 General Social Survey

─ ─ ─ ─ P E A R S O N   C O R R E L A T I O N   C O E F F I C I E N T S ─ ─ ─

	EDUC	PAEDUC	MAEDUC	AGE	AGEWED
EDUC	1.0000	.5299	.4951	−.1899	.1141
	(0)	(115)	(133)	(154)	(128)
	P= .	P= .000	P= .000	P= .018	P= .200
PAEDUC	.5299	1.0000	.7485	−.3218	.0090
	(115)	(0)	(110)	(115)	(95)
	P= .000	P= .	P= .000	P= .000	P= .931
MAEDUC	.4951	.7485	1.0000	−.4261	−.0771
	(133)	(110)	(0)	(133)	(110)
	P= .000	P= .000	P= .	P= .000	P= .423
AGE	−.1899	−.3218	−.4261	1.0000	.1119
	(154)	(115)	(133)	(0)	(128)
	P= .018	P= .000	P= .000	P= .	P= .209
AGEWED	.1141	.0090	−.0771	.1119	1.0000
	(128)	(95)	(110)	(128)	(0)
	P= .200	P= .931	P= .423	P= .209	P= .

(COEFFICIENT / (CASES) / 2-TAILED SIG)

" . " IS PRINTED IF A COEFFICIENT CANNOT BE COMPUTED

As you can tell from the command, the name of the procedure is PEARSON CORR. The names of the variables for which you want coefficients follow the command name. Option 3 requests two-tailed probabilities. (More about probabilities later.) The output from this command is shown in Figure 21.7.

Each row and column of the table represents one of the variables. In each cell of the table you have three numbers. The first is the value of the coefficient. The second is the number of cases used to calculate it. The third number is the observed significance level—the next topic to be covered in this chapter.

Testing Hypotheses about the Correlation Coefficient

Sometimes the correlation coefficient is used simply to summarize the strength of a linear relationship between two variables. In other situations you may want to do more than that; you may want to test hypotheses about the population correlation coefficient. For example, you may want to test the null hypothesis that there is no linear relationship between mother's and father's education in the population.

Remember, if your data are a random sample from a particular population, you want to be able to draw conclusions about the population based on the results you observe in your sample. As was the case with other descriptive measures such as the mean, you know that the value of the correlation coefficient you calculate for your sample will not exactly equal the value that you would obtain if you had values for the entire population. You know that if you took many samples from the same population and calculated the correlation coefficients, their values would vary. That is, there is a distribution of possible values of the correlation coefficient, just as there was a distribution of possible values for sample means. If you know what the distribution is, you can calculate observed significance levels. For example, you can calculate how often you would expect to find, in samples of a particular size, a coefficient of .3 or greater when the population value is zero.

Look again at Figure 21.7. The value of the correlation coefficient for mother's education and age at marriage is $-.0771$. It is based on a sample of 110 cases. The probability that you would observe in a sample a correlation coefficient larger than .0771 or smaller than $-.0771$, when the value in the population is zero, is .424. Since the observed significance level is larger than .05 you would not reject the null hypothesis that there is no linear association between the two variables in the population.

Does *Significant* Mean *Important?*

If you reject the null hypothesis, does that mean there is an important relationship between the two variables? No. It simply means that it is unlikely that the value of the correlation coefficient is 0 in the population. For large sample sizes even very small correlation coefficients have small observed significance levels. You can have a correlation coefficient of .1 and have it be "statistically" significant. It indicates that there is a very small, but non-zero, linear relationship between the variables. You should look at both the value of the coefficient and its associated significance level when evaluating the relationships among variables.

? *If two variables are correlated, does that mean one of them causes the other?* Not at all. You can never assume that just because two variables are correlated one of them causes the other. If you find a large correlation coefficient between the ounces of coffee consumed in a day and number of auto accidents in a year, you can't conclude that coffee consumption causes auto accidents. It may well be that coffee drinkers also consume more alcohol, or are older, or more poorly coordinated than non-coffee drinkers. You can't easily tell which of the factors may influence the occurrence of accidents. ■ ■ ■

One-Tailed and Two-Tailed Significance Probabilities

If you don't know before looking at your data whether a pair of variables should be positively or negatively correlated, you must use a two-tailed significance level. You reject the null hypothesis for either large positive or large negative values of the correlation coefficient.

If you know in advance whether your variables should be positively or negatively correlated, you can use a one-tailed significance test. For example, if you're studying the relationship between total yearly income and value of housing, you know that if there is a relationship it will be positive. Poor people can't own expensive houses.

For a one-tailed test, you reject the null hypothesis only if the value of the correlation coefficient is large and in the direction you specified. For a one-tailed test, the observed significance level is one-half of the two-tailed value. That's because you only calculate the probability that you would obtain a more extreme value in one direction, not two.

If you don't specify what kind of test you want when you use the SPSS^X PEARSON CORR command, you get a one-tailed test. That's why we specified OPTION 3 in the job that produced Figure 21.7.

Assumptions about the Data

In order to test hypotheses about the Pearson correlation coefficient you have to make certain assumptions about the data. If your data are a random sample from a population in which the distribution of the two variables together is normal, the previously described procedure is appropriate.

If it seems unreasonable to assume that the variables are from normal distributions, you may have to use other statistical procedures that don't require the normality assumption. These are nonparametric procedures and are described in books such as Siegel's (1956).

Examining Many Coefficients

If your study involves many variables, you may be tempted to compute all possible correlation coefficients among them. If you're just interested in exploring possible associations among the variables, you may find the coefficients helpful in identifying possible relationships. However, you must be careful when examining the significance levels from large tables. If you have enough coefficients, you expect some of them to be statistically significant even if there is no relationship between the variables in the population. If you compute 100 coefficients, you expect somewhere around 5 of them to have observed significance levels less than 0.05 even when there is no relationship among the variables in the population. Think about it—that's what a significance level means!

Missing Values

If you look at Figure 21.7, you'll see that the number of cases used for calculating the different coefficients varies. The coefficient between mother's education and father's education is based on 110 cases, while the coefficient for age and age at marriage is based on 128 cases. Why is this so? Not all of the respondents in the General Social Survey answered all of the questions. Some may not have known how many years of education their mothers and fathers had. Those who were not married did not have a value for age at first marriage. When SPSS^X computes correlation coefficients, it uses as much available information as possible. For example, if a case has values for age and age at first marriage but not for mother's and father's education, it is used in the computation of the coefficient for age and age at first marriage, but not for any of the coefficients that involve parents' education.

Analysis of data when some of the cases have missing information can be troublesome, especially if you have reason to believe that the missing values are related to values of one of the variables you're analyzing. For example, people with low incomes may be less willing to report their financial status than more affluent people. People who are highly educated and poor may be even less likely to reveal their income than poor people in general. If this is the case it may be very difficult to draw correct conclusions about income and education from the data.

If there are missing values in the data you should see whether there is a pattern to the missing values. For example, you can calculate the average education for people who reported their income and those who did not. If these values are quite different, you have reason to suspect that the income values are not randomly missing. When values are not randomly missing you must use great caution in attempting to analyze the data. In fact, you may not be able to analyze some of it.

MORE ABOUT THE PEARSON CORR PROCEDURE

To compute all possible correlation coefficients between several variables, specify all the variables as in:

```
PEARSON CORR  EDUC PAEDUC MAEDUC
```

This command will print correlation coefficients for all three of the possible pairs of the variables, the number of cases used to compute each correlation, and the one-tailed significance levels.

To modify the output, specify one or more of the following options after the PEARSON CORR command:

1 Include missing values
2 Exclude missing values listwise
3 Two-tailed test of significance
5 Suppress count and significance level
6 Print only nonredundant coefficients

Option 2 requests "listwise" exclusion of cases with missing values. That simply means that a case with a missing value for any of the variables on your list is excluded from calculation of all the correlations, even for correlations between variables for which it has valid data. Thus all the correlations are computed from the same group of cases—cases that have valid data for all the variables used in the procedure. We have used

Option 3 in the chapter to get two-tailed significance tests. Option 5 simplifies the output by printing only the correlation coefficients, without the case counts and significance levels.

If you request STATISTICS 1 after the PEARSON CORR command, you will get the mean, standard deviation, and count for each variable.

WHAT'S NEXT?

The correlation coefficient measures the strength of a linear relationship —how tightly the points are clustered around a straight line. In Chapter 22 we'll learn more about that line itself. We'll find out how to choose the best line, and how to use it.

Summary

How can you summarize the strength of the linear relationship between two variables?

The Pearson correlation coefficient measures the strength of the linear relationship between variables.

Two variables have a positive relationship if, as the values of one variable increase, so do the values of the other.

Two variables have a negative relationship if, as the values of one variable increase, the values of the other decrease.

A correlation coefficient of +1 means that there is a perfect positive linear relationship between two variables. A value of −1 means that there is a perfect negative linear relationship.

A correlation coefficient only measures the strength of a *linear* relationship. If there is a strong nonlinear relationship between two variables, the correlation coefficient can be zero.

A correlation between two variables doesn't mean that one causes the other.

To test the null hypothesis that the correlation coefficient is zero in the population, you can calculate the observed significance level for the coefficient.

You can use a one-tailed test if you know in advance whether the relationship between two variables is positive or negative.

If you have missing values in your data, you should see whether there is a pattern to the cases for which information is missing.

EXERCISES

Syntax

1 Write the SPSS^X command to obtain correlation coefficients and two-tailed significance levels for all pairs of the following variables: MONEY INVEST SALARY WEALTH.

2 Correct the errors in the following commands:
   a. PEARSON CORR   VAR= A B C D
   b. PEARSON   ONE TWO THREE MANY
   c. PEARSON   CORR   AGE
   d. PEARSON CORR ONE TWO MANY / SIG = 2

Statistical Concepts

1 For the following pairs of variables, would you expect the correlation coefficient to be positive, negative, or zero?
   a. A person's total family income and his neighbor's total family income.
   b. Number of registered voters in a district and the number voting on election day.
   c. Number of cigarettes smoked and lung function.
   d. Calories consumed and weight.
   e. Altitude and mean temperature.
   f. Gross national product and infant mortality rate.
   g. Age at first marriage and years of education.
   h. Number of cars in a household and total family income.

2 A medical researcher studying the relationship between two variables finds a correlation coefficient of .02. She concludes that there is no relationship between the two variables. Do you agree or disagree with her conclusion? Why?

3 A mail-order house is interested in studying the relationship between income and type of product purchased. They take a random sample of orders, and then they call people to determine family income. They then calculate the correlation coefficient between income and product code. The value is .76, and the two-tailed observed significance level is .03. Based on this study what can you conclude about the relationship between income and type of product purchased? Explain.

4 A dental association is studying the relationship between ounces of orange juice consumed per week and yearly family dental bill. They find a large positive coefficient, with an observed significance level of less than .01. What do you think of their conclusion that orange juice causes tooth decay? Discuss other possible explanations for their findings.

5 A friend of yours is analyzing the relationship between a large number of variables. He's decided that the best strategy is to compute correlation coefficients among all of them and see which relationships appear to be significant. Advise him on issues he must consider when using the correlation coefficient to describe the relationships between variables.

6 The correlation coefficient between variables A and B is .62. For variables C and D it is −.62. Which of the pairs of variables is more strongly related?

7 An educator wishes to study the relationship between father's and son's educational attainment. Five hundred randomly selected fathers of sons are interviewed and the years of education are recorded for both fathers and sons. Since a fairly high proportion of "Unknown" responses was obtained, the educator divides the education variables into two groups and obtains the following table:

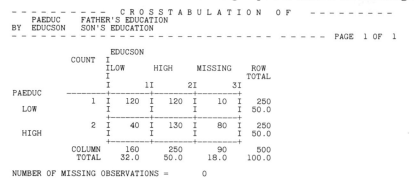

```
- - - - - - - - - -   C R O S S T A B U L A T I O N   O F   - - - - - - - -
    PAEDUC    FATHER'S EDUCATION
BY  EDUCSON   SON'S EDUCATION
- - - - - - - - - - - - - - - - - - - - - - - - - - - - - - -   PAGE  1 OF  1

                    EDUCSON
            COUNT  I
                   ILOW       HIGH       MISSING     ROW
                   I                                 TOTAL
                   I           1I         2I      3I
    PAEDUC    -----+---------+---------+---------+
            1  I     120  I    120  I    10  I     250
    LOW        I          I         I        I     50.0
               +---------+---------+---------+
            2  I      40  I    130  I    80  I     250
    HIGH       I          I         I        I     50.0
               +---------+---------+---------+
            COLUMN     160        250        90      500
            TOTAL     32.0       50.0      18.0    100.0

NUMBER OF MISSING OBSERVATIONS =         0
```

a. Is there reason to suspect that there is a relationship between father's education and non-response to son's education level? What may be going on?

b. Is there a satisfactory way to deal with the missing values when estimating the correlation coefficient between father's and son's education?

Data Analysis

1 In the previous chapter you were asked to identify four pairs of variables for which a plot was an appropriate means of displaying their relationship. Compute a correlation matrix for all possible pairs of these variables.

2 What null hypothesis are you testing when you compute the observed significance level for the correlation coefficient?

3 For males and females separately, compute the correlation coefficient between mother's education (MAEDUC) and father's education (PAEDUC). Discuss your findings.

4 Compute the correlation coefficient for age at first marriage (AGEWED) and education (EDUC), for males and females separately. Does there appear to be a relationship between these two variables? Does it differ for the two sexes?

22 Calculating Simple Regression Lines

How can you determine the line that best summarizes the linear relationship between two variables?

- How do you choose among the many lines that can be drawn through the data points?

- What does the slope tell you? The intercept?

- What is a least squares line?

- How can you predict values for one variable, based on the values of another variable?

- How can you tell how well a line fits the data?

- How can you tell what proportion of the variability in one variable is "explained" by the other?

A correlation coefficient provides you with a measure of the strength of the linear association between two variables. All it measures, though, is how *closely* the points cluster about a straight line. It doesn't tell you anything about the line itself.

In many situations it's useful to obtain information about the actual line which is drawn through the data points. For example, if there's a linear relationship between two variables, and you know the equation for the line that describes their relationship, you can use one variable to predict values of the other. If there's a linear relationship between the amount of money a company spends on advertising and its sales volume for the year, you can use the line to predict sales volume based on advertising. That's what this chapter is about. You'll learn how to calculate what's called a **regression line** and what it means.

CHOOSING THE BEST LINE

Thinking back to Chapter 21, you'll remember that the correlation coefficient was based on how closely points cluster about "a line." We didn't say anything about how we selected the line which was shown on the plots. We'll consider that now.

When the correlation coefficient is +1 or −1, all the data points fall on a single line. All you have to do is connect the points and you have a line. You don't have to worry about choosing a line. When the observations are not perfectly correlated, many different lines may be drawn through the data. How do we choose among them? Since we want a line which describes the data, it should be as close as possible to the points. There are different ways to define "as close as possible." The most commonly used method for determining the line is called the method of least squares. The **least squares line** is the line that has the smallest sum of squared vertical distances from the observed points to the line.

To understand what this means, look at Figure 22.1, which is a plot of the respondents' education and their fathers' for a sample of the cases. We took a sample of the cases in the GSS so that the plot would be easier to read and interpret.

The least squares line has been drawn on the plot. For any point on the plot you can find the vertical distance from the point to the line. The dotted line on the plot shows such a vertical distance for one of the points. If you find the vertical distances to the line for all points, square them, and then add them up you'll have the *sum of the squared distances*. If you

Figure 22.1 Least squares line

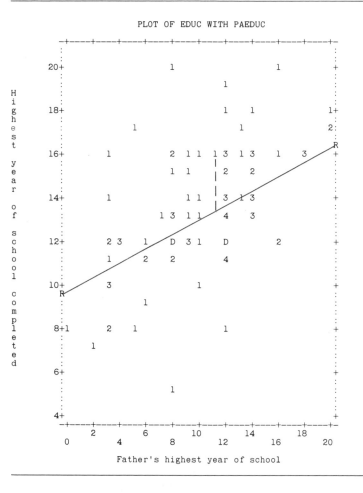

PLOT OF EDUC WITH PAEDUC

Father's highest year of school

draw any other line on the plot, it would have a larger sum of squared distances than the least squares line. That's why this particular line is the least squares line. The least squares line is the one which has the smallest sum of squared distances possible, for these points.

The Equation of a Line

Before we talk any more about lines, let's consider the equation for a straight line. Take two variables, say X and Y. Call the variable we plot on the vertical axis Y, and the variable we plot on the horizontal axis X. Then the equation is

$$Y = A + B \times X$$

Figure 22.2 Plot of a line with intercept 10 and slope .3

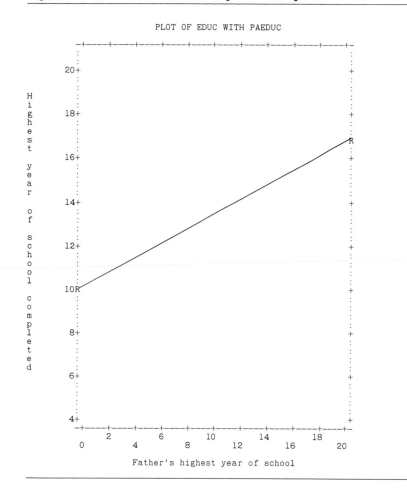

PLOT OF EDUC WITH PAEDUC

A and *B* are just numbers. The value *A* is called the **intercept**, and the value *B* is called the **slope**. To understand what the slope and intercept are (and why they're called slope and intercept), look at Figure 22.2, which is a plot of the line

EDUC = 10 + .3 × PAEDUC

The intercept, 10, is the value for child's education when father's education is 0. It is the point at which the line hits the vertical axis. The slope tells you how much increase there is in a child's education for every year of his or her father's education. In this case it's .3. If a father has 10 years of education the child should have 13 years: 10 to start off with (the intercept), and 3 more because of the father's 10 years of education (10

Figure 22.3 Plot of a line for unrelated variables

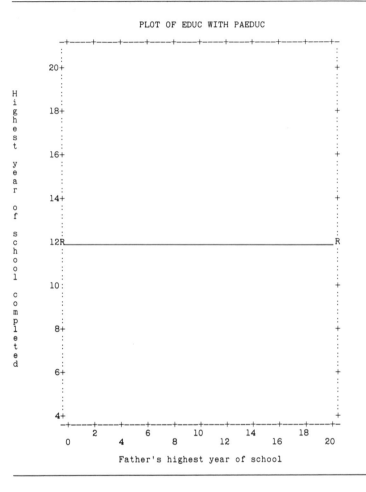

PLOT OF EDUC WITH PAEDUC

Father's highest year of school

years × .3, the slope, makes 3 years). If a father has 11 years of education the child should have 13.3 years (10 years for the intercept + 11 years × .3). The additional year of education for a father results in an additional .3 years for the child.

If the value for the slope is positive, it tells you that as one variable increases, so does the other variable. If the slope is negative, it tells you that as one variable increases, the other decreases. If the slope is large, the line is steep, indicating that a small change in the father's education would lead to a large change in the child's education. If the slope is small, there is a gradual increase or decrease. If the slope is *zero*, it means that changes in the X variable have no effect on the Y variable. If father's education and child's education were not related, the line would look something like that in Figure 22.3. This line is completely flat. Its equation is

EDUC = 12 + 0.0 × PAEDUC

Predicting Values from the Regression Line

The equation for the least squares regression line in Figure 22.1 is

Predicted EDUC = 9.68 + .34 × PAEDUC

The line is drawn on the plot by connecting the two Rs which appear on the edges of the plot. The values for the slope and intercept are obtained from Figure 22.4, which contains the regression statistics from the PLOT procedure.

? *So the intercept is where the R appears along the left border of the plot?* The R on the border of the plot tells you where the line crosses the border. The intercept is where the line crosses *zero*, that is, where the line is when the independent variable equals zero. On this plot they're the same, because the border is at zero years of father's education. You can't count on that, though. ■ ■ ■

From the last line in Figure 22.4 you can see that the value for the intercept is 9.68 while the value for the slope is 0.34. The standard errors for the slope and the intercept are in parentheses. (The standard errors of the slope and intercept are indicators of how much variability is associated with them. These standard errors are discussed further in Chapter 23.)

Figure 22.4 Regression statistics from PLOT

```
115 cases plotted. Regression statistics of EDUC on PAEDUC:

Correlation  .52991 R Squared  .28081  S.E. of Est   2.26987 Sig.  .0000
Intercept(S.E.)    9.67783(   .55881)  Slope(S.E.)      .33997(  .05118)
```

Notice that we placed the word "predicted" in front of EDUC in the equation relating father's education (PAEDUC) and child's education (EDUC), at the beginning of this section. That's because the relationship between the two variables is not perfect. For a particular value of father's education we cannot exactly say what the child's education is. From the regression line we can only predict what the value would be if all of the points fell exactly on the regression line.

Calculating the Predicted Values

Once you have a regression equation, it's easy to obtain predicted values. All you have to do is substitute the value of the independent variable into the equation. To predict child's education when the father has eight years of education, use

$$\text{Predicted EDUC} = 9.68 + .34 \times \text{PAEDUC}$$
$$= 9.68 + .34 \times 8$$
$$= 9.68 + 2.72$$
$$= 12.40$$

Choosing the Dependent Variable

When we are computing correlation coefficients it doesn't matter which variable we plot on the horizontal axis and which we plot on the vertical. The correlation coefficient is exactly the same. That's not usually true for regression. The slope and the intercept will differ depending on which variable is the Y variable in the equation and which is the X variable. Since regression analysis is used to predict values of a dependent variable from values of an independent variable, Y is taken to be the dependent variable and X the independent.

In this example, it's natural to consider the child's education as the dependent variable and father's education as the independent variable. We know that the child's education is not likely to influence the father's education. However, it is possible that the father's education may influence the child's. Child's education is *dependent* on father's education. To calculate the regression line with child's education as the dependent variable it must be plotted on the vertical axis in the PLOT procedure. As we said in Chapter 20, the first variable named, the one before WITH, goes on the vertical axis—so we name EDUC first:

```
FILE HANDLE GSS / (system-specific information)
GET FILE=GSS
SAMPLE .10
PLOT     HSIZE = 50 / VSIZE = 42 /
   FORMAT = REGRESSION /
  PLOT = EDUC WITH PAEDUC
```

DETERMINING HOW WELL THE LINE FITS

Although the regression line is a useful summary of the relationship between two variables, the values of the slope and intercept alone don't indicate how well the line actually fits the data. We need some measure of **goodness of fit.** We know that if the regression line fits the data perfectly, the observed values for the dependent variable equal the predicted values. They all fall exactly on the line. The poorer the line fits, the more discrepancy we would expect between the line and the actual values.

Figure 22.5 Correlation of EDUC with predicted EDUC

```
FILE:      1984 General Social Survey
- - - -  P E A R S O N    C O R R E L A T I O N    C O E F F I C I E N T S  - - -

                   EDUC        PREDEDUC
EDUC              1.0000         .5299
                 (    0)       (   115)
                 P= .          P= .000

PREDEDUC           .5299        1.0000
                 (   115)      (    0)
                 P= .000       P= .

(COEFFICIENT / (CASES) / 1-TAILED SIG)

" . " IS PRINTED IF A COEFFICIENT CANNOT BE COMPUTED
```

Correlating Predicted and Observed Values

One way we can measure how well the line fits is to calculate a correlation coefficient (as in Chapter 21) between the observed values of the dependent variable and those predicted from the regression equation. The value will be 1 if there is a perfect fit and close to 0 if the fit is poor.

Let's use SPSS^X to do this. To calculate the predicted values for each case type:

```
COMPUTE PREDEDUC = 9.6778 + .34 * PAEDUC
```

Here is the whole job to calculate the correlation coefficient between the two variables:

```
FILE HANDLE GSS / (system-specific information)
GET FILE=GSS
SAMPLE .10
COMPUTE PREDEDUC = 9.6778  +  .34 * PAEDUC
VARIABLE LABELS PREDEDUC 'Predicted values of EDUC from PAEDUC'
PEARSON CORR EDUC PREDEDUC
```

Figure 22.5 contains the output from these commands.

The correlation coefficient between the observed and predicted values is 0.53, exactly the same value we obtained for the correlation of father's and child's education in Chapter 21. Thus we have yet another interpretation of the correlation coefficient. It is a measure of the strength of the linear relationship between the *observed* values of the dependent variable and those *predicted* by the regression line. The correlation coefficient tells us how well the least squares line fits the data.

This interpretation applies only to the *absolute value* of the correlation coefficient (its value if you disregard the sign). That's because even if the relationship between two variables is negative, the relationship between the observed and predicted values will be positive.

Explaining Variability

If you square the value of the correlation coefficient, you obtain yet another useful statistic. The square of the correlation coefficient tells you *what proportion of the variability* in the dependent variable is "explained" by the regression.

What do we mean when we say that the regression "explains" variability? Consider father's and child's education again. We know that there is variability in the education of the children. All children do not have the same amount of education. If there is a relationship between father's education and child's education, we can attribute some of the observed variability in children's education to variability in their fathers' education.

Consider the situation where the regression line fits the data points exactly. In this case there is still variability in children's education. However, the regression line perfectly explains the differences. The different amounts of father's education perfectly predict child's education. All children with fathers of the same education have exactly the same amount of education. In this situation we would say that father's education explains all of the variation in child's education. Data points all lie exactly on the regression line when the line perfectly explains the data.

In general, the distance between a point and the regression line is a measure of how much variability we *can't* explain with the regression line. If you compare the sum of the squared distances from the data points to the regression line, with the total variability in the dependent variable, you can calculate what percent of the total variability is *un*explained by the regression. The remainder of the variability *is* explained.

This is what the square of the correlation coefficient tells you. It is the proportion of the total variability in the dependent variable which can be accounted for by the independent variable. In our example, the square of the correlation coefficient is $0.53^2 = 0.28$. (SPSS^X reported this among the regression statistics in Figure 22.4.) This means that 28% of the variability in children's education can be explained by father's education.

MORE ABOUT REGRESSION WITH THE PLOT PROCEDURE

Now you understand what the *R*s mean in the margins of a plot. When you enter the command

```
PLOT  FORMAT = REGRESSION /
  PLOT = EDUC WITH PAEDUC
```

SPSS[X] calculates the regression line, prints the regression statistics shown in Figure 22.4, and places the letter R at the two places where the regression line crosses the borders of the plot. You must enter the dependent variable in the regression *first* on the PLOT subcommand, so that it will be plotted on the vertical axis.

That's all you can do with regression lines in the PLOT procedure. However, SPSS[X] does have a more powerful REGRESSION procedure, as we're about to see.

WHAT'S NEXT?

In this chapter we considered only the very basics of calculating a regression line. In Chapter 23 we'll use the REGRESSION procedure to consider the problem of drawing conclusions about the population line from the sample line. We'll also consider other methods for establishing how well a linear regression model fits the data.

Summary

How can you determine the line that best summarizes the linear relationship between two variables?

In the equation for a straight line, $Y = A + B \times X$, the intercept A is the value of Y when X is zero. It is the point at which the line crosses the vertical axis.

The slope B tells you how much Y increases or decreases for a one-unit change in X.

The least squares line has, of all possible lines, the smallest sum of squared distances from the points to the line.

By using the least squares line, you can predict values for the dependent variable based on values of the independent variables.

You can find the correlation coefficient between the observed values and the predicted values by taking the absolute value of the Pearson correlation coefficient between the two variables.

The square of the Pearson correlation coefficient tells you what proportion of the variability in the dependent variable is explained by the independent variable.

EXERCISES

Syntax

1 Correct the errors in the following commands:

a. PLOT PLOT DEP WITH INDEP / FORMAT REGRESSION

b. PLOT FOR=REG / DEP WITH INDEP

c. PLOT PLOT FORMAT REG / FATIGUE BY HOMEWORK

d. PLOT   PLOT FORMAT=NOREG / PLOT= GRADE WITH EFFORT

2 Write the SPSS[X] commands to obtain a plot of AGEDEATH and EDUCATION. Obtain the regression statistics, with age at death being the dependent variable and years of education the independent variable.

3 Repeat the previous analysis with education as the dependent variable and age at death as the independent variable.

4 Describe what output the following job produces:

```
GET FILE=PHYSIQUE
TEMPORARY
SELECT IF (SEX EQ 1)
PLOT FORM REG/PLOT WEIGHT WITH HEIGHT
TEMPORARY
SELECT IF (SEX EQ 2)
PLOT FORMAT=REG/PLOT HEIGHT WITH WEIGHT
```

Statistical Concepts

1 Plot the following two points and write the equation of the straight line that passes through them:

Point 1   age = 20   income = 20,000
Point 2   age = 30   income = 25,000

2 In the previous question, what is the value for the intercept? For the slope? If the line you've calculated predicts income exactly, what would be the income for a 40-year-old?

3 Consider the following plot:

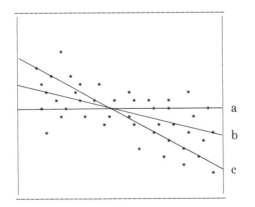

a. Of the three lines drawn on the plot, which one is most likely to be the regression line?

b. Is the correlation between the two variables positive, negative, or can you not tell from the plot? Why?

4 Consider the following plot and statistics obtained from procedure PLOT:

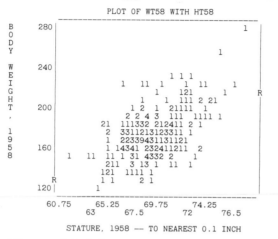

PLOT OF WT58 WITH HT58

STATURE, 1958 — TO NEAREST 0.1 INCH

240 cases plotted. Regression statistics of WT58 on HT58:
Correlation .53553 R Squared .28679 S.E. of Est 20.92697 Sig. .0000
Intercept(S.E.) −166.51879(34.77567) Slope(S.E.) 4.96169(.50719)

a. Write the equation predicting WT58 from HT58 and draw the line on the plot.

b. For a case with an observed value of 68 for HT58 and 200 for WT58, calculate the predicted value for WT58 and the residual.

c. Draw a line that represents the residual on the plot.

5 Here are the equations for two regression lines:

Predicted weight = 100 + 5 × Adjusted height

Predicted weight = 105 + 50 × Ring size

Is the correlation coefficient larger for weight and adjusted height, or for weight and ring size? How can you tell?

Data Analysis

1 Obtain regression statistics for the pairs of variables you were analyzing in Chapter 21. Write out each of the regression equations.

2 For which pairs of variables do you think the regression line provides a good summary of the data?

3 Show how you would use each of the previous regression lines to predict values for new cases. Under what conditions would you expect the prediction to be good?

4 Take one of the previous pairs of variables and reverse the regression. That is, interchange the dependent and independent variables. How do the results of this analysis compare to the one you obtained previously? Which statistics change and which remain the same? Why?

23 Testing Regression Hypotheses

How can you test hypotheses about the population regression line, based on the values you obtain in a sample?

- What is the population regression line?
- What assumptions do you have to make about the data to test hypotheses about the population regression line?
- How do you test the null hypothesis that the slope is zero in the population?
- What is the meaning of the confidence interval for the slope?
- What does the analysis of variance table for the regression analysis tell you?

A regression line is a good way to describe and summarize the linear relationship between two variables. Often, however, you want to do more than that. You want to draw conclusions about the relationship of the two variables in the population from which the sample was selected. You want to draw conclusions, for example, about the relationship between child's education and father's education for all people in the United States—not just those included in the General Social Survey. In this chapter you'll learn what's involved in testing hypotheses about the population regression line.

THE POPULATION REGRESSION LINE

When you calculate a regression line which is used only to *describe* an observed relationship between two variables, you have two concerns. Are the variables measured on an interval or ratio scale, and does their relationship appear to be linear? It makes no sense to calculate a regression line relating religious preference to the region in which someone lives. There is no order to the categories of either of these variables, and a statistic like the slope is meaningless. Even if the two variables are measured on an interval scale, but their relationship is not linear, it makes no sense to calculate a regression line. You may need to fit some other mathematical function besides a straight line, or perhaps change the scale on which the variables are measured. Those topics are mostly beyond the scope of this book, but we'll talk a little about them in Chapter 24.

When you're interested in drawing conclusions about the *population* regression line, you need additional assumptions. First, let's clarify what we mean by a "population regression line." In all of our previous discussions about hypothesis testing, we considered our data to be a random sample from some underlying population. We thought of the people included in the General Social Survey as a sample of the population of adults in the United States. We wanted to draw conclusions about the *population* based on what we saw in our *sample*. When we computed a sample mean, we considered it to be our best guess of the population mean. When we computed a correlation coefficient, we considered it our best guess for the value of the correlation coefficient in the population.

What we'll be doing now is very similar. We'll try to draw conclusions about the relationship of two variables in the population based on the results we see in our sample. If we had been able to include our entire population in the study, we could calculate a regression line which describes the relationship between the two variables in the population. This would be the "true" or **population regression line.** We don't know what the true line is, since all we have is a sample from the population. We don't know the true slope or the true intercept. We do have some evidence about what they are, however. Our best guess for the population line is the results observed in our sample.

Additional Assumptions

To be able to test hypotheses about the population line statistically, we must make some assumptions about the population. We need these assumptions so we'll know that the sampling distributions of the slope and intercept will be normal. (The sampling distribution of the slope is the distribution of the values of the slope that you would get if you took all possible samples of a particular size from a population. The sampling distribution of the intercept is defined similarly.) As before, our computations of the observed significance level will be based on these normal distributions.

Normality and Equal Variances

If I tell you that a person's father has four years of college, would you expect to be able to predict exactly how many years of education the child has? Probably not. Even if there is a strong relationship between two variables, it is unlikely to be perfect. Look at Figure 23.1, which is a histogram of years of education for only those people whose fathers have exactly four years of college. The most frequent value of the child's education is exactly four years of college, but some children did not even finish high school. Others have several years of graduate education. There is a distribution of the values of children's education for each value of father's education.

For hypothesis testing, we'll have to make the assumptions that, in the population

- For each year of father's education, the distribution of children's education is normal.

- All of these distributions have the same variance.

That is, the variance in children's education is the same for those whose fathers had eight years of education, twelve years of education, or twenty years of education.

Linearity

We've just stated that to test hypotheses about the population line, we need to assume that the distributions of the dependent variable must be

Figure 23.1 Education when father's education equals 16

```
FILE:      1984 General Social Survey

EDUC       Highest year of school completed

     COUNT      VALUE   ONE SYMBOL EQUALS APPROXIMATELY   .40 OCCURRENCES

        1       10.00   ***
        2       11.00   *****
       10       12.00   ************************
        8       13.00   *******************
       10       14.00   ************************
       12       15.00   *****************************
       18       16.00   *********************************************
        7       17.00   *****************
        4       18.00   **********
        2       19.00   *****
        5       20.00   *************
                        I.........I.........I.........I.........I.........I
                        0         4         8        12        16        20
                                       HISTOGRAM FREQUENCY

VALID CASES       79    MISSING CASES    0
```

Figure 23.2 Regression assumptions

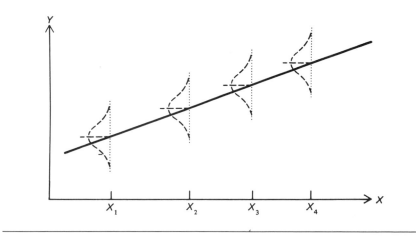

normal for each value of the independent variable, and that the variances of those distributions must be equal. Now, what about the means of the distributions?

If there is a linear relationship in the population between father's and child's education, then *the means of all of the population distributions must fall on a straight line*. To test regression hypotheses, we must assume that this is true.

Look at Figure 23.2, which schematically shows the assumptions we've been talking about. In the population there is a *true* regression line which specifies the relationship between father's education and child's education. This line is drawn in on the plot. For each value of the independent variable there is a distribution of the values of the dependent variable. These distributions are all normal and have the same variance. The means of all of these distributions fall on a straight line.

Independence

The last assumption that we need for linear regression analysis is that *all observations are selected independently*. That is, including one person in the sample should not in any way alter the chance of any other person being included. For example, if we're studying the relationship between parent's and child's education, and we include all children in each family in the sample, the observations are not independent. The same father could be included several times (once with each child).

SOME HYPOTHESES OF INTEREST

We'll return in Chapter 24 to the question of how you can examine your data to see if they violate any of these assumptions. Meanwhile, suppose that the data do satisfy all of the assumptions outlined above. What sorts of hypotheses can we now test? We can test hypotheses about the values of the population slope and the population intercept, and hypotheses about how well the regression model fits the data.

Testing Hypotheses with the REGRESSION Command

The PLOT command is convenient for displaying the data and fitting a simple regression line. The REGRESSION command lets you test hypotheses about regression models and fit more complicated models. To obtain hypothesis tests for whether the population slope and intercept are zero, type

```
FILE HANDLE GSS / (system-specific information)
GET FILE=GSS
REGRESSION VARIABLES = PAEDUC EDUC
    / DEPENDENT = EDUC
    / METHOD = ENTER
```

The VARIABLES subcommand simply specifies the names of the two variables in the regression equation. The DEPENDENT subcommand identifies which of the two is the dependent variable. The METHOD subcommand tells SPSS^X what method to use for including independent variables in the regression equation. Since we only have one independent variable in our model (the variable PAEDUC, or father's education), the subcommand METHOD = ENTER includes, or "enters," that variable in the model. Other methods can be used for regression equations with more than one independent variable.

Figure 23.3 Output from a REGRESSION command

```
FILE:     1984 General Social Survey

          * * * *   M U L T I P L E   R E G R E S S I O N   * * * *

Listwise Deletion of Missing Data

Equation Number 1    Dependent Variable..    EDUC   Highest year of school comple

Beginning Block Number  1.  Method:  Enter      PAEDUC

Variable(s) Entered on Step Number
   1..     PAEDUC    Father's highest year of school

Multiple R            .48221
R Square              .23253
Adjusted R Square     .23181
Standard Error       2.56857

Analysis of Variance
                    DF       Sum of Squares      Mean Square
Regression           1          2126.84923       2126.84923
Residual          1064          7019.77366          6.59753

F =     322.37045      Signif F =  .0000


------------------ Variables in the Equation ------------------

Variable            B         SE B       Beta        T  Sig T

PAEDUC          .347027     .019328     .482212   17.955  .0000
(Constant)     9.451633     .209802               45.050  .0000

End Block Number   1   All requested variables entered.
```

Regression Coefficients

The regression coefficients and associated statistics are shown in Figure 23.3. The values of the regression coefficients are in the column labeled B. You should recognize the values in this figure as quite close to the values on the PLOT output in Chapter 22. The slope is .35, and the intercept, sometimes called the *constant*, is 9.45. Instead of thinking of these values as descriptions of the sample, we will now treat them as our best guesses, or *estimates*, of the unknown population values of the slope and intercept.

? *But why aren't the values from* REGRESSION *exactly the same as the values from* PLOT? *They're the same variables, aren't they?* Yes, but they're not all the same cases. In Chapter 22 we took a smaller sample, so there wouldn't be too many cases to plot. We'd expect the slope and intercept in Figure 23.3 to be better estimates of the population values than the values in Chapter 22, since these are now based on more cases. ■ ■ ■

The next column in Figure 23.3, labeled SE B, contains the standard errors of the slope and intercept. The standard errors are estimates of the standard deviation of the sampling distributions of the slope and the intercept. Remember, the slope and intercept we have calculated are based on one sample from a population. If you took another sample and calculated values for the slope and intercept they would differ. The values of the slope and intercept from repeated samples from the same population have a distribution. The standard deviation of this distribution is called the standard error. It's just like the standard error of the mean, back in Chapter 14.

Are the Population Values Zero?

If there is no linear relationship between two variables in the population, the true slope is zero. All of the means of the distributions are the same. The predicted value for child's education is the same, regardless of father's education. Even if the population value is zero, of course, you wouldn't expect the sample value for the slope to be *exactly* zero. You hope that it wouldn't be too far from zero. To test the null hypothesis, that the value of the slope is zero in the population, we can calculate the probability of obtaining a slope at least as large as the one we've observed, when the null hypothesis is true. As usual, if this probability is small we will reject the null hypothesis that the slope is zero.

The observed significance level is based on the *t*-statistic shown in Figure 23.3 in the column labeled T. This *t*-statistic is calculated (like any *t*-statistic) by dividing a sample value by its standard error. In this case, the *t* values are the sample slope and the sample intercept, divided by their standard errors.

In the column labeled SIG T are the two-tailed significance levels for the tests of the hypotheses that the slope and intercept are zero in the population. In this example, the values .0000 are printed. This indicates that the probability is less than .00005 that a sample slope would occur at least as large as the one we've observed (in absolute value), if the true slope is zero. The same interpretation holds for the significance of the intercept.

When testing whether there is a linear relationship between two variables, the important test is the test of the *slope*. The intercept is simply the value of the dependent variable when the independent variable is zero. All that the test of the intercept tells us is whether the regression line goes through the **origin.** (The origin is the point at the intersection of the two axes. It is the point where both variables are zero.) In this example, you wouldn't predict zero years of education for a child whose parents had zero years of education. You would predict 9.45 years, because that's the intercept.

Figure 23.4 Confidence intervals for regression coefficients

```
---------------------- Variables in the Equation ----------------------

Variable              B      SE B   95% Confdnce Intrvl B      Beta

PAEDUC           .347027   .019328    .309102    .384952    .482212
(Constant)      9.451633   .209802   9.039960   9.863306


----------- in ------------

Variable         T   Sig T

PAEDUC       17.955  .0000
(Constant)   45.050  .0000

End Block Number   1   All requested variables entered.
```

Confidence Intervals for Regression Coefficients

The sample values for the slope and intercept are our best guesses for the population values. However, we know it's unlikely that they are exactly on target. As we've discussed before, it's possible to calculate a confidence interval for the population value. A confidence interval is a range of values which, with a designated likelihood, contains the unknown population value. To obtain 95% confidence intervals for the slope and intercept using SPSS^X REGRESSION, we must add an additional specification to the command. It's called the STATISTICS subcommand, and it tells the system what values we want to see printed:

```
FILE HANDLE GSS / (system-specific information)
GET FILE=GSS
REGRESSION VARIABLES = PAEDUC EDUC
    /STATISTICS = DEFAULT CI
    /DEPENDENT = EDUC
   /METHOD = ENTER
```

The keyword DEFAULT on the STATISTICS subcommand tells the system to print the usual regression output. The keyword CI tells it to print the confidence intervals also. The regression statistics and their confidence intervals are shown in Figure 23.4. The 95% confidence interval for the slope ranges from .309 to .385.

Remember what *95% confidence* means: if we draw repeated samples from a population, under the same conditions, and compute 95% confidence intervals for the slope and intercept, 95% of these intervals should include the unknown *population* values for the slope and intercept. Of course, since the true population values are not known, it isn't possible to tell whether any particular interval contains the population values.

Notice that in this example, neither the confidence interval for the slope nor the one for the intercept contains the value zero. An interval will only include zero if you *can't* reject the null hypothesis that the slope or intercept is zero, at an observed significance level of .05 or less.

GOODNESS OF FIT OF THE MODEL

In Chapter 22 we discussed the importance of assessing how well the regression model actually fits the data. The REGRESSION command prints several statistics which describe the "goodness of fit." Look at the first part of Figure 23.5, which is part of the output from the same job that produced Figure 23.4. The entry labeled Multiple R is just the absolute value of the correlation coefficient between the dependent variable and the single independent variable. It's also the correlation coefficient between the values *predicted* by the regression model and the actual *observed* values. If the value is close to 1, the regression model fits the data well. If the value is close to zero, the regression model does not fit well.

Another way of looking at how well the regression model fits is to see what proportion of the total variability (or variance) in the dependent variable can be "explained" by the independent variable. The variability in the dependent variable is divided into two components: variability explained by the regression, and variability not explained by the regression. Because of the way they're calculated, these two components are termed **sums of squares.** Indeed, they are conceptually very similar to the sums of squares we discussed in Chapter 18.

The two sums of squares are displayed in the Analysis of Variance table in the second half of Figure 23.5. The sums of squares explained by the regression equation are labeled Regression, while the unexplained variability is labeled Residual. You can obtain the total variability in the dependent variable by adding up these two sums of squares.

To calculate what proportion of the total variability is explained by the regression, all you have to do is divide the regression sum of squares by the total sum of squares. For this example, the value is

$$\text{Variance explained} = \frac{2127}{2127 + 7020} = 0.23$$

There's an easier way to calculate this proportion. All you have to do is square the correlation coefficient. This value is shown in Figure 23.5 next to the label R Square. From R^2 we see that in our sample we can explain 23% of the variability in children's education by knowing their fathers' education.

Figure 23.5 Goodness-of-fit statistics

```
FILE:    1984 General Social Survey
              * * * *   M U L T I P L E   R E G R E S S I O N   * * * *

Listwise Deletion of Missing Data

Equation Number 1   Dependent Variable..   EDUC   Highest year of school comple

Beginning Block Number  1.  Method:  Enter


Variable(s) Entered on Step Number
   1..   PAEDUC    Father's highest year of school


Multiple R          .48221
R Square            .23253
Adjusted R Square   .23181
Standard Error     2.56857

Analysis of Variance
                    DF      Sum of Squares      Mean Square
Regression           1         2126.84923       2126.84923
Residual          1064         7019.77366          6.59753

F =      322.37045      Signif F =  .0000
```

Another Test for a Linear Relationship

The analysis of variance table in Figure 23.5 can also be used to test the null hypothesis that there is no linear relationship between the two variables. Below the analysis of variance table you see the label F. This is for the same kind of F-statistic we discussed in Chapter 18. Just as in that chapter, F is the ratio of the mean square for regression to the mean square for the residual, and the mean squares are the sums of squares divided by their respective degrees of freedom.

You can find these mean squares in the column labeled Mean Square. If there is *no* linear relationship between the two variables, then each of these mean squares provides an estimate of the variance, or variability, of the dependent variable. If there *is* a linear relationship, then the variability estimate based on the regression mean square will be much larger than the estimate of variability based on the residuals. Large F-values suggest that there is a linear relationship between the two variables. In this example, the F-value is 322 and the observed significance level associated with it is less than .00005. We reject the null hypothesis that there is no linear relationship between the two variables.

> **?** *Is there any relationship of this F-statistic to the test that the slope is zero? It seems like we're testing the same hypothesis in both situations.* Yes, the two tests are evaluating exactly the same hypothesis when there's only one independent variable. In fact there's a relationship between the two statistics. If you square the *t*-value for the test that the slope is zero, you will come up with the *F*-value in the analysis of variance table. (Try it!) For a simple equation like this, you don't learn anything from the analysis of variance table that you didn't already know from the test of the slope. ▪ ▪ ▪

Other Regression Statistics

There are several statistics in Figure 23.5 that we haven't discussed yet. The number labeled Standard Error is an estimate of the standard deviation of the distributions of the dependent variable. Remember, we assumed that for each value of the independent variable there is a distribution of values of the dependent variable. All of these distributions are normal and have the same standard deviation. Our estimate of it is the standard error.

The number labeled Adjusted R Square is most useful when you have a model with several independent variables. This statistic adjusts the value of R^2 to take into account the fact that a regression model always fits the particular data on which it was developed better than it will fit the population. When there is only one independent variable, and a reasonably large number of cases, the adjusted R^2 will be very close to the unadjusted value.

MORE ABOUT THE REGRESSION PROCEDURE

To obtain regression coefficients and goodness-of-fit statistics for the dependent variable DEP, as predicted by the independent variable INDEP, type:

```
REGRESSION  VARIABLES = DEP, INDEP /
   DEPENDENT = DEP /
  METHOD = ENTER
```

You must enter these three subcommands in this order: VARIABLES, DEPENDENT, and then METHOD. To get confidence intervals for the regression parameters in addition to the default statistics, type:

```
REGRESSION VARIABLES = DEP, INDEP /
   STATISTICS = DEFAULT CI /
   DEPENDENT = DEP /
  METHOD = ENTER
```

If you also want descriptive statistics about the variables you are using, type:

```
REGRESSION  VARIABLES = DEP, INDEP /
  DESCRIPTIVES = ALL /
  STATISTICS = DEFAULT CI /
  DEPENDENT = DEP /
 METHOD = ENTER
```

Note that the DESCRIPTIVES and STATISTICS subcommands must be placed before the DEPENDENT subcommand.

REGRESSION can use more than one independent variable in the same equation ("multiple regression"), but we don't discuss multiple regression in this book. Additional features and subcommands are discussed in Chapter 24.

WHAT'S NEXT?

Regression is a powerful technique, but you must make a number of assumptions in order to use it. The SPSS[X] REGRESSION procedure provides several optional plots and statistics that make it easy to determine whether your data satisfy these assumptions, and help you decide what to do if they don't. That's what we'll talk about next.

Summary

How can you test hypotheses about the population regression line, based on the values you obtain in a sample?

To draw conclusions about the population regression line, you must assume that for each value of the independent variable, the distribution of values of the dependent variable is normal, with the same variance. The means of these distributions must all fall on a straight line.

The test of the null hypothesis that the slope is zero is a test of whether there is a linear relationship between the two variables.

The confidence interval for the population slope provides you with a range of values that, with a designated likelihood, includes the population value.

When there is a single independent variable, the analysis of variance table for the regression is equivalent to the test that the slope is zero.

EXERCISES

Syntax

1 Correct the errors in the following commands:

   a. REGRESSION VAR=IQ / DEP=GPA / ENTER IQ

   b. REGRESSION VAR=IQ GPA/ENTER IQ/DEP GPA

   c. REGRESSION VAR=IQ POPIQ/DEP=POPIQ/ENTER MIQ

   d. REGRESSION VAR=IQ GPA/DEP GPA/ENTER GPA

2 Write the SPSS[X] commands to calculate a regression equation when SBPRES is the dependent variable and AGE is the independent variable. Obtain the default regression statistics and the confidence interval for the regression coefficient.

3 When you run the command

   REGRESSION VAR=IQ GPA / DEP GPA / ENTER IQ / STATISTICS DEF CI

   the following error message is obtained:

   ```
   >ERROR   10595 LINE    4, (END OF COMMAND)
   >INVALID REGRESSION SUBCOMMAND ORDER--CRITERIA, STATISTICS, ORIGIN or NOORIGIN
   >subcommands should be placed directly before the DEPENDENT subcommand for the
   >equation to which they apply.  They should not be placed before the position
   >indicated above.
   ```

   Identify the error and correct the command.

Statistical Concepts

1 A personnel manager is interested in studying the relationship between salary and years on the job for rodent exterminators. She also wants to see whether males and females are similarly reimbursed. She has obtained salary and experience data from a sample of 1000 exterminators.

   a. Outline the steps you would recommend for analyzing the data.

   b. The three variables are named SALARY, EXPER, and SEX (coded 0=male; 1=female). Write the SPSS[X] commands to produce the analysis you recommended in (a).

2 Assume that in question 1 the personnel manager did find a a fairly good linear relationship for salaries and experience in the 1- to 5-year range. She did not include people with less than 1 year of experience or with more than 5 years of experience in the study. Discuss some of the problems she may encounter if she attempts to use her regression equation to determine compensation for people with more than five years of experience or less than 1.

3 Here's a hypothetical plot of salary and work experience.

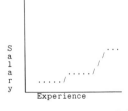

   a. Discuss the possible use of regression analysis for this problem.

   b. What ways can you think of for summarizing the relationship between the two variables? 5. Based on the following statistics

4 Based on the following statistics

```
----------------- VARIABLES IN THE EQUATION ------------------
VARIABLE          B        SE B      BETA       T   SIG T
X              1.70000    .82260    .76642    2.067  .1307
(CONSTANT)     4.30000   2.72825              1.576  .2131
```

  a. Would you reject the null hypothesis that there is no linear relationship between X and the dependent variable?

  b. On what do you base your conclusion?

  c. What is the two-tailed observed significance level for the test of the null hypothesis that the correlation coefficient is 0?

  d. What would be the value of the F statistic and its associated observed significance level in the ANOVA table for the previous regression?

4 You are reading an article about the relationship between college GPA and IQ. The authors present the following equation:

$$GPA = 3.54 + .001 \times IQ$$

The observed significance level for the slope is reported as .03.

  a. Is it possible to have both a small slope and a small observed significance level for the test that the slope is zero?

  b. How does the intercept affect the test of the null hypothesis that the slope is zero?

  c. Is it possible to reject the null hypothesis that the slope is zero and not reject the null hypothesis that there is no linear relationship between the two variables?

  d. From the value of the slope can you tell how well the model fits the data?

  e. Interpret the observed significance level reported for the equation.

Data Analysis

1 In this chapter we looked at the relationship between a person's education and the father's education.

  a. Perform a regression analysis to examine the relationship between a person's education and the mother's education.

  b. Summarize the results.

  c. Discuss the similarities and differences between the results of the two analyses (PAEDUC and EDUC; MAEDUC and EDUC). Is there a stronger linear relationship between father's education and a person's education, or between mother's education and the person's education?

2 Using the SELECT IF command, repeat the previous analyses for males and for females separately. Summarize your results. Comment on whether father's education is a better predictor of son's education than of daughter's education.

3 Develop a regression equation for predicting husband's education from wife's education. Perform any other analyses which you think would be helpful in studying the relationship between two variables. Write a short paper presenting the results of all of your analyses. Be sure to include discussion of the hypotheses you are testing and the statistics you are using.

4 Is there a relationship between the age at which a woman first marries and her mother's educational attainment? Analyze this question and summarize your results.

24 Analyzing Residuals

How can you tell whether the assumptions necessary for a regression analysis appear to be violated?

- What is a residual and what does it tell you?

- How can you use residuals to check whether the assumption of normality appears to be violated?

- How can you use residuals to check whether the assumption of constant variance appears to be violated?

- How can you use residuals to check whether the assumption of linearity appears to be violated?

- What can you do if you suspect that some of the assumptions are being violated?

- What are transformations and how can they help you?

When you begin studying the relationship between two variables you usually don't know whether the assumptions needed for regression analysis are satisfied. You don't know whether there is a linear relationship between the two variables, much less whether the distribution of the dependent variable is normal, and has the same variance, for all values of the independent variable. One of the goals of regression analysis is to check whether the required assumptions of linearity, normality, and constant variance are met. In this chapter we'll discuss several procedures for looking for violations of the assumptions.

RESIDUALS

A quantity called the **residual** plays a very important role when you're fitting models to data. You can think of a residual as what's left over after a model is fit. In a linear regression the residual is the difference between the observed and predicted values of the dependent variable. If a person has 12 years of education and your model predicts 9, the residual for the case is $12 - 9 = 3$. You have three years of education left over or not explained by the model.

Looking at Residuals

By looking at the residual for each case you can see how well a model fits. If a model fits the data perfectly all of the residuals are zero. Cases for which the model doesn't fit well have large residuals.

You can use the REGRESSION procedure to calculate the residuals for all of the cases. Type

```
FILE HANDLE GSS / (system-specific information)
GET FILE=GSS
REGRESSION VARIABLES = PAEDUC EDUC
   / DEPENDENT = EDUC
   / METHOD = ENTER
   / CASEWISE = ALL DEPENDENT PRED RESID ZRESID
```

Figure 24.1 Casewise plot and residuals from REGRESSION

```
FILE:     1984 General Social Survey

          * * * *   M U L T I P L E   R E G R E S S I O N   * * * *

Equation Number 1    Dependent Variable..   EDUC   Highest year of school comple

Casewise Plot of Standardized Residual

*: Selected   M: Missing

          -3.0      0.0      3.0
          0:.....:.........:0     EDUC      *PRED      *RESID     *ZRESID
Case #
   1      .         .         .     12         .          .           .
   2      .         .*        .     16      15.0041      .9959       .3877
   3      .         .         .     15         .          .           .
   4      .         .  *      .     16      12.5749     3.4251      1.3335
   5      .         .*        .     16      15.0041      .9959       .3877
   6      .         .  *      .     17      13.6160     3.3840      1.3175
   7      .         .     *   .     18      12.2278     5.7722      2.2472
   8      .     *   .         .     12      15.0041    -3.0041     -1.1695
   9      .         .         .     10         .          .           .
  10      .     *   .         .     12      15.0041    -3.0041     -1.1695
  11      .         .         .     12         .          .           .
  12      .         *         .     12      12.2278     -.2278      -.0887
  13      .         .         .     11         .          .           .
  14      .         .         .      9         .          .           .
  15      .     *   .         .     13      16.3922    -3.3922     -1.3206
  ...
```

This is the same job we used in Chapter 23, except that the CASEWISE subcommand has been added. This subcommand prints information about residuals for each case ("casewise"). It has quite a few possible specifications, which are listed in "More about the Regression Procedure" at the end of this chapter. Here the keyword ALL instructs SPSS^X to print residual values for all of the cases. The other keywords tell it what to print. The keyword DEPENDENT stands for the observed dependent value, PRED for the predicted value, RESID for the residual, and ZRESID for the standardized residual.

Reading the Casewise Results

Part of the output from the previous command is shown in Figure 24.1. The column labeled Case # tells you the number of the case for which the results are printed. The first column to the right of the plot shows the actual value of EDUC for each case. EDUC is the dependent variable, so it's the "target" for the predictions. *PRED is the predicted value for the dependent variable based on the regression equation. The residual is in the column labeled *RESID. For example, case 2 has 16 years of education. The predicted value of education, based on the regression equation using father's education, is 15.0041. The residual is therefore $16 - 15.0041 = 0.9959$. (When father's education is missing for a case there is no prediction, so for such cases SPSS^X prints periods instead of predictions and residuals.)

Judging the Size of the Residuals

How can you tell whether a residual is big or small? If I tell you that a case has a residual of 500, can you say whether the model gives a reasonably good prediction for the case? On first thought, 500 seems like a pretty large number, an indication that a model doesn't fit that case. However, if you're predicting income in dollars, a residual of 500 may not be all that large. Predicting a person's income to the nearest 500 dollars is pretty good. On the other hand, if you're predicting years of education, a residual of 500 should send you searching for a new and improved model.

One way to modify the residuals so that they would be easier to interpret is to standardize them. That is, divide each residual by an estimate of its standard deviation.

? *How come you're only dividing the residual by its standard deviation? Why aren't you first subtracting off the mean, like you did before, when computing standardized values?* There's no need to subtract the mean of the residuals before dividing by the standard deviation, because the mean of the residuals is zero. If you add up all of the residuals you'll find that their sum, and therefore their mean, is zero. That's always true for a regression model which includes a constant. ■ ■ ■

The standardized residuals are shown in the column labeled *ZRESID. For most cases they range in value from −2 to +2. (Remember that in a normal distribution with a mean of 0 and a standard deviation of 1, about 95 percent of the cases fall within +2 and −2.) Whenever you see a standardized residual larger than +2 or smaller than −2, you should examine the case to see if there's some explanation for why the model doesn't fit. The standardized residuals are plotted on the chart on the left side of Figure 24.1. Whenever a value is larger than 3, it is plotted in the border.

Looking for Outliers

If you have a large number of cases, as in the GSS, you may not want to look at the values of the residuals for all of the cases. Instead you may want to look only at the cases with "large" residuals. Such cases are called OUTLIERS. This is easy to do with the REGRESSION procedure. Just leave off the keyword ALL on the CASEWISE subcommand:

```
FILE HANDLE GSS / (system-specific information)
GET FILE=GSS
REGRESSION VARIABLES = PAEDUC EDUC
   / DEPENDENT = EDUC
   / METHOD = ENTER
  / CASEWISE = DEPENDENT PRED RESID ZRESID
```

Figure 24.2 Residuals for outliers only

```
FILE:    1984 General Social Survey

         * * * *   M U L T I P L E   R E G R E S S I O N   * * * *

Equation Number 1   Dependent Variable..   EDUC   Highest year of school comple


Casewise Plot of Standardized Residual

Outliers = 3.    *: Selected   M: Missing

         -6.    -3.  3.    6.
  Case #  0:.......:  :.......:0      EDUC      *PRED      *RESID     *ZRESID
      78  .       *..         .          2    10.8397     -8.8397     -3.4415
     100  .      *..          .          3    11.5338     -8.5338     -3.3224
     188  .          ..*      .         20    12.2278      7.7722      3.0259
     361  .       *..         .          4    12.2278     -8.2278     -3.2033
     836  .     *  ..         .          4    13.9630     -9.9630     -3.8788
    1188  .          ..*      .         20    12.2278      7.7722      3.0259
    1444  .          ..*      .         20    12.2278      7.7722      3.0259


         7 Outliers found.
```

This is just like the previous regression command. The only difference is that the keyword ALL no longer appears on the CASEWISE subcommand. If you don't tell SPSS^X to print all cases, it prints only those whose standardized residuals are greater than 3 or less than −3.

Output from this command is shown in Figure 24.2. You see that there are 7 cases with large standardized residuals. It's interesting that four of the cases have very little education (four years or less), while the other three have a lot of education (twenty years). You can tell that the model predicts too little education for the people with a lot of education. Their residuals are positive, meaning that they have more education than the model predicts. The model predicts too much education for the people with little education: their residuals are negative. By looking at the characteristics of the outliers you can see situations where the model doesn't work well.

CHECKING ASSUMPTIONS WITH RESIDUALS

Residuals are the primary tools for checking whether the assumptions necessary for linear regression appear to be violated. We can draw histograms of the residuals, plot them against the observed and predicted values, recompute them excluding certain cases, and manipulate them in other ways. By examining the resulting plots and statistics, we can learn much about how appropriate the regression model is for a particular data set. Let's consider how to check each of the assumptions in turn.

Figure 24.3 Histogram of standardized residuals

```
Histogram — Standardized Residual
   N   Exp N        (* = 3 Cases,    . : = Normal Curve)
   0     .82    Out
   4    1.63    3.00 :
   0    4.16    2.67 .
  23    9.51    2.33 **:*****
  30   19.45    2.00 *****:****
  21   35.64    1.67 *******     .
  49   58.49    1.33 ***************  .
  80   85.98    1.00 ************************** .
  90  113.22     .67 *****************************  .
 110  133.55     .33 **************************************  .
 186  141.10     .00 ***************************************************:***************
 140  133.55    -.33 ***********************************************:**
 162  113.22    -.67 **************************************:***************
  73   85.98   -1.00 *********************** .
  38   58.49   -1.33 *************   .
  26   35.64   -1.67 *********  .
  11   19.45   -2.00 **** .
  10    9.51   -2.33 **:
   6    4.16   -2.67 :*
   3    1.63   -3.00 :
   4     .82    Out *
```

Normality

If the relationship is linear and in the population the dependent variable is normally distributed for each value of the independent variable, then the distribution of the residuals should also be approximately normal. Figure 24.3 is a histogram of the residuals for the current example. The figure was produced by these commands:

```
FILE HANDLE GSS / (system-specific information)
GET FILE=GSS
REGRESSION VARIABLES = PAEDUC EDUC
  / DEPENDENT = EDUC
  / METHOD = ENTER
  / RESIDUALS = HISTOGRAM
```

The distribution of the residuals appears to be fairly normal, though it is a bit more "peaked" than you would expect. Remember, the periods and colons indicate what a normal distribution with the same mean and variance would look like.

When the distribution of residuals doesn't appear to be normal you can sometimes transform the data to make it appear more normal. When you "transform" a variable you change its values by taking square roots, or logarithms, or some other mathematical function of the data. If the distribution of residuals is not symmetric but has a tail in the positive direction, it's sometimes helpful to take logs of the dependent variable. If the tail is in the negative direction and all data values are positive, taking

Figure 24.4 Before log transformation

```
  N   Exp N         (* = 2 Cases,    . : = Normal Curve)
  7    .37    Out ****
  2    .73   3.00  *
  4   1.85   2.67  :*
  2   4.23   2.33  *.
  6   8.65   2.00  ***.
 12  15.85   1.67  ****** .
  7  26.01   1.33  ****           .
 18  38.23   1.00  ********          .
 35  50.34    .67  ******************        .
 63  59.38    .33  ******************************:.************
 87  62.74    .00  *******************************.*************
114  59.38   -.33  ******************************:***************************
 64  50.34   -.67  ************************:*******
 32  38.23  -1.00  ****************    .
  9  26.01  -1.33  *****         .
  6  15.85  -1.67  ***       .        "
  1   8.65  -2.00  *   .
  1   4.23  -2.33  *.
  2   1.85  -2.67  :
  0    .73  -3.00
  2    .37    Out *
```

Figure 24.5 After log transformation

```
  N  Exp N         (* = 1 Cases,    . : = Normal Curve)
  3   .37    Out ***
  1   .73   3.00  :
  3  1.85   2.67  *:*
  4  4.23   2.33  ***:
 10  8.65   2.00  ********:*
 14 15.85   1.67  *************  .
 21 26.01   1.33  *******************    .
 31 38.23   1.00  *****************************        .
 48 50.34    .67  ***********************************************  .
 55 59.38    .33  ******************************************************  .
 63 62.74    .00  ************************************************************:
 64 59.38   -.33  ***********************************************:*****
 62 50.34   -.67  **************************************************:************
 44 38.23  -1.00  ****************************************:******
 28 26.01  -1.33  ************************:**
 14 15.85  -1.67  **************  .
  7  8.65  -2.00  *******  .
  1  4.23  -2.33  *   .
  1  1.85  -2.67  *.
  0   .73  -3.00  .
  0   .37    Out
```

the square root of the data may be helpful. Figures 24.4 and 24.5 show histograms (for a different data set) of the residuals before and after a log transformation.

The distribution of your residuals may appear not to be normal for several reasons besides a population in which the distributions are not normal. If you have a variance which is not constant for different values of the independent variable, or if you simply have a small number of residuals, your histogram may also appear not to be normal. So it's possible that after you've remedied some of these problems the distribution of residuals may look more normal.

Constant Variance

To check whether the variance appears to be constant, you can plot the residuals against the predicted values, and also against the values of the independent variable. This is done in SPSS^X with a simple addition to the usual regression command. Type:

```
FILE HANDLE GSS / (system-specific information)
GET FILE=GSS
REGRESSION VARIABLES = PAEDUC EDUC
  / DEPENDENT = EDUC
  / METHOD = ENTER
  / SCATTERPLOT = (*RESID, *PRED) (*RESID, PAEDUC)
```

The additional subcommand SCATTERPLOT causes the system to plot the residuals against the predicted values and the residuals against the independent variable.

? *What are all those words beginning with asterisks, on the* SCATTERPLOT *subcommand?* Those are just the names of the temporary variables you can use to analyze residuals in REGRESSION. You saw some of them at the tops of the columns in Figures 24.1 and 24.2. There's a list of them at the end of this chapter. You have to put asterisks in front of their names when you use them on the SCATTERPLOT subcommand, because the SCATTERPLOT subcommand also accepts ordinary variables, like PAEDUC. ■ ■ ■

The plots produced by this job are shown in Figure 24.6. If the spread of the residuals increases or decreases either with the values of the independent variable or with the predicted values, you have reason to suspect that the variance is not constant. In both of our plots there doesn't appear to be any pattern to the spread of the residuals. The residuals form a horizontal band.

Figure 24.6 Scatterplots of residuals

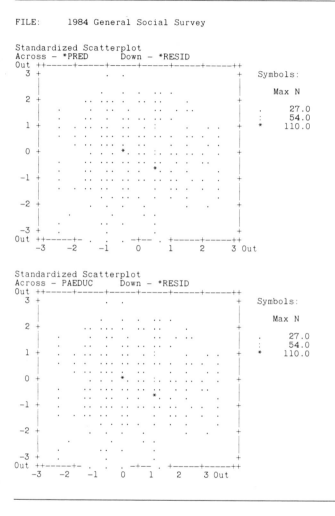

FILE: 1984 General Social Survey

```
Standardized Scatterplot
Across - *PRED      Down - *RESID
Out ++-----+-----+-----+-----+-----+-----++
  3 +               .  .                   +      Symbols:
    |             .   .   .   . . .        |
  2 +          ..  ...   ..  .      .       +        Max N
    |      .      .   . .  .     .. .  .    |
    |      .      .   .. . .  .    . . ..   |        .       27.0
  1 +      .  .  .. ..  ..  .:    .   . .   +        :       54.0
    |      .      .   .   .   .  .  .    .  |        *      110.0
    |      .      .   .    .   .  .  .      |
  0 +         .   .  . *..   .. :. .   . .  +
    |         .   .. .. ..  . .  . .   .    |
    |         .   .   .   *.  .  . .  .     |
 -1 +      .      .   .. . .  .  .  .  .    +
    |         .   .   .    .   .   .        |
    |         .      .   .    .   .         |
 -2 +            .      .      .      .     +
    |         .      .. .      .           |
 -3 +      .         .  .      .            +
Out ++-----+- .   .   . -+-- . +-----+-----++
    -3    -2    -1     0     1     2     3 Out
```

```
Standardized Scatterplot
Across - PAEDUC     Down - *RESID
Out ++-----+-----+-----+-----+-----+-----++
  3 +               .  .                   +      Symbols:
    |             .   .   .   . . .        |
  2 +          ..  ...   ..  .      .       +        Max N
    |      .      .   . .  .     .. .  .    |
    |      .      .   .. . .  .    . . ..   |        .       27.0
  1 +      .  .  .. ..  ..  .:    .   . .   +        :       54.0
    |      .      .   .   .   .  .  .    .  |        *      110.0
    |      .      .   .    .   .  .  .      |
  0 +         .   .  . *..   .. :. .   . .  +
    |         .   .. .. ..  . .  . .   .    |
    |         .   .   .   *.  .  . .  .     |
 -1 +      .      .   .. . .  .  .  .  .    +
    |         .   .   .    .   .   .        |
    |         .      .   .    .   .         |
 -2 +            .      .      .      .     +
    |         .      .. .      .           |
 -3 +      .         .  .      .            +
Out ++-----+- .   .   . -+-- . +-----+-----++
    -3    -2    -1     0     1     2     3 Out
```

This won't always be the case. In Figure 24.7 the spread of the residuals increases with increasing values of the independent variable. The residuals form a funnel pattern. This suggests that the variance of the dependent variable increases over the values of the independent variable. This is a common occurrence. If you're studying the relation-

Figure 24.7 Variance increasing with independent variable

```
Standardized Scatterplot
Across - PAEDUC     Down - *RESID
Out ++-----+-----+- . .-+- . -+- . -+-----++
  3 +                        . .        .     +    Symbols:
    |             .     . .         .          |
  2 +        .  .   . .  ..  ..   .  .   +        Max N
    |        .   .  :: .  ..   .  .  ..   |
    |     .. ..  :  ..  ::  .. *   . .    |    .       9.0
  1 +  .   .. ...  :  .. *  . .  .  .   +        :      18.0
    |     :  . .. .. *. .. *. . .  .      |    *      39.0
  0 +   .   .: .::  *.   *  . . .       +
    |    .  : .. .  *.   *. ..  .        |
    |     . .. ..  *.   *. .  . .        |
 -1 +    .  .. ..   :  *. .  .  .       +
    |       .  . .. .  :  . .            |
 -2 +      .       . .  ..  . .    .     +
    |             .   .   :  .  .        |
 -3 +                :   .  .  .         +
Out ++-----+-----+-----+-----+-----+-----++
    -3    -2    -1    0     1     2    3 Out
```

ship between children's weights and ages, you would expect that there is more variability in the weights of twelve-year-olds than in the weights of one-year-olds. As age increases so does the variability of the weights.

There are some common transformations which may help when the variance does not appear to be constant. If the variance increases linearly with the values of the independent variable, and all values of the dependent variable are positive, take the square root of the dependent variable. If it's the standard deviation which is increasing linearly with values of the independent variable, try taking logs of the data.

Linearity

To see whether it's appropriate to assume a linear relationship, you should always plot the dependent variable against the independent variable (as in Chapter 20). If the points don't seem to cluster around a straight line, you shouldn't fit a linear regression model.

Another way to see whether a relationship is linear is to look at the plots of the residuals against the predicted values and the residuals against the values of the independent variable. (These are the plots shown in Figure 24.6, above.) If you see any type of pattern to the residuals—that is, if they don't fall in a horizontal band—you have reason

Figure 24.8 Residuals from nonlinear relationships

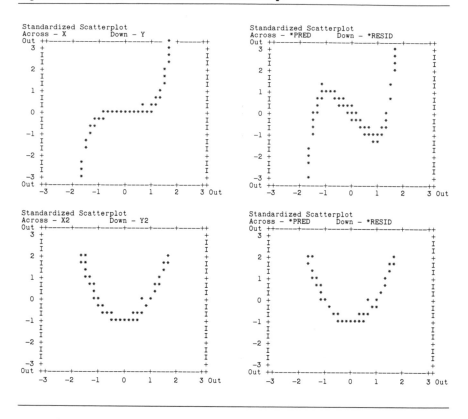

to suspect that the relationship is not linear. Figure 24.8 contains plots of the residuals against the predicted values when the relationships are not linear. Two of the plots show the original data, and the other two show the residuals and predicted values.

Sometimes when the relationship between two variables doesn't appear to be linear, it's possible to transform the variables and make it linear. Then you can study the relationship between the transformed variables using linear regression. For example, look at Figure 24.9. The relationship between the two variables doesn't look quite linear. However, if you take the log of the dependent variable you get the relationship shown in Figure 24.10. The relationship between the x and the *log* of y appears to be fairly linear.

Figure 24.9 Nonlinear relationship

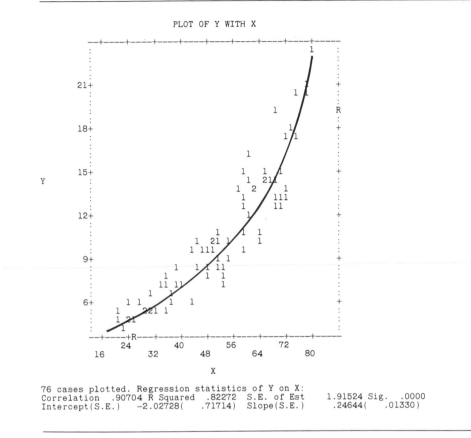

PLOT OF Y WITH X

76 cases plotted. Regression statistics of Y on X:
Correlation .90704 R Squared   .82272 S.E. of Est   1.91524 Sig.   .0000
Intercept(S.E.)   −2.02728(.71714) Slope(S.E.)   .24644(.01330)

? *Isn't transforming the data more or less cheating, or at least distorting the true picture?* No. All that transforming a variable does is change the scale on which it's measured. Instead of saying that there is a linear relationship between work experience and salary, you say that there is a linear relationship between work experience and the log of salary. It's much easier to build models for relationships that are linear than those that are not. That's why transforming variables is often a convenient tactic. ■ ■ ■

Figure 24.10 After log transformation

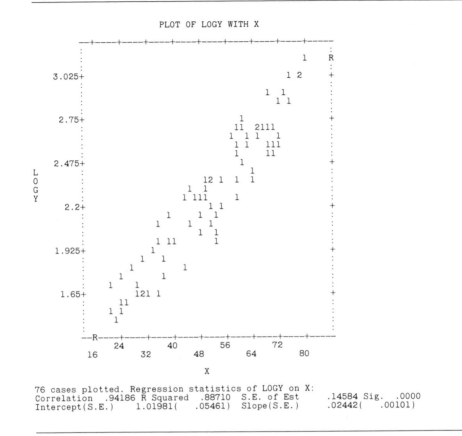

```
                    PLOT OF LOGY WITH X
       --+----+----+----+----+----+----+----+----+-----
       :                                        1    R
3.025+ :                                     1  2    +
       :                                  1  1
       :                                   1 1
2.75+  :                             1                +
       :                           11   2111
       :                          1  1  1   1
       :                          1 1    111
       :                          1      11
2.475+ :                        1  .                  +
L      :                          1
O      :                    12 1   1  1
G      :                  1  1
Y      :                1 111     1
2.2+   :                   11                         +
       :              1    1 1
       :             1      1 1
       :                    1 1
       :             1 11     1
1.925+ :            1                                 +
       :         1   1
       :       1      1
       :      1    1
       :    1    1
1.65+  :      121 1                                   +
       :     11
       :    1 1
       :     1
       --R----+----+----+----+----+----+----+----+-----
          24        40        56        72
       16        32        48        64        80
                             X
```

76 cases plotted. Regression statistics of LOGY on X:
Correlation .94186 R Squared .88710 S.E. of Est   .14584 Sig.   .0000
Intercept(S.E.)   1.01981(.05461) Slope(S.E.)   .02442(.00101)

Choosing a Transformation

How do you decide what transformation to use? Sometimes you might know what the mathematical formula is that relates two variables. In that case you can use mathematics to figure out what transformation you need. This situation happens more often in the physical or biological sciences than in the social sciences.

If the true model isn't known, you choose a transformation by looking at the plot of the data. Often, a relationship appears to be nearly linear for part of the data but is curved for the rest. The log transformation is useful for "straightening out" such a relationship. Sometimes taking the square root of the dependent variable may also straighten a curved relationship. These are two of the most common transformations, but others can be used.

Figure 24.11 Residuals that are not independent

```
CASEWISE PLOT OF STUDENTIZED RESIDUAL
                   -3.0      0.0      3.0     LIFE      *PRED    *RESID   *SRESID
     SEQNUM   TIME  0:........:........:0
        1    78012     .  *    .        .    15.0000   19.5624  -4.5624   -2.2598
        2    78055     .  *    .        .    13.5000   17.8974  -4.3974   -2.1856
        3    78122     .   *   .        .     9.9000   13.8390  -3.9390   -1.9871
        4    78134     .    *  .        .    15.5000   18.5218  -3.0218   -1.4997
        5    78233     .    *  .        .    35.0000   38.2933  -3.2933   -1.7466
        6    78298     .     * .        .    14.7000   16.6487  -1.9487    -.9720
        7    78344     .      *.        .    34.8000   36.0040  -1.2040    -.6258
        8    79002     .      *.        .    20.8000   20.8111   -.0111    -.0055
        9    79008     .       . *      .    15.9000   14.8796   1.0204    .5123
       10    79039     .       *        .    22.0000   21.6436    .3564    .1762
       11    79101     .       . *      .    13.7000   11.7578   1.9422    .9910
       12    79129     .       . *      .    14.2000   11.4456   2.7544   1.4082
       13    79178     .       .   *    .    33.2000   30.3847   2.8153   1.4144
       14    79188     .       .  *     .    26.2000   22.4761   3.7239   1.8401
       15    79189     .       .   *    .    37.4000   33.2984   4.1016   2.0920
      ...
```

When you try to make a relationship linear, you can transform either the independent variable, the dependent variable, or both. If you transform only the independent variable you're not changing the distribution of the dependent variable. If it was normally distributed with a constant variance for each value of the independent variable, that remains unchanged. However, if you transform the dependent variable you change its distribution. For example, if you take logs of the dependent variable, then the log of the dependent variable—not the original dependent variable—must be normally distributed with a constant variance. In other words, the regression assumptions must hold for the variables you actually use in the regression equation.

Independence

Another assumption that we made was that all observations are independent. (The same person isn't included in the data twice on separate occasions. One person's values don't influence the others'.) When data are collected in sequence it's possible to check this assumption. You should plot the residuals against the sequence variable. If you see any kind of pattern, for example that seen in Figure 24.11, you should be concerned. (This plot was obtained, from different data, with the CASEWISE keyword, as shown for Figure 24.1.)

In this figure the value of the residual is related to the order in which the experiment was conducted. Early subjects had large negative residuals, while later subjects had large positive residuals. This might occur, for example, when you give a test of facts to subjects one at a time, and word of its contents spreads. The first people taking the test will do worse than later people who know the questions and answers.

A Final Comment on Assumptions

It's important to examine the data for violation of the assumptions since significance levels, confidence intervals, and other regression tests are sensitive to certain types of violations and cannot be interpreted in the usual fashion if serious departures exist. If you carefully examine the residuals, you'll have an idea of what sorts of problems might exist in your data. Transformations provide you with an opportunity to try to remedy some of the problems. You can then be more confident that the regression model is appropriate for your data.

MORE ABOUT THE REGRESSION PROCEDURE

To get listings of all residuals that are greater than 3 or less than -3, type:

```
REGRESSION  VARIABLES = DEP, INDEP /
   DEPENDENT = DEP /
   METHOD = ENTER /
  CASEWISE = DEPENDENT PRED RESID ZRESID
```

This prints a listing of the dependent variable (which is DEP in this example) and three of the temporary variables that SPSS^X calculates automatically. Twelve temporary variables are available in all:

PRED   Unstandardized predicted values.

RESID   Unstandardized residuals.

DRESID   Deleted residuals.

ADJPRED   Adjusted predicted values.

ZPRED   Standardized predicted values.

ZRESID   Standardized residuals.

SRESID   Studentized residuals.

SDRESID   Studentized deleted residuals.

SEPRED   Standard errors of the predicted values.

MAHAL   Mahalanobis' distances.

COOK   Cook's distances.

LEVER   Leverage values.

To get a listing of residuals for all cases, specify ALL on the CASEWISE subcommand:

```
REGRESSION  VARIABLES = DEP, INDEP /
   DEPENDENT = DEP /
   METHOD = ENTER /
  CASEWISE = ALL DEPENDENT PRED RESID ZRESID
```

You can use any of the twelve temporary variables and the keyword DEPENDENT on the CASEWISE subcommand.

Histograms

To get histograms of standardized residuals, type:

```
REGRESSION  VARIABLES = DEP, INDEP /
   DEPENDENT = DEP /
   METHOD = ENTER /
   RESIDUALS = HISTOGRAM
```

You can specify PRED, RESID, ZPRED, ZRESID, DRESID, ADJPRED, SRESID, or SDRESID in parentheses after the HISTOGRAM keyword, to get histograms of those temporary variables. All histograms will show the standardized versions of the temporary variables.

Scatterplots

To get scatterplots involving the temporary residual variables, with one another or with the variables in your regression, use the SCATTERPLOT subcommand. Give the variable names in parentheses after the subcommand. Since this subcommand accepts ordinary variable names as well as the temporary variables, you must place an asterisk before the names of the temporary variables:

```
REGRESSION  VARIABLES = DEP, INDEP /
   DEPENDENT = DEP /
   METHOD = ENTER /
   SCATTERPLOT = (*RESID, *PRED) (*RESID, INDEP)
```

This command prints scatterplots of the residuals (*RESID) with both the predicted values (*PRED) and the independent variable, which is named INDEP in this example. Scatterplots, like histograms, always use the standardized versions of the temporary variables.

WHAT'S NEXT?

You've reached the end of the book. However, it's by no means the end of what you can learn about data analysis. To whet your appetite for more, Chapter 25 briefly describes some of the more advanced methods you can use. They're all based on the material you've studied in this book. If you understand these fundamentals, you're well on your way to understanding the more powerful techniques. As you learn to use them, though, always remember: start simply.

Summary

How can you tell whether the assumptions necessary for a regression analysis appear to be violated?

A residual is the difference between the observed value of the dependent variable and the value predicted by the regression model.

To check the assumption of normality, make a histogram of the residuals. It should look approximately normal.

To check the assumption of constant variance, plot the residuals against the predicted values and against the values of the independent variable. There should be no relationship between the residuals and either of these two variables. If you note a pattern in the plots, you have reason to suspect that the assumption of constant variance is violated.

To check whether the relationship between the two variables is linear, plot the two variables. If the points do not cluster about a straight line, you have reason to believe that the relationship is not linear.

If any of the assumptions appear to be violated, transforming the data may help. The choice of the transformation depends on which assumption is violated and in what way.

EXERCISES

Syntax

1 You want to predict husband's education from wife's education using the data in the GSS. You also want to obtain a histogram of the residuals and a casewise plot of residuals which are greater than 3 in absolute value. Write *all* the SPSS^X commands required to perform this analysis.

2 You run the following command

```
REGRESSION VARIABLES=GPA IQ / STATISTICS DEF CI
    / DEPENDENT GPA / CASEWISE
```

and obtain the following error message:

```
>ERROR   10508  LINE   5, COLUMN 22, TEXT: CASEWISE
>MISPLACED SUBCOMMAND ON REGRESSION COMMAND--Only the METHOD subcommand can
>follow a DEPENDENT subcommand.
>THIS COMMAND NOT EXECUTED.

*WARNING* - REGRESSION syntax scan continues.
Further diagnostics may be misleading - interpret with care.
```

Correct the command.

3 Correct the errors in the following commands:

  a. REGRESSION CASEWISE / VARIABLES=DEP INDEP / DEPENDENT=DEP

  b. REGRESSION VARIABLES=Y X / STATISTICS=DEF CI / CASEWISE / HIST

  c. REGRESSION VAR= Y X /DEP Y/CASEWISE RESIDUALS

  d. REGRESSION VAR= HT WT/DEP WT/CASEWISE/SCAT(*RES AGE)

4 Write the SPSS^X commands for a regression analysis in which MAWEIGHT is the independent variable and MYWEIGHT is the dependent variable. Obtain as many diagnostic plots as you can.

Statistical Concepts

1 The regression equation used to predict salary from work experience is

$$SALARY = 10,000 + 1000 \times EXP$$

  a. What is the predicted salary for a person who has 10 years of experience?

  b. If a person with 10 years of experience earns $20,000, what is the residual for the case?

  c. What does a negative residual mean?

  d. What does a positive residual mean?

2 Below are regression statistics and values of the independent and dependent variables for five cases. Fill in the missing information in the casewise plot.

```
------------------- VARIABLES IN THE EQUATION -------------------

VARIABLE           B        SE B      BETA       T   SIG T

X               1.70000    .82260    .76642    2.067  .1307
(CONSTANT)      4.30000   2.72825             1.576  .2131


CASEWISE PLOT OF STANDARDIZED RESIDUAL

*: SELECTED   M: MISSING

            -3.0           0.0          3.0
   CASE # X  0:.............:.............:0    Y    *PRED     *RESID
     1 1    .              .  *          .      7   6.0000    1.0000
     2 2    .              .  *          .      9
     3 3    .       *      .             .      6
     4 4    .            * .             .     ▒▒   11.1000   -1.1000
     5 5    .              .   *         .     15   ▒▒▒▒▒▒    2.2000
   CASE # X  0:.............:.............:0    Y    *PRED     *RESID
            -3.0           0.0          3.0
```

3 What violations of assumptions, if any, are suggested by the following plots:

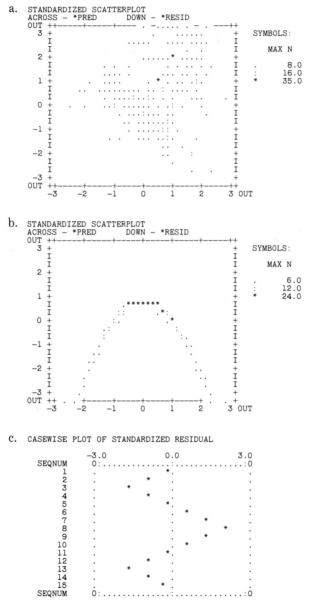

d.

```
HISTOGRAM - STANDARDIZED RESIDUAL
   N EXP N      (* = 1 CASES,     . : = NORMAL CURVE)
   0   .33    OUT
   0   .17   3.00
   0   .24   2.88
   0   .34   2.75
   0   .48   2.63
   0   .66   2.50 .
   0   .89   2.38 .
   0  1.19   2.25 .
   0  1.57   2.13 .
   0  2.03   2.00  .
   0  2.58   1.88   .
   0  3.24   1.75    .
   2  4.00   1.63 ** .
  16  4.86   1.50 ****:***********
  18  5.82   1.38 *****:*************
   9  6.85   1.25 ******:**
  12  7.95   1.13 *******:****
  12  9.07   1.00 ********:***
   8 10.20    .88 ********  .
  16 11.29    .75 *********:*****
  21 12.30    .63 **********:*********
   6 13.20    .50 ******       .
   6 13.94    .38 ******       .
   8 14.49    .25 *******      .
   6 14.83    .13 ******       :
  17 14.95    .00 **************:**
   9 14.83   -.13 *********  .
  15 14.49   -.25 **************:.*
  10 13.94   -.38 *********  .
  11 13.20   -.50 **********  .
   7 12.30   -.63 *******  .
   8 11.29   -.75 *******  .
  13 10.20   -.88 *********:***
  10  9.07  -1.00 ********:*
   8  7.95  -1.13 *******:
  11  6.85  -1.25 ******:****
  15  5.82  -1.38 *****:*********
  10  4.86  -1.50 ****:*****
  12  4.00  -1.63 ***:*******
   4  3.24  -1.75 **:*
   0  2.58  -1.88   .
   0  2.03  -2.00  .
   0  1.57  -2.13 .
   0  1.19  -2.25 .
   0   .89  -2.38 .
   0   .66  -2.50 .
   0   .48  -2.63 .
   0   .34  -2.75 .
   0   .24  -2.88 .
   0   .17  -3.00 .
   0   .33    OUT
```

4 What can you learn from a histogram of the residuals?

   a. A casewise plot of the residuals?

   b. A plot of the independent variable and the dependent variable?

   c. A plot of the residuals against the independent variable

5 You find that cases with large values of the independent variable all have large positive residuals. Otherwise there appears to be no relationship between the residuals and the independent variable. Sketch a plot illustrating when this may happen.

Data Analysis

1 Rerun all of the regression equations you developed in the previous chapter. For each one, examine how well the data seem to fit the regression assumptions. Indicate which plots suggest that the regression model may be inappropriate. Consider strategies for dealing with violations of the assumptions.

25. Looking Beyond

In the previous chapters we've analyzed the General Social Survey data in many different ways. We've described and summarized, tested hypotheses, and looked for associations among the variables. We've computed means and standard deviations, t-tests, and chi-square statistics. We've looked at measures of association and built regression equations.

Many additional statistical techniques exist for analyzing the data in still other ways. You can test more complicated hypotheses and build more complex models. This chapter gives an overview of some of these other frequently-used statistical procedures. The goal of the chapter is not to cram all remaining statistical wisdom into your skull. But you should be aware of how much more you can learn about your data with additional statistical methods. For more detail about these methods, and the SPSS^X procedures you can use to calculate them, read *The SPSS^X Advanced Statistics Guide*.

MULTIVARIATE STATISTICAL TECHNIQUES

In the previous chapters we studied the relationship between father's and child's education using linear regression. There was a single dependent variable, child's education, and a single independent variable, father's education. Even the most unenlightened of researchers would realize that father's education is but one of many variables that influence a person's educational achievements. Mother's education, size of the family, socioeconomic status, intelligence, and a myriad of other variables may affect how many years of education a person endures. What you really want to do is determine which of the many possible variables are important predictors of education, and then build a model which shows the relationship between education and these important predictor variables.

Variables such as mother's education, family size, and intelligence of offspring are not independent of one another. You can't just calculate separate regression models for each of the possible predictor variables and then "put them together" to assess the overall situation. You must use a statistical procedure which allows you to examine the variables *together*, a technique which takes into account the correlations among the variables.

A special class of statistical techniques, called **multivariate methods,** are used for studying the relationships among several interrelated variables. The goals of such multivariate analyses may be quite different, but they share many common features. Let's look at some of the most popular ones.

Multiple Linear Regression

You can use **multiple linear regression analysis** to study the relationship between a single dependent variable and several independent variables. You can build a linear model in which a person's education is the dependent variable and variables such as mother's and father's education and number of siblings are the independent variables. For example, if PAEDUC, MAEDUC, and SIBS are the independent variables, you can examine the model

$$\text{EDUC} = \text{Constant} + B_1 \times \text{PAEDUC} + B_2 \times \text{MAEDUC} + B_3 \times \text{SIBS}$$

The model looks like the regression model in Chapter 22. The difference is that there are now several variables on the independent variable side of the model. Besides father's education, mother's education and number of siblings are also included in the model.

As before, the method of least squares can be used to estimate all of the coefficients. The coefficients for this model are shown in Figure 25.1 The coefficients for mother's and father's education are both positive, indicating that the more educated the parents, the more educated the children. The coefficient for SIBS (the number of brothers and sisters) is negative. This suggest that children from large families are less likely to continue their education than children from smaller families.

```
FILE HANDLE GSS / (system-specific information)
GET FILE=GSS
REGRESSION VARIABLES = EDUC PAEDUC MAEDUC SIBS
  / DEPENDENT = EDUC
  / METHOD = ENTER
```

Since the variables are measured in different units, you can't just compare the magnitudes of the coefficients to each other. You must standardize the variables in some fashion. The column labeled *Beta* contains the regression coefficients when all variables are standardized to a mean of 0 and a standard deviation of 1. The column labeled *Sig T* is the observed significance level for the test of the null hypothesis that the value of a coefficient is zero in the population. You can see that the null hypothesis can be rejected for all of the variables.

When you build a model with several independent variables which are interrelated, it's not easy to determine how much each variable contributes to the model. You can't just look at the coefficients and say *this* is an important variable for predicting the dependent variable and *this* one is not. The contributions of the variables are "shared."

Figure 25.1 Multiple linear regression coefficients

```
FILE:    1984 General Social Survey

         * * * *   M U L T I P L E   R E G R E S S I O N   * * * *

Listwise Deletion of Missing Data

Equation Number 1   Dependent Variable..   EDUC   Highest year of school comple

Beginning Block Number  1. Method:  Enter


Variable(s) Entered on Step Number
     1..    SIBS       Number of siblings
     2..    PAEDUC     Father's highest year of school
     3..    MAEDUC     Mother's highest year of school

(Regression statistics here--see below.)


------------------- Variables in the Equation -------------------

Variable              B         SE B       Beta         T   Sig T

SIBS           -.201871     .026952    -.210018     -7.490   .0000
PAEDUC          .207500     .024992     .290028      8.303   .0000
MAEDUC          .176143     .030834     .203262      5.713   .0000
(Constant)     9.858697     .320956                 30.717   .0000


End Block Number   1   All requested variables entered.
```

Figure 25.2 Multiple linear regression statistics

```
Multiple R            .55697
R Square              .31021
Adjusted R Square     .30814
Standard Error       2.42935

Analysis of Variance
                    DF    Sum of Squares    Mean Square
Regression           3       2648.83529      882.94510
Residual           998       5889.94016        5.90174

F =     149.60750       Signif F =   .0000
```

The goodness-of-fit statistics we considered for a regression model with one independent variable can easily be extended to a model with multiple independent variables. They are shown in Figure 25.2. You see that a regression model with these three independent variables explains almost 31 percent of the observed variability in years of education.

Selecting Independent Variables

Often you don't know which independent variables together are good predictors of the dependent variable. You want to eliminate variables which are of little use from your equation so you will have a simple, easy to interpret model. You can do this with the assistance of what are called

Figure 25.3 Classification results from discriminant analysis

CLASSIFICATION RESULTS –

ACTUAL GROUP	NO. OF CASES	PREDICTED GROUP MEMBERSHIP		
		1	2	3
GROUP 1 Exciting	652	379 58.1%	270 41.4%	3 0.5%
GROUP 2 Pretty routine	663	253 38.2%	405 61.1%	5 0.8%
GROUP 3 Dull	64	11 17.2%	51 79.7%	2 3.1%
UNGROUPED CASES	9	3 33.3%	6 66.7%	0 0.0%

PERCENT OF "GROUPED" CASES CORRECTLY CLASSIFIED: 57.00%

variable-selection methods. Based on statistical considerations, such as the percent of variance explained by one variable that is *not* explained by any other variables, SPSS^X selects a set of variables for inclusion in a regression model. Although such procedures often result in a useful model, the selected model is not necessarily best in any absolute sense.

Discriminant Analysis

You can use regression analysis to predict values of the dependent variable based on a set of independent variables. The dependent and independent variables are all measured on an interval or ratio scale. What if the dependent variable is not measured on an interval or ratio scale? Suppose you want to predict whether people find life exciting, routine, or dull, based on a set of variables such as education, age, income and hours worked per week? You can't use regression analysis, since the dependent variable is ordinal. What you might want to use is a procedure called **discriminant analysis.**

In discriminant analysis, you compute "discriminant scores" for each case to predict what group it is in. These scores are obtained by finding linear combinations of the independent variables. (A linear combination is formed by multiplying each variable by some constant, and then adding up the products.) For example, you might compute an individual's score by taking 2 times income in thousands, plus 1.5 times age, plus 1.1 times education.

Discriminant analysis uses mathematical techniques to determine the way of computing scores that results in the best *separation* among the groups (in other words, the most accurate prediction of what group each case is in). Statistical packages such as SPSS^X do all the computations for you, including selection of the best coefficients. The results of a discriminant analysis include a table like that shown in Figure 25.3. It tells you how well you are able to predict what case a groups falls into, based on the values of the independent variables.

In this example, we're able to correctly classify only 57 percent of the cases, so the independent variables don't seem to be very good predictors of whether life is viewed as exciting, routine, or dull.

Log-Linear Models

Using a crossclassification table and the chi-square statistic you were able to test whether two variables which have a small number of distinct values are independent. For example, you were able to test whether marital status and degree of excitement are related. What if you wanted to know the effect of additional variables, such as sex, race, job satisfaction, and happiness of a marriage, on the relationships that you are examining? You could always make a crosstabulation table of all of the variables, but this would be very difficult to interpret. You would have hundreds or thousands of cells and most of them would contain few cases, if any.

One way to study the relationships among a set of variables which are categorical is with **log-linear** models. With a log-linear model you try to predict the number of cases in a cell of a crosstabulation, based on the values of the individual variables and on their combinations. You see whether certain combinations of values are more likely or less likely to occur than others. This tells you about the relationships among the variables.

Factor Analysis

If you give a group of students 100 different aptitude tests, their scores on the different tests will no doubt be correlated. The tests probably measure some of the same characteristics, such as verbal skills, mathematical aptitude, reasoning ability and perceptual speed. Characteristics such as "verbal skill," "mathematical aptitude," and "reasoning ability" are not well-defined, easily measureable variables like weight or age. Instead they can be thought of as unifying concepts or labels that characterize responses to related groups of variables. A mathematically apt person would score well on all of the tests which are related to mathematical skills. In fact, that's how the definition of mathematical aptitude was arrived at. **Factor analysis** is a statistical technique which attempts to measure such concepts.

In some research situations you have a set of interrelated variables such as consumer ratings of products. You think that the ratings are correlated because people are rating the products on similar dimensions such as product quality and utility. But you don't know what these underlying dimensions, or factors, are. You can use factor analysis to help you identify these underlying concepts by using a number of variables that you can directly measure.

Cluster Analysis

If you question sick patients about their symptoms, you will undoubtedly have a very long list of complaints. You may think that there are as many combinations of symptoms as there are patients. However, if you study the types of symptoms that frequently occur together, you'll probably be able to put the patients into groups—those who have respiratory disturbances, those who have gastric problems, those who have cardiac difficulties. Classifying the patients into groups of similar individuals may be helpful both for determining treatment strategies and for understanding how the body malfunctions.

In statistics, the search for similar groups of objects or people is called **cluster analysis.** By forming clusters of objects and then studying the characteristics the objects share, as well as those in which they differ, you can gain useful insights. For example, cluster analysis has been used to cluster skulls from various archeological digs into the civilizations from which they originated. Cluster analysis is also frequently used in market research to identify groups of people for whom various marketing pitches may be particularly attractive.

Testing Hypotheses about Many Means

In the two-sample t-test we tested hypotheses about the equality of two population means. We wanted to know whether people who find life exciting live in households of the same size as people who find life routine or dull. We used the analysis of variance procedure to test hypotheses that more than two population means are equal. We tested whether there a difference in education among the three excitement groups.

What if there are several interrelated dependent variables, such as education and income, about which we wish to test hypotheses? Is there a way to test hypotheses that *both* education and income do not differ among the three excitement groups in the population? **Multivariate analysis of variance,** or MANOVA, is used to test such hypotheses. Using MANOVA you can compare four instructional methods based on student achievement levels, satisfaction, anxiety, and long-term retention of the material. Or you compare five new ice-cream flavors based on the amount consumed, a preference rating, and the price people say they would pay.

If the same variable is measured on several different ocassions, there are special "repeated measures" analysis of variance techniques which can be used to test hypotheses . These can be thought of as extensions of the simple paired t-test.

THERE'S MORE

In the previous chapters we explained some of the more widely used statistical techniques, and in this chapter we've attempted to give an idea of the more sophisticated methods available. There are still others. There are non-parametric procedures which don't require such stringent assumptions about the distributions of variables. There are procedures for analyzing specialized types of data such as test scores or survival times. There are often many different ways to look at the same problem. No one way is best for every problem; each view tells you something new.

Appendix A
Error Messages

Errors are nearly inevitable, no matter how well you know SPSS[X]. Even the best data analysts occasionally need to run programs several times before they correct all their errors. You may not get the SPSS[X] commands right the first time. Always allow more time to write the job than you think you need, especially if you are just learning SPSS[X].

MAKING ERRORS IN SPSS[X]

Several kinds of errors cause programs to run improperly or to terminate. The most common ones are errors in command syntax, in the order of commands, or in the data. Syntax errors occur if you do something like forget a slash, misspell a command, or specify a subcommand out of order. Data errors stem from a number of problems, such as embedded blanks and stray punches.

Whenever SPSS[X] encounters problems in a job, it issues a message explaining what you did wrong and what action the system is taking. Normally, the message appears immediately after the place where the program detected the error.

CORRECTING ERRORS IN SPSS[X]

Whenever you get an error, check the statement where it occurred and previous statements (if necessary) to see if you specified the commands correctly. Some common mistakes you might make are:

- Using variable names that don't conform to SPSS[X] naming conventions.
- Omitting required slashes and equals signs.
- Leaving pairs of parentheses, apostrophes, or quotation marks unmatched.
- Using subcommands out of order.

Since one mistake often triggers others, you should always correct the first problem identified before you correct any others.

377

TYPES OF MESSAGES

SPSS[X] issues notes, warnings, and three types of error messages of different severity. The following sections give some common messages you might encounter and their possible causes and solutions. If the causes and solutions don't fit your problem or you get a message that isn't on the list, start out by reading the message carefully and checking your command syntax. If you still can't figure out the problem, contact your SPSS coordinator.

Notes

Notes are the least serious of all SPSS[X] messages. Their purpose is simply to call attention to a job's peculiarities that won't affect the results of later commands but may alert you to things you don't know about. For example, the following note lets you know that SORT CASES was used to sort a file with only one case:

```
>NOTE      5802
>SORT CASES was not executed because the file has fewer than 2 cases.
```

Since presumably you'd expect more than one case, the note may mean that earlier in your job you somehow deleted every case but one on your sort variable. If so, you'll need to re-examine all prior transformation statements with the variable to see how the mistake was made.

Warnings

Warnings identify problems that will affect the results of later commands. If you get too many warnings (normally 80), the program will terminate your job. For example, here's a warning message that tells you the program found a non-numeric value in a field read with a numeric format, and that it changed the contents to the system-missing value:

```
>WARNING   652
>An invalid numeric field has been found.  The result has been set to the
>system-missing value.

COMMAND LINE:    12  CURRENT CASE:      2  CURRENT SPLITFILE GROUP:   1
FIELD CONTENTS: '    A'
RECORD NUMBER:    2  STARTING COLUMN:   1  RECORD LENGTH:    72
```

This warning could mean you're using the wrong format to read your data. However, it could also mean the data has some errors that you can correct with an editor.

Common Warning Messages

Some warning messages you may encounter are:

Warning 208.   A literal is not correctly enclosed in quotation marks on the command line. Literals may not be continued across command lines without the use of the continuation symbol '+'.

Cause: All literals (strings) in SPSS^X must be enclosed within apostrophes or quotation marks. These include all values of string variables and all titles, variable labels, and value labels. If you need to continue a literal across command lines, use the continuation symbol '+'.

Solution: Supply all missing apostrophes or quotation marks around literals where necessary.

Warning 522. An unexpected end of file has been found in the middle of reading a case. The partial case will be ignored. Check your input for a possible missing record.

Cause: This probably means you didn't allow for the right number of records per case (in fixed-format data), or you didn't separate two values with a blank or a comma (in freefield-format data). For fixed-format data, the warning could also mean that each case doesn't have the same number of records, even if the number on RECORDS is correct. For freefield-format data, it could mean that you didn't code values for all variables on each case.

Solution: For fixed-format data, see if the number of records you allowed for on RECORDS is correct and that each case has the same number of records. For freefield-format data, make sure each case has the same number of values and that each value is separated from the next with a blank or a comma.

Warning 664. An embedded blank has been found under a numeric format. The result has been set to the system-missing value.

Cause: SPSS^X encountered a field with an embedded blank in a numeric format. Blanks are allowed in the leading and trailing positions of fields but not within fields. Normally, this means your column specifications on DATA LIST are off somewhere, and you should check them.

Solution: See if you defined all your variables in the correct columns. You can use DATA LIST with keyword TABLE to examine variables and column locations. If you did, use an editor to change the blanks to something else.

Warning 4461. An unknown variable name was specified on the VAR LABELS command. The name and the label will be ignored.

Cause: A variable name on the VARIABLE LABELS command is misspelled or doesn't exist.

Solution: Chances are, you misspelled the variable name.

Warning 4492. The VALUE LABELS command included a symbol other than a value where a value (either numeric or character) was expected. For compatibility with previous systems, a parenthesized value would have been acceptable. All value labels up to the next slash will be ignored.

Cause: You probably didn't use a slash between two sets of value labels. Here, the slash was omitted after the labels for the variable SES:

```
VALUE LABELS SES 1 'AVERAGE PLUS'
                 2 'AVERAGE'
                 3 'AVERAGE MINUS'
             JOB 1 'WHITE COLLAR'
                 2 'BLUE COLLAR'
                 3 'FARMER'
                 4 'OTHER,NONE'
```

Solution: Insert slashes where necessary to separate the value labels of different variables.

Warning 11810. The left and right lists are different lengths. Some variables will be omitted.

Cause: The number of variables named or implied on each side of the keyword WITH are not the same. For example:

```
T-TEST  PAIRS=RESLTH MEMRES WITH INCOMER
OPTIONS 5
```

Solution: Adjust the variable lists so they have the same number of variables, or remove the keyword WITH to request a test of each variable with every other variable.

Errors

Error messages indicate serious problems in your job. In SPSS^X, there are three different kinds of error messages.

- The first kind forces the program to skip a command but continues processing subsequent commands. Normally, these involve procedures like BREAKDOWN or CROSSTABS, which the program can skip without affecting subsequent commands.

- The second kind of error forces SPSS^X to stop processing commands but allows the program to continue checking for errors. SPSS^X issues this kind of error message for problems that will probably make later processing meaningless. Errors on COMPUTE statements are treated this way.

- The third kind of message causes SPSS^X to terminate a job immediately. Jobs are terminated when SPSS^X encounters a "catastrophic" error, such as a damaged data file. This kind of error also occurs when SPSS^X reaches the maximum number of errors or warnings allowed for the job, or it can't access a file. No further error checking is done when SPSS^X encounters these kinds of errors.

Common Error Messages

These are some of the SPSS^X error messages you might encounter:

Error 1. Text appearing in the first column is not recognized as a command. Is it spelled correctly? If it was intended as a continuation of the previous command, the first column must be blank.

Cause: You probably misspelled a command name, but you also might have begun some text in column 1 that you didn't intend as an SPSS^X command. For example, this statement is incorrect because the variable name V29 begins in the first column:

```
FREQUENCIES VARIABLES=V1,V5,V18,V27,
V29,V57
```

All text other than the first line of a command must be indented at least one column.

Solution: Move all text that isn't the first line of an SPSS^X command out of column 1. If you need to break a string across input lines, enclose the first line of the string in apostrophes, end the first line with a plus sign, and begin the second line with an apostrophe, as in:

```
TITLE='SELLINGSWORTH COUNTY COMMISSION FOR EMERGENCY'+
   ' PREPAREDNESS AND DISASTER SERVICES'/
```

Error 543. In-line input was expected, but no BEGIN DATA command is present. It is possible that the BEGIN DATA command was misspelled or misplaced.

Cause: Chances are, you didn't use the FILE subcommand to identify the file you described on the DATA LIST command. The FILE subcommand is required when data are contained in an external file. You also may have placed more than one procedure before the BEGIN DATA command, or you may have misspelled the OPTIONS or STATISTICS commands.

Solution: Use the FILE subcommand to indicate the handle of the file described on the DATA LIST command. Make sure the file was previously defined on a FILE HANDLE command or, in the IBM/OS version of SPSS^X, has a matching DDNAME in the JCL statement. Also check to see if you specified more than one procedure before the BEGIN DATA command, or if you misspelled OPTIONS or STATISTICS.

Error 701. An undefined variable name, or a scratch or system variable was specified in a variable list which accepts only standard variables. Check spelling, and verify the existence of this variable.

Cause: You probably misspelled a variable name or used a name you didn't define on DATA LIST. You'll get the same error if you omit the slash after the last range on the VARIABLES subcommand on procedures like integer-mode BREAKDOWN. For example:

```
BREAKDOWN VARIABLES = AGE(LO,HI) LIFE(1,3) SEX (1,2)
    CROSSBREAK = AGE BY LIFE BY SEX
```

Unless you include the slash, SPSS^X will assume CROSSBREAK is a variable name, not a subcommand.

Solution: Check the spelling and existence of all the variables you named. Insert a slash after the last range specification on the VARIABLES subcommand if you omitted it.

Error 707.   Too many variables were specified.

Cause: You probably specified more variables than the procedure allows. For example, FREQUENCIES and PEARSON CORR only allow up to 500 variables.

Solution: Break up your request among more than one command. The TO convention and the keyword ALL make it easy to exceed this limitation if your data have several hundred variables. Be sure to use these keywords with caution.

Error 714.   A variable was not named or implied on the primary variable list.

Cause: Some SPSS^X procedures, like integer-mode BREAKDOWN require a VARIABLES subcommand to name all variables in an analysis. In this situation, you probably used a variable that you didn't name on the VARIABLES subcommand. In the following example, the variable INCOMER was specified on the TABLES subcommand but not on the VARIABLES subcommand:

```
BREAKDOWN VARIABLES=RESLTH INCOME EDUC RACE(0,9)/
          CROSSBREAK=RESLTH BY INCOMER BY EDUC BY RACE/
          INCOME BY EDUC BY RACE
```

Solution: See if you named all your analysis variables on the primary variables list. If you did, see if some of them are misspelled.

Error 4100.   Unrecognized text appears on the DATA LIST command in the file specification section. This text will be ignored.

Cause: You probably didn't begin the variable definition portion of the DATA LIST command with a slash. For example:

```
DATA LIST FILE=MYDATA VARA 1 VARB 2 VARC 3
```

Solution: Insert a slash before the variables list if you omitted it.

Error 4112.   The DATA LIST describes more records than its RECORDS subcommand allows for. If more than one record is to be read, a correct RECORDS value must be supplied.

Cause: Chances are, you described multiple records per case, but didn't use the RECORDS subcommand to tell the program how many to expect. You'll get the same error if you used RECORDS but allowed for a different number of records than you described on DATA LIST.

Solution: If you described multiple records per case on DATA LIST, use the RECORDS subcommand to tell SPSS[X] how many to expect. If you used RECORDS but still got this error, make sure the number of records you allowed for and the number of records you described are the same.

Error 4117.   The file specified in the FILE subcommand of the DATA LIST command does not exist.

Cause: The file on the FILE HANDLE command might be misspelled or is in a different directory or disk. It also might not exist.

Solution: See if you spelled the name of the file correctly. If the name is correct, get a directory listing to verify that the file actually does exist.

Error 4138.   Unrecognized text appears on the DATA LIST command where a variable name was expected. NO FURTHER COMMANDS WILL BE EXECUTED. ERROR SCAN CONTINUES.

Cause: You probably used an illegal variable name on the DATA LIST command. Chances are, it has more than 8 characters; it doesn't begin with either one of the 26 letters A-Z, @, #, or $; or it's an SPSS[X] reserved keyword. Reserved keywords have special meaning in SPSS[X], and cannot be used as variable names. These are the SPSS[X] reserved keywords: ALL, AND, BY, EQ, GE, GT, LE, LT, NE, NOT, OR, THRU, TO, WITH.

Solution: Check that all your variables have valid SPSS[X] names.

Error 4143.   Column format was used on the DATA LIST command, but the number of columns specified is not evenly divisible by the number of variables specified.

Cause: Either you didn't name the right number of variables, or the columns are incorrect. Whenever you specify a range of columns for more than one variable, DATA LIST divides the number of columns by the number of variables, and assigns an equal number of columns to each variable. This means that the number of columns must be an integral multiple of the number of variables. For example, the following command is incorrect since 5 variables and 8 columns were named, but 5 doesn't divide evenly into 8:

```
DATA LIST FILE=GSS / SES RELIGION JOB STATE EMPSTAT 1-8
```

Solution: Adjust either the number of variables or the column range so that the number of variables evenly divides into the number of columns. Remember that this format can only be used if the variables are recorded in adjacent columns of the same record and have the same width and format type.

Error 4195. This file handle is not defined by a matching SPSSX FILE HANDLE command or CMS FILEDEF. If the data are in the command file, don't use the FILE subcommand.

Cause: Chances are, you used the FILE subcommand on DATA LIST, but your data are in your command file. The FILE subcommand should only be used if the data are in an external file.

Solution: Omit the FILE subcommand if your data are not in an external file.

Error 4664. A string variable may not be recoded to a numeric value. Consider the CONVERT or INTO options.

Cause: A string variable cannot be changed to numeric by recoding it into itself. For example, this RECODE command is invalid:

```
RECODE GENDER ('MALE'=1)('FEMALE'=2)
```

Solution: To recode a string variable to numeric, use the keyword INTO to specify a new variable name, as in:

```
RECODE GENDER ('MALE'=1)('FEMALE'=2) INTO SEX
```

To recode string representations of numbers to their numeric representation, use the keyword CONVERT. For example:

```
RECODE JOB (CONVERT) ('-'=11)('&'=12) INTO OCCUPAT
```

The keyword CONVERT causes the program to convert all remaining values, which in this situation are those between 1 and 9, to numeric.

Error 4666. A numeric variable may not be recoded to a string value. Consider the CONVERT or INTO options.

Cause: You cannot change a numeric variable to a string by recoding it into itself. For example, this RECODE command is incorrect:

```
DATA LIST  FILE=MYDATA  / GENDER 1
RECODE GENDER (1='MALE')(2='FEMALE')
```

Solution: Use the STRING command to declare a new variable, and use the INTO option to recode the old variable into the new variables, as in:

```
STRING SEX(A6)
RECODE GENDER (1='MALE')(2='FEMALE') INTO SEX
```

Error 5210. The file named does not exist.

Cause: The file was probably defined via a FILE HANDLE command or a DD statement but was never saved with the SAVE command.

Solution: Check to see that you used the SAVE command to write the file. The FILE HANDLE command or the DD statement only defines the handle of the file. It doesn't actually create it.

Error 10040. Error in FREQUENCIES command.

Cause: This message means there's something wrong with the command syntax. Perhaps you misspelled a subcommand or left off the VARIABLES subcommand, as in:

```
FREQUENCIES SES OCCUPAT RELIGION
```

Solution: Check the command syntax. Make sure you used the VARIABLES subcommand to name the variables you want to analyze and that you spelled all other subcommands correctly.

Error 10073. There is not enough memory for general FREQUENCIES processing. Increase memory or split the task into several tasks.

Cause: You'll get this error if you request frequencies for a variable with more than the maximum number of values allowed for a table. Normally, this number is 32,767, but it depends on your available workspace.

Solution: The limitation cannot be overridden. You can break up your request with SELECT IF commands, as in:

```
TEMPORARY
SELECT IF (ID GE 1 AND ID LE 32766)
FREQUENCIES VARIABLES=ID
TEMPORARY
SELECT IF (ID GE 32767 AND ID LE 54389)
FREQUENCIES VARIABLES=ID
```

FREQUENCIES prints as many variables as it can without exceeding the value limit for a table. Whenever possible, it drops variables to stay under this limit. It only issues this error message if every variable exceeds the value limit, and it can't print any of them.

Error 10314. Syntax error in CROSSTABS command, the TABLES = subcommand is missing.

Cause: You either omitted the TABLES subcommand or misspelled it.

Solution: Use the TABLES subcommand to name the tables list if you omitted it. If you didn't, check to see if you spelled it correctly.

Error 11404. The parenthesized range appears to be missing on the ONEWAY command.

Cause: You probably omitted the value range for the independent (grouping) variable on the ONEWAY command. This range is required and must be in the form: (minimum,maximum).

Solution: Supply the value range if you omitted it.

Error 11820. An illegal keyword is used on the T-TEST command. Valid keywords are GROUPS, VARIABLES, and PAIRS.

Cause: Chances are, you used the VARIABLES subcommand before the GROUPS subcommand, as in:

```
T-TEST VARIABLES=RESLTH MEMRES
    /GROUPS=INCOMER(1,2)
```

To request an independent-samples *t*-test, you must specify GROUPS first, then VARIABLES. If you also want paired-samples tests, specify GROUPS first, then VARIABLES, and finally PAIRS.

Solution: Switch the order of the GROUPS and VARIABLES subcommands so that GROUPS comes first.

Error 14102. 'PLOT' must be the last subcommand.

Cause: PLOT probably wasn't the last subcommand on procedure PLOT. The PLOT subcommand is required to specify the variables to plot, and it must be the last subcommand. You'll get the same error if you omit the PLOT subcommand altogether.

Solution: Rearrange your subcommands so that PLOT is last. If you didn't use PLOT, be sure to include it as your last subcommand.

Appendix B
Answers to Selected Exercises

CHAPTER 2

2 The second plan provides a more effective sample, because respondents are selected independently. In the first plan, family members are likely to give similar responses to many questions. (Of course, this must be balanced against costs, which may be lower for the first plan.)

4 None of the plans is perfect. Plan *a* is most likely to give a random sample of the entire adult population, although it misses people without telephones.

5 The major problem in the *Literary Digest* poll was probably non-response. Less than a quarter of the surveys were returned, and there is evidence that those who returned the surveys differed systematically from those who did not. For many years it was believed that the *Digest* failed by taking its lists of possible respondents from telephone books, and that in 1936 these were biased toward the well-to-do. We now know that respondents were taken from many sources other than phone books—including voting rolls—and that non-response among those to whom the surveys were mailed was a greater problem than selection of the sample.

CHAPTER 3

2 Assign identification numbers to individual voters (respondents). Record age numerically, and assign numeric codes to sex, candidate, registration, and employment status. Allow for missing values, and allow an "other" category for candidate.

6 The codes for question (a) overlap at 1, while omitting responses of 4 and 7. There is no reason not to enter the number itself, instead of a code. Question (b) should allow a yes-or-no response for each price category, and should explain what the categories mean. Question (c) is remarkably confusing, and should be written as three questions about cost, food, and service. Question (d) should use a more sensible scale, such as zero to a hundred. Question (e) should be translated into English, perhaps as "Do you have any suggestions?"

CHAPTER 4

Concepts

2 Bad questions are often not detected until they have been tried out on real people. A pretest is an invaluable tool for improving the form, and should be conducted whenever possible.

CHAPTER 5

Syntax

1 a. LIST CASES 10 b. LIST must begin in column 1; c. CASES must not begin in column 1.

2 No. The data file would be replaced by the command file.

CHAPTER 6

Syntax

1 a. FIRSTNAME is more than eight characters long. b. Variable names cannot begin with numbers. c. No two variables can have the same name. d. ALL is an invalid variable name because it is an SPSS^X reserved word.

2 DATA LIST FILE=MYDATA RECORDS=3 /1 SEX 11 RACE 12 /3 VOTE 40

3 b. Use quotation marks when the label contains an apostrophe.

Concepts

1 a. Yes; b. No.

CHAPTER 7

Syntax

1 The VARIABLES keyword is missing.

2 FREQUENCIES VAR=LIFE MARITAL SEX RACE

Statistical Concepts

1 a. No; b. Yes; c. Yes; d. No; e. Yes; f. No.

4 a. Yes; b. No; c. No; d. Yes.

CHAPTER 8

Syntax

1
```
DATA LIST FREE / LOSS
FREQUENCIES VARIABLE=LOSS
STATISTICS ALL
BEGIN DATA
0 2 1 5 3
END DATA
```

4 a. FORMAT = NOTABLE; b. HISTOGRAM is not part of the FORMAT subcommand; c. AND is not part of the syntax.

Statistical Concepts

1 a. Yes (1); b. Yes (1); c. No; d. No.

3 a. Yes (1); b. Yes (1); c. Yes (1.14).

5 The mean equals the proportion coded 1.

12 a. Histogram; b. Barchart; c. Barchart; d. Histogram; e. Barchart; f. Histogram.

CHAPTER 9

Syntax

1 a. CROSSTABS TABLE=RACE BY SATJOB; c. Add OPTIONS=3.

2 c. OPTION is a separate command which must begin in column 1.

Statistical Concepts

1 c. 40%; d. 60%; e. 25%, 83%.

2 The independent variable is: a. race; b. sex; c. astrological sign; d. mother's degree; e. either one.

4 GPA is the independent variable. Use row percentages.

8 Crosstabulation would be appropriate for b.

CHAPTER 10

Syntax

1 b. RECODE SEX ('M' = 1)('F' = 2) INTO another variable name; c. A hyphen cannot be used instead of the keyword THRU.

2 The second set of commands is not equivalent to the first command.

CHAPTER 11

Syntax

1 BREAKDOWN TABLES=INCOME BY SATJOB

3 BREAKDOWN TABLES=SYSTBP BY SMOKE BY DRINK

5 All four commands are syntactically correct. However, (d) will produce reams of useless output if income is recorded in dollars. The "means" for sex can be interpreted, but you should probably obtain this information with a crosstabulation.

Statistical Concepts

1 a. BREAKDOWN; b. CROSSTABS; c. FREQUENCIES; d. BREAKDOWN; e. CROSSTABS

2 The table is meaningless.

CHAPTER 12

Syntax

1 a. The command name is missing; b. Each computation requires a separate COMPUTE command; d. Use the symbol + to add; e. The name of a command cannot be abbreviated.

2 b. Yes; c. No.

CHAPTER 13

Statistical Concepts

1 a. (10,12) (10,14) (10,16) (10,50) (12,14) (12,16) (12,50) (14,16) (14,50) (16,50); c. Both means equal 20.4.

4 a. 40; b. The survey responses differ because of sampling variation. Some values are low and some are high, as one expects in sample results. This variation does not indicate that the deans rigged their polls; c. Probability over .99 that a poll will show more than 25%; probability about .02 that a poll will show more than 55%; probability about .20 that a poll will show less than 35%.

CHAPTER 14

Statistical Concepts

2 a. 50%; c. 16%; e. 5%.

3 b. +0.5; d. −1.5.

5 b. 3 divided by the square root of 50, or about .42, for samples of 50; about .95 for samples of 10.

7 From .14 to .16.

CHAPTER 15

Syntax

1 GROUPS must precede VARIABLES.

2 T-TEST GROUPS=TREAT(0,1) / VAR=WEIGHT

4 RECODE TREAT (1,2=0) (3,4=1), followed by the command in question 2. Other commands will achieve the same results.

Statistical Concepts

1 a. On average, Republicans and Democrats earn the same income; b. On average, Republicans earn more than Democrats (this is a one-tailed test).

3 a. No; b. No; c. .006 of the time (this is a one-tailed test, remember).

5 False. The observed significance level tells the probability of observing a value of t as large or larger than yours, *if* the null hypothesis is true.

8 Yes, this is possible (although quite unlikely).

9 In fact, it's quite likely that the two population means are unequal. Nevertheless, you can't reject the null hypothesis that they are equal.

10 The results are meaningless.

CHAPTER 16

Syntax

1 Each rat is a case. Variables are the time without the drug and the time with the drug; a. DATA LIST FREE / DRUG NODRUG; b. T-TEST PAIRS = DRUG NODRUG

2 Again each rat is a case, but in this arrangement the variables are the time and the group. The command would be something like T-TEST GROUPS = AGENT(0,1) / VARIABLES = TIME.

Statistical Concepts

1 a. Paired; b. Paired; c. Independent; d. Paired; e. Paired.
4 The one-tailed significance level is half the two-tailed significance level.

CHAPTER 17

Syntax

1 CROSSTABS TABLES=DEGREE BY PADEG, followed by OPTIONS 4 and STATISTICS 1.
2 The keyword BY was omitted. (Using VAR instead of TABLES is not standard, but it will work.)
4
```
GET FILE=WTSTUDY
COMPUTE RATIO=WEIGHT/IDEAL
COMPUTE PARATIO=PAWEIGHT/PAIDEAL
COMPUTE MARATIO=MAWEIGHT/MAIDEAL
RECODE RATIO    (LOWEST THRU 1.3=0)(1.3 THRU HIGHEST=1)
                INTO OBESE
RECODE PARATIO (LOWEST THRU 1.3=0)(1.3 THRU HIGHEST=1)
                INTO PAOBESE
RECODE MARATIO (LOWEST THRU 1.3=0)(1.3 THRU HIGHEST=1)
                INTO MAOBESE
CROSSTABS TABLES=OBESE BY PAOBESE, MAOBESE
OPTIONS 4
STATISTICS 1
```

Statistical Concepts

1 (a) and (d) are probably independent; the others are probably dependent.
3 a. The variables are probably related in the population; b. Slightly less than 5% of the time; c. No.
5 Chi-square for the second table is 45.45.
7 The other investigator has more cases.

CHAPTER 18

Syntax

2 a. Needs a range of values for RACE; b. OK; c. OK; d. RANGES TUKEYB belongs on ONEWAY (after a slash), not on OPTIONS.

3
```
RECODE EDUC (MISSING = SYSMIS) (0 THRU 8=1) (9 THRU 12=2)
    (13 THRU 16=3) (16 THRU HIGHEST=4)
ONEWAY CHOL BY EDUC (1,4)
```

Statistical Concepts

2 a. No; b. There is no evidence that age of first marriage differs among the categories of whether life is exciting; c. Similar; d. No.
3 a. ONEWAY MAEDUC BY LIFE(1,3) / RANGES=TUKEYB; b. The average years of mother's education are the same for all three excitement groups in the population; c. Mother's education differs among the excitement groups. You can reject the null hypothesis; d. Each group differs from both of the other two.

CHAPTER 19

Syntax

1 RECODE AGE (LOW THRU 19=1)(20 THRU 29=2)(30 THRU 39=3)
    (40 THRU 49=4)(50 THRU 59=5)(60 THRU 69=6)(70 THRU 79=7)
    (80 THRU 89=8)(ELSE=SYSMIS)
    CROSSTABS TABLES=AGE BY SATJOB
    OPTIONS 3
    STATISTICS 6 7 8 9

Statistical Concepts

1 All four statements are false.

4 It's easier to interpret values in these ranges. In particular, it's easier to compare coefficients from different tables when you know the coefficients are restricted to these ranges.

6 Lambda = .40, with MIGRAINE dependent. The two variables are strongly related.

7 This would simply reverse the sign of gamma.

CHAPTER 20

Syntax

1 PLOT PLOT = INCOME WITH AGE

3 PLOT PLOT = INCOME WITH AGE BY SEX

5 The PLOT subcommand was omitted, as in Example 4b.

Statistical Concepts

1 a. BREAKDOWN; b. CROSSTABS; c. PLOT; d. CROSSTABS;
   e. BREAKDOWN; f. PLOT

2 a. Unrelated; d. Nonlinear (curvilinear) relationship.

CHAPTER 21

Syntax

1 PEARSON CORR MONEY INVEST SALARY WEALTH
    OPTION 3

Statistical Concepts

1 a. Positive; c. Negative; e. Negative; g. Positive.

3 The correlation coefficient is meaningless, since product code does not measure anything at the interval level.

5 The correlation coefficient is appropriate only when variables are measured at the interval or ratio level and when the relationship between them is linear. When he computes a large number of correlation coefficients, some of them will be large enough to be statistically significant because of sampling variation alone.

CHAPTER 22

Syntax

1 a. PLOT must be the last subcommand; b. The keyword PLOT is omitted from the specifications; c. The second PLOT belongs after the slash, and WITH should be used instead of BY; d. Delete the second of the three PLOT keywords in this command.

Statistical Concepts

2 The intercept is 10,000 and the slope is 500. The predicted income for a 40-year-old is $30,000.

5 You can't tell which correlation is larger.

CHAPTER 23

Syntax

1 a. The variable GPA is omitted from the variables list; b. DEP must precede ENTER; c. MIQ is not named on the variables list and is probably a misspelling of IQ; d. GPA is named as both dependent and independent variable.

3 REGRESSION VAR=IQ GPA / STATISTICS DEF CI / DEP GPA / ENTER IQ

Statistical Concepts

4 a. Yes; b. It is unrelated; c. No; d. No; e. If there is no linear relationship between the two variables, there is only a .03 probability that the authors could have obtained a slope as large as the one they obtained.

CHAPTER 24

Syntax

2 The ENTER keyword (which is a shortened form of the METHOD subcommand) should be used after the DEPENDENT subcommand.

4 REGRESSION VARS=MYWEIGHT, MAWEIGHT / DEPENDENT=MYWEIGHT
    / ENTER MAWEIGHT / RESIDUALS=HISTOGRAM
    / CASEWISE = ALL DEPENDENT PRED RESID ZRESID
    / SCATTERPLOT = (*RESID, *PRED) (*RESID, MAWEIGHT)

Statistical Concepts

1 a. $20,000; b. Zero; c. The observed value is less than the predicted value.

3 a. The variance of the residuals is not constant; b. The relationship is not linear; c. The observations are not independent of one another; d. The residuals are not normally distributed, so the dependent variable is probably not normally distributed.

Bibliography

Basic Statistics Textbooks

Blalock, H. M. 1979. *Social statistics*. New York: McGraw-Hill.

Hays, W. M. 1973. *Statistics for the social sciences*. Second edition. New York: Holt, Rinehart and Winston.

Loether, H. J., and D. G. McTavish. 1976. *Descriptive and inferential statistics: An introduction*. Boston: Allyn & Bacon.

Books on Designing Experiments and Surveys

Kirk, R. 1968. *Experimental design: Procedures for the behavioral sciences*. Belmont, California: Brooks, 1968.

Sudman, S., and N. M. Bradburn. 1982. *Asking questions: A practical guide to questionnaire design*. San Francisco: Jossey-Bass.

Williams, B. 1978. *A sampler on sampling*. New York: John Wiley & Sons.

Other References

Cedercreutz, C. 1978. Hypnotic treatment of 100 cases of migraine. In F. H. Frankel and H. S. Zamansky, eds. *Hypnosis at Its Bicentennial*. New York: Plenum.

Hooke, R. 1983. *How to tell the liars from the statisticians*. New York: Marcel Dekker, Inc.

Siegel, S. 1956. *Nonparametric statistics for the behavioral sciences*. New York: McGraw-Hill.

Tanur, J. M. 1978. *Statistics: A guide to the unknown*. San Francisco: Holden-Day.

Winer, B. J. 1971. *Statistical principles in experimental design*. New York: McGraw-Hill.

SPSS Manuals

Norusis, M. J. 1983. *SPSS^X introductory statistics guide*. Chicago: SPSS Inc.

Norusis, M. J. 1985. *SPSS^X advanced statistics guide*. Chicago: SPSS Inc.

Norusis, M. J., and SPSS Inc. 1986. *SPSS/PC+ for the IBM PC/XT/AT*. Chicago: SPSS Inc.

SPSS Inc. 1985. *SPSS statistical algorithms*. Chicago: SPSS Inc.

SPSS Inc. 1986. *SPSS^X user's guide*. Second edition. Chicago: SPSS Inc.

Index